SENECA

V

LCL 76

SENECA

EPISTLES
66–92

WITH AN ENGLISH TRANSLATION BY
RICHARD M. GUMMERE

HARVARD UNIVERSITY PRESS
CAMBRIDGE, MASSACHUSETTS
LONDON, ENGLAND

First published 1920
Reprinted 1930, 1953, 1962, 1970, 1991, 1996, 2001

ISBN 0-674-99085-4

Printed in Great Britain by St Edmundsbury Press Ltd, Bury St Edmunds, Suffolk, on acid-free paper.
Bound by Hunter & Foulis Ltd, Edinburgh, Scotland.

CONTENTS

CONTENTS

THE EPISTLES OF SENECA

L. ANNAEI SENECAE AD LUCILIUM EPISTULAE

LXVI.

Seneca Lucilio suo salutem

1 Claranum, condiscipulum meum, vidi post multos annos. Non, puto, exspectas, ut adiciam senem, sed mehercules viridem animo ac vigentem et cum corpusculo suo conluctantem. Inique enim se natura gessit et talem animum male conlocavit; aut fortasse voluit hoc ipsum nobis ostendere, posse ingenium fortissimum ac beatissimum sub qualibet cute latere. Vincit tamen omnia inpedimenta et ad cetera con-
2 temnenda a contemptu sui venit. Errare mihi visus est, qui dixit

gratior et pulchro veniens e[1] corpore virtus.

Non enim ullo honestamento eget; ipsa magnum sui decus est et corpus suum consecrat. Aliter[2] certe Claranum nostrum coepi intueri; formosus mihi videtur et tam rectus corpore quam est animo.
3 Potest ex casa vir magnus exire, potest et ex deformi humilique corpusculo formosus animus ac magnus. Quosdam itaque mihi videtur in hoc tales natura

[1] The Vergil MSS. give *in*.
[2] *consecrat aliter* Haase; *consecraliter* MSS.

THE EPISTLES OF SENECA

LXVI. ON VARIOUS ASPECTS OF VIRTUE

I HAVE just seen my former school-mate Claranus for the first time in many years. You need not wait for me to add that he is an old man; but I assure you that I found him hale in spirit and sturdy, although he is wrestling with a frail and feeble body. For Nature acted unfairly when she gave him a poor domicile for so rare a soul; or perhaps it was because she wished to prove to us that an absolutely strong and happy mind can lie hidden under any exterior. Be that as it may, Claranus overcomes all these hindrances, and by despising his own body has arrived at a stage where he can despise other things also. The poet who sang

> Worth shows more pleasing in a form that's fair,[a]

is, in my opinion, mistaken. For virtue needs nothing to set it off; it is its own great glory, and it hallows the body in which it dwells. At any rate, I have begun to regard Claranus in a different light; he seems to me handsome, and as well-set-up in body as in mind. A great man can spring from a hovel; so can a beautiful and great soul from an ugly and insignificant body. For this reason Nature seems to

[a] Vergil, *Aeneid*, v. 344.

generare, ut adprobet virtutem omni loco nasci. Si
posset per se nudos edere animos, fecisset; nunc,
quod amplius est, facit; quosdam enim edit corporibus inpeditos, sed nihilominus perrumpentes
4 obstantia. Claranus mihi videtur in exemplar editus,
ut scire possemus non deformitate corporis foedari
animum, sed pulchritudine animi corpus ornari.

Quamvis autem paucissimos una fecerimus dies,
tamen multi nobis sermones fuerunt, quos subinde
5 egeram et ad te permittam. Hoc primo die quaesi-
tum est: quomodo possint paria[1] bona esse, si
triplex eorum condicio est. Quaedam, ut nostris
videtur, prima bona sunt, tamquam gaudium, pax,
salus patriae; quaedam secunda, in materia infelici
expressa, tamquam tormentorum patientia et in
morbo gravi temperantia. Illa bona derecto optabi-
mus nobis, haec, si necesse erit. Sunt adhuc tertia,
tamquam modestus incessus et conpositus ac probus
6 voltus et conveniens prudenti viro gestus. Quomodo
ista inter se paria[1] esse possunt, cum alia optanda
sint, alia aversanda? Si volumus ista distinguere, ad
primum bonum revertamur et consideremus id quale
sit: animus intuens vera, peritus fugiendorum ac

[1] *paria* the later MSS.; *tria* pVPb.

---

[a] Seneca is not speaking here of the three generic virtues (physical, ethical, logical), nor of the three kinds of goods (based on bodily advantage) which were classified by the Peripatetic school; he is only speaking of three sorts of circumstances under which the good can manifest itself. And in §§ 36 ff. he shows that he regards only the first two classes as real goods. See Zeller, *Stoics*, p. 230, n. 3.

me to breed certain men of this stamp with the idea of proving that virtue springs into birth in any place whatever. Had it been possible for her to produce souls by themselves and naked, she would have done so; as it is, Nature does a still greater thing, for she produces certain men who, though hampered in their bodies, none the less break through the obstruction. I think Claranus has been produced as a pattern, that we might be enabled to understand that the soul is not disfigured by the ugliness of the body, but rather the opposite, that the body is beautified by the comeliness of the soul.

Now, though Claranus and I have spent very few days together, we have nevertheless had many conversations, which I will at once pour forth and pass on to you. The first day we investigated this problem: how can goods be equal if they are of three kinds?[a] For certain of them, according to our philosophical tenets, are primary, such as joy, peace, and the welfare of one's country. Others are of the second order, moulded in an unhappy material, such as the endurance of suffering, and self-control during severe illness. We shall pray outright for the goods of the first class; for the second class we shall pray only if the need shall arise. There is still a third variety, as, for example, a modest gait, a calm and honest countenance, and a bearing that suits the man of wisdom. Now how can these things be equal when we compare them, if you grant that we ought to pray for the one and avoid the other? If we would make distinctions among them, we had better return to the First Good, and consider what its nature is: the soul that gazes upon truth, that is skilled in what should be sought and what should

petendorum, non ex opinione, sed ex natura pretia rebus inponens, toti se inserens mundo et in omnes eius actus contemplationem suam mittens, cogitationibus actionibusque intentus, ex aequo magnus ac vehemens, asperis blandisque pariter invictus, neutri se fortunae summittens, supra omnia quae contingunt acciduntque eminens, pulcherrimus, ordinatissimus cum decore tum[1] viribus, sanus ac siccus, inperturbatus, intrepidus, quem nulla vis frangat, quem nec adtollant fortuita nec deprimant; talis animus virtus
7 est. Haec eius est facies, si sub unum veniat aspectum et semel tota se ostendat. Ceterum multae eius species sunt. Pro vitae varietate et pro actionibus explicantur; nec minor fit aut maior ipsa. Decrescere enim summum bonum non potest nec virtuti ire retro licet; sed in alias atque alias qualitates convertitur ad rerum, quas actura est, habitum
8 figurata. Quidquid attigit, in similitudinem sui adducit et tinguit; actiones, amicitias, interdum domos totas, quas intravit disposuitque, condecorat. Quidquid tractavit, id amabile, conspicuum, mirabile facit.

Itaque vis eius et magnitudo ultra non potest surgere, quando incrementum maximo non est. Nihil invenies rectius recto, non magis quam verius
9 vero, quam temperato temperatius. Omnis sine

[1] *tum* Haase; *cum* MSS.

---

[a] *Siccus* (not in the sense of *Ep.* xviii. 4) here means "vigorous," "healthy," "dry"; *i.e.*, free from dropsy, catarrh, etc.

[b] *Cf.*, from among many passages, *Ep.* lxxi. 20 f. and xcii. 16 ff.

be avoided, establishing standards of value not according to opinion, but according to nature,—the soul that penetrates the whole world and directs its contemplating gaze upon all its phenomena, paying strict attention to thoughts and actions, equally great and forceful, superior alike to hardships and blandishments, yielding itself to neither extreme of fortune, rising above all blessings and tribulations, absolutely beautiful, perfectly equipped with grace as well as with strength, healthy and sinewy,[a] unruffled, undismayed, one which no violence can shatter, one which acts of chance can neither exalt nor depress,—a soul like this is virtue itself. There you have its outward appearance, if it should ever come under a single view and show itself once in all its completeness. But there are many aspects of it. They unfold themselves according as life varies and as actions differ; but virtue itself does not become less or greater.[b] For the Supreme Good cannot diminish, nor may virtue retrograde; rather is it transformed, now into one quality and now into another, shaping itself according to the part which it is to play. Whatever it has touched it brings into likeness with itself, and dyes with its own colour. It adorns our actions, our friendships, and sometimes entire households which it has entered and set in order. Whatever it has handled it forthwith makes lovable, notable, admirable.

Therefore the power and the greatness of virtue cannot rise to greater heights, because increase is denied to that which is superlatively great. You will find nothing straighter than the straight, nothing truer than the truth, and nothing more temperate than that which is temperate. Every virtue is

modo [1] est virtus; modo certa mensura est. Constantia
non habet, quo procedat, non magis quam fiducia
aut veritas aut fides. Quid accedere perfecto potest?
Nihil, aut perfectum non erat, cui accessit. Ergo ne
virtuti quidem, cui si quid adici potest, defuit.
Honestum quoque nullam accessionem recipit;
honestum est enim propter ista, quae rettuli. Quid
porro? Decorum et iustum et legitimum non
eiusdem esse formae putas, certis terminis con-
prensum? Crescere posse inperfectae rei signum est.
10 Bonum omne in easdem cadit leges; iuncta est
privata et publica utilitas, tam mehercules quam
inseparabile est laudandum petendumque. Ergo
virtutes inter se pares sunt et opera virtutis et omnes
11 homines, quibus illae contigere. Satorum vero
animaliumque virtutes cum mortales sint, fragiles
quoque caducaeque sunt et incertae. Exiliunt
residuntque et ideo non eodem pretio aestimantur;
una inducitur humanis virtutibus regula. Una enim
est ratio recta simplexque. Nihil est divino divinius,
12 caelesti caelestius. Mortalia minuuntur, cadunt,
deteruntur, crescunt, exhauriuntur, inplentur.
Itaque illis in tam incerta sorte inaequalitas est;
divinorum una natura est. Ratio autem nihil aliud
est quam in corpus humanum pars divini spiritus

[1] *sine modo* Capps; *in modo* MSS. and Hense.

---

[a] *i.e.*, constancy, fidelity, etc.

limitless; for limits depend upon definite measurements. Constancy cannot advance further, any more than fidelity, or truthfulness, or loyalty. What can be added to that which is perfect? Nothing; otherwise that was not perfect to which something has been added. Nor can anything be added to virtue, either, for if anything can be added thereto, it must have contained a defect. Honour, also, permits of no addition; for it is honourable because of the very qualities which I have mentioned.[a] What then? Do you think that propriety, justice, lawfulness, do not also belong to the same type, and that they are kept within fixed limits? The ability to increase is proof that a thing is still imperfect.

The good, in every instance, is subject to these same laws. The advantage of the state and that of the individual are yoked together; indeed it is as impossible to separate them as to separate the commendable from the desirable. Therefore, virtues are mutually equal; and so are the works of virtue, and all men who are so fortunate as to possess these virtues. But, since the virtues of plants and of animals are perishable, they are also frail and fleeting and uncertain. They spring up, and they sink down again, and for this reason they are not rated at the same value; but to human virtues only one rule applies. For right reason is single and of but one kind. Nothing is more divine than the divine, or more heavenly than the heavenly. Mortal things decay, fall, are worn out, grow up, are exhausted, and replenished. Hence, in their case, in view of the uncertainty of their lot, there is inequality; but of things divine the nature is one. Reason, however, is nothing else than a portion of the divine spirit set

mersa. Si ratio divina est, nullum autem bonum sine ratione est, bonum omne divinum est. Nullum porro inter divina discrimen est; ergo nec inter bona. Paria itaque sunt et gaudium et fortis atque obstinata tormentorum perpessio; in utroque enim eadem est animi magnitudo, in altero remissa et
13 laeta, in altera pugnax et intenta. Quid? Tu non putas parem esse virtutem eius, qui fortiter hostium moenia expugnat, et eius, qui obsidionem patientissime sustinet? Magnus[1] Scipio, qui Numantiam cludit et conprimit cogitque invictas manus in exitium ipsas suum verti; magnus ille obsessorum animus, qui scit non esse clusum, cui mors aperta est, et in conplexu libertatis expirat. Aeque reliqua quoque inter se paria sunt, tranquillitas, simplicitas, liberalitas, constantia, aequanimitas, tolerantia. Omnibus enim istis una virtus subest, quae animum rectum et indeclinabilem praestat.

14 "Quid ergo? Nihil interest inter gaudium et dolorum inflexibilem patientiam?" Nihil, quantum ad ipsas virtutes; plurimum inter illa, in quibus virtus utraque ostenditur. In altero enim naturalis est animi remissio ac laxitas, in altero contra naturam dolor. Itaque media sunt haec, quae plurimum intervalli recipiunt; virtus in utroque par est.
15 Virtutem materia non mutat; nec peiorem facit dura

[1] *et magnus* MSS.; Haase deletes *et.*

---

[a] *Ratio* (λόγος) is also defined as God, as Absolute Truth, Destiny, etc. The same idea is evident in the definition of *sapientia* (the object of philosophy) as *rerum divinarum et humanarum . . . scientia* (Cic. *Off.* ii. 2. 5, etc.), and *nosse divina et humana et horum causas*, etc.

[b] A Spanish city, reduced and razed to the ground in 133 B.C. by Scipio Africanus, the conqueror of Carthage.

[c] *Cf. Ep.* xxxi. 4 and footnote (Vol. I.).

in a human body.[a] If reason is divine, and the good in no case lacks reason, then the good in every case is divine. And furthermore, there is no distinction between things divine ; hence there is none between goods, either. Therefore it follows that joy and a brave unyielding endurance of torture are equal goods ; for in both there is the same greatness of soul, relaxed and cheerful in the one case, in the other combative and braced for action. What ? Do you not think that the virtue of him who bravely storms the enemy's stronghold is equal to that of him who endures a siege with the utmost patience ? Great is Scipio when he invests Numantia,[b] and constrains and compels the hands of an enemy, whom he could not conquer, to resort to their own destruction. Great also are the souls of the defenders—men who know that, as long as the path to death lies open, the blockade is not complete, men who breathe their last in the arms of liberty. In like manner, the other virtues are also equal as compared with one another : tranquillity, simplicity, generosity, constancy, equanimity, endurance. For underlying them all is a single virtue—that which renders the soul straight and unswerving.

"What then," you say ; "is there no difference between joy and unyielding endurance of pain ?" None at all, as regards the virtues themselves ; very great, however, in the circumstances in which either of these two virtues is displayed. In the one case, there is a natural relaxation and loosening of the soul ; in the other there is an unnatural pain. Hence these circumstances, between which a great distinction can be drawn, belong to the category of indifferent things,[c] but the virtue shown in each case is equal. Virtue is not changed by the matter with

ac difficilis, nec meliorem hilaris et laeta. Necesse est ergo par sit.[1] In utraque enim quod fit, aeque recte fit, aeque prudenter, aeque honeste. Ergo aequalia sunt bona, ultra quae[2] nec hic potest se melius in hoc gaudio gerere nec ille melius in illis cruciatibus. Duo autem, quibus nihil fieri melius
16 potest, paria sunt. Nam si, quae extra virtutem posita sunt, aut minuere illam aut augere possunt, desinit unum bonum esse, quod honestum. Si hoc concesseris, omne honestum perît. Quare? Dicam: quia nihil honestum est, quod ab invito, quod coactum[3] fit. Omne honestum voluntarium est. Admisce illi pigritiam, querellam, tergiversationem, metum; quod habet in se optimum, perdidit, sibi placere. Non potest honestum esse, quod non est liberum;
17 nam quod timet, servit. Honestum omne securum est, tranquillum est; si recusat aliquid, si conplorat, si malum iudicat, perturbationem recepit et in magna discordia volutatur. Hinc enim species recti vocat, illinc suspicio mali retrahit. Itaque qui honeste aliquid facturus est, quicquid opponitur, id etiam si incommodum putat, malum non putet, velit, libens faciat. Omne honestum iniussum incoactumque est, sincerum et nulli malo mixtum.

18 Scio, quid mihi responderi hoc loco possit: "hoc

[1] *par sit* Haase; *pars sit* p etc.
[2] *ultra quae* Haase; *litteraque* MSS.
[3] *coactum* Haase; *aco actum* p; *a coacto* Vb; *aco acto* P.

---

[a] *Cf.* Cicero, *De Fin.* ii. 14 f. Rackham translates as "moral worth,"—a reminiscence of *τὸ καλόν*.

which it deals; if the matter is hard and stubborn, it does not make the virtue worse; if pleasant and joyous, it does not make it better. Therefore, virtue necessarily remains equal. For, in each case, what is done is done with equal uprightness, with equal wisdom, and with equal honour. Hence the states of goodness involved are equal, and it is impossible for a man to transcend these states of goodness by conducting himself better, either the one man in his joy, or the other amid his suffering. And two goods, neither of which can possibly be better, are equal. For if things which are extrinsic to virtue can either diminish or increase virtue, then that which is honourable [a] ceases to be the only good. If you grant this, honour has wholly perished. And why? Let me tell you: it is because no act is honourable that is done by an unwilling agent, that is compulsory. Every honourable act is voluntary. Alloy it with reluctance, complaints, cowardice, or fear, and it loses its best characteristic—self-approval. That which is not free cannot be honourable; for fear means slavery. The honourable is wholly free from anxiety and is calm; if it ever objects, laments, or regards anything as an evil, it becomes subject to disturbance and begins to flounder about amid great confusion. For on one side the semblance of right calls to it, on the other the suspicion of evil drags it back. Therefore, when a man is about to do something honourable, he should not regard any obstacles as evils, even though he regard them as inconvenient, but he should will to do the deed, and do it willingly. For every honourable act is done without commands or compulsion; it is unalloyed and contains no admixture of evil.

I know what you may reply to me at this point:

nobis persuadere conaris, nihil interesse, utrum aliquis in gaudio sit an in eculeo iaceat ac tortorem suum lasset?" Poteram respondere: Epicurus quoque ait sapientem, si in Phalaridis tauro peruratur, exclamaturum: "dulce est et ad me nihil pertinet." Quid miraris, si ego paria bona dico alterius in convivio iacentis,[1] alterius inter tormenta fortissime stantis, cum quod[2] incredibilius est dicat Epicurus, dulce
19 esse torreri? Sed[3] hoc respondeo, plurimum interesse inter gaudium et dolorem; si quaeratur electio, alterum petam, alterum vitabo. Illud secundum naturam est, hoc contra. Quamdiu sic aestimantur, magno inter se dissident spatio; cum ad virtutem ventum est, utraque par est et quae per laeta procedit
20 et quae per tristia. Nullum habet momentum vexatio et dolor et quicquid aliud incommodi est; virtute enim obruitur. Quemadmodum minuta lumina claritas solis obscurat, sic dolores, molestias, iniurias virtus magnitudine sua elidit atque opprimit et quocumque adfulsit, ibi quicquid sine illa apparet, extinguitur; nec magis ullam portionem habent incommoda, cum in virtutem inciderunt, quam in mari nimbus.

21 Hoc ut scias ita esse, ad omne pulchrum vir bonus sine ulla cunctatione procurret; stet illic licet carnifex, stet tortor atque ignis, perseverabit nec quid passurus, sed quid facturus sit, aspiciet, et se

[1] *alterius in convivio iacentis* Arg. B, according to Oberlin. Not in the other MSS.

[2] *cum quod* later MSS.; *quod cum* or *quocum* MSS.

[3] *torreri sed* Ludwig von Jan; *terroris et* MSS.

---

[a] One of the stock bits of heroism attributed to the ideal wise man. *Cf.* Epicurus (Frag. 601 Usener), Cicero, *Tusc.* ii. 7. 17, etc.

"Are you trying to make us believe that it does not matter whether a man feels joy, or whether he lies upon the rack and tires out his torturer?" I might say in answer: "Epicurus also maintains that the wise man, though he is being burned in the bull of Phalaris,[a] will cry out: ''Tis pleasant, and concerns me not at all.'" Why need you wonder, if I maintain that he who reclines at a banquet and the victim who stoutly withstands torture possess equal goods, when Epicurus maintains a thing that is harder to believe, namely, that it is pleasant to be roasted in this way? But the reply which I do make, is that there is great difference between joy and pain; if I am asked to choose, I shall seek the former and avoid the latter. The former is according to nature, the latter contrary to it. So long as they are rated by this standard, there is a great gulf between; but when it comes to a question of the virtue involved, the virtue in each case is the same, whether it comes through joy or through sorrow. Vexation and pain and other inconveniences are of no consequence, for they are overcome by virtue. Just as the brightness of the sun dims all lesser lights, so virtue, by its own greatness, shatters and overwhelms all pains, annoyances, and wrongs; and wherever its radiance reaches, all lights which shine without the help of virtue are extinguished; and inconveniences, when they come in contact with virtue, play no more important a part than does a storm-cloud at sea.

This can be proved to you by the fact that the good man will hasten unhesitatingly to any noble deed; even though he be confronted by the hangman, the torturer, and the stake, he will persist, regarding not what he must suffer, but what he must do; and

honestae rei tamquam bono viro credet; utilem illam sibi iudicabit, tutam, prosperam. Eundem locum habebit apud illum honesta res, sed tristis atque aspera, quem vir bonus pauper aut exul ac pallidus.
22 Agedum pone ex alia parte virum bonum divitiis abundantem, ex altera nihil habentem, sed in se omnia; uterque aeque vir bonus erit, etiam si fortuna dispari utetur. Idem, ut dixi, in rebus iudicium est, quod in hominibus; aeque laudabilis virtus est in corpore valido ac libero posita quam in morbido ac
23 vincto. Ergo tuam quoque virtutem non magis laudabis, si corpus illi tuum[1] integrum fortuna praestiterit quam si ex aliqua parte mutilatum; alioqui hoc erit ex servorum habitu dominum aestimare. Omnia enim ista, in quae dominium casus exercet, serva sunt, pecunia et corpus et honores, inbecilla, fluida, mortalia, possessionis incertae. Illa rursus libera et invicta opera virtutis, quae non ideo magis adpetenda sunt, si benignius a fortuna tractantur, nec minus, si aliqua iniquitate rerum premuntur.

24 Quod amicitia in hominibus est, hoc in rebus adpetitio. Non, puto, magis amares virum bonum locupletem quam pauperem, nec robustum et lacertosum quam gracilem et languidi corporis; ergo ne rem quidem magis adpetes aut amabis hilarem ac pacatam

[1] *illituum* VP; *illibatum* a MS. of Opsopoeus, perhaps correctly, as Hense thinks.

he will entrust himself as readily to an honourable deed as he would to a good man; he will consider it advantageous to himself, safe, propitious. And he will hold the same view concerning an honourable deed, even though it be fraught with sorrow and hardship, as concerning a good man who is poor or wasting away in exile. Come now, contrast a good man who is rolling in wealth with a man who has nothing, except that in himself he has all things; they will be equally good, though they experience unequal fortune. This same standard, as I have remarked, is to be applied to things as well as to men; virtue is just as praiseworthy if it dwells in a sound and free body, as in one which is sickly or in bondage. Therefore, as regards your own virtue also, you will not praise it any more, if fortune has favoured it by granting you a sound body, than if fortune has endowed you with a body that is crippled in some member, since that would mean rating a master low because he is dressed like a slave. For all those things over which Chance holds sway are chattels,—money, person, position; they are weak, shifting, prone to perish, and of uncertain tenure. On the other hand, the works of virtue are free and unsubdued, neither more worthy to be sought when fortune treats them kindly, nor less worthy when any adversity weighs upon them.

Now friendship in the case of men corresponds to desirability in the case of things. You would not, I fancy, love a good man if he were rich any more than if he were poor, nor would you love a strong and muscular person more than one who was slender and of delicate constitution. Accordingly, neither will you seek or love a good thing that is mirthful and tranquil more than one that is full of perplexity

25 quam distractam et operosam. Aut si hoc[1] est, magis diliges ex duobus aeque bonis viris nitidum et unctum quam pulverulentum et horrentem. Deinde hoc usque pervenies, ut magis diligas integrum omnibus membris et inlaesum quam debilem aut luscum. Paulatim fastidium tuum illo usque procedet, ut ex duobus aeque iustis ac prudentibus comatum et crispulum[2] malis. Ubi par in utroque virtus est, non conparet aliarum rerum inaequalitas. Omnia enim
26 alia non partes, sed accessiones sunt. Num quis tam iniquam censuram inter suos agit, ut sanum filium quam aegrum magis diligat, procerumve et excelsum quam brevem aut modicum? Fetus suos non distinguunt ferae et se in alimentum pariter omnium sternunt; aves ex aequo partiuntur cibos. Vlixes ad Ithacae suae saxa sic properat, quemadmodum Agamemnon ad Mycenarum nobiles muros. Nemo enim patriam quia magna est amat, sed quia sua.

27 Quorsus haec pertinent? Ut scias virtutem omnia opera velut fetus suos isdem oculis intueri, aeque indulgere omnibus et quidem inpensius laborantibus, quoniam quidem etiam parentium amor magis in ea, quorum miseretur, inclinat. Virtus quoque opera sua, quae videt adfici et premi, non magis amat, sed parentium bonorum more magis conplectitur ac fovet.

28 Quare non est ullum bonum altero maius? Quia

[1] *aut si hoc* Haase; *et si hoc* MSS.; *at si hoc* Schweighäuser.

[2] Buecheler suggests the addition, after *crispulum*, of *quam calvum et horridulum.*

---

[a] A slight variation of the idea in Cicero, *De Orat.* i. 196 *si nos . . . nostra patria delectat, cuius rei tanta est vis ac tanta natura, ut Ithacam illam in asperrimis saxulis tamquam nidulum adfixam sapientissimus vir immortalitati anteponeret.*

and toil. Or, if you do this, you will, in the case of two equally good men, care more for him who is neat and well-groomed than for him who is dirty and unkempt. You would next go so far as to care more for a good man who is sound in all his limbs and without blemish, than for one who is weak or purblind; and gradually your fastidiousness would reach such a point that, of two equally just and prudent men, you would choose him who has long curling hair! Whenever the virtue in each one is equal, the inequality in their other attributes is not apparent. For all other things are not parts, but merely accessories. Would any man judge his children so unfairly as to care more for a healthy son than for one who was sickly, or for a tall child of unusual stature more than for one who was short or of middling height? Wild beasts show no favouritism among their offspring; they lie down in order to suckle all alike; birds make fair distribution of their food. Ulysses hastens back to the rocks of his Ithaca as eagerly as Agamemnon speeds to the kingly walls of Mycenae. For no man loves his native land because it is great; he loves it because it is his own.[a]

And what is the purpose of all this? That you may know that virtue regards all her works in the same light, as if they were her children, showing equal kindness to all, and still deeper kindness to those which encounter hardships; for even parents lean with more affection towards those of their offspring for whom they feel pity. Virtue, too, does not necessarily love more deeply those of her works which she beholds in trouble and under heavy burdens, but, like good parents, she gives them more of her fostering care.

Why is no good greater than any other good?

non est quicquam apto aptius, quia plano nihil est planius. Non potes dicere hoc magis par esse alicui quam illud; ergo nec honesto honestius quicquam
29 est. Quod si par omnium virtutum natura est, tria genera bonorum in aequo sunt. Ita dico: in aequo est moderate gaudere et moderate dolere. Laetitia illa non vincit hanc animi firmitatem sub tortore gemitus devorantem; illa bona optabilia, haec mirabilia sunt, utraque nihilominus paria, quia quidquid incommodi est, vi tanto maioris boni tegitur
30 Quisquis haec inparia iudicat, ab ipsis virtutibus avertit oculos et exteriora circumspicit; bona vera idem pendent, idem patent. Illa falsa multum habent vani. Itaque speciosa et magna contra visentibus, cum ad pondus revocata sunt, fallunt.

31 Ita est, mi Lucili; quicquid vera ratio commendat, solidum et aeternum est, firmat animum attollitque semper futurum in excelso; illa quae temere laudantur et vulgi sententia bona sunt, inflant inanibus laetos. Rursus ea, quae timentur tamquam mala, iniciunt formidinem mentibus et illas non aliter
32 quam animalia species periculi agitant. Utraque

---

[a] *i.e.*, of the soul, of the body, and of external goods.

[b] Buecheler thinks that this alliterative phrase of Seneca's is an echo of some popular proverb or line taken from a play.

It is because nothing can be more fitting than that which is fitting, and nothing more level than that which is level. You cannot say that one thing is more equal to a given object than another thing; hence also nothing is more honourable than that which is honourable. Accordingly, if all the virtues are by nature equal, the three varieties[a] of goods are equal. This is what I mean: there is an equality between feeling joy with self-control and suffering pain with self-control. The joy in the one case does not surpass in the other the steadfastness of soul that gulps down the groan when the victim is in the clutches of the torturer; goods of the first kind are desirable, while those of the second are worthy of admiration; and in each case they are none the less equal, because whatever inconvenience attaches to the latter is compensated by the qualities of the good, which is so much greater. Any man who believes them to be unequal is turning his gaze away from the virtues themselves and is surveying mere externals; true goods have the same weight and the same width.[b] The spurious sort contain much emptiness; hence, when they are weighed in the balance, they are found wanting, although they look imposing and grand to the gaze.

Yes, my dear Lucilius, the good which true reason approves is solid and everlasting; it strengthens the spirit and exalts it, so that it will always be on the heights; but those things which are thoughtlessly praised, and are goods in the opinion of the mob, merely puff us up with empty joy. And again, those things which are feared as if they were evils merely inspire trepidation in men's minds, for the mind is disturbed by the semblance of danger, just as animals are disturbed. Hence it is without

ergo res sine causa animum et diffundit et mordet; nec illa gaudio nec haec metu digna est. Sola ratio inmutabilis et iudicii tenax est. Non enim servit, sed imperat sensibus. Ratio rationi par est, sicut rectum recto; ergo et virtus virtuti. Virtus[1] non aliud quam recta ratio est.[2] Omnes virtutes rationes sunt. Rationes sunt, si rectae sunt. Si rectae sunt,
33 et pares sunt. Qualis ratio est, tales et actiones sunt; ergo omnes pares sunt. Nam cum similes rationi sint, similes et inter se sunt. Pares autem actiones inter se esse dico, qua[3] honestae rectaeque sunt. Ceterum magna habebunt discrimina variante materia, quae modo latior est, modo angustior, modo inlustris, modo ignobilis, modo ad multos pertinens, modo ad paucos. In omnibus tamen istis id, quod
34 optimum est, par est; honestae sunt. Tamquam viri boni omnes pares sunt, qua[4] boni sunt. Sed habent differentias aetatis: alius senior est, alius iuvenior; habent corporis: alius formosus, alius deformis est; habent fortunae: ille dives, hic pauper est, ille gratiosus, potens, urbibus notus et populis, hic ignotus plerisque et obscurus. Sed per illud, quo boni sunt,
35 pares sunt. De bonis ac malis sensus non iudicat; quid utile sit, quid inutile, ignorat. Non potest ferre sententiam, nisi in rem praesentem perductus est. Nec futuri providus est nec praeteriti memor; quid sit consequens, nescit. Ex hoc autem rerum

[1] *virtuti. Virtus* added by Schweighäuser. Hilgenfeld would remove the two sentences *ratio rationi . . . recta ratio est.*

[2] *ratio est* M; *ratio* VPb.

[3] *qua* Muretus; *quia* MSS.

[4] *qua* Erasmus[2]; *quia* MSS.

---

[a] Here Seneca is reminding Lucilius, as he so often does in the earlier letters, that the evidence of the senses is only a stepping-stone to higher ideas—an Epicurean tenet.

reason that both these things distract and sting the spirit; the one is not worthy of joy, nor the other of fear. It is reason alone that is unchangeable, that holds fast to its decisions. For reason is not a slave to the senses, but a ruler over them. Reason is equal to reason, as one straight line to another; therefore virtue also is equal to virtue. Virtue is nothing else than right reason. All virtues are reasons. Reasons are reasons, if they are right reasons. If they are right, they are also equal. As reason is, so also are actions; therefore all actions are equal. For since they resemble reason, they also resemble each other. Moreover, I hold that actions are equal to each other in so far as they are honourable and right actions. There will be, of course, great differences according as the material varies, as it becomes now broader and now narrower, now glorious and now base, now manifold in scope and now limited. However, that which is best in all these cases is equal; they are all honourable. In the same way, all good men, in so far as they are good, are equal. There are, indeed, differences of age,—one is older, another younger; of body,—one is comely, another is ugly; of fortune,—this man is rich, that man poor, this one is influential, powerful, and well-known to cities and peoples, that man is unknown to most, and is obscure. But all, in respect of that wherein they are good, are equal. The senses[a] do not decide upon things good and evil; they do not know what is useful and what is not useful. They cannot record their opinion unless they are brought face to face with a fact; they can neither see into the future nor recollect the past; and they do not know what results from what. But it is from such knowledge that a sequence and

ordo seriesque contexitur et unitas vitae per rectum itura. Ratio ergo arbitra est bonorum ac malorum; aliena et externa pro vilibus habet et ea, quae neque bona sunt neque mala, accessiones minimas ac levissimas iudicat. Omne enim illi bonum in animo est.

36 Ceterum bona quaedam prima existimat, ad quae[1] ex proposito venit, tamquam victoriam, bonos liberos, salutem patriae. Quaedam secunda, quae non apparent nisi in rebus adversis, tamquam aequo animo pati morbum magnum, exilium. Quaedam media, quae nihilo magis secundum naturam sunt quam contra naturam, tamquam prudenter ambulare, conposite sedere. Non enim minus secundum

37 naturam est sedere quam stare aut ambulare. Duo illa bona superiora diversa sunt. Prima enim secundum naturam sunt: gaudere liberorum pietate, patriae incolumitate. Secunda contra naturam sunt: fortiter opstare tormentis et sitim perpeti morbo urente

38 praecordia. "Quid ergo? Aliquid contra naturam bonum est?" Minime; sed id aliquando contra naturam est, in quo bonum illud existit. Vulnerari enim et subiecto igne tabescere et adversa valetudine adfligi contra naturam est, sed inter ista servare

39 animum infatigabilem secundum naturam est. Et ut quod volo exprimam breviter, materia boni aliquando contra naturam est, bonum numquam,

[1] *ad quae* Hense; *atque* MSS.

succession of actions is woven, and a unity of life is created,—a unity which will proceed in a straight course. Reason, therefore, is the judge of good and evil; that which is foreign and external she regards as dross, and that which is neither good nor evil she judges as merely accessory, insignificant and trivial. For all her good resides in the soul.

But there are certain goods which reason regards as primary, to which she addresses herself purposely; these are, for example, victory, good children, and the welfare of one's country. Certain others she regards as secondary; these become manifest only in adversity,—for example, equanimity in enduring severe illness or exile. Certain goods are indifferent; these are no more according to nature than contrary to nature, as, for example, a discreet gait and a sedate posture in a chair. For sitting is an act that is not less according to nature than standing or walking. The two kinds of goods which are of a higher order are different; the primary are according to nature,—such as deriving joy from the dutiful behaviour of one's children and from the well-being of one's country. The secondary are contrary to nature,—such as fortitude in resisting torture or in enduring thirst when illness makes the vitals feverish. "What then," you say; "can anything that is contrary to nature be a good?" Of course not; but that in which this good takes its rise is sometimes contrary to nature. For being wounded, wasting away over a fire, being afflicted with bad health,—such things are contrary to nature; but it is in accordance with nature for a man to preserve an indomitable soul amid such distresses. To explain my thought briefly, the material with which a good is concerned is sometimes contrary to nature,

quoniam bonum sine ratione nullum est, sequitur autem ratio naturam.

"Quid est ergo ratio?" Naturae imitatio. "Quod est summum hominis bonum?" Ex naturae voluntate
40 se gerere. "Non est" inquit "dubium, quin felicior pax sit numquam lacessita quam multo reparata sanguine. Non est dubium" inquit "quin felicior res sit inconcussa valetudo quam ex gravibus morbis et extrema minitantibus in tutum vi quadam et patientia educta. Eodem modo non erit dubium, quin maius bonum sit gaudium quam obnixus animus ad perpetiendos cruciatus vulnerum aut ignium."
41 Minime. Illa enim, quae fortuita sunt, plurimum discriminis recipiunt; aestimantur enim utilitate sumentium. Bonorum unum propositum est consentire naturae; hoc in omnibus[1] par est. Cum alicuius in senatu sententiam sequimur, non potest dici: ille magis adsentitur quam ille; ab omnibus in eandem sententiam itur. Idem de virtutibus[a] dico: omnes naturae adsentiuntur. Idem de bonis dico:
42 omnia naturae adsentiuntur. Alter adulescens decessit, alter senex, aliquis praeter hos infans, cui nihil amplius contigit quam prospicere vitam. Omnes hi aeque fuere mortales, etiam si mors aliorum longius

[1] *hoc in omnibus* Muretus; *hoc contire* (*contingere* VPb) *in omnibus* p; *consentire omnibus* Haase.

---

[a] Another definition, developing further the thought expressed in § 12.

but a good itself never is contrary, since no good is without reason, and reason is in accordance with nature.

"What, then," you ask, "is reason?" It is copying nature.[a] "And what," you say, "is the greatest good that man can possess?" It is to conduct oneself according to what nature wills. "There is no doubt," says the objector, "that peace affords more happiness when it has not been assailed than when it has been recovered at the cost of great slaughter." "There is no doubt also," he continues, "that health which has not been impaired affords more happiness than health which has been restored to soundness by means of force, as it were, and by endurance of suffering, after serious illnesses that threaten life itself. And similarly there will be no doubt that joy is a greater good than a soul's struggle to endure to the bitter end the torments of wounds or burning at the stake." By no means. For things that result from hazard admit of wide distinctions, since they are rated according to their usefulness in the eyes of those who experience them; but with regard to goods, the only point to be considered is that they are in agreement with nature; and this is equal in the case of all goods. When at a meeting of the Senate we vote in favour of someone's motion, it cannot be said, "A. is more in accord with the motion than B." All alike vote for the same motion. I make the same statement with regard to virtues,—they are all in accord with nature; and I make it with regard to goods also,—they are all in accord with nature. One man dies young, another in old age, and still another in infancy, having enjoyed nothing more than a mere glimpse out into life. They have all been equally subject to death,

vitam passa est procedere, aliorum in medio flore
43 praecidit, aliorum interrupit ipsa principia. Alius inter cenandum solutus est. Alterius continuata mors somno est. Aliquem concubitus extinxit. His oppone ferro transfossos aut exanimatos serpentium morsu aut fractos[1] ruina aut per longam nervorum contractionem extortos minutatim. Aliquorum melior dici, aliquorum peior potest exitus; mors quidem omnium par est. Per quae desinunt,[2] diversa sunt; in quod[3] desinunt, unum est. Mors nulla maior aut minor est; habet enim eundem in omnibus modum, finisse vitam.

44 Idem tibi de bonis dico: hoc bonum inter meras voluptates est, hoc inter tristia et acerba. Illud fortunae indulgentiam rexit, hoc violentiam domuit. Utrumque aeque bonum est, quamvis illud plana et molli via ierit,[4] hoc aspera. Idem finis omnium est: bona sunt, laudanda sunt, virtutem rationemque comitantur; virtus aequat inter se, quicquid agnoscit.
45 Nec est, quare hoc inter nostra placita mireris; apud Epicurum duo bona sunt, ex quibus summum illud beatumque conponitur, ut corpus sine dolore sit, animus sine perturbatione. Haec bona non crescunt, si plena sunt. Quo enim crescet, quod plenum est? Dolore corpus caret; quid ad hanc accedere in-

[1] *fractos* later MSS.; *fructus* (*fluctus*) pVPb.
[2] *desinunt* Hense; *veniunt* or *venit* MSS.
[3] *in quod* Haase; *in id quod* MSS.
[4] *et molli via ierit* Gertz; *emolliverit* VPb; *et molli velerit* p; *et molli venerit* Wolters.

[a] Frag. 434 Usener.

even though death has permitted the one to proceed farther along the pathway of life, has cut off the life of the second in his flower, and has broken off the life of the third at its very beginning. Some get their release at the dinner-table. Others extend their sleep into the sleep of death. Some are blotted out during dissipation. Now contrast with these persons individuals who have been pierced by the sword, or bitten to death by snakes, or crushed in ruins, or tortured piecemeal out of existence by the prolonged twisting of their sinews. Some of these departures may be regarded as better, some as worse; but the act of dying is equal in all. The methods of ending life are different; but the end is one and the same. Death has no degrees of greater or less; for it has the same limit in all instances, —the finishing of life.

The same thing holds true, I assure you, concerning goods; you will find one amid circumstances of pure pleasure, another amid sorrow and bitterness. The one controls the favours of fortune; the other overcomes her onslaughts. Each is equally a good, although the one travels a level and easy road, and the other a rough road. And the end of them all is the same: they are goods, they are worthy of praise, they accompany virtue and reason. Virtue makes all the things that it acknowledges equal to one another. You need not wonder that this is one of our principles; we find mentioned in the works of Epicurus[a] two goods, of which his Supreme Good, or blessedness, is composed, namely, a body free from pain and a soul free from disturbance. These goods, if they are complete, do not increase; for how can that which is complete increase? The body is, let us suppose, free from pain; what increase can there be to this

dolentiam potest? Animus constat sibi et placidus est; quid accedere ad hanc tranquillitatem potest?
46 Quemadmodum serenitas caeli non recipit maiorem adhuc claritatem in sincerissimum nitorem repurgata, sic hominis corpus animumque curantis et bonum suum ex utroque nectentis perfectus est status et summam voti sui invenit, si nec aestus animo est nec dolor corpori. Si qua extra blandimenta contingunt, non augent summum bonum, sed ut ita dicam, condiunt et oblectant. Absolutum enim illud humanae naturae bonum corporis et animi pace contentum
47 est. Dabo apud Epicurum tibi etiamnunc simillimam huic nostrae divisionem bonorum. Alia enim sunt apud illum, quae malit contingere sibi, ut corporis quietem ab omni incommodo liberam et animi remissionem bonorum suorum contemplatione gaudentis. Alia sunt, quae quamvis nolit accidere, nihilominus laudat et conprobat, tamquam illam, quam paulo ante dicebam, malae valetudinis et dolorum gravissimorum perpessionem, in qua Epicurus fuit illo summo ac fortunatissimo die suo. Ait enim se vesicae et exulcerati ventris tormenta tolerare ulteriorem doloris accessionem non recipientia, esse nihilominus sibi illum beatum diem. Beatum autem agere, nisi qui est in summo bono, non potest.

48 Ergo et apud Epicurum sunt haec bona, quae malles non experiri, sed quia ita res tulit, et ample-

[a] Frag. 449 Usener. [b] Frag. 138 Usener.
[c] See above, § 47.

absence of pain? The soul is composed and calm; what increase can there be to this tranquillity? Just as fair weather, purified into the purest brilliancy, does not admit of a still greater degree of clearness; so, when a man takes care of his body and of his soul, weaving the texture of his good from both, his condition is perfect, and he has found the consummation of his prayers, if there is no commotion in his soul or pain in his body. Whatever delights fall to his lot over and above these two things do not increase his Supreme Good; they merely season it, so to speak, and add spice to it. For the absolute good of man's nature is satisfied with peace in the body and peace in the soul. I can show you at this moment in the writings of Epicurus[a] a graded list of goods just like that of our own school. For there are some things, he declares, which he prefers should fall to his lot, such as bodily rest free from all inconvenience, and relaxation of the soul as it takes delight in the contemplation of its own goods. And there are other things which, though he would prefer that they did not happen, he nevertheless praises and approves,—for example, the kind of resignation, in times of ill-health and serious suffering, to which I alluded a moment ago, and which Epicurus displayed on that last and most blessed day of his life. For he tells us[b] that he had to endure excruciating agony from a diseased bladder and from an ulcerated stomach,—so acute that it permitted no increase of pain; "and yet," he says, "that day was none the less happy." And no man can spend such a day in happiness unless he possesses the Supreme Good.

We therefore find mentioned, even by Epicurus,[c] those goods which one would prefer not to experience; which, however, because circumstances have decided

xanda et laudanda et exaequanda summis sunt. Non potest dici, hoc non esse par maximis bonum, quod beatae vitae clausulam inposuit, cui Epicurus extrema
49 voce gratias egit. Permitte mihi, Lucili virorum optime, aliquid audacius dicere: si ulla bona maiora esse aliis possent, haec ego, quae tristia videntur, mollibus illis et delicatis praetulissem, haec maiora dixissem. Maius est enim difficilia perfringere quam
50 laeta moderari. Eadem ratione fit, scio, ut aliquis felicitatem bene et ut calamitatem fortiter ferat. Aeque esse fortis potest, qui pro vallo securus excubuit nullis hostibus castra temptantibus et qui succisis poplitibus in genua se excepit nec arma dimisit; "macte virtute esto" sanguinolentis[1] ex acie redeuntibus dicitur. Itaque haec magis laudaverim bona
51 exercita et fortia et cum fortuna rixata. Ego dubitem, quin magis laudem truncam illam et retorridam manum Mucii quam cuiuslibet fortissimi salvam? Stetit hostium flammarumque contemptor et manum suam in hostili foculo destillantem perspectavit, donec Porsenna, cuius poenae favebat, gloriae invidit et ignem invito eripi iussit.

52 Hoc bonum quidni inter[2] prima numerem tantoque

[1] *et* after *sanguinolentis* deleted by Schweighäuser.
[2] *quidni inter* later MSS.; *quid inter* pVPb.

[a] *Clausula* has, among other meanings, that of "a period" (Quintil. viii. 5), and "the rhythmic close of a period" (Cic. *De Orat.* iii. 192).

[b] For a full discussion of this phrase see Conington, Excursus to Vergil's *Aeneid*, ix. 641.

[c] For the story see Livy, ii. 12 ff.

thus, must be welcomed and approved and placed on a level with the highest goods. We cannot say that the good which has rounded out [a] a happy life, the good for which Epicurus rendered thanks in the last words he uttered, is not equal to the greatest. Allow me, excellent Lucilius, to utter a still bolder word: if any goods could be greater than others, I should prefer those which seem harsh to those which are mild and alluring, and should pronounce them greater. For it is more of an accomplishment to break one's way through difficulties than to keep joy within bounds. It requires the same use of reason, I am fully aware, for a man to endure prosperity well and also to endure misfortune bravely. That man may be just as brave who sleeps in front of the ramparts without fear of danger when no enemy attacks the camp, as the man who, when the tendons of his legs have been severed, holds himself up on his knees and does not let fall his weapons; but it is to the blood-stained soldier returning from the front that men cry: "Well done, thou hero!" [b] And therefore I should bestow greater praise upon those goods that have stood trial, and show courage, and have fought it out with fortune. Should I hesitate whether to give greater praise to the maimed and shrivelled hand of Mucius [c] than to the uninjured hand of the bravest man in the world? There stood Mucius, despising the enemy and despising the fire, and watched his hand as it dripped blood over the fire on his enemy's altar, until Porsenna, envying the fame of the hero whose punishment he was advocating, ordered the fire to be removed against the will of the victim.

Why should I not reckon this good among the primary goods, and deem it in so far greater than

maius putem quam illa secura et intemptata fortunae, quanto rarius est hostem amissa manu vicisse quam armata? "Quid ergo?" inquis, "hoc bonum tibi optabis?" Quidni? Hoc enim nisi qui potest et
53 optare, non potest facere. An potius optem, ut malaxandos[a] articulos exoletis meis porrigam? Ut muliercula aut aliquis in mulierculam ex viro versus digitulos meos ducat? Quidni ego feliciorem putem Mucium, quod sic tractavit ignem, quasi illam manum tractatori praestitisset? In integrum restituit quidquid erraverat; confecit bellum inermis ac mancus et illa manu trunca reges duos[b] vicit. VALE.

LXVII.

SENECA LVCILIO SVO SALVTEM

1 Vt a communibus initium faciam, ver aperire se coepit, sed iam inclinatum in aestatem, quo tempore calere debebat, intepuit nec adhuc illi fides est. Saepe enim in hiemem revolvitur. Vis scire, quam dubium adhuc sit? Nondum me committo frigidae verae, adhuc rigorem eius infringo. "Hoc est," inquis, "nec calidum nec frigidum pati." Ita est, mi Lucili; iam aetas mea contenta est suo frigore.[c] Vix

[a] A rare word—sometimes spelled *malacisso*,—used by Plautus (*Bacch.* 73) and Laberius, but not in a technical sense.

[b] Porsenna and Tarquin.

[c] See Introduction (Vol. I. p. x), and the opening sentences of *Epp.* lxxvii., lxxxvii., and others.

those other goods which are unattended by danger and have made no trial of fortune, as it is a rarer thing to have overcome a foe with a hand lost than with a hand armed? "What then?" you say; "shall you desire this good for yourself?" Of course I shall. For this is a thing that a man cannot achieve unless he can also desire it. Should I desire, instead, to be allowed to stretch out my limbs for my slaves to massage,[a] or to have a woman, or a man changed into the likeness of a woman, pull my finger-joints? I cannot help believing that Mucius was all the more lucky because he manipulated the flames as calmly as if he were holding out his hand to the manipulator. He had wiped out all his previous mistakes; he finished the war unarmed and maimed; and with that stump of a hand he conquered two kings.[b] Farewell.

LXVII. ON ILL-HEALTH AND ENDURANCE OF SUFFERING

If I may begin with a commonplace remark,[c] spring is gradually disclosing itself; but though it is rounding into summer, when you would expect hot weather, it has kept rather cool, and one cannot yet be sure of it. For it often slides back into winter weather. Do you wish to know how uncertain it still is? I do not yet trust myself to a bath which is absolutely cold; even at this time I break its chill. You may say that this is no way to show the endurance either of heat or of cold; very true, dear Lucilius, but at my time of life one is at length contented with the natural chill of the body. I can scarcely thaw out in

2 media regelatur aestate. Itaque maior pars in vestimentis degitur. Ago gratias senectuti, quod me lectulo adfixit. Quidni gratias illi hoc nomine agam? Quicquid debebam nolle, non possum. Cum libellis mihi plurimus sermo est. Si quando intervenerunt epistulae tuae, tecum esse mihi videor et sic adficior animo, tamquam tibi non rescribam, sed respondeam. Itaque et de hoc, quod quaeris, quasi conloquar tecum, quale sit, una scrutabimur.

3 Quaeris, an omne bonum optabile sit. "Si bonum est," inquis, "fortiter torqueri et magno animo uri et patienter aegrotare, sequitur, ut ista optabilia sint. Nihil autem video ex istis voto dignum. Neminem certe adhuc scio eo nomine votum solvisse, quod flagellis caesus esset aut podagra distortus aut eculeo
4 longior factus." Distingue, mi Lucili, ista, et intelleges esse in iis aliquid optandum. Tormenta abesse a me velim; sed si sustinenda fuerint, ut me in illis fortiter, honeste, animose geram, optabo. Quidni ego malim non incidere bellum? Sed si inciderit, ut vulnera, ut famem et omnia, quae bellorum necessitas adfert, generose feram, optabo. Non sum tam demens, ut aegrotare cupiam; sed si aegrotandum fuerit, ut nihil intemperanter, nihil effeminate faciam, optabo. Ita non incommoda optabilia sunt, sed virtus, qua perferuntur incommoda.

[a] Seneca had a delicate constitution (see Introduction). In the Letters he speaks of suffering from asthma (liv.), catarrh (lxxviii.), and fever (civ.).

[b] Cf. lxxv. 1 *qualis sermo meus esset, si una sederemus aut ambularemus.*

the middle of summer. Accordingly, I spend most of the time bundled up; and I thank old age for keeping me fastened to my bed.[a] Why should I not thank old age on this account? That which I ought not to wish to do, I lack the ability to do. Most of my converse is with books. Whenever your letters arrive, I imagine that I am with you, and I have the feeling that I am about to speak my answer, instead of writing it. Therefore let us together investigate the nature of this problem of yours, just as if we were conversing with one another.[b]

You ask me whether every good is desirable. You say: "If it is a good to be brave under torture, to go to the stake with a stout heart, to endure illness with resignation, it follows that these things are desirable. But I do not see that any of them is worth praying for. At any rate I have as yet known of no man who has paid a vow by reason of having been cut to pieces by the rod, or twisted out of shape by the gout, or made taller by the rack." My dear Lucilius, you must distinguish between these cases; you will then comprehend that there is something in them that is to be desired. I should prefer to be free from torture; but if the time comes when it must be endured, I shall desire that I may conduct myself therein with bravery, honour, and courage. Of course I prefer that war should not occur; but if war does occur, I shall desire that I may nobly endure the wounds, the starvation, and all that the exigency of war brings. Nor am I so mad as to crave illness; but if I must suffer illness, I shall desire that I may do nothing which shows lack of restraint, and nothing that is unmanly. The conclusion is, not that hardships are desirable, but that virtue is desirable, which enables us patiently to endure hardships.

5 Quidam ex nostris[a] existimant omnium istorum fortem tolerantiam non esse optabilem, sed ne abominandam quidem, quia voto purum bonum peti debet et tranquillum et extra molestiam positum. Ego dissentio. Quare? Primum quia fieri non potest, ut aliqua res bona quidem sit, sed optabilis non sit. Deinde si virtus optabilis est, nullum autem sine virtute bonum est, omne bonum optabile est. Deinde etiam[1] tormentorum fortis patientia optabilis est.
6 Etiamnunc interrogo: nempe[2] fortitudo optabilis est? Atqui pericula contemnit et provocat. Pulcherrima pars eius maximeque mirabilis illa est, non cedere ignibus, obviam ire vulneribus, interdum tela ne vitare quidem, sed pectore excipere. Si fortitudo optabilis est, et tormenta patienter ferre optabile est; hoc enim fortitudinis pars est. Sed[3] separa ista, ut dixi; nihil erit quod tibi faciat errorem. Non enim pati tormenta optabile est, sed pati fortiter. Illud opto "fortiter," quod est virtus.

7 "Quis tamen umquam hoc sibi optavit?" Quaedam vota aperta et professa sunt, cum particulatim fiunt, quaedam latent, cum uno voto multa conprensa sunt. Tamquam opto mihi vitam honestam. Vita autem honesta actionibus variis constat; in hac est Reguli arca, Catonis scissum manu sua vulnus, Rutili[b] exilium, calix venenatus, qui Socraten transtulit e carcere in caelum. Ita cum optavi mihi vitam honestam, et

[1] *etiam si* MSS.; Madvig deleted *si*.
[2] *nempe* Haase; *neme* MSS.
[3] Buecheler would delete *sed*.

[a] *i.e.*, the Stoics.
[b] Banished from Rome in 92 B.C. *Cf. Ep.* xxiv. 4.

Certain of our school[a] think that, of all such qualities, a stout endurance is not desirable,—though not to be deprecated either,—because we ought to seek by prayer only the good which is unalloyed, peaceful, and beyond the reach of trouble. Personally, I do not agree with them. And why? First, because it is impossible for anything to be good without being also desirable. Because, again, if virtue is desirable, and if nothing that is good lacks virtue, then everything good is desirable. And, lastly, because a brave endurance even under torture is desirable. At this point I ask you: Is not bravery desirable? And yet bravery despises and challenges danger. The most beautiful and most admirable part of bravery is that it does not shrink from the stake, advances to meet wounds, and sometimes does not even avoid the spear, but meets it with opposing breast. If bravery is desirable, so is patient endurance of torture; for this is a part of bravery. Only sift these things, as I have suggested; then there will be nothing which can lead you astray. For it is not mere endurance of torture, but brave endurance, that is desirable. I therefore desire that "brave" endurance; and this is virtue.

"But," you say, "who ever desired such a thing for himself?" Some prayers are open and outspoken, when the requests are offered specifically; other prayers are indirectly expressed, when they include many requests under one title. For example, I desire a life of honour. Now a life of honour includes various kinds of conduct; it may include the chest in which Regulus was confined, or the wound of Cato which was torn open by Cato's own hand, or the exile of Rutilius,[b] or the cup of poison which removed Socrates from gaol to heaven. Accordingly, in praying for a life of

haec optavi, sine quibus interdum honesta non potest esse.

8 O terque quaterque beati,
Quis ante ora patrum Troiae sub moenibus altis
Contigit oppetere!

Quid interest, optes hoc alicui an optabile fuisse
9 fatearis? Decius se pro re publica devovit; in medios hostes concitato equo mortem petens inruit. Alter post hunc, paternae virtutis aemulus, conceptis sollemnibus ac iam familiaribus verbis in aciem confertissiman incucurrit, de hoc sollicitus tantum, ut litaret, optabilem rem putans[1] bonam mortem. Dubitas ergo, an optimum sit memorabilem mori et
10 in aliquo opere virtutis? Cum aliquis tormenta fortiter patitur, omnibus virtutibus utitur. Fortasse una in promptu sit et maxime appareat patientia. Ceterum illic est fortitudo, cuius patientia et perpessio et tolerantia rami sunt. Illic est prudentia, sine qua nullum initur consilium, quae suadet, quod effugere non possis, quam fortissime ferre. Illic est constantia, quae deici loco non potest et propositum nulla vi extorquente dimittit. Illic est individuus ille comitatus virtutum; quicquid honeste fit, una virtus facit, sed ex consilii sententia. Quod autem ab omnibus virtutibus conprobatur, etiam si ab una fieri videtur, optabile est.

11 Quid? Tu existimas ea tantum optabilia esse,

[1] *putans* later MSS.; *putas* pVPb.

[a] Vergil, *Aeneid*, i. 94 ff.

[b] *Cf.* Livy, viii. 9. 6 ff. . . . *legiones auxiliaque hostium mecum deis manibus Tellurique devoveo.*

[c] *Ut litaret: i.e.*, that by his sacrifice he might secure an omen of success. *Cf.* Pliny, *N.H.* viii. 45, and Suetonius, *Augustus*, 96: "At the siege of Perusia, when he found the sacrifices were not favourable (*sacrificio non litanti*), Augustus called for more victims."

honour, I have prayed also for those things without which, on some occasions, life cannot be honourable.

> O thrice and four times blest were they
> Who underneath the lofty walls of Troy
> Met happy death before their parents' eyes![a]

What does it matter whether you offer this prayer for some individual, or admit that it was desirable in the past? Decius sacrificed himself for the State; he set spurs to his horse and rushed into the midst of the foe, seeking death. The second Decius, rivalling his father's valour, reproducing the words which had become sacred[b] and already household words, dashed into the thickest of the fight, anxious only that his sacrifice might bring omen of success,[c] and regarding a noble death as a thing to be desired. Do you doubt, then, whether it is best to die glorious and performing some deed of valour? When one endures torture bravely, one is using all the virtues. Endurance may perhaps be the only virtue that is on view and most manifest; but bravery is there too, and endurance and resignation and long-suffering are its branches. There, too, is foresight; for without foresight no plan can be undertaken; it is foresight that advises one to bear as bravely as possible the things one cannot avoid. There also is steadfastness, which cannot be dislodged from its position, which the wrench of no force can cause to abandon its purpose. There is the whole inseparable company of virtues; every honourable act is the work of one single virtue, but it is in accordance with the judgment of the whole council. And that which is approved by all the virtues, even though it seems to be the work of one alone, is desirable.

What? Do you think that those things only are

quae per voluptatem et otium veniunt, quae ex-
cipiuntur foribus ornatis? Sunt quaedam tristis
voltus bona. Sunt quaedam vota, quae non gratu-
lantium coetu, sed adorantium venerantiumque
12 celebrantur. Ita tu non putas Regulum optasse, ut
ad Poenos perveniret? Indue magni viri animum
et ab opinionibus volgi secede paulisper. Cape,
quantam debes, virtutis pulcherrimae ac magnifi-
centissimae speciem, quae nobis non ture nec sertis,
13 sed sudore et sanguine colenda est. Adspice M.
Catonem sacro illi pectori purissimas manus ad-
moventem et vulnera parum alte[1] demissa laxantem.
Utrum tandem illi dicturus es "vellem quae velles"
et "moleste fero" an "feliciter quod agis"?

14 Hoc loco mihi Demetrius noster occurrit, qui
vitam securam et sine ullis fortunae incursionibus
mare mortuum vocat. Nihil habere, ad quod exciteris,
ad quod te concites, cuius denuntiatione et incursu
firmitatem animi tui temptes, sed in otio inconcusso
15 iacere non est tranquillitas; malacia[2] est. Attalus
Stoicus dicere solebat: "malo me fortuna in castris
suis quam in deliciis habeat. Torqueor, sed fortiter;
bene est. Occidor, sed fortiter; bene est." Audi
Epicurum, dicet et "dulce est." Ego tam honestae
16 rei ac severae numquam molle nomen inponam. Uror,

[1] *alte* Hense and Buecheler; *ante* Gertz; *autem* p; omitted by VPb.

[2] *malacia* (*malatia*) p; *malitia* VPb.

---

[a] *Donaria* at the doors of temples signified public rejoicing; *cf.* Tibullus, i. 15 f.

> Flava Ceres, tibi sit nostro de rure corona
> Spicea, quae templi pendeat ante fores.

Myrtle decorated the bridegroom's house-door; garlands heralded the birth of a child (Juvenal, ix. 85).

[b] *Cf.* Pliny, *N.H.* iv. 13. Besides the Dead Sea of Palestine, the term was applied to any sluggish body of water.

desirable which come to us amid pleasure and ease, and which we bedeck our doors to welcome[a]? There are certain goods whose features are forbidding. There are certain prayers which are offered by a throng, not of men who rejoice, but of men who bow down reverently and worship. Was it not in this fashion, think you, that Regulus prayed that he might reach Carthage? Clothe yourself with a hero's courage, and withdraw for a little space from the opinions of the common man. Form a proper conception of the image of virtue, a thing of exceeding beauty and grandeur; this image is not to be worshipped by us with incense or garlands, but with sweat and blood. Behold Marcus Cato, laying upon that hallowed breast his unspotted hands, and tearing apart the wounds which had not gone deep enough to kill him! Which, pray, shall you say to him: "I hope all will be as you wish," and "I am grieved," or shall it be "Good fortune in your undertaking!"?

In this connexion I think of our friend Demetrius, who calls an easy existence, untroubled by the attacks of Fortune, a "Dead Sea."[b] If you have nothing to stir you up and rouse you to action, nothing which will test your resolution by its threats and hostilities; if you recline in unshaken comfort, it is not tranquillity; it is merely a flat calm. The Stoic Attalus was wont to say: "I should prefer that Fortune keep me in her camp rather than in the lap of luxury. If I am tortured, but bear it bravely, all is well; if I die, but die bravely, it is also well." Listen to Epicurus; he will tell you that it is actually pleasant.[c] I myself shall never apply an effeminate word to an act so honourable and austere. If I go

[c] *Cf. Ep.* lxvi. 18.

sed invictus. Quidni hoc optabile putem[1]—non quod urit me ignis, sed quod non vincit? Nihil est virtute praestantius, nihil pulchrius. Et bonum est et optabile, quicquid ex huius geritur imperio. Vale.

LXVIII.

Seneca Lvcilio svo salvtem

1 Consilio tuo accedo; absconde te in otio. Sed et ipsum otium absconde. Hoc te facturum Stoicorum etiam si non praecepto, at exemplo licet scias. Sed ex praecepto quoque facies[2]; et tibi et cui[3] voles
2 adprobabis. Nec ad omnem rem publicam mittimus nec semper nec sine ullo fine. Praeterea, cum sapienti rem publicam ipso dignam dedimus, id est mundum, non est extra rem publicam, etiam si recesserit, immo fortasse relicto uno angulo in maiora atque ampliora transit et caelo inpositus intellegit, cum sellam aut tribunal ascenderet, quam humili loco sederit. Depone hoc apud te, numquam plus agere sapientem, quam quom[4] in conspectum[5] eius divina atque humana venerunt.
3 Nunc ad illud revertor, quod suadere tibi coeperam,

[1] *optabile putem* Hense; *obtabile autem* p; *optabile sit* VPb.
[2] *facies* Muretus; *facias* MSS.
[3] *cui* Buecheler; *cum* MSS.
[4] *quam quom* Hense; *quam* or *quam cum* MSS.
[5] *conspectum* later MSS.; *conspectu* pVPb.

---

[a] Stoicism preached "world-citizenship," and this was interpreted in various ways at different periods. The Greek teachers saw in it an opportunity for wider culture; the Romans, a more practical mission. For further discussion

to the stake, I shall go unbeaten. Why should I not regard this as desirable—not because the fire burns me, but because it does not overcome me? Nothing is more excellent or more beautiful than virtue; whatever we do in obedience to her orders is both good and desirable. Farewell.

LXVIII. ON WISDOM AND RETIREMENT

I fall in with your plan; retire and conceal yourself in repose. But at the same time conceal your retirement also. In doing this, you may be sure that you will be following the example of the Stoics, if not their precept. But you will be acting according to their precept also; you will thus satisfy both yourself and any Stoic you please. We Stoics[a] do not urge men to take up public life in every case, or at all times, or without any qualification. Besides, when we have assigned to our wise man that field of public life which is worthy of him,—in other words, the universe,—he is then not apart from public life, even if he withdraws; nay, perhaps he has abandoned only one little corner thereof and has passed over into greater and wider regions; and when he has been set in the heavens, he understands how lowly was the place in which he sat when he mounted the curule chair or the judgment-seat. Lay this to heart, —that the wise man is never more active in affairs than when things divine as well as things human have come within his ken.

I now return to the advice which I set out to give

of this topic in Seneca see *Ep.* lxxiii. 1 ff. Seneca's arguments are coloured by the facts of his life at this time.

ut otium tuum ignotum sit. Non est quod inscribas
tibi philosophiam aut quietem.[1] Aliud proposito
tuo nomen inpone; valetudinem et inbecillitatem
voca et desidiam. Gloriari otio iners ambitio est.
4 Animalia quaedam ne inveniri possint, vestigia sua
circa ipsum cubile confundunt; idem tibi faciendum
est. Alioqui non deerunt, qui semper sequantur.
Multi aperta transeunt, condita et abstrusa rimantur;
furem signata sollicitant. Vile videtur, quicquid
patet, aperta effractarius praeterit. Hos mores habet
populus, hos imperitissimus quisque: in secreta in-
rumpere cupit. Optimum itaque est non iactare
5 otium suum. Iactandi autem genus est nimis latere
et a conspectu hominum secedere. Ille Tarentum
se abdidit, ille Neapoli inclusus est, ille multis annis
non transît domus suae limen. Convocat turbam,
6 quisquis otio suo aliquam fabulam inposuit. Cum
secesseris, non est hoc agendum, ut de te homines
loquantur, sed ut ipse tecum loquaris. Quid autem
loqueris? Quod homines de aliis libentissime faciunt,
de te apud te male existima; adsuesces et dicere
verum et audire. Id autem maxime tracta, quod in
7 te esse infirmissimum senties. Nota habet sui
quisque corporis vitia. Itaque alius vomitu levat
stomachum, alius frequenti[2] cibo fulcit, alius inter-

[1] *aut quietem* O. Rossbach; *aut qui etiam* p; *atqui etiam* VPb.

[2] *frequenti* later MSS.; *a frequenti* pVPb.

[a] *Cf. Ep.* lv. §§ 3 ff. for the retirement of Vatia: *ille latere sciebat, non vivere.*

you,—that you keep your retirement in the background. There is no need to fasten a placard upon yourself with the words: "Philosopher and Quietist." Give your purpose some other name; call it ill-health and bodily weakness, or mere laziness. To boast of our retirement is but idle self-seeking. Certain animals hide themselves from discovery by confusing the marks of their foot-prints in the neighbourhood of their lairs. You should do the same. Otherwise, there will always be someone dogging your footsteps. Many men pass by that which is visible, and peer after things hidden and concealed; a locked room invites the thief. Things which lie in the open appear cheap; the house-breaker passes by that which is exposed to view. This is the way of the world, and the way of all ignorant men: they crave to burst in upon hidden things. It is therefore best not to vaunt one's retirement. It is, however, a sort of vaunting to make too much of one's concealment and of one's withdrawal from the sight of men. So-and-so [a] has gone into his retreat at Tarentum; that other man has shut himself up at Naples; this third person for many years has not crossed the threshold of his own house. To advertise one's retirement is to collect a crowd. When you withdraw from the world, your business is to talk with yourself, not to have men talk about you. But what shall you talk about? Do just what people are fond of doing when they talk about their neighbours,—speak ill of yourself when by yourself; then you will become accustomed both to speak and to hear the truth. Above all, however, ponder that which you come to feel is your greatest weakness. Each man knows best the defects of his own body. And so one relieves his stomach by vomiting, another props it up by frequent eating,

posito ieiunio corpus exhaurit et purgat. Ii, quorum pedes dolor repetit, aut vino aut balineo abstinent. In cetera neglegentes huic, a quo saepe infestantur, occurrunt; sic in animo nostro sunt quaedam quasi causariae partes, quibus adhibenda curatio est.

8 Quid in otio facio? Ulcus meum curo. Si ostenderem tibi pedem turgidum, lividam manum aut contracti cruris aridos nervos, permitteres mihi uno loco iacere et fovere morbum meum. Maius malum est hoc, quod non possum tibi ostendere; in pectore ipso collectio et vomica est. Nolo nolo laudes, nolo dicas: "o magnum virum! contempsit omnia et damnatis humanae vitae furoribus fugit."
9 Nihil damnavi nisi me. Non est quod proficiendi causa venire ad me velis. Erras, qui hinc aliquid auxilii speras; non medicus, sed aeger hic habitat. Malo, cum discesseris, dicas: "ego istum beatum hominem putabam et eruditum. Erexeram aures; destitutus sum. Nihil vidi, nihil audii,[1] quod concupiscerem, ad quod reverterer." Si hoc sentis, si hoc loqueris, aliquid profectum est. Malo ignoscas otio meo quam invideas.

10 "Otium," inquis, "Seneca, commendas mihi?

[1] *audii* Rossbach; *audivi* VPb; *laudi* p.

[a] *Causarii* (Livy, vi. 6) were soldiers on sick leave.

[b] For an argument of the same sort see Horace, *Epist.* i. 1. 93–104:

> Si curatus inaequali tonsore capillos
> Occurri, rides . . .
> . . . quid, mea cum pugnat sententia secum?

another drains and purges his body by periodic fasting. Those whose feet are visited by pain abstain either from wine or from the bath. In general, men who are careless in other respects go out of their way to relieve the disease which frequently afflicts them. So it is with our souls; there are in them certain parts which are, so to speak, on the sick-list,[a] and to these parts the cure must be applied.

What, then, am I myself doing with my leisure? I am trying to cure my own sores. If I were to show you a swollen foot, or an inflamed hand, or some shrivelled sinews in a withered leg, you would permit me to lie quiet in one place and to apply lotions to the diseased member.[b] But my trouble is greater than any of these, and I cannot show it to you. The abscess, or ulcer, is deep within my breast. Pray, pray, do not commend me, do not say: "What a great man! He has learned to despise all things; condemning the madnesses of man's life, he has made his escape!" I have condemned nothing except myself. There is no reason why you should desire to come to me for the sake of making progress. You are mistaken if you think that you will get any assistance from this quarter; it is not a physician that dwells here, but a sick man. I would rather have you say, on leaving my presence: "I used to think him a happy man and a learned one, and I had pricked up my ears to hear him; but I have been defrauded. I have seen nothing, heard nothing which I craved and which I came back to hear." If you feel thus, and speak thus, some progress has been made. I prefer you to pardon rather than envy my retirement.

Then you say: "Is it retirement, Seneca, that you are recommending to me? You will soon be

Ad Epicureas voces delaberis." Otium tibi commendo, in quo maiora agas et pulchriora quam quae reliquisti; pulsare superbas potentiorum fores, digerere in litteram senes orbos, plurimum in foro posse invidiosa potentia ac brevis est et, si verum
11 aestimes, sordida. Ille me gratia forensi longe antecedet, ille stipendiis militaribus et quaesita per hoc dignitate, ille clientium turba; est tanti ab omnibus vinci, dum a me fortuna vincatur, cui in turba par esse non possum;[1] plus habet gratiae.

12 Utinam quidem hoc propositum sequi olim fuisset animus tibi! Utinam de vita beata non in conspectu mortis ageremus! Sed nunc quoque non moremur.[2] Multa enim, quae supervacua esse et inimica credituri
13 fuimus rationi, nunc experientiae credimus. Quod facere solent, qui serius exierunt[3] et volunt tempus celeritate reparare, calcar addamus; haec aetas optime facit ad haec studia; iam despumavit.[4] Iam vitia primo fervore adulescentiae indomita lassavit, non multum superest ut extinguat.

14 "Et quando," inquis, "tibi proderit istud, quod in exitu discis,[5] aut in quam rem?" In hanc, ut exeam melior. Non est tamen quod existimes ullam aetatem

[1] Haase's punctuation. Hense regards *cui in turba . . . gratiae* as an interpolation.

[2] *moremur* Erasmus; *moramur* MSS.

[3] *exierunt* later MSS.; *exerunt* pVPb.

[4] *despumavit* cod. Vat. reg.; *disputavit* pVPb.

[5] *discis* later MSS.; *dicis* pVPb.

---

[a] This is a reference to the saying of Epicurus, λαθὲ βιώσας, "live in retirement."

[b] *Cf.* Horace, *Sat.* ii. 5. 23 ff.: *captes astutus ubique testamenta senum* and *vivet uter locuples sine gnatis . . . illius esto defensor*. The *captator* was a well-known figure at Rome; *cf.* also Pliny's notorious enemy Regulus, and Juvenal's many words of scorn for those who practised the art.

[c] *i.e.*, Fortune's support comes from crowds.

falling back upon the maxims of Epicurus!"[a] I do recommend retirement to you, but only that you may use it for greater and more beautiful activities than those which you have resigned; to knock at the haughty doors of the influential, to make alphabetical lists of childless old men,[b] to wield the highest authority in public life,—this kind of power exposes you to hatred, is short-lived, and, if you rate it at its true value, is tawdry. One man shall be far ahead of me as regards his influence in public life, another in salary as an army officer and in the position which results from this, another in the throng of his clients; but it is worth while to be outdone by all these men, provided that I myself can outdo Fortune. And I am no match for her in the throng; she has the greater backing.[c]

Would that in earlier days you had been minded to follow this purpose! Would that we were not discussing the happy life in plain view of death! But even now let us have no delay. For now we can take the word of experience, which tells us that there are many superfluous and hostile things; for this we should long since have taken the word of reason. Let us do what men are wont to do when they are late in setting forth, and wish to make up for lost time by increasing their speed—let us ply the spur. Our time of life is the best possible for these pursuits; for the period of boiling and foaming is now past.[d] The faults that were uncontrolled in the first fierce heat of youth are now weakened, and but little further effort is needed to extinguish them.

"And when," you ask, "will that profit you which you do not learn until your departure, and how will it profit you?" Precisely in this way, that I shall depart a better man. You need not think,

[d] *Cf. De Ira*, ii. 20 *ut nimius ille fervor despumet.*

aptiorem esse ad bonam mentem quam quae se multis experimentis, longa ac frequenti rerum paenitentia edomuit, quae ad salutaria mitigatis adfectibus venit. Hoc est huius boni tempus; quisquis senex ad sapientiam pervenit, annis pervenit. Vale.

LXIX.

Seneca Lvcilio svo salvtem

1 Mutare te loca et aliunde alio[1] transilire nolo; primum, quia tam frequens migratio instabilis animi est. Coalescere otio non potest, nisi desît circumspicere et errare. Ut animum possis continere,
2 primum corporis tui fugam siste. Deinde plurimum remedia continuata proficiunt. Interrumpenda non est quies et vitae prioris oblivio. Sine dediscere oculos tuos, sine aures adsuescere sanioribus verbis. Quotiens processeris, in ipso transitu aliqua, quae
3 renovent cupiditates tuas, tibi occurrent. Quemadmodum ei,[2] qui amorem exuere conatur, evitanda est omnis admonitio dilecti corporis, nihil enim facilius quam amor recrudescit, ita qui deponere vult desideria rerum omnium, quarum cupiditate flagravit,

[1] *aliunde alio* Haase; *alium de alio* pPb; *in alium de alio* V.
[2] *ei* later MSS.; *et* pVPb.

[a] *Cf. Ep.* ii. § 3 *nil aeque sanitatem impedit quam remediorum crebra mutatio.*

however, that any time of life is more fitted to the attainment of a sound mind than that which has gained the victory over itself by many trials and by long and oft-repeated regret for past mistakes, and, its passions assuaged, has reached a state of health. This is indeed the time to have acquired this good; he who has attained wisdom in his old age, has attained it by his years. Farewell.

LXIX. ON REST AND RESTLESSNESS

I do not like you to change your headquarters and scurry about from one place to another. My reasons are,—first, that such frequent flitting means an unsteady spirit. And the spirit cannot through retirement grow into unity unless it has ceased from its inquisitiveness and its wanderings. To be able to hold your spirit in check, you must first stop the runaway flight of the body. My second reason is, that the remedies which are most helpful are those which are not interrupted.[a] You should not allow your quiet, or the oblivion to which you have consigned your former life, to be broken into. Give your eyes time to unlearn what they have seen, and your ears to grow accustomed to more wholesome words. Whenever you stir abroad you will meet, even as you pass from one place to another, things that will bring back your old cravings. Just as he who tries to be rid of an old love must avoid every reminder of the person once held dear (for nothing grows again so easily as love), similarly, he who would lay aside his desire for all the things which he

et oculos et aures ab iis, quae reliquit, avertat. Cito
4 rebellat adfectus. Quocumque se verterit, pretium aliquod praesens occupationis suae aspiciet. Nullum sine auctoramento malum est. Avaritia pecuniam promittit, luxuria multas ac varias voluptates, ambitio purpuram et plausum et ex hoc potentiam et quic-
5 quid potest potentia.[1] Mercede te vitia sollicitant; hic tibi gratis vivendum est. Vix effici toto saeculo potest, ut vitia tam longa licentia tumida subigantur et iugum accipiant, nedum, si tam breve tempus intervallis caedimus.[2] Unam quamlibet rem vix ad
6 perfectum perducit adsidua vigilia et intentio. Si me quidem velis audire, hoc meditare et exerce, ut mortem et excipias et, si ita res suadebit, accersas. Interest nihil, illa ad nos veniat an ad illam nos. Illud imperitissimi cuiusque verbum falsum esse tibi ipse persuade: "Bella res est mori sua morte." Nemo moritur nisi sua morte. Illud praeterea tecum licet cogites: nemo nisi suo die moritur. Nihil perdis ex tuo tempore; nam quod relinquis, alienum est. VALE.

[1] *potest potentia* Hense; *potentia* VPb; *potia* p; *potentia potest* later MSS

[2] *tempus intervallis caedimus* Madvig; *intervallum discedimus* (*discidimus*) pVPb.

---

[a] Perhaps the converse idea of "living one's own life." It means "dying when the proper time comes," and is the common man's argument against suicide. The thought perhaps suggests the subject matter of the next letter.

used to crave so passionately, must turn away both eyes and ears from the objects which he has abandoned. The emotions soon return to the attack; at every turn they will notice before their eyes an object worth their attention. There is no evil that does not offer inducements. Avarice promises money; luxury, a varied assortment of pleasures; ambition, a purple robe and applause, and the influence which results from applause, and all that influence can do. Vices tempt you by the rewards which they offer; but in the life of which I speak, you must live without being paid. Scarcely will a whole life-time suffice to bring our vices into subjection and to make them accept the yoke, swollen as they are by long-continued indulgence; and still less, if we cut into our brief span by any interruptions. Even constant care and attention can scarcely bring any one undertaking to full completion. If you will give ear to my advice, ponder and practise this,—how to welcome death, or even, if circumstances commend that course, to invite it. There is no difference whether death comes to us, or whether we go to death. Make yourself believe that all ignorant men are wrong when they say: "It is a beautiful thing to die one's own death." [a] But there is no man who does not die his own death. What is more, you may reflect on this thought: No one dies except on his own day. You are throwing away none of your own time; for what you leave behind does not belong to you. Farewell.

LXX.

SENECA LVCILIO SVO SALVTEM

1 Post longum intervallum Pompeios tuos vidi. In
conspectum adulescentiae meae reductus sum. Quicquid illic iuvenis feceram, videbar mihi facere adhuc
2 posse et paulo ante fecisse. Praenavigavimus, Lucili,
vitam et quemadmodum in mari, ut ait Vergilius
noster,

> Terraeque urbesque recedunt,

sic in hoc cursu rapidissimi temporis primum pueritiam
abscondimus, deinde adulescentiam, deinde quidquid
est illud inter iuvenem et senem medium, in utriusque
confinio positum, deinde ipsius senectutis optimos
annos. Novissime incipit ostendi publicus finis
3 generis humani. Scopulum esse illum putamus
dementissimi; portus est, aliquando petendus, numquam recusandus, in quem si quis intra primos annos
delatus est, non magis queri debet quam qui cito
navigavit. Alium enim, ut scis, venti segnes ludunt
ac detinent et tranquillitatis lentissimae taedio lassant,
alium pertinax flatus celerrime perfert.

4 Idem evenire nobis puta: alios vita velocissime
adduxit, quo veniendum erat etiam cunctantibus,
alios maceravit et coxit. Quae, ut scis, non semper

---

[a] Probably the birthplace of Lucilius.
[b] *Aeneid*, iii. 72.

LXX. ON THE PROPER TIME TO SLIP THE CABLE

After a long space of time I have seen your beloved Pompeii.[a] I was thus brought again face to face with the days of my youth. And it seemed to me that I could still do, nay, had only done a short time ago, all the things which I did there when a young man. We have sailed past life, Lucilius, as if we were on a voyage, and just as when at sea, to quote from our poet Vergil,

> Lands and towns are left astern,[b]

even so, on this journey where time flies with the greatest speed, we put below the horizon first our boyhood and then our youth, and then the space which lies between young manhood and middle age and borders on both, and next, the best years of old age itself. Last of all, we begin to sight the general bourne of the race of man. Fools that we are, we believe this bourne to be a dangerous reef; but it is the harbour, where we must some day put in, which we may never refuse to enter; and if a man has reached this harbour in his early years, he has no more right to complain than a sailor who has made a quick voyage. For some sailors, as you know, are tricked and held back by sluggish winds, and grow weary and sick of the slow-moving calm; while others are carried quickly home by steady gales.

You may consider that the same thing happens to us: life has carried some men with the greatest rapidity to the harbour, the harbour they were bound to reach even if they tarried on the way, while others it has fretted and harassed. To such a life, as you

retinenda est. Non enim vivere bonum est, sed bene vivere. Itaque sapiens vivit, quantum debet, non
5 quantum potest. Videbit ubi victurus sit, cum quibus, quomodo, quid acturus. Cogitat semper, qualis vita, non quanta sit. Si multa[1] occurrunt molesta et tranquillitatem turbantia, emittit se. Nec hoc tantum in necessitate ultima facit, sed cum primum illi coepit suspecta esse fortuna, diligenter circumspicit, numquid ideo[2] desinendum sit. Nihil existimat sua referre, faciat finem an accipiat, tardius fiat an citius. Non tamquam de magno detrimento timet; nemo multum ex stilicidio potest perdere.
6 Citius mori aut tardius ad rem non pertinet, bene mori aut male ad rem pertinet. Bene autem mori est effugere male vivendi periculum.

Itaque effeminatissimam vocem illius Rhodii existimo, qui cum in caveam coniectus esset a tyranno et tamquam ferum aliquod animal aleretur, suadenti cuidam, ut abstineret cibo: "omnia," inquit, "homini, dum vivit, speranda sunt." Ut sit hoc verum, non omni pretio vita emenda est. Quaedam licet magna, licet certa sint, tamen ad illa turpi infirmitatis confessione non veniam. Ego cogitem in eo, qui vivit, omnia posse fortunam, potius quam cogitem in eo, qui scit mori, nil posse fortunam?

[1] *si multa* later MSS.; *si* (*sit* p) *simulata* pVPb.
[2] *ideo* C. Brakman; *illo* MSS.; *illo die* Muretus.

---

[a] Although Socrates says (*Phaedo*, 61 f.) that the philosopher must, according to Philolaus, not take his own life against the will of God, the Stoics interpreted the problem in different ways. Some held that a noble purpose justified suicide; others, that any reason was good enough. *Cf. Ep.* lxxvii. 5 ff.

[b] Telesphorus of Rhodes, threatened by the tyrant Lysimachus. On the proverb see Cicero, *Ad Att.* ix. 10. 3, and Terence, *Heauton.* 981 *modo liceat vivere, est spes.*

are aware, one should not always cling. For mere living is not a good, but living well. Accordingly, the wise man will live as long as he ought, not as long as he can.[a] He will mark in what place, with whom, and how he is to conduct his existence, and what he is about to do. He always reflects concerning the quality, and not the quantity, of his life. As soon as there are many events in his life that give him trouble and disturb his peace of mind, he sets himself free. And this privilege is his, not only when the crisis is upon him, but as soon as Fortune seems to be playing him false; then he looks about carefully and sees whether he ought, or ought not, to end his life on that account. He holds that it makes no difference to him whether his taking-off be natural or self-inflicted, whether it comes later or earlier. He does not regard it with fear, as if it were a great loss; for no man can lose very much when but a driblet remains. It is not a question of dying earlier or later, but of dying well or ill. And dying well means escape from the danger of living ill.

That is why I regard the words of the well-known Rhodian[b] as most unmanly. This person was thrown into a cage by his tyrant, and fed there like some wild animal. And when a certain man advised him to end his life by fasting, he replied: "A man may hope for anything while he has life." This may be true; but life is not to be purchased at any price. No matter how great or how well-assured certain rewards may be, I shall not strive to attain them at the price of a shameful confession of weakness. Shall I reflect that Fortune has all power over one who lives, rather than reflect that she has no power over one who knows how to die? There

8 Aliquando tamen, etiam si certa mors instabit et destinatum sibi supplicium sciet, non commodabit[1] poenae suae manum; sibi commodaret. Stultitia est timore mortis mori. Venit qui occidat. Expecta. Quid occupas? Quare suscipis alienae crudelitatis procurationem? Utrum invides carnifici tuo an
9 parcis? Socrates potuit abstinentia finire vitam et inedia potius quam veneno mori. Triginta tamen dies in carcere et in expectatione mortis exegit, non hoc animo tamquam omnia fieri possent, tamquam multas spes tam longum tempus reciperet, sed ut praeberet se legibus, ut fruendum amicis extremum Socraten daret. Quid erat stultius quam mortem contemnere, venenum timere?

10 Scribonia, gravis femina, amita Drusi Libonis fuit, adulescentis tam stolidi[2] quam nobilis, maiora sperantis quam illo saeculo quisquam sperare poterat aut ipse ullo. Cum aeger a senatu in lectica relatus esset non sane frequentibus exequiis, omnes enim necessarii deseruerant impie iam non reum, sed funus; habere coepit consilium, utrum conscisceret mortem an expectaret. Cui Scribonia: "Quid te,"

[1] *commodabit* later MSS.; *commendabit* VPb; *commendavit* p.
[2] *stolidi* Torrentius; *solidi* MSS.

---

[a] *i.e.*, if he must choose between helping along his punishment by suicide, or helping himself by staying alive under torture and practising the virtues thus brought into play, he will choose the latter,—*sibi commodare.*

[b] See the imaginary dialogue in Plato's *Crito* (50 ff.) between Socrates and the Laws—a passage which develops this thought.

[c] And to commit suicide in order to escape poisoning.

[d] For a more complete account of this tragedy see

are times, nevertheless, when a man, even though certain death impends and he knows that torture is in store for him, will refrain from lending a hand to his own punishment; to himself, however, he would lend a hand.[a] It is folly to die through fear of dying. The executioner is upon you; wait for him. Why anticipate him? Why assume the management of a cruel task that belongs to another? Do you grudge your executioner his privilege, or do you merely relieve him of his task? Socrates might have ended his life by fasting; he might have died by starvation rather than by poison. But instead of this he spent thirty days in prison awaiting death, not with the idea "everything may happen," or "so long an interval has room for many a hope" but in order that he might show himself submissive to the laws[b] and make the last moments of Socrates an edification to his friends. What would have been more foolish than to scorn death, and yet fear poison?[c]

Scribonia, a woman of the stern old type, was an aunt of Drusus Libo.[d] This young man was as stupid as he was well born, with higher ambitions than anyone could have been expected to entertain in that epoch, or a man like himself in any epoch at all. When Libo had been carried away ill from the senate-house in his litter, though certainly with a very scanty train of followers,—for all his kinsfolk undutifully deserted him, when he was no longer a criminal but a corpse,—he began to consider whether he should commit suicide, or await death. Scribonia said to him: "What pleasure do

Tacitus, *Annals*, ii. 27 ff. Libo was duped by Firmius Catus (16 A.D.) into seeking imperial power, was detected, and finally forced by Tiberius to commit suicide.

inquit, "delectat alienum negotium agere?" Non persuasit illi; manus sibi attulit nec sine causa. Nam post diem tertium aut quartum inimici moriturus arbitrio si vivit, alienum negotium agit.

11 Non possis itaque de re in universum pronuntiare, cum mortem vis externa denuntiat, occupanda sit an expectanda. Multa enim sunt, quae in utramque partem trahere possunt. Si altera mors cum tormento, altera simplex et facilis est, quidni huic inicienda sit manus? Quemadmodum navem eligam navigaturus et domum habitaturus, sic mortem exi-
12 turus e vita. Praeterea quemadmodum non utique melior est longior vita, sic peior est utique mors longior. In nulla re magis quam in morte morem animo gerere debemus. Exeat, qua impetum cepit; sive ferrum appetit sive laqueum sive aliquam potionem venas occupantem, pergat et vincula servitutis abrumpat. Vitam et aliis adprobare quisque debet,
13 mortem sibi. Optima est, quae placet. Stulte haec cogitantur: "aliquis dicet me parum fortiter fecisse, aliquis nimis temere, aliquis fuisse aliquod genus mortis animosius." Vis tu cogitare id in manibus esse consilium, ad quod fama non pertinet! Hoc unum intuere, ut te fortunae quam celerrime

[a] When the "natural advantages" (τὰ κατὰ φύσιν) of living are outweighed by the corresponding disadvantages, the honourable man may, according to the general Stoic view, take his departure. Socrates and Cato were right in so doing, according to Seneca; but he condemns (*Ep.* xxiv. 25) those contemporaries who had recourse to suicide as a mere whim of fashion.

you find in doing another man's work?" But he did not follow her advice; he laid violent hands upon himself. And he was right, after all; for when a man is doomed to die in two or three days at his enemy's pleasure, he is really "doing another man's work" if he continues to live.

No general statement can be made, therefore, with regard to the question whether, when a power beyond our control threatens us with death, we should anticipate death, or await it. For there are many arguments to pull us in either direction. If one death is accompanied by torture, and the other is simple and easy, why not snatch the latter? Just as I shall select my ship when I am about to go on a voyage, or my house when I propose to take a residence, so I shall choose my death when I am about to depart from life. Moreover, just as a long-drawn-out life does not necessarily mean a better one, so a long-drawn-out death necessarily means a worse one. There is no occasion when the soul should be humoured more than at the moment of death. Let the soul depart as it feels itself impelled to go;[a] whether it seeks the sword, or the halter, or some draught that attacks the veins, let it proceed and burst the bonds of its slavery. Every man ought to make his life acceptable to others besides himself, but his death to himself alone. The best form of death is the one we like. Men are foolish who reflect thus: "One person will say that my conduct was not brave enough; another, that I was too headstrong; a third, that a particular kind of death would have betokened more spirit." What you should really reflect is: "I have under consideration a purpose with which the talk of men has no concern!" Your sole aim should be to escape from Fortune as

eripias; alioquin aderunt, qui de facto tuo male existiment.

14 Invenies etiam professos sapientiam, qui vim adferendam vitae suae negent et nefas iudicent ipsum interemptorem sui fieri; expectandum esse exitum,[1] quem natura decrevit. Hoc qui dicit, non videt se libertatis viam cludere. Nil melius aeterna lex fecit, quam quod unum introitum nobis ad vitam
15 dedit, exitus multos. Ego expectem vel morbi crudelitatem vel hominis, cum possim per media exire tormenta et adversa discutere? Hoc est unum, cur de vita non possimus[2] queri: neminem tenet. Bono loco res humanae sunt, quod nemo nisi vitio suo miser est. Placet; vive. Non placet; licet eo
16 reverti, unde venisti. Ut dolorem capitis levares, sanguinem saepe misisti. Ad extenuandum corpus vena percutitur. Non opus est vasto vulnere dividere praecordia; scalpello aperitur ad illam magnam libertatem via et puncto securitas constat.

Quid ergo est, quod nos facit pigros inertesque? Nemo nostrum cogitat quandoque sibi ex hoc domicilio exeundum; sic veteres inquilinos indulgentia
17 loci et consuetudo etiam inter iniurias detinet. Vis adversus hoc corpus liber esse? Tamquam migraturus habita. Propone tibi quandoque hoc contubernio carendum; fortior eris ad necessitatem exeundi. Sed quemadmodum suus finis veniet in

[1] *exspectandum esse exitum* later MSS.; *expectanovum esse exitum* VPb.

[2] *possimus* Erasmus; *possemus* p; *possumus* VPb.

---

[a] By means of the *cucurbita*, or cupping-glass. *Cf.* Juvenal, xiv. 58 *caput ventosa cucurbita quaerat.* It was often used as a remedy for insanity or delirium.

speedily as possible; otherwise, there will be no lack of persons who will think ill of what you have done.

You can find men who have gone so far as to profess wisdom and yet maintain that one should not offer violence to one's own life, and hold it accursed for a man to be the means of his own destruction; we should wait, say they, for the end decreed by nature. But one who says this does not see that he is shutting off the path to freedom. The best thing which eternal law ever ordained was that it allowed to us one entrance into life, but many exits. Must I await the cruelty either of disease or of man, when I can depart through the midst of torture, and shake off my troubles? This is the one reason why we cannot complain of life: it keeps no one against his will. Humanity is well situated, because no man is unhappy except by his own fault. Live, if you so desire; if not, you may return to the place whence you came. You have often been cupped in order to relieve headaches.[a] You have had veins cut for the purpose of reducing your weight. If you would pierce your heart, a gaping wound is not necessary; a lancet will open the way to that great freedom, and tranquillity can be purchased at the cost of a pin-prick.

What, then, is it which makes us lazy and sluggish? None of us reflects that some day he must depart from this house of life; just so old tenants are kept from moving by fondness for a particular place and by custom, even in spite of ill-treatment. Would you be free from the restraint of your body? Live in it as if you were about to leave it. Keep thinking of the fact that some day you will be deprived of this tenure; then you will be more brave against the necessity of departing. But how will a man

18 mentem omnia sine fine concupiscentibus? Nullius rei meditatio tam necessaria est. Alia enim fortasse exercentur in supervacuum. Adversus paupertatem praeparatus est animus; permansere divitiae. Ad contemptum nos doloris armavimus; nunquam a nobis exegit huius virtutis experimentum integri ac sani felicitas corporis. Ut fortiter amissorum desideria pateremur praecepimus nobis; omnes, quos amabamus, superstites fortuna servavit. Huius unius rei usum qui exigat [1] dies veniet.

19 Non est quod existimes magnis tantum viris hoc robur fuisse, quo servitutis humanae claustra perrumperent; non est quod iudices hoc fieri nisi a Catone non posse, qui quam ferro non emiserat animam manu extraxit. Vilissimae sortis homines [2] ingenti impetu in tutum evaserunt,[3] cumque e commodo [4] mori non licuisset nec ad arbitrium suum instrumenta mortis eligere, obvia quaeque rapuerunt et quae
20 natura non erant noxia, vi sua tela fecerunt. Nuper in ludo bestiariorum unus e Germanis, cum ad matutina spectacula pararetur, secessit ad exonerandum corpus; nullum aliud illi dabatur sine custode secretum. Ibi lignum id, quod ad emundanda obscena adhaerente spongia positum est, totum in gulam farsit et interclusis [5] faucibus spiritum elisit.

[1] *exigat* later MSS.; *excitat* pVPb.

[2] *extraxit: vilissimae sortis homines* several editors, including Hense and Haase; *extraxit hutilissimae sortis hominis* p; *extraxit cum vilissimae sortis homines* VPb.

[3] *evaserunt* Haase; *evaserit* or *evaserint* MSS.

[4] *cumque e(x) commodo* C.F.G. Mueller; *cumque commodo (quomodo)* Pb; *cumque incommodo* p.

[5] *interclusis* Hense; *inperclusis* VPb; *in perclusi* p.

take thought of his own end, if he craves all things without end? And yet there is nothing so essential for us to consider. For our training in other things is perhaps superfluous. Our souls have been made ready to meet poverty; but our riches have held out. We have armed ourselves to scorn pain; but we have had the good fortune to possess sound and healthy bodies, and so have never been forced to put this virtue to the test. We have taught ourselves to endure bravely the loss of those we love; but Fortune has preserved to us all whom we loved. It is in this one matter only that the day will come which will require us to test our training.

You need not think that none but great men have had the strength to burst the bonds of human servitude; you need not believe that this cannot be done except by a Cato,—Cato, who with his hand dragged forth the spirit which he had not succeeded in freeing by the sword. Nay, men of the meanest lot in life have by a mighty impulse escaped to safety, and when they were not allowed to die at their own convenience, or to suit themselves in their choice of the instruments of death, they have snatched up whatever was lying ready to hand, and by sheer strength have turned objects which were by nature harmless into weapons of their own. For example, there was lately in a training-school for wild-beast gladiators a German, who was making ready for the morning exhibition; he withdrew in order to relieve himself,—the only thing which he was allowed to do in secret and without the presence of a guard. While so engaged, he seized the stick of wood, tipped with a sponge, which was devoted to the vilest uses, and stuffed it, just as it was, down his throat; thus he blocked up his windpipe, and choked

Hoc fuit morti contumeliam facere. Ita prorsus; parum munde et parum decenter; quid est stultius
21 quam fastidiose mori? O virum fortem, o dignum, cui fati daretur electio! Quam fortiter ille gladio usus esset, quam animose in profundam se altitudinem maris aut abscisae rupis inmisisset! Undique destitutus invenit, quemadmodum et mortem sibi deferret[1] et telum, ut scias ad moriendum nihil aliud in mora esse quam velle. Existimetur de facto hominis acerrimi, ut cuique visum erit, dum hoc constet, praeferendam esse spurcissimam mortem servituti mundissimae.

22 Quoniam coepi sordidis exemplis uti, perseverabo. Plus enim a se quisque exiget, si viderit hanc rem etiam a contemptissimis posse contemni. Catones Scipionesque et alios, quos audire cum admiratione consuevimus, supra imitationem positos putamus; iam ego istam virtutem habere tam multa exempla in ludo bestiario quam in ducibus belli civilis
23 ostendam. Cum adveheretur nuper inter custodias quidam ad matutinum spectaculum missus, tamquam somno premente nutaret, caput usque eo demisit, donec radiis insereret, et tamdiu se in sedili suo tenuit, donec cervicem circumactu rotae frangeret. Eodem vehiculo, quo ad poenam ferebatur, effugit.

24 Nihil obstat erumpere et exire cupienti. In

[1] *deferret* Hense; *deberet* MSS.

---

[a] *Custodia* in the sense of "prisoner" (abstract for concrete) is a post-Augustan usage. See *Ep.* v. 7, and Summers' note.

the breath from his body. That was truly to insult death! Yes, indeed; it was not a very elegant or becoming way to die; but what is more foolish than to be over-nice about dying? What a brave fellow! He surely deserved to be allowed to choose his fate! How bravely he would have wielded a sword! With what courage he would have hurled himself into the depths of the sea, or down a precipice! Cut off from resources on every hand, he yet found a way to furnish himself with death, and with a weapon for death. Hence you can understand that nothing but the will need postpone death. Let each man judge the deed of this most zealous fellow as he likes, provided we agree on this point,—that the foulest death is preferable to the fairest slavery.

Inasmuch as I began with an illustration taken from humble life, I shall keep on with that sort. For men will make greater demands upon themselves, if they see that death can be despised even by the most despised class of men. The Catos, the Scipios, and the others whose names we are wont to hear with admiration, we regard as beyond the sphere of imitation; but I shall now prove to you that the virtue of which I speak is found as frequently in the gladiators' training-school as among the leaders in a civil war. Lately a gladiator, who had been sent forth to the morning exhibition, was being conveyed in a cart along with the other prisoners[a]; nodding as if he were heavy with sleep, he let his head fall over so far that it was caught in the spokes; then he kept his body in position long enough to break his neck by the revolution of the wheel. So he made his escape by means of the very wagon which was carrying him to his punishment.

When a man desires to burst forth and take his

aperto nos natura custodit. Cui permittit necessitas
sua, circumspiciat exitum mollem ; cui ad manum plura
sunt, per quae sese adserat, is dilectum agat et qua
potissimum liberetur, consideret ; cui difficilis occasio
est, is proximam quamque pro optima arripiat, sit
licet inaudita, sit nova. Non deerit ad mortem
25 ingenium, cui non defuerit animus. Vides, quemadmodum extrema quoque mancipia, ubi illis stimulos
adegit dolor, excitentur et intentissimas custodias
fallant ? Ille vir magnus est, qui mortem sibi non
tantum imperavit, sed invenit.

Ex eodem tibi munere plura exempla promisi.
26 Secundo naumachiae spectaculo unus e barbaris
lanceam, quam in adversarios acceperat, totam iugulo
suo mersit. "Quare, quare," inquit, "non omne
tormentum, omne ludibrium iamdudum effugio ?
Quare ego mortem armatus expecto ?" Tanto hoc
27 speciosius spectaculum fuit, quanto honestius mori
discunt homines quam occidere.

Quid ergo ? Quod animi perditi quodque noxiosi habent, non habebunt illi, quos adversus hos casus instruxit longa meditatio et magistra rerum omnium ratio ? Illa nos docet fati varios esse accessus, finem eundem, nihil autem interesse, unde incipiat quod

departure, nothing stands in his way. It is an open space in which Nature guards us. When our plight is such as to permit it, we may look about us for an easy exit. If you have many opportunities ready to hand, by means of which you may liberate yourself, you may make a selection and think over the best way of gaining freedom; but if a chance is hard to find, instead of the best, snatch the next best, even though it be something unheard of, something new. If you do not lack the courage, you will not lack the cleverness, to die. See how even the lowest class of slave, when suffering goads him on, is aroused and discovers a way to deceive even the most watchful guards! He is truly great who not only has given himself the order to die, but has also found the means.

I have promised you, however, some more illustrations drawn from the same games. During the second event in a sham sea-fight one of the barbarians sank deep into his own throat a spear which had been given him for use against his foe. "Why, oh why," he said, "have I not long ago escaped from all this torture and all this mockery? Why should I be armed and yet wait for death to come?" This exhibition was all the more striking because of the lesson men learn from it that dying is more honourable than killing.

What, then? If such a spirit is possessed by abandoned and dangerous men, shall it not be possessed also by those who have trained themselves to meet such contingencies by long meditation, and by reason, the mistress of all things? It is reason which teaches us that fate has various ways of approach, but the same end, and that it makes no difference at what point the inevitable event begins.

28 venit. Eadem illa ratio monet, ut, si licet, moriaris quemadmodum placet; si minus,[1] quemadmodum potes, et quicquid obvenerit ad vim adferendam tibi invadas. Iniuriosum est rapto vivere, at contra pulcherrimum mori rapto. Vale.

LXXI.

Seneca Lvcilio svo salvtem

1 Subinde me de rebus singulis consulis oblitus vasto nos mari dividi. Cum magna pars consilii sit in tempore, necesse est evenire, ut de quibusdam rebus tunc ad te perferatur sententia mea, cum iam contraria potior est. Consilia enim rebus aptantur. Res nostrae feruntur, immo volvuntur. Ergo consilium nasci sub diem debet; et hoc quoque nimis tardum est; sub manu, quod aiunt, nascatur. Quemadmodum autem inveniatur, ostendam.

2 Quotiens, quid fugiendum sit aut quid petendum, voles scire, ad summum bonum, propositum totius vitae tuae, respice. Illi enim consentire debet, quicquid agimus; non disponet singula, nisi cui iam vitae suae summa proposita est. Nemo, quamvis paratos habeat colores, similitudinem reddet, nisi iam constat, quid velit pingere. Ideo peccamus, quia de partibus vitae omnes deliberamus, de tota

[1] Hense, following Schweighäuser, inserts *quemadmodum placet; si minus.*

[a] *i.e.*, by robbing oneself of life; but the antithesis to Vergil's phrase (*Aen.* ix. 613) is artificial.

[b] A similar argument is found in *Ep.* lxv. §§ 5 ff., containing the same figure of thought.

Reason, too, advises us to die, if we may, according to our taste; if this cannot be, she advises us to die according to our ability, and to seize upon whatever means shall offer itself for doing violence to ourselves. It is criminal to "live by robbery"[a]; but, on the other hand, it is most noble to "die by robbery." Farewell.

LXXI. ON THE SUPREME GOOD

You are continually referring special questions to me, forgetting that a vast stretch of sea sunders us. Since, however, the value of advice depends mostly on the time when it is given, it must necessarily result that by the time my opinion on certain matters reaches you, the opposite opinion is the better. For advice conforms to circumstances; and our circumstances are carried along, or rather whirled along. Accordingly, advice should be produced at short notice; and even this is too late; it should "grow while we work," as the saying is. And I propose to show you how you may discover the method.

As often as you wish to know what is to be avoided or what is to be sought, consider its relation to the Supreme Good, to the purpose of your whole life. For whatever we do ought to be in harmony with this; no man can set in order the details unless he has already set before himself the chief purpose of his life. The artist may have his colours all prepared, but he cannot produce a likeness unless he has already made up his mind what he wishes to paint.[b] The reason we make mistakes is because we all consider the parts of life, but never life as a whole.

3 nemo deliberat. Scire debet quid petat ille, qui sagittam vult mittere, et tunc derigere ac moderari manu telum. Errant consilia nostra, quia non habent, quo derigantur. Ignoranti, quem portum petat, nullus suus ventus est. Necesse est multum in vita
4 nostra casus possit, quia vivimus casu. Quibusdam autem evenit, ut quaedam scire se nesciant. Quemadmodum quaerimus saepe eos, cum quibus stamus, ita plerumque finem summi boni ignoramus adpositum.

Nec multis verbis nec circumitu longo, quod sit summum bonum, colliges[1]; digito, ut ita dicam, demonstrandum est nec in multa spargendum. Quid enim ad rem pertinet in particulas illud diducere, cum possis dicere: summum bonum est, quod honestum est? Et quod magis admireris: unum bonum est, quod honestum est, cetera falsa et
5 adulterina bona sunt. Hoc si persuaseris tibi et virtutem adamaveris, amare enim parum est, quicquid illa contigerit, id tibi, qualecumque aliis videbitur, faustum felixque erit. Et torqueri, si modo iacueris ipso torquente securior, et aegrotare, si non male dixeris fortunae, si non cesseris morbo, omnia denique, quae ceteris videntur mala, et mansuescent et in bonum abibunt, si super illa eminueris.

Hoc liqueat, nihil esse bonum nisi honestum, et omnia incommoda suo iure bona vocabuntur, quae

[1] *colliges* Muretus ; *colligis* MSS.

---

[a] For a definition of *honestum* see Cicero, *De Fin.* ii. 45 ff., and Rackham's note, explaining it as "τὸ καλόν, the morally beautiful or good."

The archer must know what he is seeking to hit; then he must aim and control the weapon by his skill. Our plans miscarry because they have no aim. When a man does not know what harbour he is making for, no wind is the right wind. Chance must necessarily have great influence over our lives, because we live by chance. It is the case with certain men, however, that they do not know that they know certain things. Just as we often go searching for those who stand beside us, so we are apt to forget that the goal of the Supreme Good lies near us.

To infer the nature of this Supreme Good, one does not need many words or any round-about discussion; it should be pointed out with the forefinger, so to speak, and not be dissipated into many parts. For what good is there in breaking it up into tiny bits, when you can say: the Supreme Good is that which is honourable[a]? Besides (and you may be still more surprised at this), that which is honourable is the only good; all other goods are alloyed and debased. If you once convince yourself of this, and if you come to love virtue devotedly (for mere loving is not enough), anything that has been touched by virtue will be fraught with blessing and prosperity for you, no matter how it shall be regarded by others. Torture, if only, as you lie suffering, you are more calm in mind than your very torturer; illness, if only you curse not Fortune and yield not to the disease—in short, all those things which others regard as ills will become manageable and will end in good, if you succeed in rising above them.

Let this once be clear, that there is nothing good except that which is honourable, and all hardships will have a just title to the name of "goods," when

6 modo virtus honestaverit. Multis videmur maiora promittere quam recipit humana condicio; non inmerito. Ad corpus enim respiciunt. Revertantur ad animum; iam hominem deo metientur. Erige te, Lucili virorum optime, et relinque istum ludum literarium philosophorum, qui rem magnificentissimam ad syllabas vocant, qui animum minuta docendo demittunt et conterunt; fies similis illis, qui invenerunt ista, non qui docent et id agunt, ut philosophia potius difficilis quam magna videatur.

7 Socrates qui totam philosophiam revocavit ad mores et hanc summam dixit esse sapientiam, bona malaque distinguere, "sequere," inquit, "illos, si quid apud te habeo auctoritatis, ut sis beatus, et te alicui stultum videri sine. Quisquis volet, tibi contumeliam faciat et iniuriam, tu tamen nihil patieris, si modo tecum erit virtus. Si vis," inquit, "beatus esse, si fide bona vir bonus, sine contemnat te aliquis." Hoc nemo praestabit, nisi qui omnia bona exaequaverit, quia nec bonum sine honesto est
8 et honestum in omnibus par est. "Quid[1] ergo? Nihil interest inter praeturam Catonis et repulsam? Nihil interest, utrum Pharsalica acie Cato vincatur an vincat? Hoc eius bonum, quo victis partibus

[1] Hense gives *quid ergo . . . componeret pacem?* to the supposed objector.

---

[a] See, for example, the syllogistic display which is ridiculed in *Ep.* xlviii. 6.

[b] *i.e.*, from being mere word-play.

[c] Hense suggests that Seneca may be rendering the phrase of Simonides—ἀνὴρ ἀληθῶς ἀγαθός.

once virtue has made them honourable. Many think that we Stoics are holding out expectations greater than our human lot admits of; and they have a right to think so. For they have regard to the body only. But let them turn back to the soul, and they will soon measure man by the standard of God. Rouse yourself, most excellent Lucilius, and leave off all this word-play of the philosophers, who reduce a most glorious subject to a matter of syllables, and lower and wear out the soul by teaching fragments; then you will become like the men who discovered these precepts, instead of those who by their teaching do their best to make philosophy seem difficult rather than great.[a]

Socrates, who recalled[b] the whole of philosophy to rules of conduct, and asserted that the highest wisdom consisted in distinguishing between good and evil, said: "Follow these rules, if my words carry weight with you, in order that you may be happy; and let some men think you even a fool. Allow any man who so desires to insult you and work you wrong; but if only virtue dwells with you, you will suffer nothing. If you wish to be happy, if you would be in good faith a good man,[c] let one person or another despise you." No man can accomplish this unless he has come to regard all goods as equal, for the reason that no good exists without that which is honourable, and that which is honourable is in every case equal. You may say: "What then? Is there no difference between Cato's being elected praetor and his failure at the polls? Or whether Cato is conquered or conqueror in the battle-line of Pharsalia? And when Cato could not be defeated, though his party met defeat, was not this goodness of his equal to that which would have been his if

non potest vinci, par erat illi bono, quo victor rediret in patriam et conponeret pacem?" Quidni par sit? Eadem enim virtute et mala fortuna vincitur et ordinatur bona. Virtus autem non potest maior aut
9 minor fieri; unius staturae est. "Sed Cn. Pompeius amittet exercitum, sed illud pulcherrimum rei publicae praetextum, optimates, et prima acies Pompeianarum partium, senatus ferens arma, uno proelio profligabuntur et tam magni ruina imperii in totum dissiliet orbem; aliqua pars eius in Aegypto, aliqua in Africa, aliqua in Hispania cadet. Ne hoc quidem miserae rei publicae continget, semel ruere."
10 Omnia licet fiant; Iubam in regno suo non locorum notitia adiuvet, non popularium pro rege suo virtus obstinatissima, Vticensium quoque fides malis fracta deficiat et Scipionem in Africa nominis sui fortuna destituat. Olim provisum est, ne quid Cato detrimenti caperet.

11 "Victus est tamen." Et hoc numera inter repulsas Catonis; tam magno animo feret aliquid sibi ad victoriam quam ad praeturam obstitisse. Quo die repulsus est, lusit, qua nocte periturus fuit, legit. Eodem loco habuit praetura et vita excidere; omnia, quae acciderent, ferenda esse persuaserat sibi.
12 Quidni ille mutationem rei publicae forti et aequo

---

[a] Egypt—47 B.C.; Africa (Thapsus)—46 B.C.; Spain (Munda)—45 B.C.

[b] A sort of serious parody of the *senatus consultum ultimum*. For a discussion of the history and meaning of the phrase see W. Warde Fowler's *Cicero*, pp. 151–158.

[c] Plato's *Phaedo*. Cato slew himself at Utica, 46 B.C., after Scipio's defeat at Thapsus.

he had returned victorious to his native land and arranged a peace?" Of course it was; for it is by the same virtue that evil fortune is overcome and good fortune is controlled. Virtue, however, cannot be increased or decreased; its stature is uniform. "But," you will object, "Gnaeus Pompey will lose his army; the patricians, those noblest patterns of the State's creation, and the front-rank men of Pompey's party, a senate under arms, will be routed in a single engagement; the ruins of that great oligarchy will be scattered all over the world; one division will fall in Egypt, another in Africa, and another in Spain![a] And the poor State will not be allowed even the privilege of being ruined once for all!" Yes, all this may happen; Juba's familiarity with every position in his own kingdom may be of no avail to him, of no avail the resolute bravery of his people when fighting for their king; even the men of Utica, crushed by their troubles, may waver in their allegiance; and the good fortune which ever attended men of the name of Scipio may desert Scipio in Africa. But long ago destiny "saw to it that Cato should come to no harm."[b]

"He was conquered in spite of it all!" Well, you may include this among Cato's "failures"; Cato will bear with an equally stout heart anything that thwarts him of his victory, as he bore that which thwarted him of his praetorship. The day whereon he failed of election, he spent in play; the night wherein he intended to die, he spent in reading.[c] He regarded in the same light both the loss of his praetorship and the loss of his life; he had convinced himself that he ought to endure anything which might happen. Why should he not suffer, bravely and calmly, a change in the govern-

pateretur animo? Quid enim mutationis periculo exceptum? Non terra, non caelum, non totus hic rerum omnium contextus, quamvis deo agente ducatur. Non semper tenebit hunc ordinem, sed
13 illum ex hoc cursu aliquis dies deiciet. Certis eunt cuncta temporibus; nasci debent, crescere, extingui. Quaecumque supra nos vides currere, et haec, quibus inmixti atque inpositi sumus veluti solidissimis carpentur ac desinent. Nulli non senectus sua est; inaequalibus ista spatiis eodem natura dimittit. Quicquid est, non erit, nec peribit, sed resolvetur.
14 Nobis solvi perire est, proxima enim intuemur; ad ulteriora non prospicit mens hebes et quae se corpori addixerit; alioqui fortius finem sui suorumque pateretur, si speraret, ut[1] omnia illa, sic vitam mortemque per vices ire et composita dissolvi, dissoluta componi, in hoc opere aeternam artem cuncta temperantis dei verti.

15 Itaque ut M. Cato, cum aevum animo percucurrerit, dicet: "omne humanum genus, quodque est quodque erit, morte damnatum est. Omnes, quae usquam rerum potiuntur urbes quaeque alienorum imperiorum magna sunt decora, ubi fuerint, aliquando quaeretur

[1] *ut* added by Haase.

---

[a] *Cf. Ep.* ix. 16 f. *resoluto mundo*, etc.

ment? For what is free from the risk of change? Neither earth, nor sky, nor the whole fabric of our universe, though it be controlled by the hand of God. It will not always preserve its present order; it will be thrown from its course in days to come.[a] All things move in accord with their appointed times; they are destined to be born, to grow, and to be destroyed. The stars which you see moving above us, and this seemingly immovable earth to which we cling and on which we are set, will be consumed and will cease to exist. There is nothing that does not have its old age; the intervals are merely unequal at which Nature sends forth all these things towards the same goal. Whatever is will cease to be, and yet it will not perish, but will be resolved into its elements. To our minds, this process means perishing, for we behold only that which is nearest; our sluggish mind, under allegiance to the body, does not penetrate to bournes beyond. Were it not so, the mind would endure with greater courage its own ending and that of its possessions, if only it could hope that life and death, like the whole universe about us, go by turns, that whatever has been put together is broken up again, that whatever has been broken up is put together again, and that the eternal craftsmanship of God, who controls all things, is working at this task.

Therefore the wise man will say just what a Marcus Cato would say, after reviewing his past life: "The whole race of man, both that which is and that which is to be, is condemned to die. Of all the cities that at any time have held sway over the world, and of all that have been the splendid ornaments of empires not their own, men shall some day ask where they were, and they shall be swept away

et vario exitii[1] genere tollentur; alias destruent bella, alias desidia paxque ad inertiam versa consumet et magnis opibus exitiosa res, luxus. Omnes hos fertiles campos repentina[2] maris inundatio abscondet aut in subitam cavernam considentis soli lapsus abducet. Quid est ergo quare indigner aut doleam,
16 si exiguo momento publica fata praecedo?" Magnus animus deo pareat et quicquid lex universi iubet, sine cunctatione patiatur; aut in meliorem emittitur vitam lucidius tranquilliusque inter divina mansurus aut certe sine ullo futurus incommodo sui[3] naturae remiscebitur et revertetur in totum.

Non est ergo M. Catonis maius bonum honesta vita quam mors honesta, quoniam non intenditur virtus. Idem esse dicebat Socrates veritatem et virtutem. Quomodo illa non crescit, sic ne virtus
17 quidem; habet numeros suos, plena est. Non est itaque quod mireris paria esse bona, et quae ex proposito sumenda sunt et quae si ita res tulit. Nam si hanc inaequalitatem receperis, ut fortiter torqueri in minoribus bonis numeres, numerabis etiam in malis, et infelicem Socraten dices in carcere, infelicem Catonem vulnera sua animosius quam

[1] *exitii* later MSS.; *exhilii* V; *exilii* Pb.
[2] *repentina* later MSS.; *repentini* VPb.
[3] *sui* G. Gemoll; *si* VPb.

---

[a] For a clear and full discussion regarding Stoic views of the immortality of the soul, and Seneca's own opinion thereon, see E. V. Arnold, *Roman Stoicism*, pp. 262 ff.

[b] *Cf.* § 20 of this letter: *rigida re quid amplius intendi potest?*

[c] *i.e.*, knowledge of facts, as Seneca so often says. *Cf.* Plato, *Meno*, 87 c ἐπιστήμη τις ἡ ἀρετή, and Aristotle, *Eth.* vi. 13 Σωκράτης . . . λόγους τὰς ἀρετὰς ᾤετο εἶναι, ἐπιστήμας γὰρ εἶναι πάσας.

[d] This is the accepted Stoic doctrine; see *Ep.* lxvi. 5. Goods are equal, absolute, and independent of circumstances;

by destructions of various kinds; some shall be ruined by wars, others shall be wasted away by inactivity and by the kind of peace which ends in sloth, or by that vice which is fraught with destruction even for mighty dynasties,—luxury. All these fertile plains shall be buried out of sight by a sudden overflowing of the sea, or a slipping of the soil, as it settles to lower levels, shall draw them suddenly into a yawning chasm. Why then should I be angry or feel sorrow, if I precede the general destruction by a tiny interval of time?" Let great souls comply with God's wishes, and suffer unhesitatingly whatever fate the law of the universe ordains; for the soul at death is either sent forth into a better life, destined to dwell with deity amid greater radiance and calm, or else, at least, without suffering any harm to itself, it will be mingled with nature again, and will return to the universe.[a]

Therefore Cato's honourable death was no less a good than his honourable life, since virtue admits of no stretching.[b] Socrates used to say that verity[c] and virtue were the same. Just as truth does not grow, so neither does virtue grow; for it has its due proportions and is complete. You need not, therefore, wonder that goods are equal,[d] both those which are to be deliberately chosen, and those which circumstances have imposed. For if you once adopt the view that they are unequal, deeming, for instance, a brave endurance of torture as among the lesser goods, you will be including it among the evils also; you will pronounce Socrates unhappy in his prison, Cato unhappy when he reopens his wounds with more courage than he showed in

although, as Seneca here maintains, circumstances may bring one or another of them into fuller play.

fecerat retractantem, calamitosissimum omnium Regulum fidei poenas etiam hostibus servatae pendentem. Atqui nemo hoc dicere, ne ex mollissimis quidem, ausus est. Negant enim illum esse beatum,
18 sed tamen negant miserum. Academici veteres beatum quidem esse etiam inter hos cruciatus fatentur, sed non ad perfectum nec ad plenum. Quod nullo modo potest recipi; nisi beatus est, in summo bono non est. Quod summum bonum est, supra se gradum non habet, si modo illi virtus inest, si illam adversa non minuunt, si[1] manet etiam comminuto corpore incolumis; manet autem. Virtutem enim intellego animosam et excelsam, quam incitat
19 quicquid infestat. Hunc animum, quem saepe induunt generosae indolis iuvenes, quos alicuius honestae rei pulchritudo percussit, ut omnia fortuita contemnant, profecto sapientia nobis[2] infundet et tradet. Persuadebit unum bonum esse, quod honestum; hoc nec remitti nec intendi posse, non magis quam regulam, qua rectum probari solet, flectes. Quicquid ex illa mutaveris, iniuria est recti.
20 Idem ergo de virtute dicemus: et haec recta est, flexuram non recipit. Rigida re[3] quid amplius intendi potest? Haec de omnibus rebus iudicat, de hac nulla. Si rectior ipsa non potest fieri, ne quae[4]

[1] *si* later MSS.; *sed* VPb.
[2] *nobis* Chatelain; *non* VPb.
[3] *rigida re* Capps; *rigidari* MSS.
[4] *ne quae* Haase; *neque* P; *nec quae* Vb.

---

[a] *e.g.*, Xenocrates and Speusippus; *cf. Ep.* lxxxv. 18. For another answer to the objection that the good depends upon outward circumstances *cf. Ep.* xcii. 14 f.

inflicting them, and Regulus the most ill-starred of all when he pays the penalty for keeping his word even with his enemies. And yet no man, even the most effeminate person in the world, has ever dared to maintain such an opinion. For though such persons deny that a man like Regulus is happy, yet for all that they also deny that he is wretched. The earlier Academics[a] do indeed admit that a man is happy even amid such tortures, but do not admit that he is completely or fully happy. With this view we cannot in any wise agree; for unless a man is happy, he has not attained the Supreme Good; and the good which is supreme admits of no higher degree, if only virtue exists within this man, and if adversity does not impair his virtue, and if, though the body be injured, the virtue abides unharmed. And it does abide. For I understand virtue to be high-spirited and exalted, so that it is aroused by anything that molests it. This spirit, which young men of noble breeding often assume, when they are so deeply stirred by the beauty of some honourable object that they despise all the gifts of chance, is assuredly infused in us and communicated to us by wisdom. Wisdom will bring the conviction that there is but one good—that which is honourable; that this can neither be shortened nor extended, any more than a carpenter's rule, with which straight lines are tested, can be bent. Any change in the rule means spoiling the straight line. Applying, therefore, this same figure to virtue, we shall say: Virtue also is straight, and admits of no bending. What can be made more tense than a thing which is already rigid? Such is virtue, which passes judgment on everything, but nothing passes judgment on virtue. And if this rule, virtue, cannot

ab illa fiunt quidem alia aliis rectiora sunt. Huic enim necesse est respondeant; ita paria sunt.

21 "Quid ergo?" inquis,[1] "iacere in convivio et torqueri paria sunt?" Hoc mirum videtur tibi? Illud licet magis admireris; iacere in convivio malum, in eculeo bonum est,[2] si illud turpiter, hoc honeste fit.[3] Bona ista aut mala non efficit materia, sed virtus. Haec ubicumque apparuit, omnia eiusdem
22 mensurae ac pretii sunt. In oculos nunc mihi manus intentat ille, qui omnium animum aestimat ex suo, quod dicam paria bona esse honeste iudicantis et honeste periclitantis,[4] quod dicam paria bona esse eius, qui triumphat, et eius, qui ante currum vehitur invictus animo. Non putant enim fieri, quicquid facere non possunt; ex infirmitate sua de virtute
23 ferunt sententiam. Quid miraris, si uri, vulnerari, occidi, alligari iuvat, aliquando etiam libet? Luxurioso frugalitas poena est, pigro supplicii loco labor est, delicatus miseretur industrii, desidioso studere torqueri est. Eodem modo haec, ad quae omnes inbecilli sumus, dura atque intoleranda credimus, obliti, quam multis tormentum sit vino carere aut prima luce excitari. Non ista difficilia sunt natura,

[1] *inquis* later MSS.; *inquit* VPb.

[2] This reading is based on the authority of late MSS. VPb read *iacere in eculeo bonum est.*

[3] *honeste fit* later MSS.; *honeste sit* Vb; *honestum sit* P.

[4] *et honeste periclitantis* added by Gertz.

itself be made more straight, neither can the things created by virtue be in one case straighter and in another less straight. For they must necessarily correspond to virtue; hence they are equal.

"What," you say, "do you call reclining at a banquet and submitting to torture equally good?" Does this seem surprising to you? You may be still more surprised at the following,—that reclining at a banquet is an evil, while reclining on the rack is a good, if the former act is done in a shameful, and the latter in an honourable manner. It is not the material that makes these actions good or bad; it is the virtue. All acts in which virtue has disclosed itself are of the same measure and value. At this moment the man who measures the souls of all men by his own is shaking his fist in my face because I hold that there is a parity between the goods involved in the case of one who passes sentence honourably, and of one who suffers sentence honourably; or because I hold that there is a parity between the goods of one who celebrates a triumph, and of one who, unconquered in spirit, is carried before the victor's chariot. For such critics think that whatever they themselves cannot do, is not done; they pass judgment on virtue in the light of their own weaknesses. Why do you marvel if it helps a man, and on occasion even pleases him, to be burned, wounded, slain, or bound in prison? To a luxurious man, a simple life is a penalty; to a lazy man, work is punishment; the dandy pities the diligent man; to the slothful, studies are torture. Similarly, we regard those things with respect to which we are all infirm of disposition, as hard and beyond endurance, forgetting what a torment it is to many men to abstain from wine or to be routed from their beds at break of day. These

24 sed nos fluvidi et enerves. Magno animo de rebus
magnis iudicandum est; alioqui videbitur illarum vitium
esse, quod nostrum est. Sic quaedam rectissima,
cum in aquam demissa sunt, speciem curvi praefra tique
visentibus reddunt. Non tantum quid videas, sed
quemadmodum, refert; animus noster ad vera perspi-
25 cienda caligat. Da mihi adulescentem incorruptum et
ingenio vegetum; dicet fortunatiorem sibi videri, qui
omnia rerum adversarum onera rigida cervice sustollat,
qui supra fortunam existat.[1] Non mirum est in tranquillitate non concuti; illud mirare, ibi extolli aliquem
ubi omnes deprimuntur, ibi stare ubi omnes iacent.
26 Quid est in tormentis, quid est in aliis, quae
adversa appellamus, mali? Hoc, ut opinor, succidere
mentem et incurvari et succumbere. Quorum nihil
sapienti viro potest evenire; stat rectus sub quolibet
pondere. Nulla illum res minorem facit; nihil illi
eorum, quae ferenda sunt, displicet. Nam quicquid
cadere in hominem potest, in se cecidisse non
queritur. Vires suas novit. Scit se esse oneri
27 ferendo. Non educo sapientem ex hominum numero
nec dolores ab illo sicut ab aliqua rupe nullum sensum
admittente summoveo. Memini ex duabus illum
partibus esse compositum; altera est inrationalis,
haec mordetur, uritur, dolet; altera rationalis, haec
inconcussas opiniones habet, intrepida est et indomita.

[1] *exsistat* cod. Bern.; *extat* VPb²; *exeat* b¹; *exiliat* Hermes; Hense suggests *extet*.

[a] "An oar, though quite whole, presents the appearance of being broken when seen in clear shallow water."—Seneca, *N.Q.* 1. 3 (Clarke and Geikie).

[b] This dualism of soul and body goes back to earlier religions, and especially to the Persian. The rational part (τὸ λογιστικόν), though held by most Stoics to be corporeal, or part of the world-stuff, is closely related to the ἡγεμονικόν, or "principate."

actions are not essentially difficult; it is we ourselves that are soft and flabby. We must pass judgment concerning great matters with greatness of soul; otherwise, that which is really our fault will seem to be their fault. So it is that certain objects which are perfectly straight, when sunk in water appear to the onlooker as bent or broken off.[a] It matters not only what you see, but with what eyes you see it; our souls are too dull of vision to perceive the truth. But give me an unspoiled and sturdy-minded young man; he will pronounce more fortunate one who sustains on unbending shoulders the whole weight of adversity, who stands out superior to Fortune. It is not a cause for wonder that one is not tossed about when the weather is calm; reserve your wonderment for cases where a man is lifted up when all others sink, and keeps his footing when all others are prostrate.

What element of evil is there in torture and in the other things which we call hardships? It seems to me that there is this evil,—that the mind sags, and bends, and collapses. But none of these things can happen to the sage; he stands erect under any load. Nothing can subdue him; nothing that must be endured annoys him. For he does not complain that he has been struck by that which can strike any man. He knows his own strength; he knows that he was born to carry burdens. I do not withdraw the wise man from the category of man, nor do I deny to him the sense of pain as though he were a rock that has no feelings at all. I remember that he is made up of two parts: the one part is irrational,—it is this that may be bitten, burned, or hurt; the other part is rational,—it is this which holds resolutely to opinions, is courageous, and unconquerable.[b] In the

In hac positum est summum illud hominis bonum. Antequam impleatur, incerta mentis volutatio est; cum vero perfectum est, inmota illa[1] stabilitas est.

28 Itaque inchoatus et ad summa procedens cultorque virtutis, etiam si adpropinquat perfecto bono, sed ei nondum summam manum inposuit, ibit[2] interim cessim et remittet aliquid ex intentione mentis. Nondum enim incerta transgressus est, etiamnunc versatur in lubrico. Beatus vero et virtutis exactae tunc se maxime amat, cum fortissime expertus est, et metuenda ceteris, si alicuius honesti officii pretia sunt, non tantum fert, sed amplexatur multoque audire mavult "tanto melior" quam "tanto felicior."

29 Venio nunc illo, quo me vocat expectatio tua. Ne extra rerum naturam vagari virtus nostra videatur, et tremet[3] sapiens et dolebit et expallescet. Hi enim omnes corporis sensus sunt. Ubi ergo calamitas, ubi illud malum verum est? Illic scilicet, si ista animum detrahunt, si ad confessionem servitutis

30 adducunt, si illi paenitentiam sui faciunt. Sapiens quidem vincit virtute fortunam, at multi professi sapientiam levissimis nonnumquam minis exterriti sunt. Hoc loco nostrum vitium est, qui idem a sapiente exigimus et a proficiente. Suadeo adhuc

[1] Buecheler prefers *illi*. [2] *ibit* Gruter; *ibi* VPb.
[3] *tremet* the common reading; *tremebit* VPb; Hense suggests *tremescet*.

---

[a] *i.e.*, because he has endured and conquered misfortune rather than escaped it.

[b] For a similar thought *cf. Ep.* xi. 6.

[c] Three stages of progress (προκοπή) were defined by Chrysippus. *Cf.* also Sen. *Epp.* lxxii. 6 and lxxv. 8 f.

latter is situated man's Supreme Good. Before this is completely attained, the mind wavers in uncertainty; only when it is fully achieved is the mind fixed and steady. And so when one has just begun, or is on one's way to the heights and is cultivating virtue, or even if one is drawing near the perfect good but has not yet put the finishing touch upon it, one will retrograde at times and there will be a certain slackening of mental effort. For such a man has not yet traversed the doubtful ground; he is still standing in slippery places. But the happy man, whose virtue is complete, loves himself most of all when his bravery has been submitted to the severest test, and when he not only endures but welcomes that which all other men regard with fear, if it is the price which he must pay for the performance of a duty which honour imposes, and he greatly prefers to have men say of him: "how much more noble!" rather than "how much more lucky[a]!"

And now I have reached the point to which your patient waiting summons me. You must not think that our human virtue transcends nature; the wise man will tremble, will feel pain, will turn pale.[b] For all these are sensations of the body. Where, then, is the abode of utter distress, of that which is truly an evil? In the other part of us, no doubt, if it is the mind that these trials drag down, force to a confession of its servitude, and cause to regret its existence. The wise man, indeed, overcomes Fortune by his virtue, but many who profess wisdom are sometimes frightened by the most unsubstantial threats. And at this stage it is a mistake on our part to make the same demands upon the wise man and upon the learner.[c] I still exhort myself to do

mihi ista, quae laudo, nondum persuadeo. Etiam si persuasissem, nondum tam parata haberem aut tam
31 exercitata, ut ad omnes casus procurrerent. Quemadmodum lana quosdam colores semel ducit, quosdam nisi saepius macerata et recocta non perbibit; sic alias disciplinas ingenia, cum accepere, protinus praestant, haec, nisi alte descendit et diu sedit et animum non coloravit, sed infecit, nihil ex his,
32 quae promiserat, praestat. Cito hoc potest tradi et paucissimis verbis: unum bonum esse virtutem, nullum certe sine virtute, et ipsam virtutem in parte nostri meliore, id est rationali, positam. Quid erit haec virtus? Iudicium verum et inmotum. Ab hoc enim impetus venient mentis, ab hoc omnis species,
33 quae impetum movet, redigetur ad liquidum. Huic iudicio consentaneum erit omnia, quae virtute contacta sunt, et bona iudicare et inter se paria.

Corporum autem bona corporibus quidem bona sunt, sed in totum non sunt bona. His pretium quidem erit aliquod, ceterum dignitas non erit; magnis inter se intervallis distabunt; alia minora,
34 alia maiora erunt. Et in ipsis sapientiam sectantibus magna discrimina esse fateamur necesse est. Alius iam in tantum profecit, ut contra fortunam audeat adtollere oculos, sed non pertinaciter, cadunt[1] enim nimio splendore praestricti; alius in tantum, ut

[1] *cadunt* Haase; *cedunt* or *caedunt* MSS.

[a] Ovid, *Metam.* vi. 9, speaks of *bibula lana*, and Horace, *Ep.* i. 10. 27, of *vellera potantia fucum.*

that which I recommend; but my exhortations are not yet followed. And even if this were the case, I should not have these principles so ready for practice, or so well trained, that they would rush to my assistance in every crisis. Just as wool takes up certain colours at once,[a] while there are others which it will not absorb unless it is soaked and steeped in them many times; so other systems of doctrine can be immediately applied by men's minds after once being accepted, but this system of which I speak, unless it has gone deep and has sunk in for a long time, and has not merely coloured but thoroughly permeated the soul, does not fulfil any of its promises. The matter can be imparted quickly and in very few words: "Virtue is the only good; at any rate there is no good without virtue; and virtue itself is situated in our nobler part, that is, the rational part." And what will this virtue be? A true and never-swerving judgment. For therefrom will spring all mental impulses, and by its agency every external appearance that stirs our impulses will be clarified. It will be in keeping with this judgment to judge all things that have been coloured by virtue as goods, and as equal goods.

Bodily goods are, to be sure, good for the body; but they are not absolutely good. There will indeed be some value in them; but they will possess no genuine merit, for they will differ greatly; some will be less, others greater. And we are constrained to acknowledge that there are great differences among the very followers of wisdom. One man has already made so much progress that he dares to raise his eyes and look Fortune in the face, but not persistently, for his eyes soon drop, dazzled by her overwhelming splendour; another has made

possit cum illa conferre vultum, nisi[1] iam pervenit
35 ad summum et fiduciae plenus est. Inperfecta necesse
est labent et modo prodeant, modo sublabantur aut
succidant. Sublabentur autem, nisi ire et niti
perseveraverint; si quicquam ex studio et fideli
intentione laxaverint, retro eundum est. Nemo profectum ibi invenit, ubi reliquerat. Instemus itaque
36 et perseveremus. Plus, quam profligavimus, restat,
sed magna pars est profectus velle proficere.

Huius rei conscius mihi sum; volo et mente tota
volo. Te quoque instinctum esse et magno ad pulcherrima properare impetu video. Properemus; ita
demum vita beneficium erit. Alioqui mora est, et
quidem turpis inter foeda versantibus. Id agamus,
ut nostrum omne tempus sit. Non erit autem, nisi
37 prius nos nostri esse coeperimus. Quando continget
contemnere utramque fortunam, quando continget
omnibus oppressis adfectibus et sub arbitrium suum
adductis hanc vocem emittere "vici"? Quem vicerim
quaeris? Non Persas nec extrema Medorum nec si
quid ultra Dahas bellicosum iacet, sed avaritiam, sed
ambitionem, sed metum mortis, qui victores gentium
vicit. VALE.

[1] *vultum, nisi* Hense; *vultum si* MSS.

[a] In which case, he would be completely superior to her.
[b] A nomad Scythian tribe east of the Caspian Sea.

so much progress that he is able to match glances with her,—that is, unless he has already reached the summit and is full of confidence.[a] That which is short of perfection must necessarily be unsteady, at one time progressing, at another slipping or growing faint; and it will surely slip back unless it keeps struggling ahead; for if a man slackens at all in zeal and faithful application, he must retrograde. No one can resume his progress at the point where he left off. Therefore let us press on and persevere. There remains much more of the road than we have put behind us; but the greater part of progress is the desire to progress.

I fully understand what this task is. It is a thing which I desire, and I desire it with all my heart. I see that you also have been aroused and are hastening with great zeal towards infinite beauty. Let us, then, hasten; only on these terms will life be a boon to us; otherwise, there is delay, and indeed disgraceful delay, while we busy ourselves with revolting things. Let us see to it that all time belongs to us. This, however, cannot be unless first of all our own selves begin to belong to us. And when will it be our privilege to despise both kinds of fortune? When will it be our privilege, after all the passions have been subdued and brought under our own control, to utter the words "I have conquered!"? Do you ask me whom I have conquered? Neither the Persians, nor the far-off Medes, nor any warlike race that lies beyond the Dahae[b]; not these, but greed, ambition, and the fear of death that has conquered the conquerors of the world. Farewell.

LXXII.

SENECA LVCILIO SVO SALVTEM

1 Quod quaeris a me, liquebat mihi, sic rem edidiceram, per se. Sed diu non retemptavi memoriam meam, itaque non facile me sequitur. Quod evenit libris situ cohaerentibus, hoc evenisse mihi sentio; explicandus est animus et quaecumque apud illum deposita sunt, subinde excuti debent, ut parata sint, quotiens usus exegerit. Ergo hoc in praesentia differamus; multum enim operae, multum diligentiae poscit. Cum primum longiorem eodem loco spera-
2 vero moram, tunc istud in manus sumam. Quaedam enim sunt, quae possis et in cisio scribere. Quaedam lectum et otium et secretum desiderant. Nihilominus his quoque occupatis diebus agatur aliquid et quidem totis. Numquam enim non succedent occupationes novae; serimus illas, itaque ex una exeunt plures. Deinde ipsi nobis dilationem damus: "cum hoc peregero, toto animo incumbam" et "si hanc rem molestam composuero, studio me dabo."

3 Non cum vacaveris, philosophandum est; omnia alia neglegenda, ut huic adsideamus, cui nullum

---

[a] The context furnishes no clue as to what the subject was.

[b] Seneca is fond of legal figures; *cf. Ep.* lxv. 15. For the *dilatio* see Pliny, *Ep.* i. 18. 1 *rogas ut dilationem petam.*

[c] *Cf. Ep.* liii. 9 (*philosophia*) *non est res subsiciva* ("a matter for spare time"), *ordinaria est; domina est, adesse iubet.*

LXXII. ON BUSINESS AS THE ENEMY OF PHILOSOPHY

The subject[a] concerning which you question me was once clear to my mind, and required no thought, so thoroughly had I mastered it. But I have not tested my memory of it for some time, and therefore it does not readily come back to me. I feel that I have suffered the fate of a book whose rolls have stuck together by disuse; my mind needs to be unrolled, and whatever has been stored away there ought to be examined from time to time, so that it may be ready for use when occasion demands. Let us therefore put this subject off for the present; for it demands much labour and much care. As soon as I can hope to stay for any length of time in the same place, I shall then take your question in hand. For there are certain subjects about which you can write even while travelling in a gig, and there are also subjects which need a study-chair, and quiet, and seclusion. Nevertheless I ought to accomplish something even on days like these,—days which are fully employed, and indeed from morning till night. For there is never a moment when fresh employments will not come along; we sow them, and for this reason several spring up from one. Then, too, we keep adjourning our own cases,[b] saying: "As soon as I am done with this, I shall settle down to hard work," or: "If I ever set this troublesome matter in order, I shall devote myself to study."

But the study of philosophy is not to be postponed until you have leisure;[c] everything else is to be neglected in order that we may attend to philosophy,

tempus satis magnum est, etiam si a pueritia usque
ad longissimos humani aevi terminos vita producitur.
Non multum refert, utrum omittas philosophiam an
intermittas; non enim ubi interrupta est, manet, sed
eorum more, quae intenta dissiliunt, usque ad initia
sua recurrit, quod a continuatione discessit. Resis-
tendum est occupationibus, nec explicandae, sed sub-
movendae sunt. Tempus quidem nullum parum est
idoneum studio salutari; atqui multi inter illa non
4 student, propter quae studendum est. "Incidet
aliquid, quod inpediat." Non quidem eum, cuius
animus in omni negotio laetus atque alacer est;
inperfectis adhuc interscinditur laetitia, sapientis vero
contexitur gaudium, nulla causa rumpitur, nulla
fortuna, semper et ubique tranquillus[1] est. Non
enim ex alieno pendet nec favorem fortunae aut
hominis expectat. Domestica illi felicitas est; exiret
5 ex animo, si intraret; ibi nascitur. Aliquando extrinsecus, quo admoneatur mortalitatis, intervenit,
sed id leve et quod summam cutem stringat. Aliquo,
inquam, incommodo adflatur; maximum autem illud
bonum est fixum. Ita dico: extrinsecus aliqua sunt
incommoda, velut in corpore interdum robusto
solidoque eruptiones quaedam pusularum et ulcuscula,
6 nullum in alto malum est. Hoc, inquam, interest

[1] *tranquillus* Haase; *tranquillum* MSS.

---

[a] *Cf. Ep.* xlv. 9 *intrepidus, quem aliqua vis movet, nulla perturbat, quem fortuna . . . pungit, non vulnerat, et hoc raro.*

for no amount of time is long enough for it, even though our lives be prolonged from boyhood to the uttermost bounds of time allotted to man. It makes little difference whether you leave philosophy out altogether or study it intermittently; for it does not stay as it was when you dropped it, but, because its continuity has been broken, it goes back to the position in which it was at the beginning, like things which fly apart when they are stretched taut. We must resist the affairs which occupy our time; they must not be untangled, but rather put out of the way. Indeed, there is no time that is unsuitable for helpful studies; and yet many a man fails to study amid the very circumstances which make study necessary. He says: "Something will happen to hinder me." No, not in the case of the man whose spirit, no matter what his business may be, is happy and alert. It is those who are still short of perfection whose happiness can be broken off; the joy of a wise man, on the other hand, is a woven fabric, rent by no chance happening and by no change of fortune; at all times and in all places he is at peace. For his joy depends on nothing external and looks for no boon from man or fortune. His happiness is something within himself; it would depart from his soul if it entered in from the outside; it is born there. Sometimes an external happening reminds him of his mortality, but it is a light blow, and merely grazes the surface of his skin.[a] Some trouble, I repeat, may touch him like a breath of wind, but that Supreme Good of his is unshaken. This is what I mean: there are external disadvantages, like pimples and boils that break out upon a body which is normally strong and sound; but there is no deep-seated malady. The difference, I say, between

inter consummatae sapientiae virum et alium procedentis, quod inter sanum et ex morbo gravi ac diutino emergentem, cui sanitatis loco est levior accessio: hic nisi adtendit, subinde gravatur et in eadem revolvitur, sapiens recidere non potest, ne incidere quidem amplius. Corpori enim ad tempus bona valetudo est, quam medicus, etiam si reddidit, non praestat, saepe ad eundem, qui[1] advocaverat, excitatur. Animus[2] semel in totum sanatur.

7 Dicam, quomodo intellegam[3] sanum: si se ipso contentus est, si confidit sibi, si scit omnia vota mortalium, omnia beneficia quae dantur petunturque, nullum in beata vita habere momentum. Nam cui aliquid accedere potest, id inperfectum est; cui aliquid abscedere potest, id inperpetuum est; cuius perpetua futura laetitia est, is suo gaudeat. Omnia autem, quibus vulgus inhiat, ultro citroque fluunt. Nihil dat fortuna mancipio. Sed haec quoque fortuita tunc delectant, cum illa ratio temperavit ac miscuit; haec est, quae etiam externa commendet, quorum
8 avidis usus ingratus est. Solebat Attalus hac imagine uti: "vidisti aliquando canem missa a domino frusta panis aut carnis aperto ore captantem? Quicquid excepit, protinus integrum devorat et semper ad

[1] *qui* Lipsius; *quem* MSS.
[2] *animus* added by Muretus.
[3] *intellegam* Koch; *intellegas* MSS.

[a] *Cf.* Lucretius, iii. 971 *vita mancipio nulli datur, omnibus usu.* Our lives are merely loaned to us; Nature retains the *dominium.* *Cf.* also Seneca's frequent figure of life as an inn, contrasted with a house over which one has ownership.

a man of perfect wisdom and another who is progressing in wisdom is the same as the difference between a healthy man and one who is convalescing from a severe and lingering illness, for whom "health" means only a lighter attack of his disease. If the latter does not take heed, there is an immediate relapse and a return to the same old trouble; but the wise man cannot slip back, or slip into any more illness at all. For health of body is a temporary matter which the physician cannot guarantee, even though he has restored it; nay, he is often roused from his bed to visit the same patient who summoned him before. The mind, however, once healed, is healed for good and all.

I shall tell you what I mean by health: if the mind is content with its own self; if it has confidence in itself; if it understands that all those things for which men pray, all the benefits which are bestowed and sought for, are of no importance in relation to a life of happiness; under such conditions it is sound. For anything that can be added to is imperfect; anything that can suffer loss is not lasting; but let the man whose happiness is to be lasting, rejoice in what is truly his own. Now all that which the crowd gapes after, ebbs and flows. Fortune gives us nothing which we can really own.[a] But even these gifts of Fortune please us when reason has tempered and blended them to our taste; for it is reason which makes acceptable to us even external goods that are disagreeable to use if we absorb them too greedily. Attalus used to employ the following simile: "Did you ever see a dog snapping with wide-open jaws at bits of bread or meat which his master tosses to him? Whatever he catches, he straightway swallows whole, and always

spem venturi hiat. Idem evenit nobis; quicquid expectantibus fortuna proiecit, id sine ulla voluptate demittimus statim, ad rapinam alterius erecti et adtoniti." Hoc sapienti non evenit; plenus est. Etiam si quid obvenit, secure excipit ac reponit.
9 Laetitia fruitur maxima, continua, sua. Habet aliquis bonam voluntatem, habet profectum, sed cui multum desit a summo; hic deprimitur alternis et extollitur ac modo in caelum adlevatur, modo defertur ad terram. Imperitis[1] ac rudibus nullus praecipitationis finis est; in Epicureum illud chaos decidunt, inane,
10 sine termino. Est adhuc genus tertium eorum, qui sapientiae adludunt, quam non quidem contigerunt, in conspectu tamen et, ut ita dicam, sub ictu habent; hi non concutiuntur, ne defluunt quidem. Nondum in sicco, iam in portu sunt.

11 Ergo cum tam magna sint inter summos imosque discrimina, cum medios quoque sequatur fluctus[2] suus, sequatur ingens periculum ad deteriora redeundi, non debemus occupationibus indulgere. Excludendae sunt; si semel intraverint, in locum suum alias substituent. Principiis illarum obstemus. Melius non incipient, quam desinent. VALE.

[1] *imperitis* later MSS.; *impeditis* VPb.
[2] *fluctus* later MSS.; *fructus* VPb.

[a] The Void (*inane*), or infinite space, as contrasted with the atoms which form new worlds in continuous succession.

opens his jaws in the hope of something more. So it is with ourselves; we stand expectant, and whatever Fortune has thrown to us we forthwith bolt, without any real pleasure, and then stand alert and frantic for something else to snatch." But it is not so with the wise man; he is satisfied. Even if something falls to him, he merely accepts it carelessly and lays it aside. The happiness that he enjoys is supremely great, is lasting, is his own. Assume that a man has good intentions, and has made progress, but is still far from the heights; the result is a series of ups and downs; he is now raised to heaven, now brought down to earth. For those who lack experience and training, there is no limit to the downhill course; such a one falls into the Chaos [a] of Epicurus,—empty and boundless. There is still a third class of men,—those who toy with wisdom; they have not indeed touched it, but yet are in sight of it, and have it, so to speak, within striking distance. They are not dashed about, nor do they drift back either; they are not on dry land, but are already in port.

Therefore, considering the great difference between those on the heights and those in the depths, and seeing that even those in the middle are pursued by an ebb and flow peculiar to their state, and pursued also by an enormous risk of returning to their degenerate ways, we should not give ourselves up to matters which occupy our time. They should be shut out; if they once gain an entrance, they will bring in still others to take their places. Let us resist them in their early stages. It is better that they shall never begin than that they shall be made to cease. Farewell.

LXXIII.

SENECA LVCILIO SVO SALVTEM

1 Errare mihi videntur, qui existimant philosophiae fideliter deditos contumaces esse ac refractarios, contemptores magistratuum aut regum eorumve, per quos publica administrantur. Ex contrario enim nulli adversus illos gratiores sunt; nec inmerito. Nullis enim plus praestant quam quibus frui tranquillo
2 otio licet. Itaque ii, quibus multum[1] ad propositum bene vivendi confert securitas publica, necesse est auctorem huius boni ut parentem colant, multo quidem magis quam illi inquieti et in medio positi, qui multa principibus debent, sed multa et inputant, quibus numquam tam plene occurrere ulla liberalitas potest, ut cupiditates illorum, quae crescunt, dum implentur, exsatiet. Quisquis autem de accipiendo cogitat, oblitus accepti est; nec ullum habet malum
3 cupiditas maius, quam quod ingrata est. Adice nunc, quod nemo eorum, qui in re publica versantur, quot vincat, sed a quibus vincatur, aspicit. Et illis non tam iucundum est multos post se videre quam grave aliquem ante se. Habet hoc vitium omnis ambitio; non respicit. Nec ambitio tantum instabilis est, verum cupiditas omnis, quia incipit semper a fine.

4 At ille vir sincerus ac purus, qui reliquit et curiam et forum et omnem administrationem rei publicae,

[1] *multum* Haase; *altum* VPb.

[a] This letter is especially interesting because of its autobiographical hints, and its relation to Seneca's own efforts to be rid of court life and seek the leisure of the sage. See the Introduction to Vol. I. pp. viii f.

[b] *Cf.* Horace, *Sat.* i. 1. 115 f.—

Instat equis auriga suos vincentibus, illum
Praeteritum temnens extremos inter euntem.

LXXIII. ON PHILOSOPHERS AND KINGS[a]

It seems to me erroneous to believe that those who have loyally dedicated themselves to philosophy are stubborn and rebellious, scorners of magistrates or kings or of those who control the administration of public affairs. For, on the contrary, no class of man is so popular with the philosopher as the ruler is; and rightly so, because rulers bestow upon no men a greater privilege than upon those who are allowed to enjoy peace and leisure. Hence, those who are greatly profited, as regards their purpose of right living, by the security of the State, must needs cherish as a father the author of this good; much more so, at any rate, than those restless persons who are always in the public eye, who owe much to the ruler, but also expect much from him, and are never so generously loaded with favours that their cravings, which grow by being supplied, are thoroughly satisfied. And yet he whose thoughts are of benefits to come has forgotten the benefits received; and there is no greater evil in covetousness than its ingratitude. Besides, no man in public life thinks of the many whom he has outstripped; he thinks rather of those by whom he is outstripped. And these men find it less pleasing to see many behind them than annoying to see anyone ahead of them.[b] That is the trouble with every sort of ambition; it does not look back. Nor is it ambition alone that is fickle, but also every sort of craving, because it always begins where it ought to end.

But that other man, upright and pure, who has left the senate and the bar and all affairs of state, that

ut ad ampliora secederet, diligit eos, per quos hoc ei facere tuto licet solusque[1] illis gratuitum testimonium reddit et magnam rem nescientibus debet. Quemadmodum praeceptores suos veneratur ac suspicit, quorum beneficio illis inviis exît, sic et hos,[2] sub quorum

5 tutela positus exercet artes bonas. "Verum alios quoque[3] rex viribus suis protegit." Quis negat? Sed quemadmodum Neptuno plus debere se iudicat ex is, qui eadem tranquillitate usi sunt, qui plura et pretiosiora illo mari vexit, animosius a mercatore quam a vectore solvitur votum, et ex ipsis mercatoribus effusius gratus est, qui odores ac purpuras et auro pensanda portabat quam qui vilissima quaeque et saburrae loco futura congesserat; sic huius pacis beneficium ad omnes pertinentis altius ad eos pervenit, qui illa bene utuntur.

6 Multi enim sunt ex his togatis, quibus pax operosior bello est. An idem existimas pro pace debere eos, qui illam ebrietati aut libidini inpendunt aut aliis vitiis, quae vel bello rumpenda sunt? Nisi forte tam iniquum putas esse sapientem, ut nihil viritim se debere pro communibus bonis iudicet. Soli lunaeque plurimum debeo, et non uni mihi oriuntur. Anno temperantique annum deo privatim obligatus

[1] *solusque* Muretus ; *solumque* VPb.
[2] *hos* later MSS. ; *his* VPb.
[3] *alios quoque* later MSS. ; *quoque alios* VPb.

---

[a] For an interesting account of philosophy and its relation to Roman history see E. V. Arnold, *Roman Stoicism*, chap. xvi. This subject is discussed fully by Cicero, *De Off.* i. 71 f., and by Seneca, *Ep.* xc.

he may retire to nobler affairs,[a] cherishes those who have made it possible for him to do this in security; he is the only person who returns spontaneous thanks to them, the only person who owes them a great debt without their knowledge. Just as a man honours and reveres his teachers, by whose aid he has found release from his early wanderings, so the sage honours these men, also, under whose guardianship he can put his good theories into practice. But you answer: "Other men too are protected by a king's personal power." Perfectly true. But just as, out of a number of persons who have profited by the same stretch of calm weather, a man deems that his debt to Neptune is greater if his cargo during that voyage has been more extensive and valuable, and just as the vow is paid with more of a will by the merchant than by the passenger, and just as, from among the merchants themselves, heartier thanks are uttered by the dealer in spices, purple fabrics, and objects worth their weight in gold, than by him who has gathered cheap merchandise that will be nothing but ballast for his ship; similarly, the benefits of this peace, which extends to all, are more deeply appreciated by those who make good use of it.

For there are many of our toga-clad citizens to whom peace brings more trouble than war. Or do those, think you, owe as much as we do for the peace they enjoy, who spend it in drunkenness, or in lust, or in other vices which it were worth even a war to interrupt? No, not unless you think that the wise man is so unfair as to believe that as an individual he owes nothing in return for the advantages which he enjoys with all the rest. I owe a great debt to the sun and to the moon; and yet they do not rise for me alone. I am personally beholden to the seasons

sum, quamvis nihil in meum honorem[1] discripta
7 sint. Stulta avaritia mortalium possessionem proprietatemque discernit nec quicquam suum credit esse, quod publicum est. At ille sapiens nihil iudicat suum magis quam cuius illi cum humano genere consortium est. Nec enim essent ita communia, nisi pars illorum pertineret ad singulos; socium efficit
8 etiam quod ex minima portione commune est. Adice nunc, quod magna et vera bona non sic dividuntur, ut exiguum in singulos cadat; ad unumquemque tota perveniunt. Ex congiario tantum ferunt homines, quantum in capita promissum est. Epulum et visceratio et quicquid[2] aliud manu capitur, discedit in partes. At haec individua bona, pax et libertas, et[3] tam omnium tota quam singulorum sunt.

9 Cogitat itaque, per quem sibi horum usus fructusque contingat, per quem non ad arma illum nec ad servandas vigilias nec ad tuenda moenia et multiplex belli tributum publica necessitas vocet, agitque gubernatori suo gratias. Hoc docet philosophia praecipue, bene debere[4] beneficia, bene solvere;
10 interdum autem solutio est ipsa confessio. Confitebitur ergo multum se debere ei, cuius administratione ac providentia contingit illi pingue otium et arbitrium

[1] Hense suggests the possibility of *tempora* after *honorem.*
[2] *et quicquid* later MSS.; *quid* or *quicquid* VPb.
[3] *et* later MSS.; *ea* VP.
[4] *debere* later MSS.; *dedere* VPb.

---

[a] For this figure *cf. Ep.* lxxii. 7 and note; see also the similar language of lxxxviii. 12 *hoc, quod tenes, quod tuum dicis, publicum est et quidem generis humani.*

[b] During certain festivals, either cooked or raw meat was distributed among the people.

and to the god who controls them, although in no respect have they been apportioned for my benefit. The foolish greed of mortals makes a distinction between possession and ownership,[a] and believes that it has ownership in nothing in which the general public has a share. But our philosopher considers nothing more truly his own than that which he shares in partnership with all mankind. For these things would not be common property, as indeed they are, unless every individual had his quota; even a joint interest based upon the slightest share makes one a partner. Again, the great and true goods are not divided in such a manner that each has but a slight interest; they belong in their entirety to each individual. At a distribution of grain men receive only the amount that has been promised to each person; the banquet and the meat-dole,[b] or all else that a man can carry away with him, are divided into parts. These goods, however, are indivisible,—I mean peace and liberty,—and they belong in their entirety to all men just as much as they belong to each individual.

Therefore the philosopher thinks of the person who makes it possible for him to use and enjoy these things, of the person who exempts him when the state's dire need summons to arms, to sentry duty, to the defence of the walls, and to the manifold exactions of war; and he gives thanks to the helmsman of his state. This is what philosophy teaches most of all,—honourably to avow the debt of benefits received, and honourably to pay them; sometimes, however, the acknowledgment itself constitutes payment. Our philosopher will therefore acknowledge that he owes a large debt to the ruler who makes it possible, by his management and foresight,

sui temporis et inperturbata publicis occupationibus quies.

> O Meliboee, deus nobis haec otia fecit:[a]
> Namque erit ille mihi semper deus.

11 Si illa quoque otia multum auctori suo debent, quorum munus hoc maximum est:

> Ille meas errare boves, ut cernis, et ipsum
> Ludere quae vellem calamo permisit agresti;[b]

quanti aestimamus hoc otium, quod inter deos agitur,
12 quod deos facit? Ita dico, Lucili, et te in caelum
compendiario voco.

Solebat Sextius dicere Iovem plus non posse quam
bonum virum. Plura Iuppiter habet, quae praestet
hominibus, sed inter duos bonos non est melior, qui
locupletior, non magis quam inter duos, quibus par
scientia regendi gubernaculum est, meliorem dixeris,
13 cui maius speciosiusque navigium est. Iuppiter quo
antecedit virum bonum? Diutius bonus est; sapiens
nihilo se minoris existimat, quod virtutes eius spatio
breviore cluduntur. Quemadmodum ex duobus
sapientibus qui senior decessit, non est beatior eo,
cuius intra pauciores annos terminata virtus est, sic
deus non vincit sapientem felicitate, etiam si vincit
14 aetate. Non est virtus maior, quae longior. Iuppiter
omnia habet, sed nempe aliis tradidit habenda; ad

---

[a] Vergil, *Eclogue*, i. 6 f. Vergil owes a debt to the Emperor, and regards him as a "god" because of the bestowal of earthly happiness; how much greater is the debt of the philosopher, who has the opportunity to study heavenly things!

[b] Vergil, *Eclogue*, i. 9 f.

[c] In the Christian religion, God is everything; among the Stoics, the wise man is equal to the gods. *Cf.*, for example, *Ep.* xli. 4.

for him to enjoy rich leisure, control of his own time, and a tranquillity uninterrupted by public employments.

> Shepherd ! a god this leisure gave to me,
> For he shall be my god eternally.[a]

And if even such leisure as that of our poet owes a great debt to its author, though its greatest boon is this :

> As thou canst see,
> He let me turn my cattle out to feed,
> And play what fancy pleased on rustic reed ;[b]

how highly are we to value this leisure of the philosopher, which is spent among the gods, and makes us gods? Yes, that is what I mean, Lucilius ; and I invite you to heaven by a short cut.

Sextius used to say that Jupiter had no more power than the good man. Of course, Jupiter has more gifts which he can offer to mankind ; but when you are choosing between two good men, the richer is not necessarily the better, any more than, in the case of two pilots of equal skill in managing the tiller, you would call him the better whose ship is larger and more imposing. In what respect is Jupiter superior to our good man? His goodness lasts longer ; but the wise man does not set a lower value upon himself, just because his virtues are limited by a briefer span. Or take two wise men ; he who has died at a greater age is not happier than he whose virtue has been limited to fewer years : similarly, a god has no advantage over a wise man in point of happiness,[c] even though he has such an advantage in point of years. That virtue is not greater which lasts longer. Jupiter possesses all things, but he has surely given over the possession of

ipsum hic unus usus pertinet, quod utendi omnibus
causa est. Sapiens tam aequo animo omnia apud
alios videt contemnitque quam Iuppiter et hoc se
magis suspicit, quod Iuppiter uti illis non potest,
15 sapiens non vult. Credamus itaque Sextio monstranti
pulcherrimum iter et clamanti: "hac 'itur ad astra,'
hac secundum frugalitatem, hac secundum temperantiam, hac secundum fortitudinem."

Non sunt di fastidiosi, non invidi; admittunt et
16 ascendentibus manum porrigunt. Miraris hominem
ad deos ire? Deus ad homines venit, immo quod
est propius, in homines venit; nulla sine deo mens
bona est. Semina in corporibus humanis divina
dispersa sunt, quae si bonus cultor excipit, similia
origini prodeunt et paria iis, ex quibus orta sunt,
surgunt; si malus, non aliter quam humus sterilis
ac palustris necat ac deinde creat purgamenta pro
frugibus. Vale.

LXXIV.

Seneca Lvcilio svo salvtem

1 Epistula tua delectavit me et marcentem excitavit,
memoriam quoque meam, quae iam mihi segnis ac
lenta est, evocavit.

Quidni tu, mi Lucili, maximum putes instrumentum

---

[a] Vergil, *Aeneid*, ix. 641.

[b] *Cf. Ep.* xli. §§ 1 f. *prope est a te deus, tecum est, intus est.*

them to others; the only use of them which belongs to him is this: he is the cause of their use to all men. The wise man surveys and scorns all the possessions of others as calmly as does Jupiter, and regards himself with the greater esteem because, while Jupiter cannot make use of them, he, the wise man, does not wish to do so. Let us therefore believe Sextius when he shows us the path of perfect beauty, and cries: "This is 'the way to the stars'[a]; this is the way, by observing thrift, self-restraint, and courage!"

The gods are not disdainful or envious; they open the door to you; they lend a hand as you climb. Do you marvel that man goes to the gods? God comes to men; nay, he comes nearer,—he comes into men.[b] No mind that has not God, is good. Divine seeds are scattered throughout our mortal bodies; if a good husbandman receives them, they spring up in the likeness of their source and of a parity with those from which they came. If, however, the husbandman be bad, like a barren or marshy soil, he kills the seeds, and causes tares to grow up instead of wheat. Farewell.

LXXIV. ON VIRTUE AS A REFUGE FROM WORLDLY DISTRACTIONS

Your letter has given me pleasure, and has roused me from sluggishness. It has also prompted my memory, which has been for some time slack and nerveless.

You are right, of course, my dear Lucilius, in deeming the chief means of attaining the happy life

beatae vitae hanc persuasionem, unum bonum esse, quod honestum est? Nam qui alia bona iudicat, in fortunae venit potestatem, alieni arbitrii fit; qui omne bonum honesto circumscripsit, intra se est felix.[1]

2 Hic amissis liberis maestus, hic sollicitus aegris, hic turpibus et aliquam passis infamiam tristis. Illum videbis alienae uxoris amore cruciari, illum suae. Non deerit quem repulsa distorqueat; erunt quos ipse
3 honor vexet. Illa vero maxima ex omni mortalium populo turba miserorum, quam expectatio mortis exagitat undique inpendens. Nihil enim est, unde non subeat. Itaque ut in hostili regione versantibus huc et illuc circumspiciendum est et ad omnem strepitum circumagenda cervix; nisi hic timor e pectore eiectus est, palpitantibus praecordiis vivitur.
4 Occurrent acti in exilium et evoluti bonis. Occurrent, quod genus egestatis gravissimum est, in divitiis inopes. Occurrent naufragi similiave naufragis passi, quos aut popularis ira aut invidia, perniciosum optimis telum, inopinantes securosque disiecit procellae more, quae in ipsa sereni fiducia solet emergere, aut fulminis

[1] *intra se est felix* Hense; *intra se felix* VPb; *intra se felix est* later MSS.

---

[a] A doctrine often expressed in the Letters; *cf.*, for example, lxxi. 4.

[b] *Cf.* Horace, *Carm.* iii. 16. 28 *magnas inter opes inops.*

[c] For the same thought *cf. Ep.* iv. 7 *Neminem eo fortuna provexit, ut non tantum illi minaretur, quantum permiserat. Noli huic tranquillitati confidere; momento mare evertitur. Eodem die ubi luserunt navigia, sorbentur.*

to consist in the belief that the only good lies in that which is honourable.[a] For anyone who deems other things to be good, puts himself in the power of Fortune, and goes under the control of another; but he who has in every case defined the good by the honourable, is happy with an inward happiness.

One man is saddened when his children die; another is anxious when they become ill; a third is embittered when they do something disgraceful, or suffer a taint in their reputation. One man, you will observe, is tortured by passion for his neighbour's wife, another by passion for his own. You will find men who are completely upset by failure to win an election, and others who are actually plagued by the offices which they have won. But the largest throng of unhappy men among the host of mortals are those whom the expectation of death, which threatens them on every hand, drives to despair. For there is no quarter from which death may not approach. Hence, like soldiers scouting in the enemy's country, they must look about in all directions, and turn their heads at every sound; unless the breast be rid of this fear, one lives with a palpitating heart. You will readily recall those who have been driven into exile and dispossessed of their property. You will also recall (and this is the most serious kind of destitution) those who are poor in the midst of their riches.[b] You will recall men who have suffered shipwreck, or those whose sufferings resemble shipwreck; for they were untroubled and at ease, when the anger or perhaps the envy of the populace,—a missile most deadly to those in high places,[c]—dismantled them like a storm which is wont to rise when one is most confident of continued calm, or like a sudden stroke of lightning which even causes

subiti, ad cuius ictum etiam vicina tremuerunt. Nam ut illic quisquis ab igne propior stetit, percusso similis obstipuit, sic in his per aliquam vim accidentibus unum calamitas opprimit, ceteros metus, paremque passis tristitiam facit pati posse.

5 Omnium animos mala aliena ac repentina sollicitant. Quemadmodum aves etiam inanis fundae sonus territat, nos ita non ad ictum tantum exagitamur, sed ad crepitum. Non potest ergo quisquam beatus esse, qui huic se opinioni credidit. Non enim beatum est, nisi quod intrepidum ; inter suspecta male vivitur.
6 Quisquis se multum fortuitis dedit, ingentem sibi materiam perturbationis et inexplicabilem fecit ; una haec via est ad tuta vadenti, externa despicere et honesto contentum esse. Nam qui aliquid virtute melius putat aut ullum praeter illam bonum, ad haec, quae a fortuna sparguntur, sinum expandit et
7 sollicitus missilia eius expectat. Hanc enim imaginem animo tuo propone, ludos facere fortunam et in hunc mortalium coetum honores, divitias, gratiam excutere, quorum alia inter diripientium manus scissa sunt, alia infida societate divisa, alia magno detrimento eorum, in quos devenerant, prensa. Ex quibus quaedam aliud agentibus inciderunt, quaedam, quia nimis

[a] *i.e.*, engaged upon something else. *Cf. Ep.* i. 1.

the region round about it to tremble. For just as anyone who stands near the bolt is stunned and resembles one who is struck, so in these sudden and violent mishaps, although but one person is overwhelmed by the disaster, the rest are overwhelmed by fear, and the possibility that they may suffer makes them as downcast as the actual sufferer.

Every man is troubled in spirit by evils that come suddenly upon his neighbour. Like birds, who cower even at the whirr of an empty sling, we are distracted by mere sounds as well as by blows. No man therefore can be happy if he yields himself up to such foolish fancies. For nothing brings happiness unless it also brings calm; it is a bad sort of existence that is spent in apprehension. Whoever has largely surrendered himself to the power of Fortune has made for himself a huge web of disquietude, from which he cannot get free; if one would win a way to safety, there is but one road,—to despise externals and to be contented with that which is honourable. For those who regard anything as better than virtue, or believe that there is any good except virtue, are spreading their arms to gather in that which Fortune tosses abroad, and are anxiously awaiting her favours. Picture now to yourself that Fortune is holding a festival, and is showering down honours, riches, and influence upon this mob of mortals; some of these gifts have already been torn to pieces in the hands of those who try to snatch them, others have been divided up by treacherous partnerships, and still others have been seized to the great detriment of those into whose possession they have come. Certain of these favours have fallen to men while they were absent-minded[a]; others have been lost to their seekers because they were snatching too eagerly for

captabantur, amissa et, dum avide rapiuntur, expulsa
sunt. Nulli vero etiam cui rapina feliciter cessit,
gaudium rapti duravit in posterum.

Itaque prudentissimus quisque cum primum induci
videt munuscula, a theatro fugit et scit magno parva
constare. Nemo manum conserit cum recedente,
8 nemo exeuntem ferit; circa praemium rixa est. Idem
in his evenit, quae fortuna desuper iactat: aestuamus
miseri, distringimur, multas habere cupimus manus,
modo in hanc partem,[1] modo in illam respicimus.
Nimis tarde nobis mitti videntur, quae cupiditates
nostras inritant, ad paucos perventura, expectata
9 omnibus. Ire obviam cadentibus cupimus. Gaudemus,
si quid invasimus, invadendique[2] aliquos spes
vana delusit; vilem praedam magno aliquo incommodo
luimus aut destituti fallimur.[3] Secedamus
itaque ab istis ludis et demus raptoribus locum; illi
spectent bona ista pendentia et ipsi magis pendeant.

10 Quicumque beatus esse constituet, unum esse bonum putet, quod honestum est. Nam si ullum aliud esse existimat, primum male de providentia

[1] *modo in hanc partem* VPb omit. The words are found in certain inferior MSS.

[2] *invadendique* later MSS.; *invidendique* V; *invidentique* P.

[3] *aut destituti fallimur* Buecheler; *aut de*$^{\text{fraudamur}}_{\text{aut}}$ *fallimur* V; *aut de . aut fallimus* P; *aut inde fallimur* b.

---

[a] A distribution of coins, etc., at the public games. Food was also doled out to the populace on similar occasions.

[b] This figure of the dole as applied to Fortune is sustained to an extent which is unusual with Seneca.

them, and, just because they are greedily seized upon, have been knocked from their hands. There is not a man among them all, however,—even he who has been lucky in the booty which has fallen to him,—whose joy in his spoil has lasted until the morrow.

The most sensible man, therefore, as soon as he sees the dole being brought in,[a] runs from the theatre; for he knows that one pays a high price for small favours. No one will grapple with him on the way out, or strike him as he departs; the quarrelling takes place where the prizes are. Similarly with the gifts which Fortune tosses down to us; wretches that we are, we become excited, we are torn asunder, we wish that we had many hands, we look back now in this direction and now in that. All too slowly, as it seems, are the gifts thrown in our direction; they merely excite our cravings, since they can reach but few and are awaited by all. We are keen to intercept them as they fall down. We rejoice if we have laid hold of anything; and some have been mocked by the idle hope of laying hold; we have either paid a high price for worthless plunder with some disadvantage to ourselves, or else have been defrauded and are left in the lurch. Let us therefore withdraw from a game like this, and give way to the greedy rabble; let them gaze after such "goods," which hang suspended above them, and be themselves still more in suspense.[b]

Whoever makes up his mind to be happy should conclude that the good consists only in that which is honourable. For if he regards anything else as good, he is, in the first place, passing an unfavourable judgment upon Providence because of the fact that

iudicat, quia multa incommoda iustis viris accidunt et quia, quicquid nobis dedit, breve est et exiguum, si compares mundi totius aevo.

11 Ex hac deploratione nascitur, ut ingrati divinorum interpretes simus; querimur, quod non semper, quod et pauca nobis et incerta et abitura contingant. Inde est, quod nec vivere nec mori volumus; vitae nos odium tenet, timor mortis. Natat omne consilium nec inplere nos ulla felicitas potest. Causa autem est, quod non pervenimus ad illud bonum inmensum et insuperabile, ubi necesse est resistat voluntas
12 nostra, quia ultra summum[1] non est locus. Quaeris, quare virtus nullo egeat? Praesentibus gaudet, non concupiscit absentia. Nihil non illi magnum est, quod satis.

Ab hoc discede iudicio; non pietas constabit, non fides. Multa enim utramque praestare cupienti patienda sunt ex iis, quae mala vocantur; multa inpendenda ex iis, quibus indulgemus tamquam
13 bonis. Perit fortitudo, quae periculum facere debet sui; perit magnanimitas, quae non potest eminere, nisi omnia velut minuta contempsit, quae pro maximis[2] volgus optat; perit gratia et relatio gratiae, si timemus laborem,[3] si quicquam pretiosius fide novimus, si non optima spectamus.

14 Sed ut illa praeteream, aut ista bona non sunt,

[1] *summum* later MSS.; *summam* VPb.
[2] *pro maximis* later MSS.; *proximis* VPb.
[3] *laborem* later MSS.; *labor* VPb.

---

[a] This phrase recalls the title of one of Seneca's philosophical essays: *De Providentia*, or *Quare Bonis Viris Mala Accidant cum sit Providentia.*

upright men often suffer misfortunes,[a] and that the time which is allotted to us is but short and scanty, if you compare it with the eternity which is allotted to the universe.

It is a result of complaints like these that we are unappreciative in our comments upon the gifts of heaven; we complain because they are not always granted to us, because they are few and unsure and fleeting. Hence we have not the will either to live or to die; we are possessed by hatred of life, by fear of death. Our plans are all at sea, and no amount of prosperity can satisfy us. And the reason for all this is that we have not yet attained to that good which is immeasurable and unsurpassable, in which all wishing on our part must cease, because there is no place beyond the highest. Do you ask why virtue needs nothing? Because it is pleased with what it has, and does not lust after that which it has not. Whatever is enough is abundant in the eyes of virtue.

Dissent from this judgment, and duty and loyalty will not abide. For one who desires to exhibit these two qualities must endure much that the world calls evil; we must sacrifice many things to which we are addicted, thinking them to be goods Gone is courage, which should be continually testing itself; gone is greatness of soul, which cannot stand out clearly unless it has learned to scorn as trivial everything that the crowd covets as supremely important; and gone is kindness and the repaying of kindness, if we fear toil, if we have acknowledged anything to be more precious than loyalty, if our eyes are fixed upon anything except the best.

But to pass these questions by: either these so-called goods are not goods, or else man is more

quae vocantur, aut homo felicior deo est, quoniam
quidem quae parata nobis sunt, non habet in usu
deus. Nec enim libido ad illum nec epularum
lautitiae nec opes nec quicquam ex his hominem
inescantibus et vili voluptate ducentibus pertinet.
Ergo aut non[1] incredibile est bona deo deesse aut
hoc ipsum argumentum est bona non esse, quod deo
15 desunt. Adice, quod multa, quae bona videri volunt,
animalibus quam homini pleniora contingunt. Illa
cibo avidius utuntur, venere non aeque fatigantur,
virium illis maior est et aequabilior firmitas. Sequitur,
ut multo feliciora sint homine. Nam sine nequitia,
sine fraudibus degunt. Fruuntur voluptatibus, quas
et magis capiunt et ex facili sine ullo pudoris aut
paenitentiae metu.

16 Considera tu itaque, an id bonum vocandum sit,
quo deus ab homine vincitur. Summum bonum in
animo contineamus; obsolescit, si ab optima nostri
parte ad pessimam transit et transfertur ad sensus,
qui agiliores sunt animalibus mutis. Non est summa
felicitatis nostrae in carne ponenda; bona illa sunt
vera, quae ratio dat, solida ac sempiterna, quae cadere
17 non possunt, ne decrescere quidem aut[2] minui.
Cetera opinione bona sunt et nomen quidem habent
commune cum veris, proprietas in illis boni non est.
Itaque commoda vocentur et, ut nostra lingua loquar,

[1] *non* added by Hense.
[2] *aut* later MSS.; *ac* VPb.

[a] *Cf. Ep.* lxxiii. § 14 *Iuppiter uti illis non potest.*

fortunate than God, because God has no enjoyment of the things which are given to us.[a] For lust pertains not to God, nor do elegant banquets, nor wealth, nor any of the things that allure mankind and lead him on through the influence of degrading pleasure. Therefore, it is either not incredible that there are goods which God does not possess, or else the very fact that God does not possess them is in itself a proof that these things are not goods. Besides, many things which are wont to be regarded as goods are granted to animals in fuller measure than to men. Animals eat their food with better appetite, are not in the same degree weakened by sexual indulgence, and have a greater and more uniform constancy in their strength. Consequently, they are much more fortunate than man. For there is no wickedness, no injury to themselves, in their way of living. They enjoy their pleasures and they take them more often and more easily, without any of the fear that results from shame or regret.

This being so, you should consider whether one has a right to call anything good in which God is outdone by man. Let us limit the Supreme Good to the soul; it loses its meaning if it is taken from the best part of us and applied to the worst, that is, if it is transferred to the senses; for the senses are more active in dumb beasts. The sum total of our happiness must not be placed in the flesh; the true goods are those which reason bestows, substantial and eternal; they cannot fall away, neither can they grow less or be diminished. Other things are goods according to opinion, and though they are called by the same name as the true goods, the essence of goodness is not in them. Let us therefore call them "advantages," and, to use our technical term,

producta.[a] Ceterum sciamus mancipia nostra esse, non partes; et sint apud nos, sed ita, ut meminerimus extra nos esse. Etiam si apud nos sint, inter subiecta et humilia numerentur propter quae nemo se adtollere debeat. Quid enim stultius quam aliquem
18 eo sibi placere, quod ipse non fecit? Omnia ista nobis accedant, non haereant, ut si abducentur, sine ulla nostri laceratione discedant. Utamur illis, non gloriemur, et utamur parce tamquam depositis apud nos et abituris. Quisquis illa sine ratione possedit, non diu tenuit, ipsa enim se felicitas, nisi temperatur, premit. Si fugacissimis bonis credidit, cito deseritur et, ut non deseratur, adfligitur. Paucis deponere felicitatem molliter licuit; ceteri cum iis, inter quae eminuere, labuntur et illos degravant ipsa,
19 quae extulerant. Ideo adhibebitur prudentia, quae modum illis aut parsimoniam imponat, quoniam quidem licentia opes suas praecipitat atque urget. Nec umquam inmodica durarunt, nisi illa moderatrix ratio conpescuit. Hoc multarum tibi urbium ostendet eventus, quarum in ipso flore luxuriosa imperia ceciderunt et quicquid virtute partum erat, intemperantia

[a] *Producta* is a translation of the Stoic term προηγμένα. For a clear exposition of this topic see Cicero, *De Fin.* iii. 52 ff.

"preferred" things.[a] Let us, however, recognize that they are our chattels, not parts of ourselves; and let us have them in our possession, but take heed to remember that they are outside ourselves. Even though they are in our possession, they are to be reckoned as things subordinate and poor, the possession of which gives no man a right to plume himself. For what is more foolish than being self-complacent about something which one has not accomplished by one's own efforts? Let everything of this nature be added to us, and not stick fast to us, so that, if it is withdrawn, it may come away without tearing off any part of us. Let us use these things, but not boast of them, and let us use them sparingly, as if they were given for safe-keeping and will be withdrawn. Anyone who does not employ reason in his possession of them never keeps them long; for prosperity of itself, if uncontrolled by reason, overwhelms itself. If anyone has put his trust in goods that are most fleeting, he is soon bereft of them, and, to avoid being bereft, he suffers distress. Few men have been permitted to lay aside prosperity gently. The rest all fall, together with the things amid which they have come into eminence, and they are weighted down by the very things which had before exalted them. For this reason foresight must be brought into play, to insist upon a limit or upon frugality in the use of these things, since licence overthrows and destroys its own abundance. That which has no limit has never endured, unless reason, which sets limits, has held it in check. The fate of many cities will prove the truth of this; their sway has ceased at the very prime because they were given to luxury, and excess has ruined all that had been won by virtue. We

corruit. Adversus hos casus muniendi sumus. Nullus autem contra fortunam inexpugnabilis murus est; intus instruamur. Si illa pars tuta est, pulsari homo potest, capi non potest.

20 Quod sit hoc instrumentum, scire desideras? Nihil indignetur sibi accidere sciatque illa ipsa, quibus laedi videtur, ad conservationem[1] universi pertinere et ex iis esse, quae cursum mundi officiumque consummant. Placeat homini, quicquid deo placuit; ob hoc ipsum se[2] suaque miretur, quod non potest vinci, quod mala ipsa sub se tenet, quod ratione, qua valentius nihil est, casum doloremque
21 et iniuriam subigit. Ama rationem! Huius te amor contra durissima armabit. Feras catulorum amor in venabula inpingit feritasque et inconsultus impetus praestat indomitas; iuvenilia nonnumquam ingenia cupido gloriae in contemptum tam ferri quam ignium misit; species quosdam atque umbra virtutis in mortem voluntariam trudit. Quanto his omnibus fortior ratio est, quanto constantior, tanto vehementius per metus ipsos et pericula exibit.

22 "Nihil agitis," inquit, "quod negatis ullum[3] esse aliud honesto bonum; non faciet vos haec munitio tutos a fortuna et inmunes. Dicitis enim inter bona

[1] *conservationem* later MSS.; *conversationem* VPb.
[2] *se* added by Ed. Rom.
[3] *ullum* later MSS.; *unum* VPb.

should fortify ourselves against such calamities. But no wall can be erected against Fortune which she cannot take by storm; let us strengthen our inner defences. If the inner part be safe, man can be attacked, but never captured.

Do you wish to know what this weapon of defence is? It is the ability to refrain from chafing over whatever happens to one, of knowing that the very agencies which seem to bring harm are working for the preservation of the world, and are a part of the scheme for bringing to fulfilment the order of the universe and its functions. Let man be pleased with whatever has pleased God; let him marvel at himself and his own resources for this very reason, that he cannot be overcome, that he has the very powers of evil subject to his control, and that he brings into subjection chance and pain and wrong by means of that strongest of powers—reason. Love reason! The love of reason will arm you against the greatest hardships. Wild beasts dash against the hunter's spear through love of their young, and it is their wildness and their unpremeditated onrush that keep them from being tamed; often a desire for glory has stirred the mind of youth to despise both sword and stake; the mere vision and semblance of virtue impel certain men to a self-imposed death. In proportion as reason is stouter and steadier than any of these emotions, so much the more forcefully will she make her way through the midst of utter terrors and dangers.

Men say to us: "You are mistaken if you maintain that nothing is a good except that which is honourable; a defence like this will not make you safe from Fortune and free from her assaults. For you maintain that dutiful children, and a well-

esse liberos pios et bene moratam patriam et parentes bonos; horum pericula non potestis spectare securi. Perturbabit vos obsidio patriae, liberorum mors,
23 parentum servitus." Quid adversus hos pro nobis responderi soleat, ponam; deinde tunc adiciam, quid praeterea respondendum putem.

Alia condicio est in iis, quae ablata in locum suum aliquid incommodi substituunt; tamquam bona valitudo vitiata in malam transfertur; acies oculorum exstincta caecitate nos adficit[1]; non tantum velocitas perit poplitibus incisis, sed debilitas pro illa subit. Hoc non est periculum in iis, quae paulo ante rettulimus. Quare? Si amicum bonum amisi, non est mihi pro illo perfidia patienda, nec si bonos liberos
24 extuli, in illorum locum impietas succedit. Deinde non amicorum illic[2] aut liberorum interitus, sed corporum est. Bonum autem uno modo perit, si in malum transit; quod natura non patitur, quia omnis virtus et opus omne virtutis incorruptum manet. Deinde etiam si amici perierunt, etiam si probati respondentesque voto patris liberi, est quod illorum expleat locum. Quid sit quaeris? Quod illos quo-
25 que bonos fecerat, virtus. Haec nihil vacare patitur loci, totum animum tenet, desiderium omnium tollit;

[1] *afficit* later MSS.; *adfecit* VPb.
[2] *illic* Buecheler; *illis* VPb.

[a] See *Ep.* lxvi. 6. The Stoics, unlike the Academics and the Peripatetics, maintained that the good must have "an unconditional value" (Zeller).

governed country, and good parents, are to be reckoned as goods; but you cannot see these dear objects in danger and be yourself at ease. Your calm will be disturbed by a siege conducted against your country, by the death of your children, or by the enslaving of your parents." I will first state what we Stoics usually reply [a] to these objectors, and then will add what additional answer should, in my opinion, be given.

The situation is entirely different in the case of goods whose loss entails some hardship substituted in their place; for example, when good health is impaired there is a change to ill-health; when the eye is put out, we are visited with blindness; we not only lose our speed when our leg-muscles are cut, but infirmity takes the place of speed. But no such danger is involved in the case of the goods to which we referred a moment ago. And why? If I have lost a good friend, I have no false friend whom I must endure in his place; nor if I have buried a dutiful son, must I face in exchange unfilial conduct. In the second place, this does not mean to me the taking-off of a friend or of a child; it is the mere taking-off of their bodies. But a good can be lost in only one way, by changing into what is bad; and this is impossible according to the law of nature, because every virtue, and every work of virtue, abides uncorrupted. Again, even if friends have perished, or children of approved goodness who fulfil their father's prayers for them, there is something that can fill their place. Do you ask what this is? It is that which had made them good in the first place, namely, virtue. Virtue suffers no space in us to be unoccupied; it takes possession of the whole soul and removes all sense of loss. It alone is

sola satis est, omnium enim bonorum vis et origo in ipsa est. Quid refert, an aqua decurrens intercipiatur atque abeat,[1] si fons, ex quo fluxerat, salvus est? Non dices vitam iustiorem salvis liberis quam amissis nec ordinatiorem nec prudentiorem nec honestiorem; ergo ne meliorem quidem. Non facit adiectio[2] amicorum[3] sapientiorem, non facit stultiorem detractio, ergo nec beatiorem aut miseriorem. Quamdiu virtus salva fuerit, non senties, quidquid[4]
26 abscesserit. "Quid ergo? Non est beatior et amicorum et liberorum turba succinctus?" Quidni non sit? Summum enim bonum nec infringitur nec augetur; in suo modo permanet, utcumque fortuna se gessit. Sive illi senectus longa contigit sive citra senectutem finitus est, eadem mensura summi boni est, quamvis aetatis diversa sit.

27 Utrum maiorem an minorem circulum scribas, ad spatium eius pertinet, non ad formam. Licet alter diu manserit, alterum statim obduxeris et in eum in quo scriptus est pulverem solveris, in eadem uterque forma fuit. Quod rectum est, nec magnitudine aestimatur nec numero nec tempore; non magis produci quam contrahi potest. Honestam vitam ex centum annorum numero in quantum voles corripe et in unum diem coge; aeque honesta est.

[1] *abeat* later MSS.; *habitat* Pb; *haebetaet* V; *habetat* M[1].
[2] *adiectio* Madvig; *adiecto* V; *alecto* P; *allecto* b.
[3] *amicorum* later MSS.; *amico* VPb.
[4] *quidquid* Gertz; *quid* VP; *qui* b.

[a] *Cf. Itane in geometriae pulvere haerebo?*, *Ep.* lxxxviii. 39 and note.
[b] See the argument in *Ep.* xii. 6 f., and often elsewhere.

sufficient; for the strength and beginnings of all goods exist in virtue herself. What does it matter if running water is cut off and flows away, as long as the fountain from which it has flowed is unharmed? You will not maintain that a man's life is more just if his children are unharmed than if they have passed away, nor yet better appointed, nor more intelligent, nor more honourable; therefore, no better, either. The addition of friends does not make one wiser, nor does their taking away make one more foolish; therefore, not happier or more wretched, either. As long as your virtue is unharmed, you will not feel the loss of anything that has been withdrawn from you. You may say: "Come now; is not a man happier when girt about with a large company of friends and children?" Why should this be so? For the Supreme Good is neither impaired nor increased thereby; it abides within its own limits, no matter how Fortune has conducted herself. Whether a long old age falls to one's lot, or whether the end comes on this side of old age—the measure of the Supreme Good is unvaried, in spite of the difference in years.

Whether you draw a larger or a smaller circle, its size affects its area, not its shape. One circle may remain as it is for a long time, while you may contract the other forthwith, or even merge it completely with the sand in which it was drawn;[a] yet each circle has had the same shape. That which is straight is not judged by its size, or by its number, or by its duration; it can no more be made longer than it can be made shorter. Scale down the honourable life as much as you like from the full hundred years, and reduce it to a single day; it is equally honourable.[b] Sometimes virtue is wide-

28 Modo latius virtus funditur, regna urbes provincias temperat, fert leges, colit amicitias, inter propinquos liberosque dispensat officia, modo arto fine concluditur paupertatis exilii orbitatis. Non tamen minor est, si ex altiore fastigio in privatum, ex regio
29 in humile[1] subducitur, ex publico et spatioso iure in angustias domus vel anguli coit. Aeque magna est, etiam si in se recessit undique exclusa. Nihilominus enim magni spiritus est et erecti, exactae prudentiae, indeclinabilis iustitiae. Ergo aeque beata est. Beatum enim illud uno loco positum est, in ipsa mente, grande, stabile, tranquillum, quod sine scientia divinorum humanorumque non potest effici.

30 Sequitur illud, quod me responsurum esse dicebam. Non adfligitur sapiens liberorum amissione, non amicorum. Eodem enim animo fert illorum mortem, quo suam expectat. Non magis hanc timet quam illam dolet. Virtus enim convenientia constat; omnia opera eius cum ipsa concordant et congruunt. Haec concordia perit, si animus, quem excelsum esse oportet, luctu aut desiderio summittitur. Inhonesta est omnis trepidatio et sollicitudo, in ullo actu pigritia. Honestum enim securum et expeditum est, interri-
31 tum est, in procinctu stat. "Quid ergo? Non aliquid perturbationi simile patietur? Non et color eius

[1] *humile* Haase; *humilem* VPb.

[a] See § 23.

[b] Called by the early Stoics ὁμολογία; the idea of "conformity with nature" is a fundamental doctrine of the school. See Rackham on Cicero, *De Fin.* iii. 21.

spread, governing kingdoms, cities, and provinces, creating laws, developing friendships, and regulating the duties that hold good between relatives and children; at other times it is limited by the narrow bounds of poverty, exile, or bereavement. But it is no smaller when it is reduced from prouder heights to a private station, from a royal palace to a humble dwelling, or when from a general and broad jurisdiction it is gathered into the narrow limits of a private house or a tiny corner. Virtue is just as great, even when it has retreated within itself and is shut in on all sides. For its spirit is no less great and upright, its sagacity no less complete, its justice no less inflexible. It is, therefore, equally happy. For happiness has its abode in one place only, namely, in the mind itself, and is noble, steadfast, and calm; and this state cannot be attained without a knowledge of things divine and human.

The other answer, which I promised [a] to make to your objection, follows from this reasoning. The wise man is not distressed by the loss of children or of friends. For he endures their death in the same spirit in which he awaits his own. And he fears the one as little as he grieves for the other. For the underlying principle of virtue is conformity;[b] all the works of virtue are in harmony and agreement with virtue itself. But this harmony is lost if the soul, which ought to be uplifted, is cast down by grief or a sense of loss. It is ever a dishonour for a man to be troubled and fretted, to be numbed when there is any call for activity. For that which is honourable is free from care and untrammelled, is unafraid, and stands girt for action. "What," you ask, "will the wise man experience no emotion like disturbance of spirit? Will not his features change

mutabitur et vultus agitabitur et artus refrigescent? Et quicquid aliud non ex imperio animi, sed inconsulto quodam naturae impetu geritur." Fateor; sed manebit illi persuasio eadem, nihil illorum malum esse nec dignum, ad quod mens sana deficiat. Omnia, quae facienda erunt, audaciter facit et prompte.
32 Hoc enim stultitiae proprium quis dixerit, ignave et contumaciter facere, quae faciat, et alio corpus inpellere, alio animum distrahique inter diversissimos motus. Nam propter illa ipsa, quibus extollit se miraturque, contempta est et ne illa quidem, quibus gloriatur, libenter facit. Si vero aliquod[1] timetur malum, eo proinde, dum expectat, quasi venisset, urgetur et quicquid ne patiatur timet, iam metu
33 patitur. Quemadmodum in corporibus insidentis languoris[2] signa praecurrunt, quaedam enim segnitia enervis est et sine labore ullo lassitudo et oscitatio et horror membra percurrens; sic infirmus animus multo ante quam opprimatur malis quatitur. Praesumit illa et ante tempus cadit.

Quid autem dementius quam angi futuris nec se tormento reservare, sed arcessere sibi miserias et
34 admovere? Quas optimum est differre, si discutere non possit. Vis scire futuro neminem debere torqueri? Quicumque audierit post quinquagesimum annum sibi patienda supplicia, non perturbatur, nisi

[1] *aliquod* later MSS.; *aliquid* VPb.
[2] *insidentis languoris* Hense; *insignis langore* or *insigni languore* MSS.

---

[a] *Cf. Epp.* xi. 6 and lxxi. 29.
[b] Perhaps a sort of malaria.

colour,[a] his countenance be agitated, and his limbs grow cold? And there are other things which we do, not under the influence of the will, but unconsciously and as the result of a sort of natural impulse." I admit that this is true; but the sage will retain the firm belief that none of these things is evil, or important enough to make a healthy mind break down. Whatever shall remain to be done virtue can do with courage and readiness. For anyone would admit that it is a mark of folly to do in a slothful and rebellious spirit whatever one has to do, or to direct the body in one direction and the mind in another, and thus to be torn between utterly conflicting emotions. For folly is despised precisely because of the things for which she vaunts and admires herself, and she does not do gladly even those things in which she prides herself. But if folly fears some evil, she is burdened by it in the very moment of awaiting it, just as if it had actually come,—already suffering in apprehension whatever she fears she may suffer. Just as in the body symptoms of latent ill-health precede the disease—there is, for example, a certain weak sluggishness,[b] a lassitude which is not the result of any work, a trembling, and a shivering that pervades the limbs,—so the feeble spirit is shaken by its ills a long time before it is overcome by them. It anticipates them, and totters before its time.

But what is greater madness than to be tortured by the future and not to save your strength for the actual suffering, but to invite and bring on wretchedness? If you cannot be rid of it, you ought at least to postpone it. Will you not understand that no man should be tormented by the future? The man who has been told that he will have to endure torture fifty years from now is not disturbed thereby,

si medium spatium transiluerit et se in illam saeculo post futuram sollicitudinem inmiserit; eodem modo fit, ut animos libenter aegros et captantes causas doloris vetera atque obliterata contristent. Et quae praeterierunt et quae futura sunt, absunt; neutra sentimus.[1] Non est autem nisi ex eo, quod sentias, dolor. VALE.

LXXV.

SENECA LVCILIO SVO SALVTEM

1 Minus tibi accuratas a me epistulas mitti quereris. Quis enim accurate loquitur, nisi qui vult putide loqui? Qualis sermo meus esset, si una sederemus aut ambularemus, inlaboratus et facilis, tales esse epistulas meas volo, quae nihil habent accersitum nec
2 fictum. Si fieri posset, quid sentiam, ostendere quam loqui mallem. Etiam si disputarem, nec supploderem pedem nec manum iactarem nec attollerem vocem, sed ista oratoribus reliquissem, contentus sensus meos ad te pertulisse, quos nec
3 exornassem nec abiecissem. Hoc unum plane tibi adprobare vellem: omnia me illa sentire, quae dicerem, nec tantum sentire, sed amare. Aliter homines amicam, aliter liberos osculantur; tamen in hoc quoque amplexu tam sancto et moderato satis apparet adfectus.

[1] *sentimus* later MSS.; *sentiamus* Pb; *sentiam* V.

[a] For *putidum* (that which offends the taste, *i.e.* is too artificially formal) see Cic. *De Orat.* iii. 41 *nolo exprimi litteras putidius, nolo obscurari neglegentius.*

[b] *Cf. Ep.* lxvii. 2 *si quando intervenerunt epistulae tuae, tecum esse mihi videor*, etc.

unless he has leaped over the intervening years, and has projected himself into the trouble that is destined to arrive a generation later. In the same way, souls that enjoy being sick and that seize upon excuses for sorrow are saddened by events long past and effaced from the records. Past and future are both absent; we feel neither of them. But there can be no pain except as the result of what you feel. Farewell.

LXXV. ON THE DISEASES OF THE SOUL

You have been complaining that my letters to you are rather carelessly written. Now who talks carefully unless he also desires to talk affectedly[a]? I prefer that my letters should be just what my conversation[b] would be if you and I were sitting in one another's company or taking walks together,—spontaneous and easy; for my letters have nothing strained or artificial about them. If it were possible, I should prefer to show, rather than speak, my feelings. Even if I were arguing a point, I should not stamp my foot, or toss my arms about, or raise my voice; but I should leave that sort of thing to the orator, and should be content to have conveyed my feelings to you without having either embellished them or lowered their dignity. I should like to convince you entirely of this one fact,—that I feel whatever I say, that I not only feel it, but am wedded to it. It is one sort of kiss which a man gives his mistress, and another which he gives his children; yet in the father's embrace also, holy and restrained as it is, plenty of affection is disclosed.

Non mehercules ieiuna esse et arida volo, quae
de rebus tam magnis dicentur; neque enim philosophia ingenio renuntiat. Multum tamen operae
4 inpendi verbis non oportet. Haec sit propositi
nostri summa: quod sentimus loquamur, quod
loquimur sentiamus; concordet sermo cum vita.
Ille promissum suum inplevit, qui, et cum videas
5 illum et cum audias, idem est. Videbimus, qualis
sit, quantus sit; unus sit. Non delectent verba
nostra, sed prosint. Si tamen contingere eloquentia
non sollicito potest, si aut parata est aut parvo
constat, adsit et res pulcherrimas prosequatur. Sit
talis, ut res potius quam se ostendat. Aliae artes ad
ingenium totae pertinent, hic animi negotium agitur.
6 Non quaerit aeger medicum eloquentem,[1] sed, si
ita conpetit, ut idem ille, qui sanare potest, compte
de iis, quae facienda sunt, disserat, boni consulet.
Non tamen erit, quare gratuletur sibi, quod inciderit
in medicum etiam disertum. Hoc enim tale est,
quale si peritus gubernator etiam formosus est.
7 Quid aures meas scabis? Quid oblectas? Aliud
agitur; urendus, secandus, abstinendus sum. Ad
haec adhibitus es.

Curare debes morbum veterem, gravem, publicum.
Tantum negotii habes, quantum in pestilentia

[1] *eloquentem* later MSS.; *loquentem* VPb.

---

[a] *Cf. Ep.* cxiv. 1 *talis hominibus fuit oratio qualis vita*, and *passim* in *Epp.* xl., lxxv. and cxiv.

[b] Eloquence and the other arts please mainly by their cleverness; nor does philosophy abjure such cleverness as style; but here in these letters, wherein we are discussing the soul, the graces of speech are of no concern.

I prefer, however, that our conversation on matters so important should not be meagre and dry; for even philosophy does not renounce the company of cleverness. One should not, however, bestow very much attention upon mere words. Let this be the kernel of my idea: let us say what we feel, and feel what we say; let speech harmonize with life.[a] That man has fulfilled his promise who is the same person both when you see him and when you hear him. We shall not fail to see what sort of man he is and how large a man he is, if only he is one and the same. Our words should aim not to please, but to help. If, however, you can attain eloquence without painstaking, and if you either are naturally gifted or can gain eloquence at slight cost, make the most of it and apply it to the noblest uses. But let it be of such a kind that it displays facts rather than itself. It and the other arts are wholly concerned with cleverness[b]; but our business here is the soul.

A sick man does not call in a physician who is eloquent; but if it so happens that the physician who can cure him likewise discourses elegantly about the treatment which is to be followed, the patient will take it in good part. For all that, he will not find any reason to congratulate himself on having discovered a physician who is eloquent. For the case is no different from that of a skilled pilot who is also handsome. Why do you tickle my ears? Why do you entertain me? There is other business at hand; I am to be cauterized, operated upon, or put on a diet. That is why you were summoned to treat me!

You are required to cure a disease that is chronic and serious,—one which affects the general weal. You have as serious a business on hand as a physician

medicus. Circa verba occupatus es? Iamdudum
gaude, si sufficis rebus. Quando, quae multa disces?
Quando, quae didiceris, adfiges tibi ita, ut excidere
non possint? Quando illa experieris? Non enim
ut cetera, memoriae tradidisse satis est; in opere
temptanda sunt. Non est beatus, qui scit illa, sed
8 qui facit.[1] "Quid ergo? Infra illum nulli gradus
sunt? Statim a sapientia praeceps est?" Non, ut
existimo. Nam qui proficit, in numero quidem
stultorum est, magno tamen intervallo ab illis didu-
citur. Inter ipsos quoque proficientes sunt magna
discrimina. In tres classes, ut quibusdam placet,
9 dividuntur: primi sunt, qui sapientiam nondum
habent, sed iam in vicinia eius constiterunt. Tamen
etiam quod prope est, extra[2] est. Qui sint hi
quaeris? Qui omnes iam adfectus ac vitia posuerunt,
quae erant complectenda, didicerunt, sed illis adhuc
inexperta fiducia est. Bonum suum nondum in usu
habent, iam tamen in illa, quae fugerunt, decidere
non possunt. Iam ibi sunt, unde non est retro
lapsus, sed hoc illis de se nondum liquet; quod in
quadam epistula scripsisse me memini, "scire se
nesciunt." Iam contigit illis bono suo frui, nondum
10 confidere. Quidam hoc proficientium genus, de quo
locutus sum, ita complectuntur, ut illos dicant iam
effugisse morbos animi, adfectus nondum, et adhuc

[1] *qui facit* later MSS.; *facit* VPb.
[2] *extra* later MSS.; *ex ora* (*hora*) VPb.

---

[a] Chrysippus, however, recognized only the first two classes, as did Epictetus (iv. 2).
[b] *Ep.* lxxi. 4.

has during a plague. Are you concerned about *words*? Rejoice this instant if you can cope with *things*. When shall you learn all that there is to learn? When shall you so plant in your mind that which you have learned, that it cannot escape? When shall you put it all into practice? For it is not sufficient merely to commit these things to memory, like other matters; they must be practically tested. He is not happy who only knows them, but he who does them. You reply: "What? Are there no degrees of happiness below your 'happy' man? Is there a sheer descent immediately below wisdom?" I think not. For though he who makes progress is still numbered with the fools, yet he is separated from them by a long interval. Among the very persons who are making progress there are also great spaces intervening. They fall into three classes,[a] as certain philosophers believe. First come those who have not yet attained wisdom but have already gained a place near by. Yet even that which is not far away is still outside. These, if you ask me, are men who have already laid aside all passions and vices, who have learned what things are to be embraced; but their assurance is not yet tested. They have not yet put their good into practice, yet from now on they cannot slip back into the faults which they have escaped. They have already arrived at a point from which there is no slipping back, but they are not yet aware of the fact; as I remember writing in another letter, "They are ignorant of their knowledge."[b] It has now been vouchsafed to them to enjoy their good, but not yet to be sure of it. Some define this class, of which I have been speaking,—a class of men who are making progress,—as having escaped the diseases of the mind,

in lubrico stare, quia nemo sit extra periculum malitiae, nisi qui totam eam excussit. Nemo autem illam excussit, nisi qui pro illa sapientiam adsumpsit.

11 Quid inter morbos animi intersit et adfectus, saepe iam dixi. Nunc quoque te admonebo: morbi sunt inveterata vitia et dura, ut avaritia, ut ambitio; nimio[1] artius[2] haec animum inplicuerunt et perpetua eius mala esse coeperunt. Ut breviter finiam, morbus est iudicium in pravo pertinax, tamquam valde expetenda sint, quae leviter expetenda sunt. Vel si mavis, ita finiamus: nimis inminere leviter petendis vel ex toto non petendis, aut in magno pretio habere
12 in aliquo habenda vel in nullo. Adfectus sunt motus animi inprobabiles, subiti et concitati, qui frequentes neglectique fecere morbum, sicut destillatio una nec adhuc in morem adducta tussim facit, adsidua et vetus phthisin. Itaque qui plurimum profecere, extra morbos sunt, adfectus adhuc sentiunt perfecto proximi.

13 Secundum genus est eorum, qui et maxima animi mala et adfectus deposuerunt, sed ita, ut non sit illis securitatis suae certa possessio. Possunt enim
14 in eadem relabi. Tertium illud genus extra multa

[1] *nimio* Rossbach; *nimia* VP; *ninia* b.
[2] *artius* later MSS.; *actus* VPb.

---

[a] For Seneca's own struggles with this disease *cf. Ep.* lxxviii. 1.

[b] The difference between the first and the second classes is well described in *Ep.* lxxii. 6 *hoc interest inter consummatae sapientiae virum et alium procedentis, quod inter sanum et ex morbo gravi ac diutino emergentem.*

but not yet the passions, and as still standing upon slippery ground; because no one is beyond the dangers of evil except him who has cleared himself of it wholly. But no one has so cleared himself except the man who has adopted wisdom in its stead.

I have often before explained the difference between the diseases of the mind and its passions. And I shall remind you once more: the diseases are hardened and chronic vices, such as greed and ambition; they have enfolded the mind in too close a grip, and have begun to be permanent evils thereof. To give a brief definition: by "disease" we mean a persistent perversion of the judgment, so that things which are mildly desirable are thought to be highly desirable. Or, if you prefer, we may define it thus: to be too zealous in striving for things which are only mildly desirable or not desirable at all, or to value highly things which ought to be valued but slightly or valued not at all. "Passions" are objectionable impulses of the spirit, sudden and vehement; they have come so often, and so little attention has been paid to them, that they have caused a state of disease; just as a catarrh,[a] when there has been but a single attack and the catarrh has not yet become habitual, produces a cough, but causes consumption when it has become regular and chronic. Therefore we may say that those who have made most progress are beyond the reach of the "diseases"; but they still feel the "passions" even when very near perfection.

The second class is composed of those who have laid aside both the greatest ills of the mind and its passions, but yet are not in assured possession of immunity.[b] For they can still slip back into their former state. The third class are beyond the reach

et magna vitia est, sed non extra omnia. Effugit avaritiam, sed iram adhuc sentit; iam non sollicitatur libidine, etiamnunc ambitione; iam non concupiscit, sed adhuc timet. Et in ipso metu ad quaedam satis firmus est, quibusdam cedit. Mortem contemnit, dolorem reformidat.

15 De hoc loco aliquid cogitemus. Bene nobiscum agetur, si in hunc admittimur numerum. Magna felicitate naturae magnaque et adsidua intentione studii secundus occupatur gradus; sed ne hic quidem contemnendus est color tertius. Cogita, quantum circa te videas malorum, aspice, quam nullum sit nefas sine exemplo, quantum cotidie nequitia proficiat, quantum publice privatimque peccetur; intelleges satis nos consequi, si inter pessimos non sumus.

16 "Ego vero," inquis, "spero me posse et amplioris ordinis fieri." Optaverim hoc nobis magis quam promiserim; praeoccupati sumus. Ad virtutem contendimus inter vitia districti. Pudet dicere: honesta colimus, quantum vacat. At quam grande praemium expectat, si occupationes nostras et mala tenacissima abrumpimus. Non cupiditas nos, non timor pellet.
17 Inagitati terroribus, incorrupti voluptatibus nec mortem horrebimus nec deos; sciemus mortem malum non esse, deos malo[1] non esse. Tam in-

[1] *malo* Hense; *maio* PM[1]; *maiores* V; *malos* b.

[a] This idea is a favourite with Seneca; *cf. Ep.* liii. 8 *non est quod precario philosopheris*, and § 9 (*philosophia*) *non est res subsiciva*, "an occupation for one's spare time."

of many of the vices and particularly of the great vices, but not beyond the reach of all. They have escaped avarice, for example, but still feel anger; they no longer are troubled by lust, but are still troubled by ambition; they no longer have desire, but they still have fear. And just because they fear, although they are strong enough to withstand certain things, there are certain things to which they yield; they scorn death, but are in terror of pain.

Let us reflect a moment on this topic. It will be well with us if we are admitted to this class. The second stage is gained by great good fortune with regard to our natural gifts and by great and unceasing application to study. But not even the third type is to be despised. Think of the host of evils which you see about you; behold how there is no crime that is not exemplified, how far wickedness advances every day, and how prevalent are sins in home and commonwealth. You will see, therefore, that we are making a considerable gain, if we are not numbered among the basest.

"But as for me," you say, "I hope that it is in me to rise to a higher rank than that!" I should pray, rather than promise, that we may attain this; we have been forestalled. We hasten towards virtue while hampered by vices. I am ashamed to say it; but we worship that which is honourable only in so far as we have time to spare.[a] But what a rich reward awaits us if only we break off the affairs which forestall us and the evils that cling to us with utter tenacity! Then neither desire nor fear shall rout us. Undisturbed by fears, unspoiled by pleasures, we shall be afraid neither of death nor of the gods; we shall know that death is no evil and that the gods are not powers of evil. That which harms has

becillum est quod nocet quam cui nocetur, optima
18 vi noxia carent. Expectant nos, si[1] ex hac aliquando faece in illud evadimus sublime et excelsum, tranquillitas animi et expulsis erroribus absoluta libertas. Quaeris quae sit ista? Non homines timere, non deos; nec turpia velle nec nimia; in se ipsum habere maximam potestatem. Inaestimabile bonum est suum fieri. Vale.

LXXVI.

Seneca Lvcilio svo salvtem

1 Inimicitias mihi denuntias, si quicquam ex iis, quae cotidie facio, ignoraveris. Vide, quam simpliciter tecum vivam: hoc quoque tibi committam. Philosophum audio et quidem quintum iam diem habeo, ex quo in scholam eo et ab octava disputantem audio. "Bona," inquis, "aetate." Quidni bona? Quid autem stultius est quam, quia diu non didiceris,
2 non discere? "Quid ergo? Idem faciam, quod trossuli et iuvenes?" Bene mecum agitur, si hoc unum senectutem meam dedecet.[2] Omnis aetatis homines haec schola admittit. "In hoc senescamus, ut iuvenes sequamur?" In theatrum senex ibo et

[1] *si* added by Pincianus, on the authority of "ancient MSS."

[2] *dedecet* Pincianus; *decet* VPb.

[a] Therefore death has no power to harm, since man is not harmed thereby, and the gods, who are utterly good, cannot be the source of evil.

[b] A mock-heroic nickname for the knights, derived from the town of Trossulum in Etruria, which they captured by a sensational charge. See Persius, i. 82, and Seneca, *Ep.* lxxxvii. 9.

no greater power than that which receives harm, and things which are utterly good have no power at all to harm.[a] There await us, if ever we escape from these low dregs to that sublime and lofty height, peace of mind and, when all error has been driven out, perfect liberty. You ask what this freedom is? It means not fearing either men or gods; it means not craving wickedness or excess; it means possessing supreme power over oneself. And it is a priceless good to be master of oneself. Farewell.

LXXVI. ON LEARNING WISDOM IN OLD AGE

You have been threatening me with your enmity, if I do not keep you informed about all my daily actions. But see, now, upon what frank terms you and I live: for I shall confide even the following fact to your ears. I have been hearing the lectures of a philosopher; four days have already passed since I have been attending his school and listening to the harangue, which begins at two o'clock. "A fine time of life for that!" you say. Yes, fine indeed! Now what is more foolish than refusing to learn, simply because one has not been learning for a long time? "What do you mean? Must I follow the fashion set by the fops[b] and youngsters?" But I am pretty well off if this is the only thing that discredits my declining years. Men of all ages are admitted to this class-room. You retort: "Do we grow old merely in order to tag after the youngsters?" But if I, an old man, go to the theatre, and am carried to

in circum deferar et nullum par sine me depugnabit ad philosophum ire erubescam?

3 Tamdiu discendum est, quamdiu nescias; si proverbio credimus, quamdiu vivas. Nec ulli hoc rei magis convenit quam huic: tamdiu discendum est, quemadmodum vivas, quamdiu vivas. Ego tamen illic aliquid et doceo. Quaeris, quid doceam? Etiam
4 seni esse discendum. Pudet autem me generis humani, quotiens scholam intravi. Praeter ipsum theatrum Neapolitanorum, ut scis, transeundum est Metronactis petenti[1] domum. Illud quidem fartum est et ingenti studio, quis sit pythaules bonus, iudicatur; habet tubicen quoque Graecus et praeco concursum. At in illo loco, in quo vir bonus quaeritur, in quo vir bonus discitur, paucissimi sedent, et hi plerisque videntur nihil boni negotii habere quod agant; inepti et inertes vocantur. Mihi contingat iste derisus; aequo animo audienda sunt inperitorum convicia et ad honesta vadenti contemnendus est ipse contemptus.

5 Perge, Lucili, et propera, tibi ne et ipsi[2] accidat, quod mihi, ut senex discas; immo ideo magis propera, quoniam diu[3] non adgressus es, quod perdiscere vix senex possis. "Quantum," inquis, "proficiam?"

[1] *petenti* Erasmus; *petentes* VPb; *petentibus* later MSS.
[2] *tibi ne et ipsi* Hense; *tibi nec* (*ne* Vb) *tibi* VPb; *ne tibi* later MSS.
[3] *diu* Buecheler; *id* VPb.

[a] See also *Ep.* xciii.

the races, and allow no duel in the arena to be fought to a finish without my presence, shall I blush to attend a philosopher's lecture?

You should keep learning as long as you are ignorant,—even to the end of your life, if there is anything in the proverb. And the proverb suits the present case as well as any: "As long as you live, keep learning how to live." For all that, there is also something which I can teach in that school. You ask, do you, what I can teach? That even an old man should keep learning. But I am ashamed of mankind, as often as I enter the lecture-hall. On my way to the house of Metronax[a] I am compelled to go, as you know, right past the Neapolitan Theatre. The building is jammed; men are deciding, with tremendous zeal, who is entitled to be called a good flute-player; even the Greek piper and the herald draw their crowds. But in the other place, where the question discussed is: "What is a good man?" and the lesson which we learn is, "How to be a good man," very few are in attendance, and the majority think that even these few are engaged in no good business; they have the name of being empty-headed idlers. I hope I may be blessed with that kind of mockery; for one should listen in an unruffled spirit to the railings of the ignorant; when one is marching toward the goal of honour, one should scorn scorn itself.

Proceed, then, Lucilius, and hasten, lest you yourself be compelled to learn in your old age, as is the case with me. Nay, you must hasten all the more, because for a long time you have not approached the subject, which is one that you can scarcely learn thoroughly when you are old. "How much progress shall I make?" you ask. Just as much as you try

6 Quantum temptaveris. Quid expectas? Nulli sapere
casu obtigit. Pecunia veniet ultro, honor offeretur,
gratia ac dignitas fortasse ingerentur tibi; virtus in
te non incidet. Ne levi quidem opera aut parvo
labore cognoscitur; sed est tanti laborare omnia bona
semel occupaturo. Unum est enim bonum, quod
honestum; in illis nihil invenies veri, nihil certi,
7 quaecumque famae placent. Quare autem unum sit
bonum, quod honestum, dicam, quoniam parum me
exsecutum priore epistula iudicas magisque hanc rem
tibi laudatam quam probatam putas, et in artum,
quae dicta sunt, contraham.

8 Omnia suo bono constant. Vitem fertilitas commendat et sapor vini, velocitas cervum. Quam fortia
dorso iumenta sint quaeris, quorum hic unus est usus,
sarcinam ferre. In cane sagacitas prima est, si
investigare debet feras, cursus, si consequi, audacia,
si mordere et invadere. Id in quoque optimum
9 esse debet, cui nascitur, quo censetur. In homine
optimum quid est? Ratio; hac antecedit animalia,
deos sequitur. Ratio ergo perfecta proprium bonum
est, cetera illi cum animalibus satisque communia
sunt. Valet; et leones. Formosus est; et pavones.

---

[a] *Ep.* lxxiv.

to make. Why do you wait? Wisdom comes haphazard to no man. Money will come of its own accord; titles will be given to you; influence and authority will perhaps be thrust upon you; but virtue will not fall upon you by chance. Neither is knowledge thereof to be won by light effort or small toil; but toiling is worth while when one is about to win all goods at a single stroke. For there is but a single good,—namely, that which is honourable; in all those other things of which the general opinion approves, you will find no truth or certainty. Why it is, however, that there is but one good, namely, that which is honourable, I shall now tell you, inasmuch as you judge that in my earlier letter[a] I did not carry the discussion far enough, and think that this theory was commended to you rather than proved. I shall also compress the remarks of other authors into narrow compass.

Everything is estimated by the standard of its own good. The vine is valued for its productiveness and the flavour of its wine, the stag for his speed. We ask, with regard to beasts of burden, how sturdy of back they are; for their only use is to bear burdens. If a dog is to find the trail of a wild beast, keenness of scent is of first importance; if to catch his quarry, swiftness of foot; if to attack and harry it, courage. In each thing that quality should be best for which the thing is brought into being and by which it is judged. And what quality is best in man? It is reason; by virtue of reason he surpasses the animals, and is surpassed only by the gods. Perfect reason is therefore the good peculiar to man; all other qualities he shares in some degree with animals and plants. Man is strong; so is the lion. Man is comely; so is the peacock. Man is

Velox est; et equi. Non dico, in his omnibus vincitur.
Non quaero, quid in se maximum habeat, sed quid
suum. Corpus habet; et arbores. Habet impetum
ac motum voluntarium; et bestiae et vermes. Habet
vocem; sed quanto clariorem canes, acutiorem
aquilae, graviorem tauri, dulciorem mobilioremque
10 luscinii? Quid in homine proprium? Ratio. Haec
recta et consummata felicitatem hominis implevit.[1]
Ergo si omnis res, cum bonum suum perfecit, laudabilis est et ad finem naturae suae pervenit; homini
autem suum bonum ratio est; si hanc perfecit,
laudabilis est et finem naturae suae tetigit. Haec
ratio perfecta virtus vocatur eademque honestum
est.

11 Id itaque unum bonum est in homine, quod unum
hominis est. Nunc enim non quaerimus, quid sit
bonum, sed quid sit hominis bonum. Si nullum aliud
est hominis quam ratio, haec erit unum eius bonum,
sed pensandum cum omnibus. Si sit aliquis malus,
puto improbabitur; si bonus, puto probabitur. Id
ergo in homine primum solumque est, quo et probatur
12 et inprobatur. Non dubitas, an hoc sit bonum;
dubitas an solum bonum sit. Si quis omnia alia
habeat, valetudinem, divitias, imagines multas,
frequens atrium, sed malus ex confesso sit, inprobabis

[1] The words *quid in homine . . . implevit* are suspected by Hilgenfeld.

---

[a] Literally "many masks" of his ancestors. These were placed in the *atrium*.

swift; so is the horse. I do not say that man is surpassed in all these qualities. I am not seeking to find that which is greatest in him, but that which is peculiarly his own. Man has body; so also have trees. Man has the power to act and to move at will; so have beasts and worms. Man has a voice; but how much louder is the voice of the dog, how much shriller that of the eagle, how much deeper that of the bull, how much sweeter and more melodious that of the nightingale! What then is peculiar to man? Reason. When this is right and has reached perfection, man's felicity is complete. Hence, if everything is praiseworthy and has arrived at the end intended by its nature, when it has brought its peculiar good to perfection, and if man's peculiar good is reason; then, if a man has brought his reason to perfection, he is praiseworthy and has reached the end suited to his nature. This perfect reason is called virtue, and is likewise that which is honourable.

Hence that in man is alone a good which alone belongs to man. For we are not now seeking to discover what is a good, but what good is man's. And if there is no other attribute which belongs peculiarly to man except reason, then reason will be his one peculiar good, but a good that is worth all the rest put together. If any man is bad, he will, I suppose, be regarded with disapproval; if good, I suppose he will be regarded with approval. Therefore, that attribute of man whereby he is approved or disapproved is his chief and only good. You do not doubt whether this is a good; you merely doubt whether it is the sole good. If a man possess all other things, such as health, riches, pedigree,[a] a crowded reception-hall, but is confessedly bad, you

illum. Item si quis nihil quidem eorum, quae rettuli,
habeat, deficiatur pecunia, clientium turba, nobilitate
et avorum proavorumque serie, sed ex confesso bonus
sit, probabis illum. Ergo hoc unum est bonum
hominis, quod qui habet, etiam si aliis destituitur,
laudandus est, quod qui non habet, in omnium
13 aliorum copia damnatur ac reicitur. Quae condicio
rerum, eadem hominum est. Navis bona dicitur non
quae pretiosis coloribus picta est nec cui argenteum
aut aureum rostrum est nec cuius tutela ebore caelata
est nec quae fiscis atque opibus regiis pressa est, sed
stabilis et firma et iuncturis aquam excludentibus
spissa, ad ferendum incursum maris solida, guber-
14 naculo parens, velox et non sentiens ventum. Gladium
bonum dices non cui auratus est balteus nec cuius
vagina gemmis distinguitur, sed cui et ad secandum
subtilis acies est et mucro munimentum omne
rupturus. Regula non quam formosa, sed quam recta
sit quaeritur. Eo quidque laudatur, cui comparatur,
quod illi proprium est.

15 Ergo in homine quoque nihil ad rem pertinet,
quantum aret, quantum faeneret, a quam multis
salutetur, quam pretioso incumbat lecto, quam per-
lucido poculo bibat, sed quam bonus sit. Bonus
autem est, si ratio eius explicita et recta est et
16 ad naturae suae voluntatem accommodata. Haec

---

[a] Literally "the guardian deity"; *cf.* Horace, *Od.* i. 14. 10. These were images of the gods, carried and invoked by the ancients, in the same manner as St. Nicholas to-day.

[b] The *fiscus* was the private treasury of the Roman Emperor, as contrasted with the *aerarium*, which theoretically was controlled by the Senate.

will disapprove of him. Likewise, if a man possess none of the things which I have mentioned, and lacks money, or an escort of clients, or rank and a line of grandfathers and great-grandfathers, but is confessedly good, you will approve of him. Hence, this is man's one peculiar good, and the possessor of it is to be praised even if he lacks other things; but he who does not possess it, though he possess everything else in abundance, is condemned and rejected. The same thing holds good regarding men as regarding things. A ship is said to be good not when it is decorated with costly colours, nor when its prow is covered with silver or gold or its figure-head [a] embossed in ivory, nor when it is laden with the imperial revenues [b] or with the wealth of kings, but when it is steady and staunch and taut, with seams that keep out the water, stout enough to endure the buffeting of the waves, obedient to its helm, swift and caring naught for the winds. You will speak of a sword as good, not when its sword-belt is of gold, or its scabbard studded with gems, but when its edge is fine for cutting and its point will pierce any armour. Take the carpenter's rule: we do not ask how beautiful it is, but how straight it is. Each thing is praised in regard to that attribute which is taken as its standard, in regard to that which is its peculiar quality.

Therefore in the case of man also, it is not pertinent to the question to know how many acres he ploughs, how much money he has out at interest, how many callers attend his receptions, how costly is the couch on which he lies, how transparent are the cups from which he drinks, but how good he is. He is good, however, if his reason is well-ordered and right and adapted to that which his nature has

vocatur virtus, hoc est honestum et unicum hominis bonum. Nam cum sola ratio perficiat hominem, sola ratio perfecta beatum facit; hoc autem unum bonum est, quo uno beatus efficitur. Dicimus et illa bona esse, quae a virtute profecta contractaque sunt, id est opera eius omnia; sed ideo unum ipsa bonum
17 est, quia nullum sine illa est. Si omne in animo bonum est, quicquid illum confirmat, extollit, amplificat, bonum est; validiorem autem animum et excelsiorem et ampliorem facit virtus. Nam cetera, quae cupiditates nostras inritant, deprimunt quoque animum et labefaciunt et, cum videntur adtollere, inflant ac multa vanitate deludunt. Ergo unum id bonum est, quo melior animus efficietur.

18 Omnes actiones totius vitae honesti ac turpis respectu temperantur; ad haec faciendi et non faciendi ratio derigitur. Quid sit hoc, dicam: vir bonus quod honeste se facturum putaverit, faciet, etiam si[1] laboriosum erit, faciet, etiam si damnosum erit, faciet, etiam si periculosum erit; rursus quod turpe erit, non faciet, etiam si pecuniam adferet, etiam si voluptatem, etiam si potentiam. Ab honesto nulla re deterrebitur, ad turpia nulla invitabitur.
19 Ergo si honestum utique secuturus est, turpe utique vitaturus et in omni actu vitae spectaturus haec duo,

[1] *etiam si* later MSS.; *etiam sine pecunia si* VPb.

---

[a] *i.e.*, "moral worth."

[b] *i.e.*, peace, the welfare of one's country, dutiful children, etc.

willed. It is this that is called virtue; this is what we mean by "honourable"[a]; it is man's unique good. For since reason alone brings man to perfection, reason alone, when perfected, makes man happy. This, moreover, is man's only good, the only means by which he is made happy. We do indeed say that those things also[b] are goods which are furthered and brought together by virtue,—that is, all the works of virtue; but virtue itself is for this reason the only good, because there is no good without virtue. If every good is in the soul, then whatever strengthens, uplifts, and enlarges the soul, is a good; virtue, however, does make the soul stronger, loftier, and larger. For all other things, which arouse our desires, depress the soul and weaken it, and when we think that they are uplifting the soul, they are merely puffing it up and cheating it with much emptiness. Therefore, that alone is good which will make the soul better.

All the actions of life, taken as a whole, are controlled by the consideration of what is honourable or base; it is with reference to these two things that our reason is governed in doing or not doing a particular thing. I shall explain what I mean: A good man will do what he thinks it will be honourable for him to do, even if it involves toil; he will do it even if it involves harm to him; he will do it even if it involves peril; again, he will not do that which will be base, even if it brings him money, or pleasure, or power. Nothing will deter him from that which is honourable, and nothing will tempt him into baseness. Therefore, if he is determined invariably to follow that which is honourable, invariably to avoid baseness, and in every act of his life to have regard for these two things, deeming nothing

nec aliud bonum quam honestum[1] nec aliud malum quam turpe, si una indepravata virtus est et sola permanet tenoris sui; unum est bonum virtus, cui iam accidere, ne sit bonum, non potest. Mutationis periculum effugit; stultitia ad sapientiam erepit, sapientia in stultitiam non revolvitur.

20 Dixi, si forte meministi, concupita volgo et formidata inconsulto impetu plerosque calcasse. Inventus est, qui flammis inponeret manum, cuius risum non interrumperet tortor, qui in funere liberorum lacrimam non mitteret, qui morti non trepidus occurreret. Amor enim, ira,[2] cupiditas pericula depoposcerunt. Quod potest brevis obstinatio animi aliquo stimulo excitata, quanto magis virtus, quae non ex impetu nec subito, sed aequaliter valet, cui
21 perpetuum robur est. Sequitur, ut quae ab inconsultis saepe contemnuntur, a sapientibus semper, ea nec bona sint nec mala. Unum ergo bonum ipsa virtus est, quae inter hanc fortunam et illam superba incedit cum magno utriusque contemptu.

22 Si hanc opinionem receperis, aliquid bonum esse praeter honestum, nulla non virtus laborabit. Nulla enim optineri poterit, si quicquam extra se respexerit.

[1] *nec aliud bonum nisi* (*quam* Hense) *honestum*, omitted by VPb, is supplied by the Venice edition of 1492.
[2] *amor enim, ira* Chatelain; *amor ē in ira* V; *amore in ira* Pb.

[a] *Cf. Ep.* lxxiv. 21.

else good except that which is honourable, and nothing else bad except that which is base; if virtue alone is unperverted in him and by itself keeps its even course, then virtue is that man's only good, and nothing can thenceforth happen to it which may make it anything else than good. It has escaped all risk of change; folly may creep upwards towards wisdom, but wisdom never slips back into folly.

You may perhaps remember my saying[a] that the things which have been generally desired and feared have been trampled down by many a man in moments of sudden passion. There have been found men who would place their hands in the flames, men whose smiles could not be stopped by the torturer, men who would shed not a tear at the funeral of their children, men who would meet death unflinchingly. It is love, for example, anger, lust, which have challenged dangers. If a momentary stubbornness can accomplish all this when roused by some goad that pricks the spirit, how much more can be accomplished by virtue, which does not act impulsively or suddenly, but uniformly and with a strength that is lasting! It follows that the things which are often scorned by the men who are moved with a sudden passion, and are always scorned by the wise, are neither goods nor evils. Virtue itself is therefore the only good; she marches proudly between the two extremes of fortune, with great scorn for both.

If, however, you accept the view that there is anything good besides that which is honourable, all the virtues will suffer. For it will never be possible for any virtue to be won and held, if there is anything outside itself which virtue must take into consideration. If there is any such thing, then it is at

Quod si est, rationi repugnat, ex qua virtutes sunt, et veritati, quae sine ratione non est. Quaecumque
23 autem opinio veritati repugnat, falsa est. Virum bonum concedas necesse est summae pietatis erga deos esse. Itaque quicquid illi accidit, aequo animo sustinebit; sciet enim id accidisse lege divina, qua universa procedunt. Quod si est, unum illi bonum erit, quod honestum; in hoc enim positum est et parere dis nec excandescere ad subita nec deplorare sortem suam, sed patienter excipere fatum et facere
24 imperata. Si ullum aliud est bonum quam honestum, sequetur nos aviditas vitae, aviditas rerum vitam instruentium, quod est intolerabile, infinitum, vagum. Solum ergo bonum est honestum, cui modus est.

25 Diximus futuram hominum feliciorem vitam quam deorum, si ea bona sunt, quorum nullus[1] dis usus est, tamquam pecunia, honores. Adice nunc, quod si modo solutae corporibus animae manent, felicior illis status restat quam est, dum versantur in corpore. Atqui si ista bona sunt, quibus per corpora utimur, emissis erit peius, quod contra fidem est, feliciores esse liberis et in universum datis clausas et obsessas.
26 Illud quoque dixeram, si bona sunt ea, quae tam homini contingunt quam mutis animalibus, et muta

[1] *nullus* later MSS.; *nullum* VPb.

---

[a] *Cf. Ep.* lxxiv. 14 *aut ista bona non sunt, quae vocantur, aut homo felicior deo est, quoniam quidem quae parata nobis sunt, non habet in usu deus.*

[b] *e.g.*, *Ep.* lxxiv. 16 *summum bonum . . . obsolescit, si ab optima nostri parte ad pessimam transit et transfertur ad sensus, qui agiliores sunt animalibus mutis.*

variance with reason, from which the virtues spring, and with truth also, which cannot exist without reason. Any opinion, however, which is at variance with truth, is wrong. A good man, you will admit, must have the highest sense of duty toward the gods. Hence he will endure with an unruffled spirit whatever happens to him; for he will know that it has happened as a result of the divine law, by which the whole creation moves. This being so, there will be for him one good, and only one, namely, that which is honourable; for one of its dictates is that we shall obey the gods and not blaze forth in anger at sudden misfortunes or deplore our lot, but rather patiently accept fate and obey its commands. If anything except the honourable is good, we shall be hounded by greed for life, and by greed for the things which provide life with its furnishings,—an intolerable state, subject to no limits, unstable. The only good, therefore, is that which is honourable, that which is subject to bounds.

I have declared [a] that man's life would be more blest than that of the gods, if those things which the gods do not enjoy are goods,—such as money and offices of dignity. There is this further consideration: if only it is true that our souls, when released from the body, still abide, a happier condition is in store for them than is theirs while they dwell in the body. And yet, if those things are goods which we make use of for our bodies' sake, our souls will be worse off when set free; and that is contrary to our belief, to say that the soul is happier when it is cabined and confined than when it is free and has betaken itself to the universe. I also said [b] that if those things which dumb animals possess equally with man are goods, then dumb animals also will

animalia beatam vitam actura; quod fieri nullo modo potest. Omnia pro honesto patienda sunt; quod non erat faciendum, si esset ullum aliud bonum quam honestum.

Haec quamvis latius exsecutus essem priore
27 epistula, constrinxi et breviter percucurri. Numquam autem vera tibi opinio talis videbitur, nisi animum adleves et te ipse interroges, si res exegerit, ut pro patria moriaris et salutem omnium civium tua redimas, an porrecturus sis cervicem non tantum patienter, sed etiam libenter. Si hoc facturus es, nullum aliud bonum est. Omnia enim relinquis, ut hoc habeas. Vide quanta vis honesti sit: pro re publica morieris, etiam si statim facturus hoc eris,
28 cum scieris tibi esse faciendum. Interdum ex re pulcherrima magnum gaudium etiam exiguo tempore ac brevi capitur, et quamvis fructus operis peracti nullus ad defunctum exemptumque rebus humanis pertineat, ipsa tamen contemplatio futuri operis iuvat, et vir fortis ac iustus, cum mortis suae pretia ante se posuit, libertatem patriae, salutem omnium, pro quibus dependit animam, in summa voluptate
29 est et periculo suo fruitur. Sed ille quoque, cui hoc gaudium eripitur, quod[1] tractatio operis maximi et

[1] *quod* Arg. b; *quam* VPb.

lead a happy life; which is of course impossible. One must endure all things in defence of that which is honourable; but this would not be necessary if there existed any other good besides that which is honourable.

Although this question was discussed by me pretty extensively in a previous letter,[a] I have discussed it summarily and briefly run through the argument. But an opinion of this kind will never seem true to you unless you exalt your mind and ask yourself whether, at the call of duty, you would be willing to die for your country, and buy the safety of all your fellow-citizens at the price of your own; whether you would offer your neck not only with patience, but also with gladness. If you would do this, there is no other good in your eyes. For you are giving up everything in order to acquire this good. Consider how great is the power of that which is honourable: you will die for your country, even at a moment's notice, when you know that you ought to do so. Sometimes, as a result of noble conduct, one wins great joy even in a very short and fleeting space of time; and though none of the fruits of a deed that has been done will accrue to the doer after he is dead and removed from the sphere of human affairs, yet the mere contemplation of a deed that is to be done is a delight, and the brave and upright man, picturing to himself the guerdons of his death,—guerdons such as the freedom of his country and the deliverance of all those for whom he is paying out his life,—partakes of the greatest pleasure and enjoys the fruit of his own peril. But that man also who is deprived of this joy, the joy which is afforded by the contemplation

[a] *Ep.* lxxiv., esp. § 14.

ultimi[1] praestat, nihil cunctatus desiliet in mortem, facere recte pieque contentus. Oppone etiamnunc illi multa quae dehortentur, dic: "factum tuum matura sequetur oblivio et parum grata existimatio civium"; respondebit[2] tibi: "ista omnia extra opus meum sunt. Ego ipsum contemplor. Hoc esse honestum scio. Itaque quocumque ducit ac vocat, venio."

30 Hoc ergo unum bonum est, quod non tantum perfectus animus, sed generosus quoque et indolis bonae sentit; cetera levia sunt, mutabilia. Itaque sollicite possidentur. Etiam si favente fortuna in unum congesta sunt, dominis suis incubant gravia et

31 illos semper premunt, aliquando et inlidunt.[3] Nemo ex istis, quos purpuratos vides, felix est, non magis quam ex illis, quibus sceptrum et chlamydem in scaena fabulae adsignant; cum praesente populo lati incesserunt et coturnati, simul exierunt, excalceantur et ad staturam suam redeunt. Nemo istorum, quos divitiae honoresque in altiore fastigio ponunt, magnus est. Quare ergo magnus videtur? Cum basi illum sua metiris. Non est magnus pumilio, licet in monte constiterit; colossus magnitudinem suam servabit

32 etiam si steterit in puteo. Hoc laboramus errore sic nobis imponitur, quod neminem aestimamus eo quod est, sed adicimus illi et ea, quibus adornatus

[1] *maximi et ultimi* Sanctolonius and Madvig; *—e et —e* or *—ae et —ae* MSS.
[2] *respondebit* or *respondet* later MSS.; *respondit* VPb.
[3] *inlidunt* Gruter; *inludunt* VP.

---

[a] Compare the argument in *Ep.* lxxx. § 7, "This farce of living, in which we act our parts so ill"; § 8, the loud mouthed impersonator of heroes, who sleeps on rags; and § 9 *hominem involutum aestimas?*

of some last noble effort, will leap to his death without a moment's hesitation, content to act rightly and dutifully. Moreover, you may confront him with many discouragements; you may say: "Your deed will speedily be forgotten," or "Your fellow-citizens will offer you scant thanks." He will answer: "All these matters lie outside my task. My thoughts are on the deed itself. I know that this is honourable. Therefore, whithersoever I am led and summoned by honour, I will go."

This, therefore, is the only good, and not only is every soul that has reached perfection aware of it, but also every soul that is by nature noble and of right instincts; all other goods are trivial and mutable. For this reason we are harassed if we possess them. Even though, by the kindness of Fortune, they have been heaped together, they weigh heavily upon their owners, always pressing them down and sometimes crushing them. None of those whom you behold clad in purple is happy, any more than one of these actors [a] upon whom the play bestows a sceptre and a cloak while on the stage; they strut their hour before a crowded house, with swelling port and buskined foot; but when once they make their exit the foot-gear is removed and they return to their proper stature. None of those who have been raised to a loftier height by riches and honours is really great. Why then does he seem great to you? It is because you are measuring the pedestal along with the man. A dwarf is not tall, though he stand upon a mountain-top; a colossal statue will still be tall, though you place it in a well. This is the error under which we labour; this is the reason why we are imposed upon: we value no man at what he is, but add to the man himself the trappings in

est. Atqui cum voles veram hominis aestimationem inire et scire, qualis sit, nudum inspice; ponat patrimonium, ponat honores et alia fortunae mendacia, corpus ipsum exuat. Animum intuere, qualis quantusque sit, alieno an suo magnus.

33 Si rectis oculis gladios micantes videt et si scit sua nihil interesse, utrum anima per os an per iugulum exeat, beatum voca; si cum illi denuntiata sunt corporis tormenta et quae casu veniunt et quae potentioris iniuria, si vincula et exilia et vanas humanarum formidines mentium securus audit et dicit:

> "Non ulla laborum,
> O virgo, nova mi facies inopinave surgit;
> Omnia praecepi atque animo mecum ipse peregi.

Tu hodie ista denuntias; ego semper denuntiavi mihi
34 et hominem paravi ad humana." Praecogitati mali mollis ictus venit. At stultis et fortunae credentibus omnis videtur nova rerum et inopinata facies; magna autem pars est apud imperitos mali novitas. Hoc ut scias, ea quae putaverant aspera, fortius, cum adsue-
35 vere, patiuntur. Ideo sapiens adsuescit futuris malis et quae alii diu patiendo levia faciunt, hic levia facit

---

[a] As the world-soul is spread through the universe, so the human soul (as fire, or breath) is diffused through the body, and may take its departure in various ways.

[b] Vergil, *Aeneid*, vi. 103 ff. (The answer of Aeneas to the Sibyl's prophecy.)

which he is clothed. But when you wish to inquire into a man's true worth, and to know what manner of man he is, look at him when he is naked; make him lay aside his inherited estate, his titles, and the other deceptions of fortune; let him even strip off his body. Consider his soul, its quality and its stature, and thus learn whether its greatness is borrowed, or its own.

If a man can behold with unflinching eyes the flash of a sword, if he knows that it makes no difference to him whether his soul takes flight through his mouth or through a wound in his throat,[a] you may call him happy; you may also call him happy if, when he is threatened with bodily torture, whether it be the result of accident or of the might of the stronger, he can without concern hear talk of chains, or of exile, or of all the idle fears that stir men's minds, and can say:

> "O maiden, no new sudden form of toil
> Springs up before my eyes; within my soul
> I have forestalled and surveyed everything.[b]

To-day it is you who threaten me with these terrors; but I have always threatened myself with them, and have prepared myself as a man to meet man's destiny." If an evil has been pondered beforehand, the blow is gentle when it comes. To the fool, however, and to him who trusts in fortune, each event as it arrives "comes in a new and sudden form," and a large part of evil, to the inexperienced, consists in its novelty. This is proved by the fact that men endure with greater courage, when they have once become accustomed to them, the things which they had at first regarded as hardships. Hence, the wise man accustoms himself to coming trouble, lightening by long reflection the evils which

diu cogitando. Audimus aliquando voces imperitorum dicentium: "sciebam[1] hoc mihi restare"; sapiens scit sibi omnia restare. Quicquid factum est, dicit: "sciebam." VALE.

LXXVII.

SENECA LVCILIO SVO SALVTEM

1 Subito nobis hodie Alexandrinae naves apparuerunt, quae praemitti solent et nuntiare secuturae classis adventum; tabellarias vocant. Gratus illarum Campaniae aspectus est; omnis in pilis Puteolorum turba consistit et ex ipso genere velorum Alexandrinas quamvis in magna turba navium intellegit. Solis enim licet siparum intendere, quod in alto omnes
2 habent naves. Nulla enim res aeque adiuvat cursum quam summa pars veli; illinc maxime navis urgetur. Itaque quotiens ventus increbruit maiorque est quam expedit, antemna summittitur; minus habet virium flatus ex humili. Cum intravere Capreas et promunturium, ex quo

Alta procelloso speculatur vertice Pallas,

ceterae velo iubentur esse contentae; siparum Alexandrinarum insigne est.[2]

3 In hoc omnium discursu properantium ad litus magnam ex pigritia mea sensi voluptatem, quod epistulas meorum accepturus non properavi scire, quis illic esset

[1] The old editors read *nesciebam*, which seems more in accord with the argument.

[2] *indicium* before *est* deleted by Muretus.

[a] Puteoli, in the bay of Naples, was the head-quarters in Italy of the important grain-trade with Egypt, on which the Roman magistrates relied to feed the populace.

[b] Author unknown.

others lighten by long endurance. We sometimes hear the inexperienced say: "I knew that this was in store for me." But the wise man knows that all things are in store for him. Whatever happens, he says: "I knew it." Farewell.

LXXVII. ON TAKING ONE'S OWN LIFE

Suddenly there came into our view to-day the "Alexandrian" ships, — I mean those which are usually sent ahead to announce the coming of the fleet; they are called "mail-boats." The Campanians are glad to see them; all the rabble of Puteoli[a] stand on the docks, and can recognize the "Alexandrian" boats, no matter how great the crowd of vessels, by the very trim of their sails. For they alone may keep spread their topsails, which all ships use when out at sea, because nothing sends a ship along so well as its upper canvas; that is where most of the speed is obtained. So when the breeze has stiffened and becomes stronger than is comfortable, they set their yards lower; for the wind has less force near the surface of the water. Accordingly, when they have made Capreae and the headland whence

> Tall Pallas watches on the stormy peak,[b]

all other vessels are bidden to be content with the mainsail, and the topsail stands out conspicuously on the "Alexandrian" mail-boats.

While everybody was bustling about and hurrying to the water-front, I felt great pleasure in my laziness, because, although I was soon to receive letters from my friends, I was in no hurry to know how my affairs

rerum mearum status, quid adferrent; olim iam nec perit quicquam mihi nec adquiritur. Hoc, etiam si senex non essem, fuerat sentiendum; nunc vero multo magis. Quantulumcumque haberem, tamen plus iam mihi superesset viatici quam viae, praesertim cum eam viam simus[1] ingressi, quam peragere non est necesse.
4 Iter inperfectum erit, si in media parte aut citra petitum locum steteris; vita non est inperfecta, si honesta est. Ubicumque desines, si bene desines, tota est. Saepe autem et fortiter desinendum est et non ex maximis causis; nam nec eae[2] maximae sunt, quae nos tenent.

5 Tullius Marcellinus, quem optime noveras, adulescens quietus[3] et cito senex, morbo et non insanabili correptus sed longo et molesto et multa imperante, coepit deliberare de morte. Convocavit complures amicos. Unusquisque aut quia timidus erat, id illi suadebat, quod sibi suasisset, aut quia adulator et blandus, id consilium dabat, quod de-
6 liberanti gratius fore suspicabatur; amicus noster Stoicus, homo egregius et, ut verbis illum, quibus laudari dignus est, laudem, vir fortis ac strenuus, videtur mihi optime illum cohortatus. Sic enim coepit: "Noli, mi Marcelline, torqueri, tamquam de

[1] *simus* later MSS.; *sumus* VPb.
[2] *nec eae* O. Rossbach; *nec et* VPb.
[3] J. W. Duff would read, with Kron., *vietus*, "old," "withered."

---

[a] This thought, found in *Ep.* xii. 6 and often elsewhere, is a favourite with Seneca.

[b] It is not likely that this Marcellinus is the same person as the Marcellinus of *Ep.* xxix., because of their different views on philosophy (Summers). But there is no definite evidence for or against.

[c] A Roman compliment; the Greeks would have used καλὸς κἀγαθός; cf. Horace, *Ep.* i. 7. 46

> Strenuus et fortis causisque Philippus agendis
> Clarus.

were progressing abroad, or what news the letters were bringing; for some time now I have had no losses, nor gains either. Even if I were not an old man, I could not have helped feeling pleasure at this; but as it is, my pleasure was far greater. For, however small my possessions might be, I should still have left over more travelling-money than journey to travel, especially since this journey upon which we have set out is one which need not be followed to the end. An expedition will be incomplete if one stops half-way, or anywhere on this side of one's destination; but life is not incomplete if it is honourable. At whatever point you leave off living, provided you leave off nobly, your life is a whole.[a] Often, however, one must leave off bravely, and our reasons therefore need not be momentous; for neither are the reasons momentous which hold us here.

Tullius Marcellinus,[b] a man whom you knew very well, who in youth was a quiet soul and became old prematurely, fell ill of a disease which was by no means hopeless; but it was protracted and troublesome, and it demanded much attention; hence he began to think about dying. He called many of his friends together. Each one of them gave Marcellinus advice,—the timid friend urging him to do what he had made up his mind to do; the flattering and wheedling friend giving counsel which he supposed would be more pleasing to Marcellinus when he came to think the matter over; but our Stoic friend, a rare man, and, to praise him in language which he deserves, a man of courage and vigour,[c] admonished him best of all, as it seems to me. For he began as follows: "Do not torment yourself, my dear Marcellinus, as if the question which you are

re magna deliberes. Non est res magna vivere;
omnes servi tui vivunt, omnia animalia; magnum est
honeste mori, prudenter, fortiter. Cogita, quamdiu
iam idem facias: cibus, somnus, libido, per hunc
circulum curritur. Mori velle non tantum prudens
aut fortis aut miser, etiam fastidiosus potest."

7 Non opus erat suasore illi, sed adiutore; servi
parere nolebant. Primum detraxit illis metum et
indicavit tunc familiam periculum adire, cum incertum esset, an mors domini voluntaria fuisset;
alioqui tam mali exempli esse occidere dominum
8 quam prohibere. Deinde ipsum Marcellinum ad-
monuit non esse inhumanum, quemadmodum cena
peracta reliquiae circumstantibus dividantur, sic
peracta vita aliquid porrigi iis, qui totius vitae
ministri fuissent. Erat Marcellinus facilis animi et
liberalis, etiam cum de suo fieret. Minutas itaque
summulas distribuit flentibus servis et illos ultro
9 consolatus est. Non fuit illi opus ferro, non sanguine;
triduo abstinuit et in ipso cubiculo poni taberna-
culum iussit. Solium deinde inlatum est, in quo
diu iacuit et calda subinde suffusa paulatim defecit,
ut aiebat, non sine quadam voluptate, quam adferre
solet lenis dissolutio non inexperta nobis, quos
aliquando liquit animus.

---

[a] For this frequent "banquet of life" simile see *Ep.* xcviii. 15 *ipse vitae plenus est*, etc.

[b] So that the steam might not escape. One thinks of Seneca's last hours: Tac. *Ann.* xv. 64 *stagnum calidae aquae introiit . . . exin balneo inlatus et vapore eius exanimatus.*

weighing were a matter of importance. It is not an important matter to live; all your slaves live, and so do all animals; but it is important to die honourably, sensibly, bravely. Reflect how long you have been doing the same thing: food, sleep, lust,—this is one's daily round. The desire to die may be felt, not only by the sensible man or the brave or unhappy man, but even by the man who is merely surfeited."

Marcellinus did not need someone to urge him, but rather someone to help him; his slaves refused to do his bidding. The Stoic therefore removed their fears, showing them that there was no risk involved for the household except when it was uncertain whether the master's death was self-sought or not; besides, it was as bad a practice to kill one's master as it was to prevent him forcibly from killing himself. Then he suggested to Marcellinus himself that it would be a kindly act to distribute gifts to those who had attended him throughout his whole life, when that life was finished, just as, when a banquet is finished,[a] the remaining portion is divided among the attendants who stand about the table. Marcellinus was of a compliant and generous disposition, even when it was a question of his own property; so he distributed little sums among his sorrowing slaves, and comforted them besides. No need had he of sword or of bloodshed; for three days he fasted and had a tent put up in his very bedroom.[b] Then a tub was brought in; he lay in it for a long time, and, as the hot water was continually poured over him, he gradually passed away, not without a feeling of pleasure, as he himself remarked,—such a feeling as a slow dissolution is wont to give. Those of us who have ever fainted know from experience what this feeling is.

10 In fabellam excessi non ingratam tibi. Exitum
enim amici tui cognosces non difficilem nec miserum.
Quamvis enim mortem sibi consciverit, tamen mollis-
sime excessit et vita elapsus est. Sed ne inutilis
quidem haec fabella fuerit. Saepe enim talia
exempla necessitas exigit. Saepe debemus mori nec
11 volumus, morimur nec volumus. Nemo tam imperitus
est, ut nesciat quandoque moriendum; tamen cum
prope accessit, tergiversatur, tremit, plorat. Nonne
tibi videbitur stultissimus omnium, qui flevit, quod
ante annos mille non vixerat? Aeque stultus est,
qui flet, quod post annos mille non vivet. Haec
paria sunt; non eris nec fuisti. Utrumque tempus
12 alienum est. In hoc punctum coniectus es, quod ut
extendas, quo usque extendes? Quid fles? Quid
optas? Perdis operam.

> Desine fata deum flecti sperare precando.

Rata et fixa sunt et magna atque aeterna necessitate
ducuntur. Eo ibis, quo omnia eunt. Quid tibi novi
est? Ad hanc legem natus es. Hoc patri tuo
accidit, hoc matri, hoc maioribus, hoc omnibus ante
te, hoc omnibus post te. Series invicta et nulla
13 mutabilis ope inligavit ac trahit cuncta. Quantus te
populus moriturorum sequetur? Quantus comita-

---

[a] For the same thought *cf. Ep.* xlix. 3 *punctum est quod vivimus et adhuc puncto minus.*

[b] Vergil, *Aeneid*, vi. 376.

This little anecdote into which I have digressed will not be displeasing to you. For you will see that your friend departed neither with difficulty nor with suffering. Though he committed suicide, yet he withdrew most gently, gliding out of life. The anecdote may also be of some use; for often a crisis demands just such examples. There are times when we ought to die and are unwilling; sometimes we die and are unwilling. No one is so ignorant as not to know that we must at some time die; nevertheless, when one draws near death, one turns to flight, trembles, and laments. Would you not think him an utter fool who wept because he was not alive a thousand years ago? And is he not just as much of a fool who weeps because he will not be alive a thousand years from now? It is all the same; you will not be, and you were not. Neither of these periods of time belongs to you. You have been cast upon this point of time;[a] if you would make it longer, how much longer shall you make it? Why weep? Why pray? You are taking pains to no purpose.

> Give over thinking that your prayers can bend
> Divine decrees from their predestined end.[b]

These decrees are unalterable and fixed; they are governed by a mighty and everlasting compulsion. Your goal will be the goal of all things. What is there strange in this to you? You were born to be subject to this law; this fate befell your father, your mother, your ancestors, all who came before you; and it will befall all who shall come after you. A sequence which cannot be broken or altered by any power binds all things together and draws all things in its course. Think of the multitudes of men doomed to death who will come after you, of the

bitur? Fortior, ut opinor, esses, si multa milia tibi commorerentur; atqui multa milia et hominum et animalium hoc ipso momento, quo tu mori dubitas, animam variis generibus emittunt. Tu autem non putabas te aliquando ad id perventurum, ad quod semper ibas? Nullum sine exitu iter est.

14 Exempla nunc magnorum virorum me tibi iudicas relaturum? Puerorum referam. Lacon ille memoriae traditur inpubis adhuc, qui captus clamabat "non serviam" sua illa Dorica lingua, et verbis fidem inposuit; ut primum iussus est servili fungi et contumelioso ministerio, adferre enim vas obscenum
15 iubebatur, inlisum parieti caput rupit. Tam prope libertas est; et servit aliquis? Ita non sic perire filium tuum malles quam per inertiam senem fieri? Quid ergo est, cur perturberis, si mori fortiter etiam puerile est? Puta nolle te sequi; duceris. Fac tui iuris, quod alieni est. Non sumes pueri spiritum, ut dicas "non servio"? Infelix, servis hominibus, servis rebus, servis vitae. Nam vita, si moriendi virtus abest, servitus est.

16 Ecquid habes, propter quod expectes? Voluptates ipsas, quae te morantur ac retinent, consumpsisti. Nulla tibi nova est, nulla non iam odiosa ipsa satie-

---

[a] See Plutarch, *Mor.* 234 b, for a similar act of the Spartan boy captured by King Antigonus. Hense (*Rhein. Mus.* xlvii. pp. 220 f.) thinks that this story may be taken from Bion, the third-century satirist and moral philosopher.

multitudes who will go with you! You would die more bravely, I suppose, in the company of many thousands; and yet there are many thousands, both of men and of animals, who at this very moment, while you are irresolute about death, are breathing their last, in their several ways. But you,—did you believe that you would not some day reach the goal towards which you have always been travelling? No journey but has its end.

You think, I suppose, that it is now in order for me to cite some examples of great men. No, I shall cite rather the case of a boy. The story of the Spartan lad has been preserved: taken captive while still a stripling, he kept crying in his Doric dialect, "I will not be a slave!" and he made good his word; for the very first time he was ordered to perform a menial and degrading service,—and the command was to fetch a chamber-pot,—he dashed out his brains against the wall.[a] So near at hand is freedom, and is anyone still a slave? Would you not rather have your own son die thus than reach old age by weakly yielding? Why therefore are you distressed, when even a boy can die so bravely? Suppose that you refuse to follow him; you will be led. Take into your own control that which is now under the control of another. Will you not borrow that boy's courage, and say: "I am no slave!"? Unhappy fellow, you are a slave to men, you are a slave to your business, you are a slave to life. For life, if courage to die be lacking, is slavery.

Have you anything worth waiting for? Your very pleasures, which cause you to tarry and hold you back, have already been exhausted by you. None of them is a novelty to you, and there is none that has not already become hateful because you are

tate. Quis sit vini, quis mulsi sapor, scis. Nihil interest, centum per vesicam tuam an mille amphorae transeant; saccus es.[1] Quid sapiat ostreum, quid mullus, optime nosti; nihil tibi luxuria tua in futuros annos intactum reservavit; atqui haec sunt, a quibus
17 invitus divelleris. Quid est aliud, quod tibi eripi doleas? Amicos? Quis enim tibi potest[2] amicus esse? Patriam? Tanti enim illam putas, ut tardius cenes? Solem? Quem, si posses, extingueres. Quid enim umquam fecisti luce dignum? Confitere non curiae te, non fori, non ipsius rerum naturae desiderio tardiorem ad moriendum fieri; invitus relinquis macellum, in quo nihil reliquisti.

18 Mortem times; at quomodo illam media boletatione contemnis? Vivere vis; scis enim? Mori times; quid porro? Ista vita non mors est? C. Caesar,[3] cum illum transeuntem per Latinam viam unus ex custodiarum agmine demissa usque in pectus vetere barba rogaret mortem: "nunc enim," inquit, "vivis?" Hoc istis respondendum est, quibus succursura mors est: mori times; nunc enim vivis?
19 "Sed ego," inquit, "vivere volo, qui multa honeste

[1] *es* later MSS.; *est* VPb.
[2] *amicos? quis enim tibi potest* added by Madvig.
[3] *C. Caesar* Bentley and O. Rossbach; *t. caesar* VO; *caesar* Pb.

---

[a] About 5¾ gallons.
[b] *Cf.* Pliny, xiv. 22 *quin immo ut plus capiamus, sacco frangimus vires.* Strained wine could be drunk in greater quantities without intoxication.
[c] *Cf.* Dio Cassius, xl. 54, for the exiled Milo's enjoyment of the mullets of Marseilles.
[d] Probably the strong tone of disapproval used in this paragraph is directed against the Roman in general rather than against the industrious Lucilius. It is characteristic of the diatribe.

cloyed with it. You know the taste of wine and cordials. It makes no difference whether a hundred or a thousand measures[a] pass through your bladder; you are nothing but a wine-strainer.[b] You are a connoisseur in the flavour of the oyster and of the mullet[c]; your luxury has not left you anything untasted for the years that are to come; and yet these are the things from which you are torn away unwillingly. What else is there which you would regret to have taken from you? Friends? But who can be a friend to you? Country? What? Do you think enough of your country to be late to dinner? The light of the sun? You would extinguish it, if you could; for what have you ever done that was fit to be seen in the light? Confess the truth; it is not because you long for the senate-chamber or the forum, or even for the world of nature, that you would fain put off dying; it is because you are loth to leave the fish-market, though you have exhausted its stores.[d]

You are afraid of death; but how can you scorn it in the midst of a mushroom supper[e]? You wish to live; well, do you know how to live? You are afraid to die. But come now: is this life of yours anything but death? Gaius Caesar was passing along the Via Latina, when a man stepped out from the ranks of the prisoners, his grey beard hanging down even to his breast, and begged to be put to death. "What!" said Caesar, "are you alive now?" That is the answer which should be given to men to whom death would come as a relief. "You are afraid to die; what! are you alive now?" "But," says one, "I wish to live, for I am engaged in many

[e] Seneca may be recalling the death of the Emperor Claudius.

facio. Invitus relinquo officia vitae, quibus fideliter et industrie fungor." Quid? Tu nescis unum esse ex vitae officiis et mori? Nullum officium relinquis. Non enim certus numerus, quem debeas explere,
20 finitur. Nulla vita est non brevis. Nam si ad naturam rerum respexeris, etiam Nestoris et Sattiae brevis est, quae inscribi monumento suo iussit annis se nonaginta novem vixisse. Vides aliquem gloriari senectute longa. Quis illam ferre potuisset, si contigisset centesimum implere? Quomodo fabula, sic vita non quam diu, sed quam bene acta sit, refert. Nihil ad rem pertinet, quo loco desinas. Quocumque voles desine; tantum bonam clausulam inpone. Vale.

LXXVIII.

Seneca Lvcilio svo salvtem

1 Vexari te destillationibus crebris ac febriculis, quae longas destillationes et in consuetudinem adductas secuntur, eo molestius mihi est, quia expertus sum hoc genus valetudinis, quod inter initia contempsi; poterat adhuc adulescentia iniurias ferre et se adversus morbos contumaciter gerere. Deinde succubui et eo perductus sum, ut ipse destillarem ad
2 summam maciem deductus. Saepe impetum cepi abrumpendae vitae; patris me indulgentissimi senectus retinuit. Cogitavi enim non quam fortiter ego

[a] A traditional example of old age, mentioned by Martial and the elder Pliny.

[b] Compare the last words of the Emperor Augustus: *amicos percontatus ecquid iis videretur mimum vitae commode transegisse* (Suet. *Aug.* 99).

[c] To such a degree that Seneca's enemy Caligula refrained from executing him, on the ground that he would soon die.

honourable pursuits. I am loth to leave life's duties, which I am fulfilling with loyalty and zeal." Surely you are aware that dying is also one of life's duties? You are deserting no duty; for there is no definite number established which you are bound to complete. There is no life that is not short. Compared with the world of nature, even Nestor's life was a short one, or Sattia's,[a] the woman who bade carve on her tombstone that she had lived ninety and nine years. Some persons, you see, boast of their long lives; but who could have endured the old lady if she had had the luck to complete her hundredth year? It is with life as it is with a play,—it matters not how long the action is spun out, but how good the acting is. It makes no difference at what point you stop. Stop whenever you choose; only see to it that the closing period is well turned.[b] Farewell.

LXXVIII.

ON THE HEALING POWER OF THE MIND

That you are frequently troubled by the snuffling of catarrh and by short attacks of fever which follow after long and chronic catarrhal seizures, I am sorry to hear; particularly because I have experienced this sort of illness myself, and scorned it in its early stages. For when I was still young, I could put up with hardships and show a bold front to illness. But I finally succumbed, and arrived at such a state that I could do nothing but snuffle, reduced as I was to the extremity of thinness.[c] I often entertained the impulse of ending my life then and there; but the thought of my kind old father kept me back. For I reflected, not how bravely I

mori possem, sed quam ille fortiter desiderare non posset. Itaque imperavi mihi, ut viverem. Aliquando enim et vivere fortiter facere est.

3 Quae mihi tunc fuerint solacio dicam, si prius hoc dixero,[1] haec ipsa, quibus adquiescebam, medicinae vim habuisse. In remedium cedunt honesta solacia, et quicquid animum erexit, etiam corpori prodest. Studia mihi nostra saluti fuerunt. Philosophiae acceptum fero, quod surrexi, quod convalui. Illi
4 vitam debeo et nihil illi minus debeo. Multum mihi contulerunt ad bonam valetudinem amici, quorum adhortationibus, vigiliis, sermonibus adlevabar. Nihil aeque, Lucili, virorum optime, aegrum reficit atque adiuvat quam amicorum adfectus; nihil aeque expectationem mortis ac metum subripit. Non iudicabam me, cum illos superstites relinquerem,[2] mori. Putabam, inquam, me victurum non cum illis, sed per illos. Non effundere mihi spiritum videbar, sed tradere.[3]

Haec mihi dederunt voluntatem adiuvandi me et patiendi omne tormentum; alioqui miserrimum est, cum animum moriendi proieceris, non habere vivendi.
5 Ad haec ergo remedia te confer. Medicus tibi quantum ambules, quantum exercearis, monstrabit; ne indulgeas otio, ad quod vergit iners valetudo; ut legas clarius et spiritum, cuius iter ac receptaculum

[1] *dixero* or *dixerim* later MSS.; *dixeris* VPb.
[2] *relinquerem* later MSS.; *relinquere* VPb.
[3] *tradere* Muretus; *trahere* VPb.

[a] *Cf. Ep.* xv. 7 f.

had the power to die, but how little power he had to bear bravely the loss of me. And so I commanded myself to live. For sometimes it is an act of bravery even to live.

Now I shall tell you what consoled me during those days, stating at the outset that these very aids to my peace of mind were as efficacious as medicine. Honourable consolation results in a cure; and whatever has uplifted the soul helps the body also. My studies were my salvation. I place it to the credit of philosophy that I recovered and regained my strength. I owe my life to philosophy, and that is the least of my obligations! My friends, too, helped me greatly toward good health; I used to be comforted by their cheering words, by the hours they spent at my bedside, and by their conversation. Nothing, my excellent Lucilius, refreshes and aids a sick man so much as the affection of his friends; nothing so steals away the expectation and the fear of death. In fact, I could not believe that, if they survived me, I should be dying at all. Yes, I repeat, it seemed to me that I should continue to live, not with them, but through them. I imagined myself not to be yielding up my soul, but to be making it over to them.

All these things gave me the inclination to succour myself and to endure any torture; besides, it is a most miserable state to have lost one's zest for dying, and to have no zest in living. These, then, are the remedies to which you should have recourse. The physician will prescribe your walks and your exercise; he will warn you not to become addicted to idleness, as is the tendency of the inactive invalid; he will order you to read in a louder voice and to exercise your lungs,[a] the passages

laborat, exerceas; ut naviges et viscera molli iactatione concutias; quibus cibis utaris, vinum quando virium causa advoces, quando intermittas, ne inritet et exasperet tussim. Ego tibi illud praecipio, quod non tantum huius morbi, sed totius vitae remedium est: contemne mortem. Nihil triste est, cum huius
6 metum effugimus. Tria haec in omni morbo gravia sunt: metus mortis, dolor corporis, intermissio voluptatum. De morte satis dictum est; hoc unum dicam, non morbi hunc esse sed naturae metum. Multorum mortem distulit morbus et saluti illis fuit videri perire. Morieris, non quia aegrotas, sed quia vivis. Ista te res et sanatum manet; cum convalueris, non mortem, sed valetudinem effugies.

7 Ad illud nunc proprium incommodum revertamur: magnos cruciatus habet morbus. Sed hos tolerabiles intervalla faciunt. Nam summi doloris intentio invenit finem. Nemo potest valde dolere et diu; sic nos amantissima nostri natura disposuit, ut dolorem
8 aut tolerabilem aut brevem faceret. Maximi dolores consistunt in macerrimis corporis partibus; nervi articulique et quicquid aliud exile est, acerrime saevit, cum in arto vitia concepit. Sed cito hae partes obstupescunt et ipso dolore sensum doloris amittunt,

---

[a] *i.e.*, men have become healthier after passing through serious illness.

[b] *Cf.* Epicurus, Frag. 446 Usener.

[c] Compare, from among many parallels, *Ep.* xxiv. 14 (*dolor*) *levis es, si ferre possum, brevis es, si ferre non possum.*

and cavity of which are affected; or to sail and shake up your bowels by a little mild motion; he will recommend the proper food, and the suitable time for aiding your strength with wine or refraining from it in order to keep your cough from being irritated and hacking. But as for me, my counsel to you is this,—and it is a cure, not merely of this disease of yours, but of your whole life,—"Despise death." There is no sorrow in the world, when we have escaped from the fear of death. There are these three serious elements in every disease: fear of death, bodily pain, and interruption of pleasures. Concerning death enough has been said, and I shall add only a word: this fear is not a fear of disease, but a fear of nature. Disease has often postponed death, and a vision of dying has been many a man's salvation.[a] You will die, not because you are ill, but because you are alive; even when you have been cured, the same end awaits you; when you have recovered, it will be not death, but ill-health, that you have escaped.

Let us now return to the consideration of the characteristic disadvantage of disease: it is accompanied by great suffering. The suffering, however, is rendered endurable by interruptions; for the strain of extreme pain must come to an end.[b] No man can suffer both severely and for a long time; Nature, who loves us most tenderly, has so constituted us as to make pain either endurable or short.[c] The severest pains have their seat in the most slender parts of our body; nerves, joints, and any other of the narrow passages, hurt most cruelly when they have developed trouble within their contracted spaces. But these parts soon become numb, and by reason of the pain itself lose the sensation of pain,

sive quia spiritus naturali prohibitus cursu et mutatus in peius vim suam, qua viget admonetque nos, perdit, sive quia corruptus umor, cum desiit habere, quo confluat, ipse se elidit et iis, quae nimis implevit,
9 excutit sensum. Sic podagra et cheragra et omnis vertebrarum dolor nervorumque[1] interquiescit,[2] cum illa, quae torquebat, hebetavit[3]; omnium istorum prima verminatio vexat, impetus mora extinguitur et finis dolendi est optorpuisse. Dentium, oculorum, aurium dolor ob hoc ipsum acutissimus est, quod inter angusta corporis nascitur, non minus, mehercule, quam capitis ipsius; sed si incitatior est, in aliena-
10 tionem soporemque convertitur. Hoc itaque solacium vasti doloris est, quod necesse est desinas illum sentire, si nimis senseris. Illud autem est, quod imperitos in vexatione corporis male habet: non adsueverunt animo esse contenti. Multum illis cum corpore fuit. Ideo vir magnus ac prudens animum diducit a corpore et multum cum meliore ac divina parte versatur, cum hac querula et fragili quantum necesse est.

11 "Sed molestum est," inquit, "carere adsuetis voluptatibus, abstinere cibo, sitire, esurire." Haec prima abstinentia gravia sunt. Deinde cupiditas relanguescit ipsis per quae[4] cupimus fatigatis ac

[1] *nervorumque* later MSS.; *et nervorumq.* PbV'; *et nervorum* edition of Mentelin.
[2] *interquiescit* later MSS.; *interciet* (*sciet* b) *scit* Pb; *in tertiae scitscit* V.
[3] *hebetavit* later MSS.; *hebetabit* VPb.
[4] *per quae* Muretus; *per se quae* MSS.

[a] See also *Ep.* xcv. 17. The word literally means "maggots," "bots," in horses or cattle.

whether because the life-force, when checked in its natural course and changed for the worse, loses the peculiar power through which it thrives and through which it warns us, or because the diseased humours of the body, when they cease to have a place into which they may flow, are thrown back upon themselves, and deprive of sensation the parts where they have caused congestion. So gout, both in the feet and in the hands, and all pain in the vertebrae and in the nerves, have their intervals of rest at the times when they have dulled the parts which they before had tortured; the first twinges,[a] in all such cases, are what cause the distress, and their onset is checked by lapse of time, so that there is an end of pain when numbness has set in. Pain in the teeth, eyes, and ears is most acute for the very reason that it begins among the narrow spaces of the body,—no less acute, indeed, than in the head itself. But if it is more violent than usual, it turns to delirium and stupor. This is, accordingly, a consolation for excessive pain,—that you cannot help ceasing to feel it if you feel it to excess. The reason, however, why the inexperienced are impatient when their bodies suffer is, that they have not accustomed themselves to be contented in spirit. They have been closely associated with the body. Therefore a high-minded and sensible man divorces soul from body, and dwells much with the better or divine part, and only as far as he must with this complaining and frail portion.

"But it is a hardship," men say, "to do without our customary pleasures,—to fast, to feel thirst and hunger." These are indeed serious when one first abstains from them. Later the desire dies down, because the appetites themselves which lead to

deficientibus; inde morosus est stomachus, inde cuius[1] fuit aviditas cibi, odium est. Desideria ipsa moriuntur. Non est autem acerbum carere eo, quod
12 cupere desieris. Adice, quod nullus non intermittitur dolor aut certe remittitur. Adice, quod licet cavere venturum et obsistere inminenti remediis. Nullus enim non signa praemittit, utique qui ex solito revertitur. Tolerabilis est morbi patientia, si
13 contempseris id quod extremum minatur. Noli mala tua facere tibi ipse[2] graviora et te querellis onerare. Levis est dolor, si nihil illi opinio adiecerit; contra, si exhortari te coeperis ac dicere: "Nihil est aut certe exiguum est. Duremus; iam desinet"; levem illum, dum putas, facies. Omnia ex opinione suspensa sunt; non ambitio tantum ad illam respicit et luxuria et avaritia. Ad opinionem dolemus. Tam miser est
14 quisque quam credidit. Detrahendas praeteritorum dolorum conquestiones puto et illa verba: "Nulli umquam fuit peius. Quos cruciatus, quanta mala pertuli! Nemo me surrecturum putavit. Quotiens deploratus sum a meis, quotiens a medicis relictus! In eculeum inpositi non sic distrahuntur.[3]" Etiam si sunt vera ista, transierunt. Quid iuvat praeteritos dolores retractare et miserum esse, quia fueris? Quid, quod nemo non multum malis suis adicit et

[1] *cuius* Madvig; *quibus* MSS.
[2] *ipse* Haase; *ipsi* MSS.
[3] *distrahuntur* later MSS.; *detra(h)untur* VPb.

desire are wearied and forsake us; then the stomach becomes petulant, then the food which we craved before becomes hateful. Our very wants die away. But there is no bitterness in doing without that which you have ceased to desire. Moreover, every pain sometimes stops, or at any rate slackens; moreover, one may take precautions against its return, and, when it threatens, may check it by means of remedies. Every variety of pain has its premonitory symptoms; this is true, at any rate, of pain that is habitual and recurrent. One can endure the suffering which disease entails, if one has come to regard its results with scorn. But do not of your own accord make your troubles heavier to bear and burden yourself with complaining. Pain is slight if opinion has added nothing to it; but if, on the other hand, you begin to encourage yourself and say, "It is nothing,—a trifling matter at most; keep a stout heart and it will soon cease"; then in thinking it slight, you will make it slight. Everything depends on opinion; ambition, luxury, greed, hark back to opinion. It is according to opinion that we suffer. A man is as wretched as he has convinced himself that he is. I hold that we should do away with complaint about past sufferings and with all language like this: "None has ever been worse off than I. What sufferings, what evils have I endured! No one has thought that I shall recover. How often have my family bewailed me, and the physicians given me over! Men who are placed on the rack are not torn asunder with such agony!" However, even if all this is true, it is over and gone. What benefit is there in reviewing past sufferings, and in being unhappy, just because once you were unhappy? Besides, every one adds much to his own

sibi ipse mentitur? Deinde quod acerbum fuit
ferre,[1] tulisse iucundum est; naturale est mali sui
fine gaudere.

Circumcidenda ergo duo sunt, et futuri timor et
veteris incommodi memoria; hoc ad me iam non
15 pertinet, illud nondum. In ipsis positus difficultati-
bus dicat:

> Forsan et haec olim meminisse iuvabit.

Toto contra ille[2] pugnet animo; vincetur, si cesserit,
vincet, si se contra dolorem suum intenderit. Nunc
hoc plerique faciunt, adtrahunt in se ruinam, cui
obstandum est. Istud quod premit, quod inpendet,
quod urget, si subducere te coeperis, sequetur et
gravius incumbet; si contra steteris et obniti volueris,
16 repelletur. Athletae quantum plagarum ore, quantum toto corpore excipiunt? Ferunt tamen omne
tormentum gloriae cupiditate nec tantum quia pug-
nant, ista patiuntur, sed ut pugnent. Exercitatio
ipsa tormentum est. Nos quoque evincamus omnia,
quorum praemium non corona nec palma est nec
tubicen praedicationi nominis nostri silentium faciens,
sed virtus et firmitas animi et pax in ceterum parta,
si semel in aliquo certamine debellata fortuna est.
17 "Dolorem gravem sentio." Quid ergo? Non sentis,

[1] *fuit ferre, tulisse* Bartsch; *fuit retulisse* MSS.
[2] *ille* Hense; *illa* or *illum* MSS.

[a] Vergil, *Aeneid*, i. 203.

ills, and tells lies to himself. And that which was bitter to bear is pleasant to have borne; it is natural to rejoice at the ending of one's ills.

Two elements must therefore be rooted out once for all,—the fear of future suffering, and the recollection of past suffering; since the latter no longer concerns me, and the former concerns me not yet. But when set in the very midst of troubles one should say:

> Perchance some day the memory of this sorrow
> Will even bring delight.[a]

Let such a man fight against them with all his might: if he once gives way, he will be vanquished; but if he strives against his sufferings, he will conquer. As it is, however, what most men do is to drag down upon their own heads a falling ruin which they ought to try to support. If you begin to withdraw your support from that which thrusts toward you and totters and is ready to plunge, it will follow you and lean more heavily upon you; but if you hold your ground and make up your mind to push against it, it will be forced back. What blows do athletes receive on their faces and all over their bodies! Nevertheless, through their desire for fame they endure every torture, and they undergo these things not only because they are fighting but in order to be able to fight. Their very training means torture. So let us also win the way to victory in all our struggles,—for the reward is not a garland or a palm or a trumpeter who calls for silence at the proclamation of our names, but rather virtue, steadfastness of soul, and a peace that is won for all time, if fortune has once been utterly vanquished in any combat. You say, "I feel severe pain." What then; are

si illum muliebriter tuleris? Quemadmodum perniciosior est hostis fugientibus, sic omne fortuitum incommodum magis instat cedenti et averso. "Sed grave est." Quid? Nos ad hoc fortes sumus, ut levia portemus? Utrum vis longum esse morbum an concitatum[1] et brevem? Si longus est, habet intercapedinem, dat refectioni locum, multum temporis donat, necesse est, ut exurgit,[2] et desinat. Brevis morbus ac praeceps alterutrum faciet: aut extinguetur aut extinguet. Quid autem interest, non sit an non sim? In utroque finis dolendi est.

18 Illud quoque proderit, ad alias cogitationes avertere animum et a dolore discedere. Cogita quid honeste, quid fortiter feceris; bonas partes tecum ipse tracta. Memoriam in ea, quae maxime miratus es, sparge. Tunc tibi fortissimus quisque et victor doloris occurrat: ille, qui cum[3] varices exsecandas praeberet, legere librum perseveravit; ille, qui non desiit ridere, cum hoc ipsum irati tortores omnia instrumenta crudelitatis suae experirentur. Non vincetur dolor
19 ratione, qui victus est risu? Quicquid vis nunc licet dicas, destillationes et vim continuae tussis egerentem viscerum partes et febrem praecordia ipsa torrentem et sitim et artus in diversum articulis exeuntibus tortos; plus est flamma et eculeus et lammina et vulneribus ipsis intumescentibus quod illa renovaret

[1] *concitatum* later MSS.; *cogitatum* VPb.
[2] *exurgit* Haase; *ex(s)urgat* MSS.
[3] *cum* Haase; *dum* MSS.

---

[a] Literally, perhaps, "the noble rôles which you have played." Summers compares *Ep.* xiv. 13 *ultimas partes Catonis*—"the closing scenes of Cato's life."

you relieved from feeling it, if you endure it like a woman? Just as an enemy is more dangerous to a retreating army, so every trouble that fortune brings attacks us all the harder if we yield and turn our backs. "But the trouble is serious." What? Is it for this purpose that we are strong,—that we may have light burdens to bear? Would you have your illness long-drawn-out, or would you have it quick and short? If it is long, it means a respite, allows you a period for resting yourself, bestows upon you the boon of time in plenty; as it arises, so it must also subside. A short and rapid illness will do one of two things: it will quench or be quenched. And what difference does it make whether it is not or I am not? In either case there is an end of pain.

This, too, will help—to turn the mind aside to thoughts of other things and thus to depart from pain. Call to mind what honourable or brave deeds you have done; consider the good side of your own life.[a] Run over in your memory those things which you have particularly admired. Then think of all the brave men who have conquered pain: of him who continued to read his book as he allowed the cutting out of varicose veins; of him who did not cease to smile, though that very smile so enraged his torturers that they tried upon him every instrument of their cruelty. If pain can be conquered by a smile, will it not be conquered by reason? You may tell me now of whatever you like—of colds, hard coughing-spells that bring up parts of our entrails, fever that parches our very vitals, thirst, limbs so twisted that the joints protrude in different directions; yet worse than these are the stake, the rack, the red-hot plates, the instrument that reopens wounds while the wounds themselves are still swollen

et altius urgeret inpressum. Inter haec tamen aliquis non gemuit. "Parum est"; non rogavit. "Parum est"; non respondit. "Parum est"; risit et quidem ex animo. Vis tu post hoc dolorem deridere?

20 "Sed nihil," inquit, "agere sinit morbus, qui me omnibus abduxit officiis." Corpus tuum valetudo tenet, non et animum. Itaque cursoris moratur pedes, sutoris aut fabri manus inpediet; si animus tibi esse in usu solet, suadebis docebis, audies disces,[1] quaeres recordaberis. Quid porro? Nihil agere te credis, si temperans aeger sis? Ostendes morbum
21 posse superari vel certe sustineri. Est, mihi crede, virtuti etiam in lectulo locus. Non tantum arma et acies dant argumenta alacris animi indomitique terroribus; et in vestimentis vir fortis apparet. Habes, quod agas: bene luctare cum morbo. Si nihil te coegerit, si nihil exoraverit, insigne prodis exemplum. O quam magna erat gloriae materia, si spectaremur aegri! Ipse te specta,[2] ipse te lauda.

22 Praeterea duo genera sunt voluptatum. Corporales morbus inhibet, non tamen tollit. Immo, si verum aestimes, incitat; magis iuvat bibere sitientem;

[1] *disces* later MSS.; *dices* VPb.
[2] *specta* later MSS.; *expecta* VPb.

---

[a] *Cf. Ep.* xiv. 4 f. and the *crucibus adfixi, flamma usti* etc., of Tac. *Ann.* xv. 44.

and that drives their imprint still deeper.[a] Nevertheless there have been men who have not uttered a moan amid these tortures. "More yet!" says the torturer; but the victim has not begged for release. "More yet!" he says again; but no answer has come. "More yet!" the victim has smiled, and heartily, too. Can you not bring yourself, after an example like this, to make a mock at pain?

"But," you object, "my illness does not allow me to be doing anything; it has withdrawn me from all my duties." It is your body that is hampered by ill-health, and not your soul as well. It is for this reason that it clogs the feet of the runner and will hinder the handiwork of the cobbler or the artisan; but if your soul be habitually in practice, you will plead and teach, listen and learn, investigate and meditate. What more is necessary? Do you think that you are doing nothing if you possess self-control in your illness? You will be showing that a disease can be overcome, or at any rate endured. There is, I assure you, a place for virtue even upon a bed of sickness. It is not only the sword and the battle-line that prove the soul alert and unconquered by fear; a man can display bravery even when wrapped in his bed-clothes. You have something to do: wrestle bravely with disease. If it shall compel you to nothing, beguile you to nothing, it is a notable example that you display. O what ample matter were there for renown, if we could have spectators of our sickness! Be your own spectator; seek your own applause.

Again, there are two kinds of pleasures. Disease checks the pleasures of the body, but does not do away with them. Nay, if the truth is to be considered, it serves to excite them; for the thirstier

gratior est esurienti cibus. Quicquid ex abstinentia contigit, avidius excipitur. Illas vero animi voluptates, quae maiores certioresque sunt, nemo medicus aegro negat. Has quisquis sequitur et bene intellegit
23 omnia sensuum blandimenta contemnit. "O infelicem aegrum!" Quare? Quia non vino nivem diluit? Quia non rigorem potionis suae, quam capac scypho miscuit, renovat fracta insuper glacie? Quia non ostrea illi Lucrina in ipsa mensa aperiuntur Quia non circa cenationem eius tumultus cocorum est ipsos cum opsoniis focos transferentium? Hoc enim iam luxuria commenta est: ne quis intepesca cibus, ne quid palato iam calloso parum ferveat
24 cenam culina prosequitur. "O infelicem aegrum!" edet, quantum concoquat. Non iacebit in conspectu aper ut vilis caro a mensa relegatus, nec in repositorio eius pectora avium, totas enim videre fastidium est congesta ponentur. Quid tibi mali factum est Cenabis tamquam aeger, immo aliquando tamquam sanus.

25 Sed omnia ista facile perferemus, sorbitionem aquam calidam et quicquid aliud intolerabile videtur delicatis et luxu fluentibus magisque animo quam corpore morbidis; tantum mortem desinamus horrere Desinemus autem, si fines bonorum ac malorum

---

[a] The *lacus Lucrinus* was a salt-water lagoon, near Baiae in Campania.

[b] *i.e.*, to be looked at; there are better dainties on the table.

[c] *Sanus* is used (1) as signifying "sound in body" and (2) as the opposite of *insanus*.

a man is, the more he enjoys a drink; the hungrier he is, the more pleasure he takes in food. Whatever falls to one's lot after a period of abstinence is welcomed with greater zest. The other kind, however, the pleasures of the mind, which are higher and less uncertain, no physician can refuse to the sick man. Whoever seeks these and knows well what they are, scorns all the blandishments of the senses. Men say, "Poor sick fellow!" But why? Is it because he does not mix snow with his wine, or because he does not revive the chill of his drink—mixed as it is in a good-sized bowl—by chipping ice into it? Or because he does not have Lucrine [a] oysters opened fresh at his table? Or because there is no din of cooks about his dining-hall, as they bring in their very cooking apparatus along with their viands? For luxury has already devised this fashion—of having the kitchen accompany the dinner, so that the food may not grow luke-warm, or fail to be hot enough for a palate which has already become hardened. "Poor sick fellow!"—he will eat as much as he can digest. There will be no boar lying before his eyes,[b] banished from the table as if it were a common meat; and on his sideboard there will be heaped together no breast-meat of birds, because it sickens him to see birds served whole. But what evil has been done to you? You will dine like a sick man, nay, sometimes like a sound man.[c]

All these things, however, can be easily endured—gruel, warm water, and anything else that seems insupportable to a fastidious man, to one who is wallowing in luxury, sick in soul rather than in body—if only we cease to shudder at death. And we shall cease, if once we have gained a knowledge of

cognoverimus; ita demum nec vita taedio erit nec
26 mors timori. Vitam enim occupare satietas sui non
potest tot res varias, magnas, divinas percensentem;
in odium illam sui adducere solet iners otium. Rerum
naturam peragranti numquam in fastidium veritas
27 veniet; falsa satiabunt. Rursus si mors accedit et
vocat, licet inmatura sit, licet mediam praecidat
aetatem, perceptus longissimae [1] fructus est. Cognita
est illi ex magna parte natura. Scit tempore honesta
non crescere; iis necesse est videri omnem vitam
brevem, qui illam voluptatibus vanis et ideo infinitis
metiuntur.

28 His te cogitationibus recrea et interim epistulis
nostris vaca. Veniet aliquando [2] tempus, quod nos
iterum iungat ac misceat; quantulumlibet sit illud,
longum faciet scientia utendi. Nam, ut Posidonius
ait, "unus dies hominum eruditorum plus patet quam
29 inperitis longissima aetas." Interim hoc tene, hoc
morde: adversis non succumbere, laetis non credere,
omnem fortunae licentiam in oculis habere, tamquam
quicquid potest facere, factura sit. Quicquid expectatum est diu, lenius [3] accedit. VALE.

[1] *longissimae* Madvig; *longissime* VPb.
[2] *vaca. veniet aliquando* P. Thomas; *vacando venie[t] aliquod* (*aliquando*) MSS.
[3] *lenius* Wolters; *levius* MSS.

---

[a] Perhaps a reminiscence of Lucretius i. 74 *omne im[mensum] mensum peragravit mente animoque.*

[b] Seneca often quotes Posidonius, as does Cicero also. These words may have been taken from his Προτρεπτικά (o[r] Λόγοι προτρεπτικοί), *Exhortations*, a work in which he main[tained] tained that men should make a close study of philosophy in spite of the varying opinions of its expositors.

the limits of good and evil; then, and then only, life will not weary us, neither will death make us afraid. For surfeit of self can never seize upon a life that surveys all the things which are manifold, great, divine; only idle leisure is wont to make men hate their lives. To one who roams [a] through the universe, the truth can never pall; it will be the untruths that will cloy. And, on the other hand, if death comes near with its summons, even though it be untimely in its arrival, though it cut one off in one's prime, a man has had a taste of all that the longest life can give. Such a man has in great measure come to understand the universe. He knows that honourable things do not depend on time for their growth; but any life must seem short to those who measure its length by pleasures which are empty and for that reason unbounded.

Refresh yourself with such thoughts as these, and meanwhile reserve some hours for our letters. There will come a time when we shall be united again and brought together; however short this time may be, we shall make it long by knowing how to employ it. For, as Posidonius says [b]: "A single day among the learned lasts longer than the longest life of the ignorant." Meanwhile, hold fast to this thought, and grip it close: yield not to adversity; trust not to prosperity; keep before your eyes the full scope of Fortune's power, as if she would surely do whatever is in her power to do. That which has been long expected comes more gently. Farewell.

LXXIX.

Seneca Lvcilio svo salvtem

1 Expecto epistulas tuas, quibus mihi indices, circuitus Siciliae totius quid tibi novi ostenderit, et ante[1] omnia de ipsa Charybdi certiora. Nam Scyllam saxum esse et quidem non terribile navigantibus optime scio; Charybdis an respondeat fabulis, perscribi mihi desidero et, si forte observaveris, dignum est autem quod observes, fac nos certiores, utrum uno tantum vento agatur in vertices an omnis tempestas aeque mare illud contorqueat, et an verum sit, quicquid illo freti turbine abreptum est, per multa milia trahi conditum et circa Tauromenitanum litus
2 emergere. Si haec mihi perscripseris, tunc tibi audebo mandare, ut in honorem meum Aetnam quoque ascendas, quam consumi et sensim subsidere ex hoc colligunt quidam, quod aliquando longius navigantibus solebat ostendi. Potest hoc accidere, non quia montis altitudo descendit, sed quia ignis evanuit et minus vehemens ac largus effertur, ob eandem causam fumo quoque per diem segniore.[2] Neutrum autem incredibile est, nec montem, qui

[1] *ante* added by Wolters.
[2] *segniore* Pincianus ; *segnior* MSS.

---

[a] Ellis suggests that the poem *Aetna*, of uncertain authorship, may have been written by Lucilius in response to this letter. His view is plausible, but not universally accepted.
[b] See *Ep*. xiv. § 8 and note (Vol. I.).
[c] The modern Taormina.

EPISTLE LXXIX.

LXXIX. ON THE REWARDS OF SCIENTIFIC DISCOVERY

I have been awaiting a letter from you, that you might inform me what new matter was revealed to you during your trip round Sicily,[a] and especially that you might give me further information regarding Charybdis itself.[b] I know very well that Scylla is a rock—and indeed a rock not dreaded by mariners; but with regard to Charybdis I should like to have a full description, in order to see whether it agrees with the accounts in mythology; and, if you have by chance investigated it (for it is indeed worthy of your investigation), please enlighten me concerning the following: Is it lashed into a whirlpool by a wind from only one direction, or do all storms alike serve to disturb its depths? Is it true that objects snatched downwards by the whirlpool in that strait are carried for many miles under water, and then come to the surface on the beach near Tauromenium[c]? If you will write me a full account of these matters, I shall then have the boldness to ask you to perform another task,—also to climb Aetna at my special request. Certain naturalists have inferred that the mountain is wasting away and gradually settling, because sailors used to be able to see it from a greater distance. The reason for this may be, not that the height of the mountain is decreasing, but because the flames have become dim and the eruptions less strong and less copious, and because for the same reason the smoke also is less active by day. However, either of these two things is possible to believe: that on the one hand the mountain is

devoretur cotidie, minui, nec manere eundem, quia non ipsum exest,[1] sed in aliqua inferna valle conceptus exaestuat et aliis pascitur. In ipso monte non
3 alimentum habet, sed viam. In Lycia regio notissima est, Hephaestion incolae vocant, foratum pluribus locis solum, quod sine ullo nascentium damno ignis innoxius circumit. Laeta itaque regio est et herbida nihil flammis adurentibus, sed tantum vi remissa ac languida refulgentibus.

4 Sed reservemus ista tunc quaesituri, cum tu mihi scripseris, quantum ab ipso ore montis nives absint, quas ne aestas quidem solvit; adeo tutae sunt ab igne vicino. Non est autem quod istam curam imputes mihi. Morbo enim tuo daturus eras, etiam si
5 nemo mandaret. Quid tibi do, ne Aetnam describas[2] in tuo carmine, ne hunc sollemnem omnibus poetis locum adtingas? Quem quo minus Ovidius tractaret, nihil obstitit, quod iam Vergilius impleverat. Ne Severum quidem Cornelium uterque deterruit. Omnibus praeterea feliciter hic locus se dedit et qui praecesserant, non praeripuisse mihi videntur, quae dici poterant, sed aperuisse.

6 Multum[3] interest, utrum ad consumptam materiam

[1] *ipsum exest* Haase; *ipsum exesse* or *ipsum ex se est* MSS.
[2] *nemo . . . describas* Rubenius; *nemo quid mandaret tibi donec aetnam describas* (*t*) MSS.
[3] *sed* before *multum* deleted by Madvig.

---

[a] Another description of this region is given by Pliny, *N.H.* ii. 106, who says that the stones in the rivers were red-hot! The phenomenon is usually explained by supposing springs of burning naphtha.
[b] *i.e.*, merely as an episode, instead of devoting a whole poem to the subject.
[c] *Metam.* xv. 340 ff.
[d] *Aeneid*, iii. 570 ff.

growing smaller because it is consumed from day to day, and that, on the other hand, it remains the same in size because the mountain is not devouring itself, but instead of this the matter which seethes forth collects in some subterranean valley and is fed by other material, finding in the mountain itself not the food which it requires, but simply a passage-way out. There is a well-known place in Lycia—called by the inhabitants "Hephaestion"[a]—where the ground is full of holes in many places and is surrounded by a harmless fire, which does no injury to the plants that grow there. Hence the place is fertile and luxuriant with growth, because the flames do not scorch but merely shine with a force that is mild and feeble.

But let us postpone this discussion, and look into the matter when you have given me a description just how far distant the snow lies from the crater,—I mean the snow which does not melt even in summer, so safe is it from the adjacent fire. But there is no ground for your charging this work to my account; for you were about to gratify your own craze for fine writing, without a commission from anyone at all. Nay, what am I to offer you *not* merely to describe[b] Aetna in your poem, and *not* to touch lightly upon a topic which is a matter of ritual for all poets? Ovid[c] could not be prevented from using this theme simply because Vergil[d] had already fully covered it; nor could either of these writers frighten off Cornelius Severus. Besides, the topic has served them all with happy results, and those who have gone before seem to me not to have forestalled all that could be said, but merely to have opened the way.

It makes a great deal of difference whether you

an ad subactam accedas; crescit in dies et inventuris inventa non obstant. Praeterea condicio optima est ultimi; parata verba invenit, quae aliter instructa novam faciem habent. Nec illis manus inicit tam-
7 quam alienis. Sunt enim publica.[1] Aut ego te non novi aut Aetna tibi salivam movet. Iam cupis grande aliquid et par prioribus scribere. Plus enim sperare modestia tibi tua non permittit, quae tanta in te est, ut videaris mihi retracturus ingenii tui vires, si vincendi periculum sit; tanta tibi priorum reverentia
8 est. Inter cetera hoc habet boni sapientia: nemo ab altero potest vinci, nisi dum ascenditur. Cum[2] ad summum perveneris, paria sunt, non est incremento locus, statur. Numquid sol magnitudini suae adicit? Numquid ultra quam solet, luna procedit? Maria non crescunt. Mundus eundem habitum ac
9 modum servat. Extollere se, quae iustam magnitudinem implevere, non possunt. Quicumque fuerint sapientes, pares erunt et aequales. Habebit unusquisque ex iis proprias dotes: alius erit adfabilior, alius expeditior, alius promptior in eloquendo, alius facundior; illud, de quo agitur, quod beatum facit,
10 aequalest[3] in omnibus. An Aetna tua possit sublabi

[1] The phrase *iurisconsulti negant quicquam publicum usu capi*, which occurs here in the MSS., is transferred by Wolters to *Ep.* 88. 12, where it suits the context.
[2] *cum ad* Gronovius; *dum ad* MSS.
[3] *aequale est* later MSS.; *aequale* VPb.

---

[a] The usual meaning of *paria esse*, or *paria facere* (a favourite phrase with Seneca—see for example *Ep.* ci. 7), is "to square the account," "balance even."
[b] "Qualities desirable in themselves, but not *essential* for the possession of wisdom, the προηγμένα of the Stoics (Summers).

approach a subject that has been exhausted, or one where the ground has merely been broken; in the latter case, the topic grows day by day, and what is already discovered does not hinder new discoveries. Besides, he who writes last has the best of the bargain; he finds already at hand words which, when marshalled in a different way, show a new face. And he is not pilfering them, as if they belonged to someone else, when he uses them, for they are common property. Now if Aetna does not make your mouth water, I am mistaken in you. You have for some time been desirous of writing something in the grand style and on the level of the older school. For your modesty does not allow you to set your hopes any higher; this quality of yours is so pronounced that, it seems to me, you are likely to curb the force of your natural ability, if there should be any danger of outdoing others; so greatly do you reverence the old masters. Wisdom has this advantage, among others,—that no man can be outdone by another, except during the climb. But when you have arrived at the top, it is a draw [a]; there is no room for further ascent, the game is over. Can the sun add to his size? Can the moon advance beyond her usual fulness? The seas do not increase in bulk. The universe keeps the same character, the same limits. Things which have reached their full stature cannot grow higher. Men who have attained wisdom will therefore be equal and on the same footing. Each of them will possess his own peculiar gifts [b]: one will be more affable, another more facile, another more ready of speech, a fourth more eloquent; but as regards the quality under discussion,—the element that produces happiness,—it is equal in them all. I do not know whether this Aetna of

et in se ruere, an hoc excelsum cacumen et conspicuum per vasti maris spatia detrahat adsidua vis ignium, nescio; virtutem non flamma, non ruina inferius adducet. Haec una maiestas deprimi nescit. Nec proferri ultra nec referri potest. Sic huius, ut caelestium, stata magnitudo est. Ad hanc nos conemur educere.

11 Iam multum operis effecti est; immo, si verum fateri volo, non multum. Nec enim bonitas est pessimis esse meliorem. Quis oculis glorietur, qui suspicetur diem? Cui sol per caliginem splendet, licet contentus interim sit effugisse tenebras, adhuc
12 non fruitur bono lucis. Tunc animus noster habebit, quod gratuletur sibi, cum emissus his tenebris, in quibus volutatur, non tenui visu clara prospexerit, sed totum diem admiserit et redditus caelo suo fuerit, cum receperit locum, quem occupavit sorte nascendi. Sursum illum vocant initia sua. Erit autem illic etiam antequam hac custodia exsolvatur, cum vitia disiecerit purusque ac levis in cogitationes divinas emicuerit.

13 Hoc nos agere, Lucili carissime, in hoc ire impetu toto, licet pauci sciant, licet nemo, iuvat. Gloria umbra virtutis est; etiam invitam[1] comitabitur. Sed

[1] *invitam* Velz.; *invita* VPb.

yours can collapse and fall in ruins, whether this lofty summit, visible for many miles over the deep sea, is wasted by the incessant power of the flames; but I do know that virtue will not be brought down to a lower plane either by flames or by ruins. Hers is the only greatness that knows no lowering; there can be for her no further rising or sinking. Her stature, like that of the stars in the heavens, is fixed. Let us therefore strive to raise ourselves to this altitude.

Already much of the task is accomplished; nay, rather, if I can bring myself to confess the truth, not much. For goodness does not mean merely being better than the lowest. Who that could catch but a mere glimpse of the daylight would boast his powers of vision? One who sees the sun shining through a mist may be contented meanwhile that he has escaped darkness, but he does not yet enjoy the blessing of light. Our souls will not have reason to rejoice in their lot until, freed from this darkness in which they grope, they have not merely glimpsed the brightness with feeble vision, but have absorbed the full light of day and have been restored to their place in the sky,—until, indeed, they have regained the place which they held at the allotment of their birth. The soul is summoned upward by its very origin. And it will reach that goal even before it is released from its prison below, as soon as it has cast off sin and, in purity and lightness, has leaped up into celestial realms of thought.

I am glad, beloved Lucilius, that we are occupied with this ideal, that we pursue it with all our might, even though few know it, or none. Fame is the shadow of virtue; it will attend virtue even against

quemadmodum umbra aliquando antecedit, aliquand sequitur vel a tergo est, ita gloria aliquando ante no est visendamque se praebet, aliquando in averso es
14 maiorque quo serior, ubi invidia secessit. Quamdi videbatur furere Democritus! Vix recepit Socrate fama. Quamdiu Catonem civitas ignoravit! Respui nec intellexit, nisi cum perdidit. Rutili innocentia a virtus lateret, nisi accepisset iniuriam; dum violatur effulsit. Numquid non sorti suae gratias egit e exilium suum complexus est? De his loquor, quo inlustravit fortuna, dum vexat; quam multorum pro fectus in notitiam evasere post ipsos! Quam multo
15 fama non excepit, sed eruit! Vides Epicurum quant opere non tantum eruditiores, sed haec quoque im peritorum turba miretur. Hic ignotus ipsis Atheni fuit, circa quas delituerat. Multis itaque iam anni Metrodoro suo superstes in quadam epistula, cun amicitiam suam et Metrodori grata commemoration cecinisset, hoc novissime adiecit, nihil sibi et Metro doro inter bona tanta nocuisse, quod ipsos illa nobili Graecia non ignotos solum habuisset, sed paen
16 inauditos. Numquid ergo non postea quam ess desierat, inventus est? Numquid non opinio eiu enituit? Hoc Metrodorus quoque in quadam epistul

---

[a] There is an unauthenticated story that the men o Abdera called in Hippocrates to treat his malady.

[b] *Cf. Ep.* xxiv. 4 *exilium . . . tulit Rutilius etiam libenter*

[c] Frag. 188 Usener.

[d] Frag. 43 Körte.

her will. But, as the shadow sometimes precedes and sometimes follows or even lags behind, so fame sometimes goes before us and shows herself in plain sight, and sometimes is in the rear, and is all the greater in proportion as she is late in coming, when once envy has beaten a retreat. How long did men believe Democritus [a] to be mad! Glory barely came to Socrates. And how long did our state remain in ignorance of Cato! They rejected him, and did not know his worth until they had lost him. If Rutilius [b] had not resigned himself to wrong, his innocence and virtue would have escaped notice; the hour of his suffering was the hour of his triumph. Did he not give thanks for his lot, and welcome his exile with open arms? I have mentioned thus far those to whom Fortune has brought renown at the very moment of persecution; but how many there are whose progress toward virtue has come to light only after their death! And how many have been ruined, not rescued, by their reputation? There is Epicurus, for example; mark how greatly he is admired, not only by the more cultured, but also by this ignorant rabble. This man, however, was unknown to Athens itself, near which he had hidden himself away. And so, when he had already survived by many years his friend Metrodorus, he added in a letter these last words, proclaiming with thankful appreciation the friendship that had existed between them: "So greatly blest were Metrodorus and I that it has been no harm to us to be unknown, and almost unheard of, in this well-known land of Greece." [c] Is it not true, therefore, that men did not discover him until after he had ceased to be? Has not his renown shone forth, for all that? Metrodorus also admits this fact in one of his letters [d]: that Epicurus

confitetur, se et Epicurum non satis enotuisse; sed post se et Epicurum magnum paratumque nomen habituros, qui voluissent per eadem ire vestigia.

17 Nulla virtus latet, et latuisse non ipsius est damnum. Veniet qui conditam et saeculi sui malignitate conpressam dies publicet. Paucis natus est, qui populum aetatis suae cogitat. Multa annorum milia, multa populorum supervenient; ad illa respice. Etiam si omnibus tecum viventibus silentium livor indixerit, venient qui sine offensa, sine gratia iudicent. Si quod est pretium virtutis ex fama, nec hoc interit. Ad nos quidem nihil pertinebit posterorum sermo; tamen etiam non sentientes colet ac frequentabit.

18 Nulli non virtus et vivo et mortuo rettulit gratiam, si modo illam bona secutus est fide, si se non exornavit et pinxit, sed idem fuit, sive ex denuntiato videbatur, sive inparatus ac subito. Nihil simulatio proficit. Paucis inponit leviter extrinsecus inducta facies; veritas in omnem partem sui eadem est. Quae decipiunt, nihil habent solidi. Tenue est mendacium; perlucet, si diligenter inspexeris. Vale.

and he were not well known to the public; but he declares that after the lifetime of Epicurus and himself any man who might wish to follow in their footsteps would win great and ready-made renown.

Virtue is never lost to view; and yet to have been lost to view is no loss. There will come a day which will reveal her, though hidden away or suppressed by the spite of her contemporaries. That man is born merely for a few, who thinks only of the people of his own generation. Many thousands of years and many thousands of peoples will come after you; it is to these that you should have regard. Malice may have imposed silence upon the mouths of all who were alive in your day; but there will come men who will judge you without prejudice and without favour. If there is any reward that virtue receives at the hands of fame, not even this can pass away. We ourselves, indeed, shall not be affected by the talk of posterity; nevertheless, posterity will cherish and celebrate us even though we are not conscious thereof. Virtue has never failed to reward a man, both during his life and after his death, provided he has followed her loyally, provided he has not decked himself out or painted himself up, but has been always the same, whether he appeared before men's eyes after being announced, or suddenly and without preparation. Pretence accomplishes nothing. Few are deceived by a mask that is easily drawn over the face. Truth is the same in every part. Things which deceive us have no real substance. Lies are thin stuff; they are transparent, if you examine them with care. Farewell.

LXXX.

SENECA LVCILIO SVO SALVTEM

1 Hodierno die non tantum meo beneficio mihi vaco, sed spectaculi, quod omnes molestos ad sphaeromachian avocavit. Nemo inrumpet, nemo cogitationem meam impediet, quae hac ipsa fiducia procedit audacius. Non crepuit subinde ostium, non adlevabitur velum; licebit tuto vadere,[1] quod magis necessarium est per se eunti et suam sequenti viam. Non ergo sequor priores? Facio, sed permitto mihi et invenire aliquid et mutare et relinquere. Non servio illis, sed adsentior.

2 Magnum tamen verbum dixi, qui mihi silentium promittebam et sine interpellatore secretum. Ecce ingens clamor ex stadio perfertur et me non excutit mihi, sed in huius ipsius rei contentionem transfert. Cogito mecum, quam multi corpora exerceant, ingenia quam pauci; quantus ad spectaculum non fidele et lusorium fiat concursus, quanta sit circa artes bonas solitudo; quam inbecilli animo sint, quorum lacertos
3 umerosque miramur. Illud maxime revolvo mecum: si corpus perduci exercitatione ad hanc patientiam potest, qua et pugnos pariter et calces non unius hominis ferat, qua solem ardentissimum in ferventissimo pulvere sustinens aliquis et sanguine suo madens

[1] *tuto vadere* Hense; *uno vadere* MSS.

[a] Probably a contest in which the participants attached leaden weights to their hands in order to increase the force of the blows.

[b] Compare Pliny's "den" (*Ep.* ii. 17. 21): *quae specularibus et velis obductis reductisve modo adicitur cubiculo modo aufertur.*

[c] Compare the ideas expressed in *Ep.* xv. 2 f.

EPISTLE LXXX.

LXXX. ON WORLDLY DECEPTIONS

To-day I have some free time, thanks not so much to myself as to the games, which have attracted all the bores to the boxing-match.[a] No one will interrupt me or disturb the train of my thoughts, which go ahead more boldly as the result of my very confidence. My door has not been continually creaking on its hinges nor will my curtain be pulled aside;[b] my thoughts may march safely on,—and that is all the more necessary for one who goes independently and follows out his own path. Do I then follow no predecessors? Yes, but I allow myself to discover something new, to alter, to reject. I am not a slave to them, although I give them my approval.

And yet that was a very bold word which I spoke when I assured myself that I should have some quiet, and some uninterrupted retirement. For lo, a great cheer comes from the stadium, and while it does not drive me distracted, yet it shifts my thought to a contrast suggested by this very noise. How many men, I say to myself, train their bodies, and how few train their minds![c] What crowds flock to the games,—spurious as they are and arranged merely for pastime,—and what a solitude reigns where the good arts are taught! How feather-brained are the athletes whose muscles and shoulders we admire! The question which I ponder most of all is this: if the body can be trained to such a degree of endurance that it will stand the blows and kicks of several opponents at once, and to such a degree that a man can last out the day and resist the scorching sun in the midst of the burning dust, drenched all the while

diem ducat; quanto facilius animus conroborari possit, ut fortunae ictus invictus excipiat, ut proiectus, ut conculcatus exsurgat.

Corpus enim multis eget rebus, ut valeat; animus ex se crescit, se ipse alit, se exercet. Illis multo cibo, multa potione opus est, multo oleo, longa denique opera; tibi continget virtus sine apparatu, sine inpensa. Quicquid facere te potest bonum,
4 tecum est. Quid tibi opus est, ut sis bonus? Velle. Quid autem melius potes velle quam eripere te huic servituti, quae omnes premit, quam mancipia quoque condicionis extremae et in his sordibus nata omni modo exuere conantur? Peculium suum, quod conparaverunt ventre fraudato, pro capite numerant; tu non concupisces quanticumque ad libertatem
5 pervenire, qui te in illa putas natum? Quid ad arcam tuam respicis? Emi non potest. Itaque in tabulas vanum coicitur nomen libertatis, quam nec qui emerunt, habent nec qui vendiderunt. Tibi des oportet istud bonum, a te petas.

Libera te primum metu mortis: illa nobis iugum
6 inponit; deinde metu paupertatis. Si vis scire, quam nihil in illa mali sit, compara inter se pauperum et divitum vultus; saepius pauper et fidelius ridet;

---

[a] For this figure see the "lucellum," "diurna mercedula," etc., of the opening letters of the correspondence (Vol. I.).

with his own blood,—if this can be done, how much more easily might the mind be toughened so that it could receive the blows of Fortune and not be conquered, so that it might struggle to its feet again after it has been laid low, after it has been trampled under foot?

For although the body needs many things in order to be strong, yet the mind grows from within, giving to itself nourishment and exercise. Yonder athletes must have copious food, copious drink, copious quantities of oil, and long training besides; but you can acquire virtue without equipment and without expense. All that goes to make you a good man lies within yourself. And what do you need in order to become good? To wish it. But what better thing could you wish for than to break away from this slavery,—a slavery that oppresses us all, a slavery which even chattels of the lowest estate, born amid such degradation, strive in every possible way to strip off? In exchange for freedom they pay out the savings which they have scraped together by cheating their own bellies; shall *you* not be eager to attain liberty at any price, seeing that you claim it as your birthright? Why cast glances toward your strong-box? Liberty cannot be bought. It is therefore useless to enter in your ledger[a] the item of "Freedom," for freedom is possessed neither by those who have bought it nor by those who have sold it. You must give this good to yourself, and seek it from yourself.

First of all, free yourself from the fear of death, for death puts the yoke about our necks; then free yourself from the fear of poverty. If you would know how little evil there is in poverty, compare the faces of the poor with those of the rich; the poor

nulla sollicitudo in alto est; etiam si qua incidit cura, velut nubes levis transit. Horum, qui felices vocantur, hilaritas ficta est at[1] gravis et subpurata tristitia, eo quidem gravior, quia interdum non licet palam esse miseros, sed inter aerumnas cor ipsum
7 exedentes necesse est agere felicem. Saepius hoc exemplo mihi utendum est, nec enim ullo efficacius exprimitur hic humanae vitae mimus, qui nobis partes, quas male agamus, adsignat. Ille, qui in scaena latus incedit et haec resupinus dicit

> En impero Argis; regna mihi liquit Pelops,
> Qua ponto ab Helles atque ab Ionio mari
> Urgetur Isthmos,

servus est, quinque modios accipit et quinque de-
8 narios; ille qui superbus atque inpotens et fiducia virium tumidus ait:

> Quod nisi quieris, Menelae, hac dextra occides,

diurnum accipit, in centunculo dormit. Idem de istis licet omnibus dicas, quos supra capita hominum supraque turbam delicatos lectica suspendit; omnium istorum personata felicitas est. Contemnes illos, si despoliaveris.

9 Equum empturus solvi iubes stratum, detrahis vestimenta venalibus, ne qua vitia corporis lateant;

[1] *at* Madvig; *aut* MSS.

[a] Authors-unknown; Ribbeck, *Frag. Trag.* pp. 289 and 276. The first passage (with one change) is also quoted by Quintilian, ix. 4. 140. See, however, Tyrrell, *Latin Poetry*, p. 39, who calls this passage the beginning of Attius's *Atreus*.

man smiles more often and more genuinely; his troubles do not go deep down; even if any anxiety comes upon him, it passes like a fitful cloud. But the merriment of those whom men call happy is feigned, while their sadness is heavy and festering, and all the heavier because they may not meanwhile display their grief, but must act the part of happiness in the midst of sorrows that eat out their very hearts. I often feel called upon to use the following illustration, and it seems to me that none expresses more effectively this drama of human life, wherein we are assigned the parts which we are to play so badly. Yonder is the man who stalks upon the stage with swelling port and head thrown back, and says:

> Lo, I am he whom Argos hails as lord,
> Whom Pelops left the heir of lands that spread
> From Hellespont and from th' Ionian sea
> E'en to the Isthmian straits.[a]

And who is this fellow? He is but a slave; his wage is five measures of grain and five denarii. Yon other who, proud and wayward and puffed up by confidence in his power, declaims:

> Peace, Menelaus, or this hand shall slay thee![a]

receives a daily pittance and sleeps on rags. You may speak in the same way about all these dandies whom you see riding in litters above the heads of men and above the crowd; in every case their happiness is put on like the actor's mask. Tear it off, and you will scorn them.

When you buy a horse, you order its blanket to be removed; you pull off the garments from slaves that are advertised for sale, so that no bodily flaws may escape your notice; if you judge a man, do you

hominem involutum aestimas? Mangones quicquid
est, quod displiceat, aliquo lenocinio abscondunt,
itaque ementibus ornamenta ipsa suspecta sunt. Sive
crus alligatum sive brachium aspiceres, nudari iuberes
10 et ipsum tibi corpus ostendi. Vides illum Scythiae
Sarmatiaeve regem insigni capitis decorum? Si vis
illum aestimare totumque scire, qualis sit, fasciam
solve; multum mali sub illa latet. Quid de aliis
loquor? Si perpendere te voles, sepone pecuniam,
domum, dignitatem, intus te ipse considera. Nunc
qualis sis, aliis credis. VALE

LXXXI.

SENECA LVCILIO SVO SALVTEM

1 Quereris incidisse te in hominem ingratum. Si
hoc nunc primum, age aut fortunae aut diligentiae
tuae gratias. Sed nihil facere hoc loco diligentia
potest nisi te malignum. Nam si hoc periculum
vitare volueris, non dabis beneficia; ita ne apud alium
pereant, apud te peribunt.

Non respondeant potius quam non dentur. Et
post malam segetem serendum est; saepe quicquid
perierat adsidua infelicis soli sterilitate, unius anni
2 restituit ubertas. Est tanti, ut gratum invenias,
experiri et ingratos. Nemo habet tam certam in

---

[a] A favourite trick; *cf.* Quintil. ii. 15. 25 *mangones, qui colorem fuco et verum robur inani sagina mentiuntur.*

[b] The reader will be interested to compare this letter with the treatise (or essay) *Of Benefits*, translated by Thomas Lodge in 1614 from Seneca's work *De Beneficiis*, which was dedicated to Aebutius Liberalis, the subject of *Ep.* xci.

judge him when he is wrapped in a disguise? Slave-dealers hide under some sort of finery any defect which may give offence,[a] and for that reason the very trappings arouse the suspicion of the buyer. If you catch sight of a leg or an arm that is bound up in cloths, you demand that it be stripped and that the body itself be revealed to you. Do you see yonder Scythian or Sarmatian king, his head adorned with the badge of his office? If you wish to see what he amounts to, and to know his full worth, take off his diadem; much evil lurks beneath it. But why do I speak of others? If you wish to set a value on yourself, put away your money, your estates, your honours, and look into your own soul. At present, you are taking the word of others for what you are. Farewell.

LXXXI. ON BENEFITS.[b]

You complain that you have met with an ungrateful person. If this is your first experience of that sort, you should offer thanks either to your good luck or to your caution. In this case, however, caution can effect nothing but to make you ungenerous. For if you wish to avoid such a danger, you will not confer benefits; and so, that benefits may not be lost with another man, they will be lost to yourself.

It is better, however, to get no return than to confer no benefits. Even after a poor crop one should sow again; for often losses due to continued barrenness of an unproductive soil have been made good by one year's fertility. In order to discover one grateful person, it is worth while to make trial of many ungrateful ones. No man has so unerring

beneficiis manum, ut non saepe fallatur; aberrent, ut aliquando haereant. Post naufragium maria temptantur. Faeneratorem non fugat a foro decoctor.[1] Cito inerti otio vita torpebit, si relinquendum est, quicquid offendit; te vero benigniorem haec ipsa res faciat. Nam cuius rei eventus incertus est, id ut
3 aliquando procedat, saepe temptandum est. Sed de isto satis multa in iis libris locuti sumus, qui de beneficiis inscribuntur.

Illud magis quaerendum videtur, quod non satis, ut existimo, explicatum est, an is, qui[2] profuit nobis, si postea nocuit, paria fecerit et nos debito solverit. Adice, si vis, et illud: multo plus postea nocuit quam
4 ante profuerat. Si rectam illam rigidi iudicis sententiam quaeris, alterum ab altero absolvet et dicet: "Quamvis iniuriae praeponderent, tamen beneficiis donetur, quod ex iniuria superest." Plus nocuit; sed prius[3] profuit. Itaque habeatur et temporis ratio.
5 Iam illa manifestiora sunt, quam ut admoneri debeas quaerendum esse, quam libenter profuerit, quam invitus nocuerit, quoniam animo et beneficia et iniuriae constant. "Nolui beneficium dare; victus

[1] *decoctor* Muretus, "from an old MS."; *coctor*, *coactor*, *tortor*, various hands of VPb.
[2] *is qui* later MSS.; *id quod* VPb.
[3] *prius* Pincianus; *pius* or *plus* MSS.

[a] See *De Ben.* i. 1. 9 f. *non est autem quod tardiores faciat ad bene merendum turba ingratorum.*

a hand when he confers benefits that he is not frequently deceived; it is well for the traveller to wander, that he may again cleave to the path. After a shipwreck, sailors try the sea again. The banker is not frightened away from the forum by the swindler. If one were compelled to drop everything that caused trouble, life would soon grow dull amid sluggish idleness; but in your case this very condition may prompt you to become more charitable. For when the outcome of any undertaking is unsure, you must try again and again, in order to succeed ultimately. I have, however, discussed the matter with sufficient fulness in the volumes which I have written, entitled "On Benefits." [a]

What I think should rather be investigated is this,—a question which I feel has not been made sufficiently clear: "Whether he who has helped us has squared the account and has freed us from our debt, if he has done us harm later." You may add this question also, if you like: "when the harm done later has been more than the help rendered previously." If you are seeking for the formal and just decision of a strict judge, you will find that he checks off one act by the other, and declares: "Though the injuries outweigh the benefits, yet we should credit to the benefits anything that stands over even after the injury." The harm done was indeed greater, but the helpful act was done first. Hence the time also should be taken into account. Other cases are so clear that I need not remind you that you should also look into such points as: How gladly was the help offered, and how reluctantly was the harm done,—since benefits, as well as injuries, depend on the spirit. "I did not wish to confer the benefit; but I was won over by my

sum aut verecundia aut instantis pertinacia aut spe."
6 Eo animo quidque debetur, quo datur, nec quantum
sit, sed a quali profectum voluntate, perpenditur.
Nunc coniectura tollatur; et illud beneficium fuit et hoc, quod modum beneficii prioris excessit, iniuria est. Vir bonus utrosque calculos sic ponit, ut se ipse circumscribat; beneficio adicit, iniuriae demit.

Alter ille remissior iudex, quem esse me malo,
7 iniuriae oblivisci iubebit,[1] officii meminisse. "Hoc
certe," inquis,[2] "iustitiae convenit, suum cuique reddere, beneficio gratiam, iniuriae talionem aut certe malam gratiam." Verum erit istud, cum alius iniuriam fecerit, alius beneficium dederit; nam si idem est, beneficio vis iniuriae extinguitur. Nam cui, etiam si merita non antecessissent, oportebat ignosci, post beneficia laedenti plus quam venia debe-
8 tur. Non pono utrique par pretium. Pluris aestimo
beneficium quam iniuriam. Non omnes grati sciunt debere beneficium; potest etiam inprudens et rudis et unus e turba, utique dum prope est ab accepto; ignorat autem, quantum pro eo debeat. Uni sapienti notum est, quanti res quaeque taxanda sit. Nam

[1] *iubebit* Gertz ; *debebit* VPb.
[2] *inquis* later MSS. ; *inquam* VPb.

---

[a] *Calculi* were counters, spread out on the *abacus*, or counting-board ; they ran in columns, by millions, hundred thousands, etc.

[b] *Talio* (from *talis*, "just so much ") is the old Roman law of "eye for eye and tooth for tooth." As law became less crude, it gave way to fines.

respect for the man, or by the importunity of his request, or by hope." Our feeling about every obligation depends in each case upon the spirit in which the benefit is conferred; we weigh not the bulk of the gift, but the quality of the good-will which prompted it. So now let us do away with guess-work; the former deed was a benefit, and the latter, which transcended the earlier benefit, is an injury. The good man so arranges the two sides of his ledger[a] that he voluntarily cheats himself by adding to the benefit and subtracting from the injury.

The more indulgent magistrate, however (and I should rather be such a one), will order us to forget the injury and remember the accommodation. "But surely," you say, "it is the part of justice to render to each that which is his due,—thanks in return for a benefit, and retribution,[b] or at any rate ill-will, in return for an injury!" This, I say, will be true when it is one man who has inflicted the injury, and a different man who has conferred the benefit; for if it is the same man, the force of the injury is nullified by the benefit conferred. Indeed, a man who ought to be pardoned, even though there were no good deeds credited to him in the past, should receive something more than mere leniency if he commits a wrong when he has a benefit to his credit. I do not set an equal value on benefits and injuries. I reckon a benefit at a higher rate than an injury. Not all grateful persons know what it involves to be in debt for a benefit; even a thoughtless, crude fellow, one of the common herd, may know, especially soon after he has received the gift; but he does not know how deeply he stands in debt therefor. Only the wise man knows exactly what value should be put

ille, de quo loquebar modo, stultus etiam si bonae
voluntatis est, aut minus quam debet aut alio quam
debet tempore[1] aut quo non debet loco reddit. Id
9 quod referendum est, effundit atque abicit. Mira in
quibusdam rebus verborum proprietas est et consuetudo sermonis antiqui quaedam efficacissimis et
officia docentibus notis signat. Sic certe solemus
loqui: "ille illi gratiam rettulit." Referre est ultro,
quod debeas, adferre. Non dicimus "gratiam reddidit," reddunt enim et qui reposcuntur et qui in-
viti et qui ubilibet et qui per alium. Non dicimus
"reposuit beneficium" aut "solvit"; nullum nobis
10 placuit, quod aeri alieno convenit, verbum. Referre
est ad eum, a quo acceperis, rem ferre. Haec vox
significat voluntariam relationem; qui rettulit, ipse
se appellavit.

Sapiens omnia examinabit secum: quantum acceperit, a quo, quando, ubi, quemadmodum. Itaque
negamus quemquam scire gratiam referre nisi sapientem; non magis quam beneficium dare quisquam scit
nisi sapiens, hic scilicet, qui magis dato gaudet quam
11 alius accepto. Hoc aliquis inter illa numerat, quae

[1] *aut alio quam debet tempore* Buecheler; *aut tempore* MSS.

---

[a] This "long-established terminology" applies to the *verborum proprietas* of philosophic diction, with special reference to τὰ καθήκοντα, the appropriate duties of the philosopher and the seeker after wisdom. Thus, *referre* is distinguished from *reddere*, *reponere*, *solvere*, and other financial terms.

[b] *i.e.*, the Stoics.

upon everything; for the fool whom I just mentioned, no matter how good his intentions may be, either pays less than he owes, or pays it at the wrong time or the wrong place. That for which he should make return he wastes and loses. There is a marvellously accurate phraseology applied to certain subjects,[a] a long-established terminology which indicates certain acts by means of symbols that are most efficient and that serve to outline men's duties. We are, as you know, wont to speak thus: "A. has made a return for the favour bestowed by B." Making a return means handing over of your own accord that which you owe. We do not say, "He has paid back the favour"; for "pay back" is used of a man upon whom a demand for payment is made, of those who pay against their will, of those who pay under any circumstances whatsoever, and of those who pay through a third party. We do not say, "He has 'restored' the benefit," or 'settled' it; we have never been satisfied with a word which applies properly to a debt of money. Making a return means offering something to him from whom you have received something. The phrase implies a voluntary return; he who has made such a return has served the writ upon himself.

The wise man will inquire in his own mind into all the circumstances: how much he has received, from whom, when, where, how. And so we[b] declare that none but the wise man knows how to make return for a favour; moreover, none but the wise man knows how to confer a benefit,—that man, I mean, who enjoys the giving more than the recipient enjoys the receiving. Now some person will reckon this remark as one of the generally surprising state-

videmur inopinata omnibus dicere, παράδοξα Graeci vocant, et ait: "Nemo ergo scit praeter sapientem referre gratiam? Ergo nec quod debet, creditori suo reponere quisquam scit alius nec, cum emit aliquam rem, pretium venditori persolvere?" Ne nobis fiat invidia, scito idem dicere Epicurum. Metrodorus certe ait solum sapientem referre gratiam scire.
12 Deinde idem admiratur, cum dicimus: "Solus sapiens scit amare. Solus sapiens amicus est." Atqui et amoris et amicitiae pars est referre gratiam, immo hoc magis vulgare est et in plures cadit quam vera amicitia. Deinde idem admiratur, quod dicimus fidem nisi in sapiente non esse, tamquam non ipse idem dicat. An tibi videtur fidem habere, qui referre
13 gratiam nescit? Desinant itaque infamare nos tamquam incredibilia iactantes et sciant apud sapientem esse ipsa honesta, apud vulgum simulacra rerum honestarum et effigies. Nemo referre gratiam scit nisi sapiens. Stultus quoque, utcumque scit et quemadmodum potest, referat; scientia illi potius quam voluntas desit. Velle non discitur.

14 Sapiens inter se omnia conparabit, maius enim aut minus fit, quamvis idem sit, tempore, loco, causa. Saepe enim hoc non potuere divitiae in domum

[a] *e.g.*, "Only the wise man is king," "there is no mean between virtue and vice," "pain is no evil," "only the wise man is free," "riches are not a good" etc.

[b] Frag. 54 Körte.

ments such as we Stoics are wont to make and such as the Greeks call "paradoxes," [a] and will say: "Do you maintain, then, that only the wise man knows how to return a favour? Do you maintain that no one else knows how to make restoration to a creditor for a debt? Or, on buying a commodity, to pay full value to the seller?" In order not to bring any odium upon myself, let me tell you that Epicurus says the same thing. At any rate, Metrodorus remarks [b] that only the wise man knows how to return a favour. Again, the objector mentioned above wonders at our saying: "The wise man alone knows how to love, the wise man alone is a real friend." And yet it is a part of love and of friendship to return favours; nay, further, it is an ordinary act, and happens more frequently than real friendship. Again, this same objector wonders at our saying, "There is no loyalty except in the wise man," just as if he himself does not say the same thing! Or do you think that there is any loyalty in him who does not know how to return a favour? These men, accordingly, should cease to discredit us, just as if we were uttering an impossible boast; they should understand that the essence of honour resides in the wise man, while among the crowd we find only the ghost and the semblance of honour. None but the wise man knows how to return a favour. Even a fool can return it in proportion to his knowledge and his power; his fault would be a lack of knowledge rather than a lack of will or desire. To will does not come by teaching.

The wise man will compare all things with one another; for the very same object becomes greater or smaller, according to the time, the place, and the cause. Often the riches that are spent in profusion upon a palace cannot accomplish as much as a

infusae, quod opportune dati mille denarii. Multum
enim interest, donaveris an succurreris, servaverit
illum tua liberalitas an instruxerit. Saepe quod
datur, exiguum est, quod sequitur ex eo, magnum.
Quantum autem existimas interesse, utrum aliquis
quod derat a se,[1] quod praestabat, sumpserit an
beneficium acceperit ut daret?

15 Sed ne in eadem, quae satis scrutati sumus, re-
volvamur. In hac conparatione beneficii et iniuriae
vir bonus iudicabit quidem quod erit aequissimum,
sed beneficio favebit; in hanc erit partem proclivior.
16 Plurimum autem momenti persona solet adferre in
rebus eiusmodi: "Dedisti mihi beneficium in servo,
iniuriam fecisti in patre. Servasti mihi filium, sed
patrem[2] abstulisti." Alia deinceps, per quae procedit
omnis conlatio, prosequetur et, si pusillum erit, quod
intersit, dissimulabit. Etiam si multum fuerit, sed
si id donari salva pietate ac fide poterit, remittet; id
17 est, si ad ipsum tota pertinebit iniuria. Summa res
haec est: facilis erit in conmutando. Patietur plus
inputari sibi. Invitus beneficium per conpensationem
iniuriae solvet. In hanc partem inclinabit, huc
verget, ut cupiat debere gratiam, cupiat referre.

[1] *derat a se* Haase; *derata sed* VP; *dederat sed* b; *dare a se, quod praesto erat* Madvig.
[2] *patrem* edd.; *patri* Vb; *patiā* P.

thousand *denarii* given at the right time. Now it makes a great deal of difference whether you give outright, or come to a man's assistance, whether your generosity saves him, or sets him up in life. Often the gift is small, but the consequences great. And what a distinction do you imagine there is between taking something which one lacks,—something which was offered,—and receiving a benefit in order to confer one in return?

But we should not slip back into the subject which we have already sufficiently investigated. In this balancing of benefits and injuries, the good man will, to be sure, judge with the highest degree of fairness, but he will incline towards the side of the benefit; he will turn more readily in this direction. Moreover, in affairs of this kind the person concerned is wont to count for a great deal. Men say: "You conferred a benefit upon me in that matter of the slave, but you did me an injury in the case of my father"; or, "You saved my son, but robbed me of a father." Similarly, he will follow up all other matters in which comparisons can be made, and if the difference be very slight, he will pretend not to notice it. Even though the difference be great, yet if the concession can be made without impairment of duty and loyalty, our good man will overlook it—that is, provided the injury exclusively affects the good man himself. To sum up, the matter stands thus: the good man will be easy-going in striking a balance; he will allow too much to be set against his credit. He will be unwilling to pay a benefit by balancing the injury against it. The side towards which he will lean, the tendency which he will exhibit, is the desire to be under obligations for the favour, and the desire to make return therefor. For

Errat enim, si quis beneficium accipit libentius quam reddit. Quanto hilarior est, qui solvit quam qui mutuatur, tanto debet laetior esse, qui se maximo aere alieno accepti benefici exonerat, quam qui cum
18 maxime obligatur. Nam in hoc quoque falluntur ingrati, quod creditori quidem praeter sortem extra ordinem numerant, beneficiorum autem usum esse gratuitum putant. Et illa crescunt mora tantoque plus solvendum est, quanto tardius. Ingratus est, qui beneficium reddit sine usura. Itaque huius quoque rei habebitur ratio, cum conferentur accepta et
19 expensa. Omnia facienda sunt, ut quam gratissimi simus.

Nostrum enim hoc bonum est, quemadmodum iustitia non est, ut vulgo creditur, ad alios pertinens; magna pars eius in se redit. Nemo non, cum alteri prodest, sibi profuit, non eo nomine dico, quod volet adiuvare adiutus, protegere defensus, quod bonum exemplum circuitu ad facientem revertitur, sicut mala exempla recidunt in auctores nec ulla miseratio contingit iis, qui patiuntur iniurias, quas posse fieri faciendo docuerunt, sed quod virtutum omnium pretium in ipsis est. Non enim exercentur ad prae-
20 mium; recte facti fecisse merces est. Gratus sum, non ut alius mihi libentius praestet priore inritatus

[a] Literally, "more than the capital and in addition to the rate of interest."

[b] Beneficence is a subdivision of the second cardinal virtue of the Stoics, Justice. Cicero discusses this topic at length in *De Off.* i. 42 ff.

anyone who receives a benefit more gladly than he repays it is mistaken. By as much as he who pays is more light-hearted than he who borrows, by so much ought he to be more joyful who unburdens himself of the greatest debt—a benefit received—than he who incurs the greatest obligations. For ungrateful men make mistakes in this respect also: they have to pay their creditors both capital and interest,[a] but they think that benefits are currency which they can use without interest. So the debts grow through postponement, and the later the action is postponed the more remains to be paid. A man is an ingrate if he repays a favour without interest. Therefore, interest also should be allowed for, when you compare your receipts and your expenses. We should try by all means to be as grateful as possible.

For gratitude is a good thing for ourselves, in a sense in which justice, that is commonly supposed to concern other persons, is not; gratitude returns in large measure unto itself. There is not a man who, when he has benefited his neighbour, has not benefited himself,—I do not mean for the reason that he whom you have aided will desire to aid you, or that he whom you have defended will desire to protect you, or that an example of good conduct returns in a circle to benefit the doer, just as examples of bad conduct recoil upon their authors, and as men find no pity if they suffer wrongs which they themselves have demonstrated the possibility of committing; but that the reward for all the virtues lies in the virtues themselves. For they are not practised with a view to recompense; the wages of a good deed is to have done it.[b] I am grateful, not in order that my neighbour, provoked by the earlier act of kindness, may be more ready to benefit me, but simply

exemplo, sed ut rem iucundissimam ac pulcherrimam faciam; gratus sum, non quia expedit, sed quia iuvat. Hoc ut scias ita esse, si gratum esse non licebit, nisi ut videar ingratus, si reddere beneficium non aliter quam per speciem iniuriae potero, aequissimo animo ad honestum consilium per mediam infamiam tendam. Nemo mihi videtur pluris aestimare virtutem, nemo illi magis esse devotus quam qui boni viri famam
21 perdidit, ne conscientiam perderet. Itaque, ut dixi, maiori tuo quam alterius bono gratus es. Illi enim vulgaris et cottidiana res contigit, recipere, quod dederat, tibi magna et ex beatissimo animi statu profecta, gratum fuisse. Nam si malitia miseros facit, virtus beatos, gratum autem esse virtus est, rem usitatam reddidisti, inaestimabilem consecutus es, conscientiam grati, quae nisi in animum divinum fortunatumque non pervenit. Contrarium autem huic adfectum summa infelicitas urget; nemo si ingratus est, miser erit. Non differo illum, statim miser est.

22 Itaque ingrati esse vitemus, non aliena causa, sed nostra. Minimum ex nequitia levissimumque ad alios redundat. Quod pessimum ex illa est et, ut ita dicam

in order that I may perform a most pleasant and beautiful act; I feel grateful, not because it profits me, but because it pleases me. And, to prove the truth of this to you, I declare that even if I may not be grateful without seeming ungrateful, even if I am able to return a benefit only by an act which resembles an injury; even so, I shall strive in the utmost calmness of spirit toward the purpose which honour demands, in the very midst of disgrace. No one, I think, rates virtue higher or is more consecrated to virtue than he who has lost his reputation for being a good man in order to keep from losing the approval of his conscience. Thus, as I have said, your being grateful is more conducive to your own good than to your neighbour's good. For while your neighbour has had a common, everyday experience,—namely, receiving back the gift which he had bestowed,—you have had a great experience which is the outcome of an utterly happy condition of soul,—to have felt gratitude. For if wickedness makes men unhappy and virtue makes men blest, and if it is a virtue to be grateful, then the return which you have made is only the customary thing, but the thing to which you have attained is priceless,—the consciousness of gratitude, which comes only to the soul that is divine and blessed. The opposite feeling to this, however, is immediately attended by the greatest unhappiness; no man, if he be ungrateful, will be unhappy in the future. I allow him no day of grace; he is unhappy forthwith.

Let us therefore avoid being ungrateful, not for the sake of others, but for our own sakes. When we do wrong, only the least and lightest portion of it flows back upon our neighbour; the worst and, if

spississimum, domi remanet et premit habentem, quemadmodum Attalus noster dicere solebat: "malitia ipsa maximam partem veneni sui bibit." Illud venenum, quod serpentes in alienam perniciem proferunt, sine sua continent, non est huic simile; hoc
23 habentibus pessimum est. Torquet ingratus se et macerat; odit, quae accepit, quia redditurus est, et extenuat, iniurias vero dilatat atque auget. Quid autem eo miserius, cui beneficia excidunt haerent iniuriae?

At contra sapientia exornat omne beneficium ac sibi ipsa commendat et se adsidua eius commemora-
24 tione delectat. Malis una voluptas est et haec brevis, dum accipiunt beneficia, ex quibus sapienti longum gaudium manet ac perenne. Non enim illum accipere, sed accepisse delectat, quod inmortale est et adsiduum. Illa contemnit, quibus laesus est, nec
25 obliviscitur per neglegentiam, sed volens. Non vertit omnia in peius nec quaerit, cui inputet casum, et peccata hominum ad fortunam potius refert. Non calumniatur verba nec vultus; quicquid accidit, benigne interpretando levat. Non offensae potius quam officii meminit. Quantum potest, in priore ac meliore se memoria detinet nec mutat animum adversus bene

[a] Perhaps a figure from the vintage. For the same metaphor, though in a different connexion, see *Ep.* i. 5, and *Ep.* cviii. 26: *quemadmodum ex amphora primum, quod est sincerissimum, effluit, gravissimum quodque turbidumque subsidit, sic in aetate nostra quod est optimum, in primo est.*

[b] *Cf.* § 6: "The good man so arranges the two sides of his ledger that he voluntarily cheats himself by adding to the benefit and subtracting from the injury." *Cf.* also § 17: "The good man will be easy-going in striking a balance; he will allow too much to be set against his credit."

I may use the term, the densest portion of it stays at home and troubles the owner.[a] My master Attalus used to say: "Evil herself drinks the largest portion of her own poison." The poison which serpents carry for the destruction of others, and secrete without harm to themselves, is not like this poison; for this sort is ruinous to the possessor. The ungrateful man tortures and torments himself; he hates the gifts which he has accepted, because he must make a return for them, and he tries to belittle their value, but he really enlarges and exaggerates the injuries which he has received. And what is more wretched than a man who forgets his benefits and clings to his injuries?

Wisdom, on the other hand, lends grace to every benefit, and of her own free will commends it to her own favour, and delights her soul by continued recollection thereof. Evil men have but one pleasure in benefits, and a very short-lived pleasure at that; it lasts only while they are receiving them. But the wise man derives therefrom an abiding and eternal joy. For he takes delight not so much in receiving the gift as in having received it; and this joy never perishes; it abides with him always. He despises the wrongs done him; he forgets them, not accidentally, but voluntarily. He does not put a wrong construction upon everything, or seek for someone whom he may hold responsible for each happening; he rather ascribes even the sins of men to chance. He will not misinterpret a word or a look; he makes light of all mishaps by interpreting them in a generous way.[b] He does not remember an injury rather than a service. As far as possible, he lets his memory rest upon the earlier and the better deed, never changing his attitude towards those who have

meritos, nisi multum male facta praecedunt et manifestum etiam coniventi[1] discrimen est; tunc quoque in hoc dumtaxat, ut talis sit post maiorem iniuriam qualis ante beneficium. Nam cum beneficio par est iniuria, aliquid in animo benivolentiae remanet.
26 Quemadmodum reus sententiis paribus absolvitur et semper quicquid dubium est humanitas inclinat in melius, sic animus[2] sapientis, ubi paria maleficiis merita sunt, desinet quidem debere, sed non desinit velle debere et hoc facit, quod qui post tabulas novas solvunt.

27 Nemo autem gratus esse potest, nisi contempsit ista, propter quae vulgus insanit; si referre vis gratiam, et in exilium eundum est et effundendus sanguis et suscipienda egestas et ipsa innocentia saepe maculanda indignisque obicienda rumoribus.
28 Non parvo sibi constat homo gratus. Nihil carius aestimamus quam beneficium, quamdiu petimus, nihil vilius, cum accepimus. Quaeris quid sit, quod oblivionem nobis acceptorum faciat? Cupiditas accipiendorum. Cogitamus non quid inpetratum, sed quid petendum sit. Abstrahunt a recto divitiae, honores, potentia et cetera, quae opinione nostra cara
29 sunt, pretio suo vilia. Nescimus aestimare res, de

[1] *conniventi* later MSS.; *contuenti* VPb.
[2] *animus* later MSS.; *animo* VPb.

[a] When by law or special enactment *novae tabellae* were granted to special classes of debtors, their debts, as in our bankruptcy courts, were cancelled.
[b] *Cf. Ep.* xxxi. 6 *quid ergo est bonum? rerum scientia.*

deserved well of him, except in cases where the bad deeds far outdistance the good, and the space between them is obvious even to one who closes his eyes to it; even then only to this extent, that he strives, after receiving the preponderant injury, to resume the attitude which he held before he received the benefit. For when the injury merely equals the benefit, a certain amount of kindly feeling is left over. Just as a defendant is acquitted when the votes are equal, and just as the spirit of kindliness always tries to bend every doubtful case toward the better interpretation, so the mind of the wise man, when another's merits merely equal his bad deeds, will, to be sure, cease to feel an obligation, but does not cease to desire to feel it, and acts precisely like the man who pays his debts even after they have been legally cancelled.[a]

But no man can be grateful unless he has learned to scorn the things which drive the common herd to distraction; if you wish to make return for a favour, you must be willing to go into exile, or to pour forth your blood, or to undergo poverty, or,—and this will frequently happen,—even to let your very innocence be stained and exposed to shameful slanders. It is no slight price that a man must pay for being grateful. We hold nothing dearer than a benefit, so long as we are seeking one; we hold nothing cheaper after we have received it. Do you ask what it is that makes us forget benefits received? It is our extreme greed for receiving others. We consider not what we have obtained, but what we are to seek. We are deflected from the right course by riches, titles, power, and everything which is valuable in our opinion but worthless when rated at its real value. We do not know how to weigh matters[b];

quibus non cum fama, sed cum rerum natura deliberandum est; nihil habent ista magnificum, quo mentes in se nostras trahant, praeter hoc, quod mirari illa consuevimus. Non enim, quia concupiscenda sunt, laudantur, sed concupiscuntur, quia laudata sunt, et cum singulorum error publicum fecerit, singulorum errorem facit publicus.

30 Sed quemadmodum illa credidimus, sic et hoc eidem populo credamus, nihil esse grato animo honestius. Omnes hoc urbes, omnes etiam ex barbaris regionibus gentes conclamabunt. In hoc bonis
31 malisque conveniet. Erunt qui voluptates laudent, erunt qui labores malint; erunt qui dolorem maximum malum dicant, erunt qui ne malum quidem appellent; divitias aliquis ad summum bonum admittet, alius illas dicet malo vitae humanae repertas, nihil esse eo locupletius, cui quod donet fortuna non invenit. In tanta iudiciorum diversitate referendam bene merentibus gratiam omnes tibi uno, quod aiunt, ore adfirmabunt. In hoc tam discors turba consentiet; cum interim iniurias pro beneficiis reddimus, et prima causa est, cur quis ingratus sit, si satis
32 gratus esse non potuit. Eo perductus est furor, ut periculosissima res sit beneficia in aliquem magna conferre; nam quia putat turpe non reddere, non vult esse, cui reddat. Tibi habe, quod accepisti;

we should take counsel regarding them, not with their reputation but with their nature; those things possess no grandeur wherewith to enthral our minds, except the fact that we have become accustomed to marvel at them. For they are not praised because they ought to be desired, but they are desired because they have been praised; and when the error of individuals has once created error on the part of the public, then the public error goes on creating error on the part of individuals.

But just as we take on faith such estimates of values, so let us take on the faith of the people this truth, that nothing is more honourable than a grateful heart. This phrase will be echoed by all cities, and by all races, even those from savage countries. Upon this point good and bad will agree. Some praise pleasure, some prefer toil; some say that pain is the greatest of evils, some say it is no evil at all; some will include riches in the Supreme Good, others will say that their discovery meant harm to the human race, and that none is richer than he to whom Fortune has found nothing to give. Amid all this diversity of opinion all men will yet with one voice, as the saying is, vote "aye" to the proposition that thanks should be returned to those who have deserved well of us. On this question the common herd, rebellious as they are, will all agree, but at present we keep paying back injuries instead of benefits, and the primary reason why a man is ungrateful is that he has found it impossible to be grateful enough. Our madness has gone to such lengths that it is a very dangerous thing to confer great benefits upon a person; for just because he thinks it shameful not to repay, so he would have none left alive whom he should repay. "Keep for yourself what you

non repeto, non exigo. Profuisse tutum sit. Nullum est odium perniciosius quam e beneficii violati pudore. VALE.

LXXXII.

SENECA LVCILIO SVO SALVTEM

1 Desii iam de te esse sollicitus. "Quem," inquis, "deorum sponsorem accepisti?" Eum scilicet, qui neminem fallit, animum recti ac boni amatorem. In tuto pars tui melior est. Potest fortuna tibi iniuriam facere; quod ad rem magis pertinet, non timeo, ne tu facias tibi. I, qua ire coepisti et in isto te vitae
2 habitu conpone placide, non molliter. Male mihi esse malo quam molliter; male[1] nunc sic excipe, quemadmodum a populo solet dici: dure, aspere, laboriose. Audire solemus sic quorundam vitam laudari, quibus invidetur: "molliter vivit"; hoc dicunt: "mollis est." Paulatim enim effeminatur animus atque in similitudinem otii sui et pigritiae, in qua iacet, solvitur. Quid ergo? Viro non vel obrigescere satius est? Deinde idem delicati timent,[2] cui vitam suam fecere similem. Multum interest

[1] *male* added by Muretus.
[2] *morti* after *timent* deleted by Madvig.

---

[a] The words are put into the mouth of an imaginary benefactor who fears for his own life.
[b] *Cf.* Tac. *Agric.* 42 *proprium humani ingenii est odisse quem laeseris.*
[c] One who incurs liability by taking upon himself the debt of another. It is part of the process known as *intercessio*.
[d] Rather than *mollis*.

have received; I do not ask it back; I do not demand it. Let it be safe to have conferred a favour."[a] There is no worse hatred than that which springs from shame at the desecration of a benefit.[b] Farewell.

LXXXII. ON THE NATURAL FEAR OF DEATH

I have already ceased to be anxious about you. "Whom then of the gods," you ask, "have you found as your voucher?"[c] A god, let me tell you, who deceives no one,—a soul in love with that which is upright and good. The better part of yourself is on safe ground. Fortune can inflict injury upon you; what is more pertinent is that I have no fears lest you do injury to yourself. Proceed as you have begun, and settle yourself in this way of living, not luxuriously, but calmly. I prefer to be in trouble rather than in luxury; and you had better interpret the term "in trouble" as popular usage is wont to interpret it: living a "hard," "rough," "toilsome" life. We are wont to hear the lives of certain men praised as follows, when they are objects of unpopularity: "So-and-So lives luxuriously"; but by this they mean: "He is softened by luxury." For the soul is made womanish by degrees, and is weakened until it matches the ease and laziness in which it lies. Lo, is it not better for one who is really a man even to become hardened[d]? Next, these same dandies fear that which they have made their own lives resemble. Much difference is there between

3 inter otium et conditivum. "Quid ergo?" inquis, "non satius est vel sic iacere quam in istis officiorum verticibus volutari?" Utraque res detestabilis est, et contractio et torpor. Puto, aeque qui in odoribus iacet, mortuus est quam qui rapitur unco.

Otium sine litteris mors est et hominis vivi
4 sepultura. Quid deinde prodest secessisse? Tamquam non trans maria nos sollicitudinum causae persequantur! Quae latebra est, in quam non intret metus mortis? Quae tam emunita et in altum subducta vitae quies, quam non dolor territet? Quacumque te abdideris, mala humana circumstrepent. Multa extra sunt, quae circumeunt nos, quo aut[1] fallant aut urgeant, multa intus, quae in media solitudine exaestuant.

5 Philosophia circumdanda est, inexpugnabilis murus, quem fortuna multis machinis lacessitum non transit. In insuperabili loco stat animus, qui externa deseruit, et arce se sua vindicat; infra illum omne telum cadit. Non habet, ut putamus, fortuna longas manus; nemi-
6 nem occupat nisi haerentem sibi. Itaque quantum possumus, ab illa resiliamus; quod sola praestabit sui naturaeque cognitio.[2] Sciat, quo iturus sit, unde ortus, quod illi bonum, quod malum sit, quid petat, quid evitet, quae sit illa ratio, quae adpetenda ac

[1] *quo aut* later MSS.; *quae aut* VPb.
[2] *cognitio* later MSS.; *conditio* Vb; *condicio* p.

---

[a] *Conditivum* (more frequently and properly *conditorium*) is a grim jest. The word is mostly found in an adjectival sense applying to fruits and grain *stored* for later use.

[b] Compare Arnold's nineteenth-century definition of culture.

lying idle and lying buried[a]! "But," you say, "is it not better even to lie idle than to whirl round in these eddies of business distraction?" Both extremes are to be deprecated—both tension and sluggishness. I hold that he who lies on a perfumed couch is no less dead than he who is dragged along by the executioner's hook.

Leisure without study is death; it is a tomb for the living man. What then is the advantage of retirement? As if the real causes of our anxieties did not follow us across the seas! What hiding-place is there, where the fear of death does not enter? What peaceful haunts are there, so fortified and so far withdrawn that pain does not fill them with fear? Wherever you hide yourself, human ills will make an uproar all around. There are many external things which compass us about, to deceive us or to weigh upon us; there are many things within which, even amid solitude, fret and ferment.

Therefore, gird yourself about with philosophy, an impregnable wall. Though it be assaulted by many engines, Fortune can find no passage into it. The soul stands on unassailable ground, if it has abandoned external things; it is independent in its own fortress; and every weapon that is hurled falls short of the mark. Fortune has not the long reach with which we credit her; she can seize none except him that clings to her. Let us then recoil from her as far as we are able. This will be possible for us only through knowledge of self and of the world[b] of Nature. The soul should know whither it is going and whence it came, what is good for it and what is evil, what it seeks and what it avoids, and what is that Reason which distinguishes between the desirable and the undesirable, and thereby tames

fugienda discernat, qua cupiditatum mansuescit insania, timorum saevitia conpescitur.

7 Haec quidam[1] putant ipsos etiam sine philosophia repressisse. Sed, cum securos aliquis casus expertus est, exprimitur sera confessio. Magna verba excidunt, cum tortor poposcit manum, cum mors propius[2] accessit. Possis illi dicere: facile provocabas mala absentia; ecce dolor, quem tolerabilem esse dicebas, ecce mors, quam contra multa animose locutus es; sonant flagella, gladius micat:

> Nunc animis opus, Aenea, nunc pectore firmo.

8 Faciet autem illud firmum adsidua meditatio, si non verba exercueris, sed animum, si contra mortem te praeparaveris, adversus quam non exhortabitur nec adtollet, qui cavillationibus tibi persuadere temptaverit mortem malum non esse. Libet enim, Lucili virorum optime, ridere ineptias Graecas, quas nondum,
9 quamvis mirer, excussi. Zenon noster hac collectione utitur: "nullum malum gloriosum est; mors autem gloriosa est; mors ergo non est malum." Profecisti; liberatus sum metu; post hoc non dubitabo porrigere cervicem. Non vis severius loqui nec morituro risum

[1] *quidam* later MSS.; *quidem* VPb.
[2] *propius* later MSS.; *potius* VPb.

---

[a] Vergil, *Aeneid*, vi. 261.
[b] Frag. 196 von Arnim.

the madness of our desires and calms the violence of our fears.

Some men flatter themselves that they have checked these evils by themselves even without the aid of philosophy; but when some accident catches them off their guard, a tardy confession of error is wrung from them. Their boastful words perish from their lips when the torturer commands them to stretch forth their hands, and when death draws nearer! You might say to such a man: "It was easy for you to challenge evils that were not near-by; but here comes pain, which you declared you could endure; here comes death, against which you uttered many a courageous boast! The whip cracks, the sword flashes:

> Ah now, Aeneas, thou must needs be stout
> And strong of heart!"[a]

This strength of heart, however, will come from constant study, provided that you practise, not with the tongue but with the soul, and provided that you prepare yourself to meet death. To enable yourself to meet death, you may expect no encouragement or cheer from those who try to make you believe, by means of their hair-splitting logic, that death is no evil. For I take pleasure, excellent Lucilius, in poking fun at the absurdities of the Greeks, of which, to my continual surprise, I have not yet succeeded in ridding myself. Our master Zeno[b] uses a syllogism like this: "No evil is glorious; but death is glorious; therefore death is no evil." A cure, Zeno! I have been freed from fear; henceforth I shall not hesitate to bare my neck on the scaffold. Will you not utter sterner words instead of rousing a dying man to laughter? Indeed, Lucilius, I could

movere? Non mehercules facile tibi dixerim, utrum ineptior fuerit, qui se hac interrogatione iudicavit mortis metum extinguere, an qui hoc, tamquam ad
10 rem pertineret, conatus est solvere. Nam et ipse interrogationem contrariam opposuit ex eo natam, quod mortem inter indifferentia ponimus, quae ἀδιάφορα Graeci vocant. "Nihil," inquit, "indifferens gloriosum est; mors autem gloriosum est; ergo mors non est indifferens." Haec interrogatio vides ubi obrepat: mors non est gloriosa, sed fortiter mori gloriosum est. Et cum dicis: "indifferens nihil gloriosum est," concedo tibi ita, ut dicam nihil gloriosum esse nisi circa indifferentia. Tamquam indifferentia esse dico, id est nec bona nec mala, morbum, dolorem, paupertatem, exilium, mortem.
11 Nihil horum per se gloriosum est, nihil tamen sine his. Laudatur enim non paupertas, sed ille, quem paupertas[1] non summittit nec[2] incurvat. Laudatur non exilium, sed ille qui in exilium ivit tanquam[3] misisset. Laudatur non dolor, sed ille, quem nihil coegit dolor. Nemo mortem laudat, sed eum, cuius
12 mors ante abstulit animum quam conturbavit. Omnia ista per se non sunt honesta nec gloriosa, sed quicquid ex illis virtus adiit tractavitque, honestum et gloriosum facit; illa in medio posita sunt; interest, utrum malitia illis an virtus manum admoverit. Mors enim illa, quae in Catone gloriosa est, in Bruto statim

[1] Pb and V^1 omit *sed . . . paupertas*.
[2] *nec* later MSS.; *sed* VPb.
[3] *sed ille qui in exilium ivit tanquam* Madvig; . . . *ut quam* MSS.

[a] Defined by the Greeks as "things which have no direct connexion either with happiness or with unhappiness." See Cicero, *De Finibus*, iii. 50 ff.
[b] *i.e.*, are "indifferent" (*cf.* § 14 *indifferentia ac media dicuntur*).

not easily tell you whether he who thought that he was quenching the fear of death by setting up this syllogism was the more foolish, or he who attempted to refute it, just as if it had anything to do with the matter! For the refuter himself proposed a counter-syllogism, based upon the proposition that we regard death as "indifferent,"—one of the things which the Greeks call ἀδιάφορα.[a] "Nothing," he says, "that is indifferent can be glorious; death is glorious; therefore death is not indifferent." You comprehend the tricky fallacy which is contained in this syllogism: mere death is, in fact, not glorious; but a brave death is glorious. And when you say: "Nothing that is indifferent is glorious," I grant you this much, and declare that nothing is glorious except as it deals with indifferent things. I classify as "indifferent,"—that is, neither good nor evil,—sickness, pain, poverty, exile, death. None of these things is intrinsically glorious; but nothing can be glorious apart from them. For it is not poverty that we praise, it is the man whom poverty cannot humble or bend. Nor is it exile that we praise, it is the man who withdraws into exile in the spirit in which he would have sent another into exile. It is not pain that we praise, it is the man whom pain has not coerced. One praises not death, but the man whose soul death takes away before it can confound it. All these things are in themselves neither honourable nor glorious; but any one of them that virtue has visited and touched is made honourable and glorious by virtue; they merely lie in between,[b] and the decisive question is only whether wickedness or virtue has laid hold upon them. For instance, the death which in Cato's case is glorious, is in the case

turpis est et erubescenda. Hic est enim Brutus, qu
cum periturus mortis moras quaereret, ad exonerandun
ventrem secessit et evocatus ad mortem iussusque
praebere cervicem: "praebebo," inquit, "ita vivam."
Quae dementia est fugere, cum retro ire non possis
"Praebebo," inquit, "ita vivam." Paene adiecit
"vel sub Antonio." O hominem dignum, qui vita
dederetur!

13 Sed, ut coeperam dicere, vides ipsam mortem ne
malum esse nec bonum; Cato illa honestissime usu
est, turpissime Brutus. Omnis res quod non habui
decus, virtute addita sumit. Cubiculum lucidun
14 dicimus, hoc idem obscurissimum est nocte. Die
illi lucem infundit, nox eripit; sic istis, quae a nobi
indifferentia ac media dicuntur, divitiis, viribus, for
mae, honoribus, regno et contra morti, exilio, mala
valetudini, doloribus quaeque alia aut minus aut magi
pertimuimus, aut malitia aut virtus dat boni vel ma
nomen. Massa per se nec calida nec frigida est; i
fornacem coniecta concaluit, in aquam demissa[1] re
frixit. Mors honesta est per illud, quod honestum
est, id est virtus et animus extrema contemnens.

15 Est et horum, Lucili, quae appellamus medi
grande discrimen. Non enim sic mors indifferen
est, quomodo utrum capillos pares an inpares
habeas. Mors inter illa est, quae mala quidem no
sunt, tamen habent mali speciem; sui amor est

[1] Haase; *remissa* VPb. [2] Later MSS.; *honesta* VP
[3] *an impares* added by Koch.

---

[a] Presumably D. Junius Brutus, who finally incurred th enmity of both Octavian and Antony. He was ignominious put to death by a Gaul while fleeing to join M. Brutus Macedonia.

[b] *media*: a technical word in Stoic philosophy, meani neither good nor bad.

of Brutus[a] forthwith base and disgraceful. For this Brutus, condemned to death, was trying to obtain postponement; he withdrew a moment in order to ease himself; when summoned to die and ordered to bare his throat, he exclaimed: "I will bare my throat, if only I may live!" What madness it is to run away, when it is impossible to turn back! "I will bare my throat, if only I may live!" He came very near saying also: "even under Antony!" This fellow deserved indeed to be consigned to *life*!

But, as I was going on to remark, you see that death in itself is neither an evil nor a good; Cato experienced death most honourably, Brutus most basely. Everything, if you add virtue, assumes a glory which it did not possess before. We speak of a sunny room, even though the same room is pitch-dark at night. It is the day which fills it with light, and the night which steals the light away; thus it is with the things which we call indifferent and "middle,[b]" like riches, strength, beauty, titles, kingship, and their opposites,—death, exile, ill-health, pain, and all such evils, the fear of which upsets us to a greater or less extent; it is the wickedness or the virtue that bestows the name of good or evil. An object is not by its own essence either hot or cold; it is heated when thrown into a furnace, and chilled when dropped into water. Death is honourable when related to that which is honourable; by this I mean virtue and a soul that despises the worst hardships.

Furthermore, there are vast distinctions among these qualities which we call "middle." For example, death is not so indifferent as the question whether your hair should be worn evenly or unevenly. Death belongs among those things which are not indeed evils, but still have in them a semblance of evil;

permanendi conservandique se insita voluntas atque aspernatio dissolutionis, quia videtur multa nobis bona eripere et nos ex hac, cui adsuevimus, rerum copia educere. Illa quoque res morti nos alienat, quod haec iam novimus, illa, ad quae transituri sumus, nescimus, qualia sint, et horremus ignota. Naturalis praeterea tenebrarum metus est, in quas
16 adductura mors creditur. Itaque etiam si indifferens mors est, non tamen ea est, quae facile neglegi possit. Magna exercitatione durandus est animus, ut conspectum eius accessumque patiatur.

Mors contemni debet magis quam solet. Multa enim de illa credidimus. Multorum ingeniis certatum est ad augendam eius infamiam. Descriptus est carcer infernus et perpetua nocte oppressa regio, in qua

> Ingens ianitor Orci
> Ossa super recubans antro semesa cruento,
> Aeternum latrans exsangues terreat umbras.

Etiam cum persuaseris istas fabulas esse nec quicquam defunctis superesse, quod timeant, subit alius metus. Aeque enim timent, ne apud inferos sint, quam ne nusquam.

17 His adversantibus, quae nobis offundit longa persuasio, fortiter pati mortem quidni gloriosum sit et

[a] See Vergil, *Aeneid*, vi. 400 f. and viii. 296 f.

for there are implanted in us love of self, a desire for existence and self-preservation, and also an abhorrence of dissolution, because death seems to rob us of many goods and to withdraw us from the abundance to which we have become accustomed. And there is another element which estranges us from death: we are already familiar with the present, but are ignorant of the future into which we shall transfer ourselves, and we shrink from the unknown. Moreover, it is natural to fear the world of shades, whither death is supposed to lead. Therefore, although death is something indifferent, it is nevertheless not a thing which we can easily ignore. The soul must be hardened by long practice, so that it may learn to endure the sight and the approach of death.

Death ought to be despised more than it is wont to be despised. For we believe too many of the stories about death. Many thinkers have striven hard to increase its ill repute; they have portrayed the prison in the world below and the land overwhelmed by everlasting night, where

> Within his blood-stained cave Hell's warder huge
> Doth sprawl his ugly length on half-crunched bones,
> And terrifies the disembodied ghosts
> With never-ceasing bark.[a]

Even if you can win your point and prove that these are mere stories and that nothing is left for the dead to fear, another fear steals upon you. For the fear of going to the underworld is equalled by the fear of going nowhere.

In the face of these notions, which long-standing opinion has dinned in our ears, how can brave endurance of death be anything else than glorious, and fit to rank among the greatest accomplishments of the

inter maxima opera mentis humanae? Quae numquam ad virtutem exsurget, si mortem malum esse crediderit; exsurget, si putabit indifferens esse. Non recipit rerum natura, ut aliquis magno animo accedat ad id, quod malum iudicat; pigre veniet et cunctanter. Non est autem gloriosum, quod ab invito et tergiversante fit; nihil facit virtus, quia necesse
18 est. Adice nunc, quod nihil honeste fit, nisi cui totus animus incubuit atque adfuit, cui nulla parte sui repugnavit. Ubi autem ad malum acceditur aut peiorum metu aut spe bonorum, ad quae pervenire tanti sit devorata unius mali patientia, dissident inter se iudicia facientis. Hinc est, quod iubeat proposita perficere, illinc, quod retrahat et ab re suspecta ac periculosa fugiat. Igitur in diversa distrahitur; si hoc est, perit gloria. Virtus enim concordi animo decreta peragit. Non timet, quod facit.

> Tu ne cede malis, sed contra audentior ito
> Qua tua te fortuna sinet.

19 Non ibis audentior, si mala illa esse credideris. Eximendum hoc e pectore est; alioqui haesitabit inpetum moratura suspicio. Trudetur in id, quod invadendum est.

Nostri quidem videri volunt Zenonis interroga-

[a] Vergil, *Aeneid*, vi. 95 f., the advice of the Sibyl to Aeneas.

human mind? For the mind will never rise to virtue if it believes that death is an evil; but it will so rise if it holds that death is a matter of indifference. It is not in the order of nature that a man shall proceed with a great heart to a destiny which he believes to be evil; he will go sluggishly and with reluctance. But nothing glorious can result from unwillingness and cowardice; virtue does nothing under compulsion. Besides, no deed that a man does is honourable unless he has devoted himself thereto and attended to it with all his heart, rebelling against it with no portion of his being. When, however, a man goes to face an evil, either through fear of worse evils or in the hope of goods whose attainment is of sufficient moment to him that he can swallow the one evil which he must endure,—in that case the judgment of the agent is drawn in two directions. On the one side is the motive which bids him carry out his purpose; on the other, the motive which restrains him and makes him flee from something which has aroused his apprehension or leads to danger. Hence he is torn in different directions; and if this happens, the glory of his act is gone. For virtue accomplishes its plans only when the spirit is in harmony with itself. There is no element of fear in any of its actions.

> Yield not to evils, but, still braver, go
> Where'er thy fortune shall allow.[a]

You cannot "still braver go," if you are persuaded that those things are the real evils. Root out this idea from your soul; otherwise your apprehensions will remain undecided and will thus check the impulse to action. You will be pushed into that towards which you ought to advance like a soldier.

Those of our school, it is true, would have men

tionem veram esse, fallacem autem alteram et falsam, quae illi opponitur. Ego non redigo ista ad legem dialecticam et ad illos artificii veternosissimi nodos. Totum genus istuc exturbandum iudico, quo circumscribi se, qui interrogatur, existimat et ad confessionem perductus aliud respondet, aliud putat. Pro veritate simplicius agendum est, contra metum
20 fortius. Haec ipsa, quae volvuntur ab illis, solvere malim et expendere, ut persuadeam, non ut inponam.

In aciem educturus exercitum pro coniugibus ac liberis mortem obiturum quomodo exhortabitur? Do tibi Fabios totum rei publicae bellum in unam transferentes domum. Laconas tibi ostendo in ipsis Thermopylarum angustiis positos. Nec victoriam sperant nec reditum. Ille locus illis sepulchrum
21 futurus est. Quemadmodum exhortaris, ut totius gentis ruinam obiectis corporibus excipiant et vita potius quam loco cedant? Dices: "quod malum est, gloriosum non est; mors gloriosa est; mors ergo non malum"? O efficacem contionem! Quis post hanc dubitet se infestis ingerere mucronibus et stans mori! At ille Leonidas quam fortiter illos adlocutus est! "Sic," inquit, "commilitones, prandete tamquam apud inferos cenaturi." Non in ore crevit cibus, non

---

[a] *Cf.* §§ 9 and 10. [b] *Cf. Ep.* xlviii. 4 ff.

[c] *Cf.* Livy, ii. 49. 1 *familiam unam subisse civitatis onus.*

[d] Οὕτως ἀριστᾶτε ὡς ἐν ᾅδου δειπνήσοντες,—quoted by Stobaeus, Plutarch, and Diodorus. Cicero says (*Tusc.* i. 101) *hodie apud inferos fortasse cenabimus.*

think that Zeno's syllogism[a] is correct, but that the second[a] I mentioned, which is set up against his, is deceptive and wrong. But I for my part decline to reduce such questions to a matter of dialectical rules or to the subtleties of an utterly worn-out system. Away, I say, with all that sort of thing, which makes a man feel, when a question is propounded to him, that he is hemmed in, and forces him to admit a premiss, and then makes him say one thing in his answer when his real opinion is another.[b] When truth is at stake, we must act more frankly; and when fear is to be combated, we must act more bravely. Such questions, which the dialecticians involve in subtleties, I prefer to solve and weigh rationally, with the purpose of winning conviction and not of forcing the judgment.

When a general is about to lead into action an army prepared to meet death for their wives and children, how will he exhort them to battle? I remind you of the Fabii,[c] who took upon a single clan a war which concerned the whole state. I point out to you the Lacedaemonians in position at the very pass of Thermopylae! They have no hope of victory, no hope of returning. The place where they stand is to be their tomb. In what language do you encourage them to bar the way with their bodies and take upon themselves the ruin of their whole tribe, and to retreat from life rather than from their post? Shall you say: "That which is evil is not glorious; but death is glorious; therefore death is not an evil"? What a powerful discourse! After such words, who would hesitate to throw himself upon the serried spears of the foemen, and die in his tracks? But take Leonidas: how bravely did he address his men! He said: "Fellow-soldiers, let us to our breakfast, knowing that we shall sup in Hades!"[d] The food

haesit in faucibus, non elapsus est manibus; alacres
22 et ad prandium illi promiserunt et ad cenam. Quid?
Dux ille Romanus, qui ad occupandum locum milites missos, cum per ingentem hostium exercitum ituri essent, sic adlocutus est: "ire, commilitones, illo necesse est, unde redire non est necesse."

Vides, quam simplex et imperiosa virtus sit; quem mortalium circumscriptiones vestrae fortiorem facere, quem erectiorem possunt? Frangunt animum, qui numquam minus contrahendus est et in minuta ac spinosa cogendus, quam cum aliquid grande com-
23 ponitur. Non trecentis, sed omnibus mortalibus mortis timor detrahi debet. Quomodo illos doces malum non esse? Quomodo opiniones totius aevi, quibus protinus infantia inbuitur, evincis? Quod auxilium invenis[1] inbecillitati humanae? Quid dicis, quo inflammati in media pericula inruant? Qua oratione hunc timendi consensum, quibus ingeni viribus obnixam contra te persuasionem humani generis avertis? Verba mihi captiosa conponis et interrogatiunculas nectis? Magnis telis magna por-
24 tenta feriuntur. Serpentem illam in Africa saevam et Romanis legionibus bello ipso terribiliorem frustra sagittis fundisque petierunt; ne Pythio quidem vulnerabilis erat, cum ingens magnitudo pro vastitate

[1] After *invenis*, Gertz removed *quid dicis* . . .

---

[a] Calpurnius, in Sicily, during the first Punic war. *Cf.* Livy, xxii. 60. 11.

[b] The soldiers of Leonidas.

[c] An especially large machine for assaulting walls; a nickname, like the modern " Long Tom."

of these men did not grow lumpy in their mouths, or stick in their throats, or slip from their fingers; eagerly did they accept the invitation to breakfast, and to supper also! Think, too, of the famous Roman general;[a] his soldiers had been dispatched to seize a position, and when they were about to make their way through a huge army of the enemy, he addressed them with the words: "You must go now, fellow-soldiers, to yonder place, whence there is no 'must' about your returning!"

You see, then, how straightforward and peremptory virtue is; but what man on earth can your deceptive logic make more courageous or more upright? Rather does it break the spirit, which should never be less straitened or forced to deal with petty and thorny problems than when some great work is being planned. It is not the Three Hundred,[b] —it is all mankind that should be relieved of the fear of death. But how can you prove to all those men that death is no evil? How can you overcome the notions of all our past life,—notions with which we are tinged from our very infancy? What succour can you discover for man's helplessness? What can you say that will make men rush, burning with zeal, into the midst of danger? By what persuasive speech can you turn aside this universal feeling of fear, by what strength of wit can you turn aside the conviction of the human race which steadfastly opposes you? Do you propose to construct catchwords for me, or to string together petty syllogisms? It takes great weapons to strike down great monsters. You recall the fierce serpent in Africa, more frightful to the Roman legions than the war itself, and assailed in vain by arrows and slings; it could not be wounded even by "Pythius,"[c] since its huge size, and the

corporis solida ferrum et quicquid humanae torserant manus reiceret. Molaribus demum fracta saxis est. Et adversus mortem tu tam[1] minuta iacularis? Subula leonem excipis? Acuta sunt ista, quae dicis; nihil est acutius arista. Quaedam inutilia et inefficacia ipsa subtilitas reddit. Vale.

LXXXIII.

Seneca Lvcilio svo salvtem

1 Singulos dies tibi meos et quidem totos indicari iubes; bene de me iudicas, si nihil esse in illis putas, quod abscondam. Sic certe vivendum est, tamquam in conspectu vivamus; sic cogitandum, tamquam aliquis in pectus intimum introspicere[2] possit; et potest. Quid enim prodest ab homine aliquid esse secretum? Nihil deo clusum est. Interest animis nostris et cogitationibus mediis intervenit—sic inter-
2 venit, dico, tamquam aliquando discedat. Faciam ergo, quod iubes, et quid agam et quo ordine, libenter tibi scribam. Observabo me protinus et, quod est utilissimum, diem meum recognoscam. Hoc nos pessimos facit, quod nemo vitam suam respicit. Quid facturi simus cogitamus. Atqui consilium futuri ex praeterito venit.

[1] *tu tam* later MSS.; *totam* VPb.
[2] *introspicere* Hense; *prospicere* VPb.

---

[a] *Cf. Ep.* lxxxv. 1 *pudet in aciem descendere pro dis hominibusque susceptam subula armatum.*

[b] *Cf. Ep.* xli. 2 *sacer intra nos spiritus, . . . malorum bonorumque nostrorum observator et custos.*

[c] *Cf. Ep.* i. 4 *ratio constat inpensae* (referring to his attempt to employ his time profitably).

toughness which matched its bulk, made spears, or any weapon hurled by the hand of man, glance off. It was finally destroyed by rocks equal in size to millstones. Are you, then, hurling petty weapons like yours even against death? Can you stop a lion's charge by an awl?[a] Your arguments are indeed sharp; but there is nothing sharper than a stalk of grain. And certain arguments are rendered useless and unavailing by their very subtlety. Farewell.

LXXXIII. ON DRUNKENNESS

You bid me give you an account of each separate day, and of the whole day too; so you must have a good opinion of me if you think that in these days of mine there is nothing to hide. At any rate, it is thus that we should live,—as if we lived in plain sight of all men; and it is thus that we should think,—as if there were someone who could look into our inmost souls; and there is one who can so look. For what avails it that something is hidden from man? Nothing is shut off from the sight of God. He is witness of our souls,[b] and he comes into the very midst of our thoughts—comes into them, I say, as one who may at any time depart. I shall therefore do as you bid, and shall gladly inform you by letter what I am doing, and in what sequence. I shall keep watching myself continually, and—a most useful habit—shall review each day.[c] For this is what makes us wicked: that no one of us looks back over his own life. Our thoughts are devoted only to what we are about to do. And yet our plans for the future always depend on the past.

3 Hodiernus dies solidus est; nemo ex illo quicquam mihi eripuit. Totus inter stratum lectionemque divisus est. Minimum exercitationi corporis datum, et hoc nomine ago gratias senectuti: non magno mihi constat; cum me movi, lassus sum. Hic autem
4 est exercitationis etiam fortissimis finis. Progymnastas meos quaeris? Unus mihi sufficit Pharius[1] puer, ut scis, amabilis, sed mutabitur. Iam aliquem teneriorem quaero. Hic quidem ait nos eandem crisin habere, quia utrique dentes cadunt. Sed iam vix illum adsequor currentem et intra paucissimos dies non potero; vide, quid exercitatio cotidiana proficiat. Cito magnum intervallum fit inter duos in diversum euntes. Eodem tempore ille adscendit, ego descendo, nec ignoras, quanto ex his velocius alterum fiat. Mentitus sum; iam enim aetas nostra non de-
5 scendit, sed cadit. Quomodo tamen hodiernum certamen nobis cesserit quaeris? Quod raro cursoribus evenit, hieran fecimus. Ab hac fatigatione magis quam exercitatione in frigidam descendi; hoc apud me vocatur parum calda. Ille tantus psychrolutes, qui kalendis Ianuariis euripum salutabam, qui anno novo quemadmodum legere, scribere, dicere aliquid, sic auspicabar in Virginem desilire, primum ad Tiberim transtuli castra, deinde ad hoc solium, quod,

[1] *Pharius* some MSS.; *farvius* b; *farivus* PV; *Earinus* Erasmus.

[a] See *Ep.* xii. 3 for a similar witticism.

[b] *Hieran* (*coronam*), as Lipsius thinks, when the result was doubtful, the garland was offered to the gods. From the Greek ἱερός, sacred.

[c] Constructed by Marcus Agrippa; now the fountain of Trevi.

EPISTLE LXXXIII.

To-day has been unbroken; no one has filched the slightest part of it from me. The whole time has been divided between rest and reading. A brief space has been given over to bodily exercise, and on this ground I can thank old age—my exercise costs very little effort; as soon as I stir, I am tired. And weariness is the aim and end of exercise, no matter how strong one is. Do you ask who are my pace-makers? One is enough for me,—the slave Pharius, a pleasant fellow, as you know; but I shall exchange him for another. At my time of life I need one who is of still more tender years. Pharius, at any rate, says that he and I are at the same period of life; for we are both losing our teeth.[a] Yet even now I can scarcely follow his pace as he runs, and within a very short time I shall not be able to follow him at all; so you see what profit we get from daily exercise. Very soon does a wide interval open between two persons who travel different ways. My slave is climbing up at the very moment when I am coming down, and you surely know how much quicker the latter is. Nay, I was wrong; for now my life is not coming down; it is falling outright. Do you ask, for all that, how our race resulted to-day? We raced to a tie,[b]—something which rarely happens in a running contest. After tiring myself out in this way (for I cannot call it exercise), I took a cold bath; this, at my house, means just short of hot. I, the former cold-water enthusiast, who used to celebrate the new year by taking a plunge into the canal, who, just as naturally as I would set out to do some reading or writing, or to compose a speech, used to inaugurate the first of the year with a plunge into the Virgo aqueduct,[c] have changed my allegiance, first to the Tiber, and then to my favourite tank, which is warmed only by the

cum fortissimus sum et omnia bona fide fiunt, sol temperat. Non multum mihi ad balneum superest.
6 Panis deinde siccus et sine mensa prandium, post quod non sunt lavandae manus. Dormio minimum. Consuetudinem meam nosti: brevissimo somno utor et quasi interiungo. Satis est mihi vigilare desisse. Aliquando dormisse me scio, aliquando suspicor.

7 Ecce circensium obstrepit clamor. Subita aliqua et universa voce feriuntur aures meae. Nec cogitationem meam excutiunt, ne interrumpunt quidem. Fremitum patientissime fero. Multae voces et in unum confusae pro fluctu mihi sunt aut vento silvam verberante et ceteris sine intellectu sonantibus.

8 Quid ergo est nunc, cui animum adiecerim? Dicam. Superest ex hesterno mihi cogitatio: quid sibi voluerint prudentissimi viri, qui rerum maximarum probationes levissimas et perplexas fecerunt, quae ut
9 sint verae, tamen mendacio similes sunt. Vult nos ab ebrietate deterrere Zenon, vir maximus, huius sectae fortissimae ac sanctissimae conditor. Audi ergo, quemadmodum colligat virum bonum non futurum ebrium: "ebrio secretum sermonem nemo committit; viro autem bono committit; ergo vir bonus ebrius non erit." Quemadmodum opposita interrogatione simili derideatur, adtende. Satis est enim unam

---

[a] The same word is used by Seneca in *De Tranq. An.* xvii. 7 *quidam medio die interiunxerunt et in postmeridianas horas aliquid levioris operae distulerunt.*

[b] *Cf. Ep.* lvi. 3 *istum fremitum non magis curo quam fluctum aut deiectum aquae.*

[c] Zeno, Frag. 229 von Arnim,—quoting also Philo's *εἰ τῷ μεθύοντι οὐκ ἄν τις εὐλόγως λόγον ἀπόρρητον παρακατάθοιτο . . . οὐκ ἄρα μεθύει ὁ ἀστεῖος.*

sun, at times when I am most robust and when there is not a flaw in my bodily processes. I have very little energy left for bathing. After the bath, some stale bread and breakfast without a table; no need to wash the hands after such a meal. Then comes a very short nap. You know my habit; I avail myself of a scanty bit of sleep, — unharnessing, as it were.[a] For I am satisfied if I can just stop staying awake. Sometimes I know that I have slept; at other times, I have a mere suspicion.

Lo, now the din of the Races sounds about me! My ears are smitten with sudden and general cheering. But this does not upset my thoughts or even break their continuity. I can endure an uproar with complete resignation. The medley of voices blended in one note sounds to me like the dashing of waves,[b] or like the wind that lashes the tree-tops, or like any other sound which conveys no meaning.

What is it, then, you ask, to which I have been giving my attention? I will tell you. A thought sticks in my mind, left over from yesterday,—namely, what men of the greatest sagacity have meant when they have offered the most trifling and intricate proofs for problems of the greatest importance, — proofs which may be true, but none the less resemble fallacies. Zeno, that greatest of men, the revered founder of our brave and holy school of philosophy, wishes to discourage us from drunkenness. Listen, then, to his arguments proving that the good man will not get drunk: "No one entrusts a secret to a drunken man; but one will entrust a secret to a good man; therefore, the good man will not get drunk."[c] Mark how ridiculous Zeno is made when we set up a similar syllogism in contrast with his. There are

ponere ex multis: "dormienti nemo secretum sermonem committit; viro autem bono committit;
10 vir bonus ergo non dormit." Quo uno modo potest, Posidonius Zenonis nostri causam agit, sed ne sic quidem, ut existimo, agi potest. Ait enim ebrium duobus modis dici: altero, cum aliquis vino gravis est et inpos sui; altero, si solet ebrius fieri et huic obnoxius vitio est. Hunc a Zenone dici, qui soleat fieri ebrius, non qui sit. Huic autem neminem com-
11 missurum arcana, quae per vinum eloqui possit. Quod est falsum. Prima enim illa interrogatio conplectitur eum, qui est ebrius, non eum, qui futurus est. Plurimum enim interesse concedes et inter ebrium et ebriosum. Potest et qui ebrius est, tunc primum esse nec habere hoc vitium, et qui ebriosus est, saepe extra ebrietatem esse. Itaque id intellego, quod significari verbo isto solet, praesertim cum ab homine diligentiam professo ponatur et verba examinante. Adice nunc quod, si hoc intellexit Zenon et nos intellegere voluit, ambiguitate verbi quaesiit locum fraudi, quod faciendum non est, ubi veritas quaeritur.

12 Sed sane hoc senserit; quod sequitur, falsum est, ei qui soleat ebrius fieri, non committi sermonem secretum. Cogita enim, quam multis militibus non semper sobriis et imperator et tribunus et centurio

---

[a] *Cf. Ep.* xlix. 8 *quod non perdidisti, habes; cornua autem non perdidisti; cornua ergo habes*,—and the syllogisms given in *Ep.* xlviii.

many, but one will be enough : "No one entrusts a secret to a man when he is asleep ; but one entrusts a secret to a good man ; therefore, the good man does not go to sleep." [a] Posidonius pleads the cause of our master Zeno in the only possible way ; but it cannot, I hold, be pleaded even in this way. For Posidonius maintains that the word "drunken" is used in two ways,—in the one case of a man who is loaded with wine and has no control over himself; in the other, of a man who is accustomed to get drunk, and is a slave to the habit. Zeno, he says, meant the latter, —the man who is accustomed to get drunk, not the man who is drunk ; and no one would entrust to this person any secret, for it might be blabbed out when the man was in his cups. This is a fallacy. For the first syllogism refers to him who is actually drunk and not to him who is about to get drunk. You will surely admit that there is a great difference between a man who is drunk and a drunkard. He who is actually drunk may be in this state for the first time and may not have the habit, while the drunkard is often free from drunkenness. I therefore interpret the word in its usual meaning, especially since the syllogism is set up by a man who makes a business of the careful use of words, and who weighs his language. Moreover, if this is what Zeno meant, and what he wished it to mean to us, he was trying to avail himself of an equivocal word in order to work in a fallacy ; and no man ought to do this when truth is the object of inquiry.

But let us admit, indeed, that he meant what Posidonius says ; even so, the conclusion is false,— that secrets are not entrusted to an habitual drunkard. Think how many soldiers who are not always sober have been entrusted by a general or a captain or a centurion with messages which might not be divulged!

tacenda mandaverint. De illa C. Caesaris caede,
illius dico, qui superato Pompeio rem publicam
tenuit, tam creditum est Tillio Cimbro[1] quam C.
Cassio. Cassius tota vita aquam bibit, Tillius Cimber
et nimius erat in vino et scordalus. In hanc rem
locutus est ipse: "ego," inquit, "quemquam feram,
13 qui vinum ferre non possum?" Sibi quisque nunc
nominet eos, quibus scit et vinum male credi et
sermonem bene, unum tamen exemplum, quod
occurrit mihi, referam, ne intercidat. Instruenda
est enim vita exemplis inlustribus. Non semper
confugiamus ad vetera.

14 L. Piso, urbis custos, ebrius ex quo semel factus
est, fuit. Maiorem noctis partem in convivio
exigebat; usque in horam fere sextam dormiebat;
hoc eius erat matutinum. Officium tamen suum, quo
tutela urbis continebatur, diligentissime administravit.
Huic et divus Augustus dedit secreta mandata, cum
illum praeponeret Thraciae, quam perdomuit, et
Tiberius proficiscens in Campaniam, cum multa in
15 urbe et suspecta relinqueret et invisa. Puto, quia
illi bene cesserat Pisonis ebrietas, postea Cossum fecit
urbis praefectum, virum gravem, moderatum, sed
mersum et vino madentem, adeo ut ex senatu
aliquando, in quem e convivio venerat, obpressus
inexcitabili somno tolleretur. Huic tamen Tiberius

[1] *Tillio Cimbro* Muretus; *illi Cimbro* V; *illinc imbro* P; *illic imbro* b.

---

[a] In 11 B.C., when the Thracians were attacking Macedonia. The campaign lasted for three years, and Piso was rewarded with a triumph at its close.

With regard to the notorious plot to murder Gaius Caesar,—I mean the Caesar who conquered Pompey and got control of the state,—Tillius Cimber was trusted with it no less than Gaius Cassius. Now Cassius throughout his life drank water; while Tillius Cimber was a sot as well as a brawler. Cimber himself alluded to this fact, saying: "*I* carry a master? I cannot carry my liquor!" So let each one call to mind those who, to his knowledge, can be ill trusted with wine, but well trusted with the spoken word; and yet one case occurs to my mind, which I shall relate, lest it fall into oblivion. For life should be provided with conspicuous illustrations. Let us not always be harking back to the dim past.

Lucius Piso, the Director of Public Safety at Rome, was drunk from the very time of his appointment. He used to spend the greater part of the night at banquets, and would sleep until noon. That was the way he spent his morning hours. Nevertheless, he applied himself most diligently to his official duties, which included the guardianship of the city. Even the sainted Augustus trusted him with secret orders when he placed him in command of Thrace.[a] Piso conquered that country. Tiberius, too, trusted him when he took his holiday in Campania, leaving behind him in the city many a critical matter that aroused both suspicion and hatred. I fancy that it was because Piso's drunkenness turned out well for the Emperor that he appointed to the office of city prefect Cossus, a man of authority and balance, but so soaked and steeped in drink that once, at a meeting of the Senate, whither he had come after banqueting, he was overcome by a slumber from which he could not be roused, and had to be carried home. It was to this man that Tiberius sent many

multa sua manu scripsit, quae committenda ne ministris quidem suis iudicabat. Nullum Cosso aut privatum secretum aut publicum elapsum est.

16 Itaque declamationes istas de medio removeamus: "Non est animus in sua potestate ebrietate devinctus. Quemadmodum musto dolia ipsa rumpuntur et omne, quod in imo iacet, in summam partem vis caloris eiectat; sic vino exaestuante, quicquid in imo iacet abditum, effertur et prodit in medium. Onerati mero quemadmodum non continent cibum vino redundante, ita ne secretum quidem. Quod suum
17 alienumque est, pariter effundunt." Sed quamvis hoc soleat accidere, ita et illud solet, ut cum iis, quos sciamus libentius bibere, de rebus necessariis deliberemus. Falsum ergo est hoc, quod patrocinii loco ponitur, ei qui soleat ebrius fieri, non dari tacitum.

Quanto satius est aperte accusare ebrietatem et vitia eius exponere, quae etiam tolerabilis homo vitaverit, nedum perfectus ac sapiens, cui satis est sitim extinguere, qui, etiam si quando hortata est hilaritas aliena causa producta longius, tamen citra
18 ebrietatem resistit. Nam de illo videbimus, an sapientis animus nimio vino turbetur et faciat ebriis solita; interim, si hoc colligere vis virum bonum non debere ebrium fieri, cur syllogismis agis? Dic, quam turpe sit plus sibi ingerere quam capiat et stomachi sui non nosse mensuram, quam multa ebrii

orders, written in his own hand, — orders which he believed he ought not to trust even to the officials of his household. Cossus never let a single secret slip out, whether personal or public.

So let us abolish all such harangues as this: "No man in the bonds of drunkenness has power over his soul. As the very vats are burst by new wine, and as the dregs at the bottom are raised to the surface by the strength of the fermentation; so, when the wine effervesces, whatever lies hidden below is brought up and made visible. As a man overcome by liquor cannot keep down his food when he has over-indulged in wine, so he cannot keep back a secret either. He pours forth impartially both his own secrets and those of other persons." This, of course, is what commonly happens, but so does this,—that we take counsel on serious subjects with those whom we know to be in the habit of drinking freely. Therefore this proposition, which is laid down in the guise of a defence of Zeno's syllogism, is false,—that secrets are not entrusted to the habitual drunkard.

How much better it is to arraign drunkenness frankly and to expose its vices! For even the middling good man avoids them, not to mention the perfect sage, who is satisfied with slaking his thirst; the sage, even if now and then he is led on by good cheer which, for a friend's sake, is carried somewhat too far, yet always stops short of drunkenness. We shall investigate later the question whether the mind of the sage is upset by too much wine and commits follies like those of the toper; but meanwhile, if you wish to prove that a good man ought not to get drunk, why work it out by logic? Show how base it is to pour down more liquor than one can carry, and not to know the capacity of one's own stomach; show

faciant, quibus sobrii erubescant, nihil aliud esse ebrietatem quam voluntariam insaniam. Extende in plures dies illum ebrii habitum; numquid de furore
19 dubitabis? Nunc quoque non est minor, sed brevior.
Refer Alexandri Macedonis exemplum, qui Clitum, carissimum sibi ac fidelissimum, inter epulas transfodit et intellecto facinore mori voluit, certe debuit.[1]

Omne vitium ebrietas et incendit et detegit, obstantem malis conatibus verecundiam removet. Plures enim pudore peccandi quam bona voluntate
20 prohibitis abstinent. Ubi possedit animum nimia vis
vini, quicquid mali latebat, emergit. Non facit ebrietas vitia, sed protrahit; tunc libidinosus ne cubiculum quidem expectat, sed cupiditatibus suis quantum petierunt sine dilatione permittit; tunc inpudicus morbum profitetur ac publicat; tunc petulans non linguam, non manum continet. Crescit insolenti superbia, crudelitas saevo, malignitas livido.
21 Omne vitium laxatur[2] et prodit. Adice illam
ignorationem sui, dubia et parum explanata verba, incertos oculos, gradum errantem, vertiginem capitis, tecta ipsa mobilia velut aliquo turbine circumagente totam domum, stomachi tormenta, cum effervescit merum ac viscera ipsa distendit. Tunc tamen

[1] *debuit* Lipsius; *deruit* VPb; *meruit* Gruter.
[2] *laxatur* Lipsius; *taxatur* or *texatur* MSS.

---

[a] Like anger, which was interpreted by the ancients as "short-lived madness."

[b] For a dramatic account of the murder see Plutarch's *Alexander*, ch. 51.

[c] This is the firm conviction of Seneca, himself a most temperate man. §§ 14 and 15 admit that natural genius may triumph over drunkenness; § 17 may allow (with Chrysippus) a certain amount of hilarity; but the general conclusion is obvious.

how often the drunkard does things which make him blush when he is sober; state that drunkenness [a] is nothing but a condition of insanity purposely assumed. Prolong the drunkard's condition to several days; will you have any doubt about his madness? Even as it is, the madness is no less; it merely lasts a shorter time. Think of Alexander of Macedon,[b] who stabbed Clitus, his dearest and most loyal friend, at a banquet; after Alexander understood what he had done, he wished to die, and assuredly he ought to have died.

Drunkenness kindles and discloses every kind of vice, and removes the sense of shame that veils our evil undertakings.[c] For more men abstain from forbidden actions because they are ashamed of sinning than because their inclinations are good. When the strength of wine has become too great and has gained control over the mind, every lurking evil comes forth from its hiding-place. Drunkenness does not create vice, it merely brings it into view; at such times the lustful man does not wait even for the privacy of a bedroom, but without postponement gives free play to the demands of his passions; at such times the unchaste man proclaims and publishes his malady; at such times your cross-grained fellow does not restrain his tongue or his hand. The haughty man increases his arrogance, the ruthless man his cruelty, the slanderer his spitefulness. Every vice is given free play and comes to the front. Besides, we forget who we are, we utter words that are halting and poorly enunciated, the glance is unsteady, the step falters, the head is dizzy, the very ceiling moves about as if a cyclone were whirling the whole house, and the stomach suffers torture when the wine generates gas and causes our very bowels to swell.

utcumque tolerabile est, dum illi vis sua est; quid, cum somno vitiatur et quae ebrietas fuit, cruditas facta est?

22 Cogita, quas clades ediderit publica ebrietas; haec acerrimas gentes bellicosasque hostibus tradidit, haec multorum annorum pertinaci[1] bello defensa moenia patefecit, haec contumacissimos et iugum recusantes in alienum egit arbitrium, haec invictos acie mero
23 domuit. Alexandrum, cuius modo feci mentionem, tot itinera, tot proelia, tot hiemes, per quas victa temporum locorumque difficultate transierat, tot flumina ex ignoto cadentia, tot maria tutum dimiserunt; intemperantia bibendi et ille Herculaneus ac fatalis scyphus condidit.

24 Quae gloria est capere multum? Cum penes te palma fuerit et propinationes tuas strati somno ac vomitantes recusaverint, cum superstes toti convivio fueris, cum omnes viceris virtute magnifica et nemo
25 vini tam capax fuerit, vinceris a dolio. M. Antonium, magnum virum et ingenii nobilis, quae alia res perdidit et in externos mores ac vitia non Romana traiecit quam ebrietas nec minor vino Cleopatrae amor? Haec illum res hostem rei publicae, haec

[1] *pertinaci* later MSS.; *pertinacia* VPb.

[a] Lipsius quotes Athenaeus as saying that Boeotian silver cups of large size were so called because the Boeotian Hercules drank from them; Servius, however, on Verg. *Aen.* viii. 278, declared that the name was derived from the large wooden bowl brought by Hercules to Italy and used for sacrificial purposes.

However, at the time, these troubles can be endured, so long as the man retains his natural strength; but what can he do when sleep impairs his powers, and when that which was drunkenness becomes indigestion?

Think of the calamities caused by drunkenness in a nation! This evil has betrayed to their enemies the most spirited and warlike races; this evil has made breaches in walls defended by the stubborn warfare of many years; this evil has forced under alien sway peoples who were utterly unyielding and defiant of the yoke; this evil has conquered by the wine-cup those who in the field were invincible. Alexander, whom I have just mentioned, passed through his many marches, his many battles, his many winter campaigns (through which he worked his way by overcoming disadvantages of time or place), the many rivers which flowed from unknown sources, and the many seas, all in safety; it was intemperance in drinking that laid him low, and the famous death-dealing bowl of Hercules.[a]

What glory is there in carrying much liquor? When you have won the prize, and the other banqueters, sprawling asleep or vomiting, have declined your challenge to still other toasts; when you are the last survivor of the revels; when you have vanquished every one by your magnificent show of prowess and there is no man who has proved himself of so great capacity as you,—you are vanquished by the cask. Mark Antony was a great man, a man of distinguished ability; but what ruined him and drove him into foreign habits and un-Roman vices, if it was not drunkenness and—no less potent than wine—love of Cleopatra? This it was that made him an enemy of the state; this it was that rendered him

hostibus suis imparem reddidit; haec crudelem fecit, cum capita principum civitatis cenanti referrentur, cum inter apparatissimas epulas luxusque regales ora ac manus proscriptorum recognosceret, cum vino gravis sitiret tamen sanguinem. Intolerabile erat, quod ebrius fiebat, cum haec faceret; quanto intolerabilius, quod haec in ipsa ebrietate faciebat!

26 Fere vinolentiam crudelitas sequitur; vitiatur enim exasperaturque sanitas mentis. Ut querulos difficilesque[1] faciunt diutini morbi et ad minimam rabidos[2] offensionem, ita ebrietates continuae efferant animos. Nam cum saepe apud se non sint,[3] consuetudo insaniae durat et[4] vitia vino concepta etiam sine illo valent.

27 Dic ergo, quare sapiens non debeat ebrius fieri. Deformitatem rei et inportunitatem ostende rebus, non verbis. Quod facillimum est, proba istas, quae voluptates vocantur, ubi transcenderunt modum, poenas esse. Nam si illud argumentaberis, sapientem multo vino inebriari et retinere rectum tenorem, etiam si temulentus sit; licet colligas nec veneno poto moriturum nec sopore sumpto dormiturum nec elleboro accepto, quicquid in visceribus haerebit, eiecturum deiecturumque. Sed si temptantur pedes,

[1] *ut querulos difficilesque* Madvig; *quem difficilesque* VPb.
[2] *rabidos* Haupt; *radios* VPb; *habidos* Arg b.
[3] *sint* later MSS.; *sunt* VPb.
[4] *durat et* Wolters; *durata*, *duracta*, or *durat ac* MSS.

---

[a] "Antony gave orders to those that were to kill Cicero, to cut off his head and right hand . . . ; and, when they were brought before him, he regarded them joyfully, actually bursting out more than once into laughter, and, when he had satiated himself with the sight of them, ordered them to be hung up . . . in the forum" (Clough's translation of Plutarch's *Antony*, p. 172).

[b] A plant which possessed cathartic properties and was

no match for his enemies; this it was that made him cruel, when as he sat at table the heads of the leaders of the state were brought in; when amid the most elaborate feasts and royal luxury he would identify the faces and hands of men whom he had proscribed;[a] when, though heavy with wine, he yet thirsted for blood. It was intolerable that he was getting drunk while he did such things; how much more intolerable that he did these things while actually drunk! Cruelty usually follows wine-bibbing; for a man's soundness of mind is corrupted and made savage. Just as a lingering illness makes men querulous and irritable and drives them wild at the least crossing of their desires, so continued bouts of drunkenness bestialize the soul. For when people are often beside themselves, the habit of madness lasts on, and the vices which liquor generated retain their power even when the liquor is gone.

Therefore you should state why the wise man ought not to get drunk. Explain by facts, and not by mere words, the hideousness of the thing, and its haunting evils. Do that which is easiest of all—namely, demonstrate that what men call pleasures are punishments as soon as they have exceeded due bounds. For if you try to prove that the wise man can souse himself with much wine and yet keep his course straight, even though he be in his cups, you may go on to infer by syllogisms that he will not die if he swallows poison, that he will not sleep if he takes a sleeping-potion, that he will not vomit and reject the matter which clogs his stomach when you give him hellebore.[b] But, when a man's feet totter

widely used by the ancients. It was also applied in cases of mental derangement. The native Latin term is *veratrum*.

lingua non constat, quid est, quare illum existimes in parte sobrium esse, in parte ebrium? Vale.

LXXXIV.

Seneca Lvcilio svo salvtem

1 Itinera ista, quae segnitiam mihi excutiunt, et valitudini meae prodesse iudico et studiis. Quare valitudinem adiuvent, vides: cum pigrum me[1] et neglegentem corporis litterarum amor faciat, aliena opera exerceor; studio quare prosint, indicabo: a lectionibus nihil[2] recessi. Sunt autem, ut existimo, necessariae, primum ne sim me uno contentus; deinde ut, cum ab aliis quaesita cognovero, tum et de inventis iudicem et cogitem de inveniendis. Alit lectio ingenium et studio fatigatum, non sine studio
2 tamen, reficit. Nec scribere tantum nec tantum legere debemus; altera res contristabit vires et exhauriet, de stilo dico, altera solvet ac diluet. Invicem hoc et illo commeandum est et alterum altero temperandum, ut quicquid lectione collectum est, stilus redigat in corpus.

3 Apes, ut aiunt, debemus imitari, quae vagantur et flores ad mel faciendum idoneos carpunt, deinde quicquid attulere, disponunt ac per favos digerunt et, ut Vergilius noster ait,

[1] *me* later MSS.; *viae* VPb.
[2] *nihil* added by Buecheler, omitted by VPb.

[a] A considerable part of this letter is found in the preface to the *Saturnalia* of Macrobius, without any acknowledgment of indebtedness.

and his tongue is unsteady, what reason have you for believing that he is half sober and half drunk? Farewell.

LXXXIV. ON GATHERING IDEAS[a]

The journeys to which you refer—journeys that shake the laziness out of my system—I hold to be profitable both for my health and for my studies. You see why they benefit my health: since my passion for literature makes me lazy and careless about my body, I can take exercise by deputy; as for my studies, I shall show you why my journeys help them, for I have not stopped my reading in the slightest degree. And reading, I hold, is indispensable—primarily, to keep me from being satisfied with myself alone, and besides, after I have learned what others have found out by their studies, to enable me to pass judgment on their discoveries and reflect upon discoveries that remain to be made. Reading nourishes the mind and refreshes it when it is wearied with study; nevertheless, this refreshment is not obtained without study. We ought not to confine ourselves either to writing or to reading; the one, continuous writing, will cast a gloom over our strength, and exhaust it; the other will make our strength flabby and watery. It is better to have recourse to them alternately, and to blend one with the other, so that the fruits of one's reading may be reduced to concrete form by the pen.

We should follow, men say, the example of the bees, who flit about and cull the flowers that are suitable for producing honey, and then arrange and assort in their cells all that they have brought in; these bees, as our Vergil says,

liquentia mella
Stipant et dulci distendunt nectare cellas.

4 De illis non satis constat, utrum sucum ex floribus ducant, qui protinus mel sit, an quae collegerunt, in hunc saporem mixtura quadam et proprietate spiritus sui mutent. Quibusdam enim placet non faciendi mellis scientiam esse illis, sed colligendi. Aiunt inveniri apud Indos mel in arundinum foliis, quod aut ros illius caeli aut ipsius arundinis umor dulcis et pinguior gignat. In nostris quoque herbis vim eandem, sed minus manifestam et notabilem poni, quam persequatur et contrahat animal huic rei genitum. Quidam existimant conditura et dispositione in hanc qualitatem verti, quae ex tenerrimis virentium florentiumque decerpserint, non sine quodam, ut ita dicam, fermento, quo in unum diversa coalescunt.

5 Sed ne ad aliud quam de quo agitur abducar,[1] nos quoque has apes debemus imitari et quaecumque ex diversa lectione congessimus, separare, melius enim distincta servantur, deinde adhibita ingenii nostri cura et facultate in unum saporem varia illa libamenta confundere, ut etiam si apparuerit, unde sumptum sit, aliud tamen esse quam unde sumptum est, appareat. Quod in corpore nostro videmus sine
6 ulla opera nostra facere naturam: alimenta, quae

[1] *abducar* Erasmus; *adducar* VPb.

---

[a] *Aeneid*, i. 432 f.

[b] Cf. *mel in harundinibus collectum* (from India) in Pliny, *N.H.* xii. 32 (Summers).

pack close the flowing honey,
And swell their cells with nectar sweet.[a]

It is not certain whether the juice which they obtain from the flowers forms at once into honey, or whether they change that which they have gathered into this delicious object by blending something therewith and by a certain property of their breath. For some authorities believe that bees do not possess the art of making honey, but only of gathering it; and they say that in India honey has been found on the leaves of certain reeds, produced by a dew peculiar to that climate, or by the juice of the reed itself, which has an unusual sweetness and richness.[b] And in our own grasses too, they say, the same quality exists, although less clear and less evident; and a creature born to fulfil such a function could hunt it out and collect it. Certain others maintain that the materials which the bees have culled from the most delicate of blooming and flowering plants is transformed into this peculiar substance by a process of preserving and careful storing away, aided by what might be called fermentation,—whereby separate elements are united into one substance.

But I must not be led astray into another subject than that which we are discussing. We also, I say, ought to copy these bees, and sift whatever we have gathered from a varied course of reading, for such things are better preserved if they are kept separate; then, by applying the supervising care with which our nature has endowed us,—in other words, our natural gifts,—we should so blend those several flavours into one delicious compound that, even though it betrays its origin, yet it nevertheless is clearly a different thing from that whence it came. This is what we see nature doing in our own bodies without any labour

accepimus, quamdiu in sua qualitate perdurant et solida innatant stomacho, onera sunt; at cum ex eo, quod erant, mutata sunt, tum demum in vires et in sanguinem transeunt. Idem in his, quibus aluntur ingenia, praestemus, ut quaecumque hausimus, non
7 patiamur integra esse, ne aliena sint. Concoquamus illa; alioqui in memoriam ibunt, non in ingenium. Adsentiamur illis fideliter et nostra faciamus, ut unum quiddam fiat ex multis, sicut unus numerus fit ex singulis, cum minores summas et dissidentes conputatio una comprendit. Hoc faciat animus noster: omnia, quibus est adiutus, abscondat, ipsum
8 tantum ostendat, quod effecit. Etiam si cuius in te comparebit similitudo, quem admiratio tibi altius fixerit, similem esse te volo quomodo filium, non quomodo imaginem; imago res mortua est.

"Quid ergo? Non intellegetur, cuius imiteris orationem, cuius argumentationem, cuius sententias?" Puto aliquando ne intellegi quidem posse, si imago vera sit; haec enim[1] omnibus, quae ex quo velut exemplari traxit, formam suam inpressit, ut in uni-
9 tatem illa conpetant.[2] Non vides, quam multorum vocibus chorus constet? Unus tamen ex omnibus redditur; aliqua illic acuta est, aliqua gravis, aliqua

[1] *si imago vera sit; haec enim* Madvig; *si magni viri nec enim* VPb.

[2] *competant* later MSS.; *conparavit* or *conpetat* MSS.

---

[a] The same figure is used with reference to reading, in *Ep.* ii. 2 f., *non prodest cibus nec corpori accedit, qui statim sumptus emittitur*, etc.

on our part; the food we have eaten, as long as it retains its original quality and floats in our stomachs as an undiluted mass, is a burden;[a] but it passes into tissue and blood only when it has been changed from its original form. So it is with the food which nourishes our higher nature,—we should see to it that whatever we have absorbed should not be allowed to remain unchanged, or it will be no part of us. We must digest it; otherwise it will merely enter the memory and not the reasoning power. Let us loyally welcome such foods and make them our own, so that something that is one may be formed out of many elements, just as one number is formed of several elements whenever, by our reckoning, lesser sums, each different from the others, are brought together. This is what our mind should do: it should hide away all the materials by which it has been aided, and bring to light only what it has made of them. Even if there shall appear in you a likeness to him who, by reason of your admiration, has left a deep impress upon you, I would have you resemble him as a child resembles his father, and not as a picture resembles its original; for a picture is a lifeless thing.

"What," you say, "will it not be seen whose style you are imitating, whose method of reasoning, whose pungent sayings?" I think that sometimes it is impossible for it to be seen who is being imitated, if the copy is a true one; for a true copy stamps its own form upon all the features which it has drawn from what we may call the original, in such a way that they are combined into a unity. Do you not see how many voices there are in a chorus? Yet out of the many only one voice results. In that chorus one voice takes the tenor, another the bass,

media. Accedunt viris feminae, interponuntur tibiae.
10 Singulorum illic latent voces, omnium apparent. De choro dico, quem veteres philosophi noverant; in commissionibus nostris plus cantorum est quam in theatris olim spectatorum fuit. Cum omnes vias ordo canentium inplevit et cavea aenatoribus[1] cincta est et ex pulpito omne tibiarum genus organorumque consonuit, fit concentus ex dissonis.

Talem animum nostrum esse volo; multae in illo artes, multa praecepta sint, multarum aetatum
11 exempla, sed in unum conspirata. "Quomodo," inquis, "hoc effici poterit?" Adsidua intentione; si nihil egerimus nisi ratione suadente. Hanc si audire volueris, dicet tibi: relinque ista iamdudum, ad quae discurritur. Relinque divitias, aut periculum possidentium aut onus. Relinque corporis atque animi voluptates; molliunt et enervant. Relinque ambitum; tumida res est, vana, ventosa, nullum habet terminum, tam sollicita est, ne quem ante se videat, quam ne quem post se.[2] Laborat invidia et quidem duplici; vides autem, quam miser sit, si is cui invidetur et invidet.

12 Intueris illas potentium domos, illa tumultuosa rixa salutantium limina? Multum habent contu-

[1] *aenatoribus* Buecheler; *aeneatoribus* VPb; *cantoribus* Arg.b; *a venatoribus* later MSS.
[2] *ne quem post se* Hense; *ne se* VPb; *ne post se* later MSS.

---

[a] *Commissio* means an entertainment, or a concert; cf. Pliny, *Panegyric* 54, *ludis et commissionibus*

another the baritone. There are women, too, as well as men, and the flute is mingled with them. In that chorus the voices of the individual singers are hidden; what we hear is the voices of all together. To be sure, I am referring to the chorus which the old-time philosophers knew; in our present-day exhibitions[a] we have a larger number of singers than there used to be spectators in the theatres of old. All the aisles are filled with rows of singers; brass instruments surround the auditorium; the stage resounds with flutes and instruments of every description; and yet from the discordant sounds a harmony is produced.

I would have my mind of such a quality as this; it should be equipped with many arts, many precepts, and patterns of conduct taken from many epochs of history; but all should blend harmoniously into one. "How," you ask, "can this be accomplished?" By constant effort, and by doing nothing without the approval of reason. And if you are willing to hear her voice, she will say to you: "Abandon those pursuits which heretofore have caused you to run hither and thither. Abandon riches, which are either a danger or a burden to the possessor. Abandon the pleasures of the body and of the mind; they only soften and weaken you. Abandon your quest for office; it is a swollen, idle, and empty thing, a thing that has no goal, as anxious to see no one outstrip it as to see no one at its heels. It is afflicted with envy, and in truth with a twofold envy; and you see how wretched a man's plight is if he who is the object of envy feels envy also."

Do you behold yonder homes of the great, yonder thresholds uproarious with the brawling of those who would pay their respects? They have many

meliarum, ut intres, plus, cum intraveris. Praeteri istos gradus divitum et magno adgestu suspensa vestibula; non in praerupto tantum istic stabis, sed in lubrico. Huc potius te ad sapientiam derige tranquillissimasque res eius et simul amplissimas pete.
13 Quaecumque videntur eminere in rebus humanis, quamvis pusilla sint et comparatione humillimorum extent, per difficiles tamen et arduos tramites adeuntur. Confragosa in fastigium dignitatis via est; at si conscendere hunc verticem libet, cui se fortuna summisit, omnia quidem sub te, quae pro excelsissimis habentur, aspicies, sed tamen venies ad summa per planum. Vale.

LXXXV.

Seneca Lvcilio svo salvtem

1 Peperceram tibi et quicquid nodosi adhuc super erat, praeterieram, contentus quasi gustum tibi dare eorum, quae a nostris dicuntur, ut probetur virtus ad explendam beatam vitam sola satis efficax. Iubes me quicquid est interrogationum aut nostrarum aut ad traductionem nostram excogitatarum comprendere. Quod si facere voluero, non erit epistula, sed liber. Illud totiens testor, hoc me argumentorum genere

---

[a] For such treatment cf. Juvenal iii. 152 f.—

> Nil habet infelix paupertas durius in se
> Quam quod ridiculos homines facit, etc.

[b] Such as that in *Ep.* lxxxiii. 9 (constructed, however, by Seneca himself) *dormienti nemo secretum sermonem committit*, etc. See *ad loc.* and *n.*

an insult[a] for you as you enter the door, and still more after you have entered. Pass by the steps that mount to rich men's houses, and the porches rendered hazardous by the huge throng; for there you will be standing, not merely on the edge of a precipice but also on slippery ground. Instead of this, direct your course hither to wisdom, and seek her ways, which are ways of surpassing peace and plenty. Whatever seems conspicuous in the affairs of men—however petty it may really be and prominent only by contrast with the lowest objects—is nevertheless approached by a difficult and toilsome pathway. It is a rough road that leads to the heights of greatness; but if you desire to scale this peak, which lies far above the range of Fortune, you will indeed look down from above upon all that men regard as most lofty, but none the less you can proceed to the top over level ground. Farewell.

LXXXV. ON SOME VAIN SYLLOGISMS

I had been inclined to spare you, and had omitted any knotty problems that still remained undiscussed; I was satisfied to give you a sort of taste of the views held by the men of our school, who desire to prove that virtue is of itself sufficiently capable of rounding out the happy life. But now you bid me include the entire bulk either of our own syllogisms or of those which have been devised[b] by other schools for the purpose of belittling us. If I shall be willing to do this, the result will be a book, instead of a letter. And I declare again and again that I take no pleasure in such proofs. I am ashamed to

non delectari. Pudet in aciem descendere pro dis hominibusque susceptam subula armatum.

2 "Qui prudens est, et temperans est. Qui temperans est, et constans. Qui constans est, inperturbatus est. Qui inperturbatus est, sine tristitia est. Qui sine tristitia est, beatus est; ergo prudens beatus est et prudentia ad beatam vitam satis est."

3 Huic collectioni hoc modo Peripatetici quidam respondent, ut inperturbatum et constantem et sine tristitia sic interpretentur, tamquam inperturbatus dicatur, qui raro perturbatur et modice, non qui numquam. Item sine tristitia eum dici aiunt, qui non est obnoxius tristitiae nec frequens nimiusve in hoc vitio. Illud enim humanam naturam negare, alicuius animum inmunem esse tristitia. Sapientem non vinci maerore, ceterum tangi. Et cetera in hunc modum

4 sectae suae respondentia. Non his tollunt adfectus, sed temperant. Quantulum autem sapienti damus, si inbecillissimis fortior est et maestissimis laetior et effrenatissimis moderatior et humillimis maior? Quid, si miretur velocitatem suam Ladas[1] ad claudos debilesque respiciens?

Illa vel intactae segetis per summa volaret
Gramina nec cursu teneras laesisset aristas,
Vel mare per medium fluctu suspensa tumenti
Ferret iter celeres nec tingueret aequore plantas.

[1] *Ladas* Lipsius; *laudans* VPb.

---

[a] Cf. *Ep.* lxxxii. 24 *subula leonem excipis?*

[b] E. V. Arnold (*Roman Stoicism*, p. 333) calls attention to the passion of anger, for example, which the Peripatetics believed should be kept under control, but not stamped out.

[c] Vergil, *Aeneid*, vii. 808 ff. The lines describe Camilla, the Volscian warrior-huntress.

enter the arena and undertake battle on behalf of gods and men armed only with an awl.[a]

"He that possesses prudence is also self-restrained; he that possesses self-restraint is also unwavering; he that is unwavering is unperturbed; he that is unperturbed is free from sadness; he that is free from sadness is happy. Therefore, the prudent man is happy, and prudence is sufficient to constitute the happy life."

Certain of the Peripatetics[b] reply to this syllogism by interpreting "unperturbed," "unwavering," and "free from sadness" in such a way as to make "unperturbed" mean one who is rarely perturbed and only to a moderate degree, and not one who is never perturbed. Likewise, they say that a person is called "free from sadness" who is not subject to sadness, one who falls into this objectionable state not often nor in too great a degree. It is not, they say, the way of human nature that a man's spirit should be exempt from sadness, or that the wise man is not overcome by grief but is merely touched by it, and other arguments of this sort, all in accordance with the teachings of their school. They do not abolish the passions in this way; they only moderate them. But how petty is the superiority which we attribute to the wise man, if he is merely braver than the most craven, happier than the most dejected, more self-controlled than the most unbridled, and greater than the lowliest! Would Ladas boast his swiftness in running by comparing himself with the halt and the weak?

> For she could skim the topmost blades of corn
> And touch them not, nor bruise the tender ears;
> Or travel over seas, well-poised above
> The swollen floods, nor dip her flying feet
> In ocean's waters.[c]

Haec est pernicitas per se aestimata, non quae tardis-
simorum conlatione laudatur. Quid, si sanum voces
leviter febricitantem? Non est bona valitudo medio-
5 critas morbi. "Sic," inquit, "sapiens inperturbatus
dicitur, quomodo apyrina dicuntur, non quibus nulla
inest duritia granorum, sed quibus minor." Falsum
est. Non enim deminutionem malorum in bono viro
intellego, sed vacationem; nulla debent esse, non
parva. Nam si ulla sunt, crescent et interim in-
pedient. Quomodo oculos maior et perfecta suffusio
excaecat, sic modica turbat.

6 Si das aliquos adfectus sapienti, inpar illis erit
ratio et velut torrente quodam auferetur, praesertim
cum illi non unum adfectum des,[1] cum quo con-
luctetur, sed omnis. Plus potest quamvis mediocrium
7 turba quam posset unius magni violentia. Habet
pecuniae cupiditatem, sed modicam. Habet ambitionem, sed non concitatam. Habet iracundiam,
sed placabilem. Habet inconstantiam, sed minus
vagam ac mobilem. Habet libidinem non insanam.
Melius cum illo ageretur, qui unum vitium integrum
haberet, quam cum eo, qui leviora quidem, sed omnia.
8 Deinde nihil interest, quam magnus sit adfectus;

[1] *des* later MSS.; *sed* Pb; *sit* corr. from *sed* V.

---

[a] Seneca uses *suffusio* of jaundice in *Ep.* xcv. 16. Celsus, vii. 7. 14, explains the cause of cataracts, *vel ex morbo vel e ictu concrescit humor*, and outlines the treatment.

This is speed estimated by its own standard, not the kind which wins praise by comparison with that which is slowest. Would you call a man well who has a light case of fever? No, for good health does not mean moderate illness. They say, "The wise man is called unperturbed in the sense in which pomegranates are called mellow—not that there is no hardness at all in their seeds, but that the hardness is less than it was before." That view is wrong; for I am not referring to the gradual weeding out of evils in a good man, but to the complete absence of evils; there should be in him no evils at all, not even any small ones. For if there are any, they will grow, and as they grow will hamper him. Just as a large and complete cataract [a] wholly blinds the eyes, so a medium-sized cataract dulls their vision.

If by your definition the wise man has any passions whatever, his reason will be no match for them and will be carried swiftly along, as it were, on a rushing stream,—particularly if you assign to him, not one passion with which he must wrestle, but all the passions. And a throng of such, even though they be moderate, can affect him more than the violence of one powerful passion. He has a craving for money, although in a moderate degree. He has ambition, but it is not yet fully aroused. He has a hot temper, but it can be appeased. He has inconstancy, but not the kind that is very capricious or easily set in motion. He has lust, but not the violent kind. We could deal better with a person who possessed one full-fledged vice, than with one who possessed all the vices, but none of them in extreme form. Again, it makes no difference how great the passion is; no matter what its size may

quantuscumque est, parere nescit, consilium non accipit. Quemadmodum rationi nullum animal optemperat, non ferum, non domesticum et mite, natura enim illorum est surda suadenti; sic non secuntur, non audiunt adfectus, quantulicumque sunt. Tigres leonesque numquam feritatem exuunt, aliquando summittunt, et cum minime expectaveris, exasperatur torvitas mitigata. Numquam bona fide
9 vitia mansuescunt. Deinde, si ratio proficit, ne incipient quidem adfectus; si invita ratione coeperint, invita perseverabunt. Facilius est enim initia illorum prohibere quam impetum regere. Falsa est itaque ista mediocritas et inutilis, eodem loco habenda, quo si quis diceret modice insaniendum, modice
10 aegrotandum. Sola virtus habet, non recipiunt animi mala temperamentum. Facilius sustuleris illa quam rexeris. Numquid dubium est, quin vitia mentis humanae inveterata et dura, quae morbos vocamus, inmoderata sint, ut avaritia, ut crudelitas, ut inpotentia[1]? Ergo inmoderati sunt et adfectus.
11 Ab his enim ad illa transitur. Deinde si das aliquid iuris tristitiae, timori, cupiditati, ceteris motibus[2] pravis, non erunt in nostra potestate. Quare? Quia extra nos sunt, quibus inritantur. Itaque crescent, prout magnas habuerint[3] minoresve causas, quibus concitentur. Maior erit timor, si plus, quo exterreatur, aut propius aspexerit, acrior cupiditas, quo

[1] *inpietas*, after *inpotentia*, removed by Madvig as a gloss; *inpotentia* later MSS.; *innocentia* VPb; *inimicitia* V^2.
[2] *motibus* later MSS.; *moribus* VPb.
[3] *habuerint* later MSS.; *habuerunt* VPb.

[a] Another reply to the Peripatetic claim of § 3.

be, it knows no obedience, and does not welcome advice.[a] Just as no animal, whether wild or tamed and gentle, obeys reason, since nature made it deaf to advice; so the passions do not follow or listen, however slight they are. Tigers and lions never put off their wildness; they sometimes moderate it, and then, when you are least prepared, their softened fierceness is roused to madness. Vices are never genuinely tamed. Again, if reason prevails, the passions will not even get a start; but if they get under way against the will of reason, they will maintain themselves against the will of reason. For it is easier to stop them in the beginning than to control them when they gather force. This half-way ground is accordingly misleading and useless; it is to be regarded just as the declaration that we ought to be "moderately" insane, or "moderately" ill. Virtue alone possesses moderation; the evils that afflict the mind do not admit of moderation. You can more easily remove than control them. Can one doubt that the vices of the human mind, when they have become chronic and callous ("diseases" we call them), are beyond control, as, for example, greed, cruelty, and wantonness? Therefore the passions also are beyond control; for it is from the passions that we pass over to the vices. Again, if you grant any privileges to sadness, fear, desire, and all the other wrong impulses, they will cease to lie within our jurisdiction. And why? Simply because the means of arousing them lie outside our own power. They will accordingly increase in proportion as the causes by which they are stirred up are greater or less. Fear will grow to greater proportions, if that which causes the terror is seen to be of greater magnitude or in closer proximity; and desire will grow keener

12 illam amplioris rei spes evocaverit. Si in nostra potestate non est, an sint adfectus, ne illud quidem est, quanti sint; si ipsis permisisti incipere, cum causis suis crescent tantique erunt, quanti fient. Adice nunc, quod ista, quamvis exigua sint, in maius excedunt. Numquam perniciosa servant modum. Quamvis levia initia morborum serpunt et aegra corpora minima interdum mergit accessio.

13 Illud vero cuius dementiae est, credere, quarum rerum extra nostrum arbitrium posita principia sunt, earum nostri esse arbitrii terminos? Quomodo ad id finiendum satis valeo, ad quod prohibendum parum valui, cum facilius sit excludere quam admissa com-
14 primere? Quidam ita distinxerunt, ut dicerent: "Temperans ac prudens positione quidem mentis et habitu tranquillus est, eventu non est. Nam, quantum ad habitum mentis suae, non perturbatur, nec contristatur nec timet, sed multae extrinsecus causae
15 incidunt, quae illi perturbationem adferant." Tale est, quod volunt dicere: iracundum quidem illum non esse, irasci tamen aliquando; et timidum quidem non esse, timere tamen aliquando; id est, vitio timoris carere, adfectu non carere. Quod si recipitur, usu frequenti timor transibit in vitium, et ira in

[a] For this topic of emotions as possible sources of the vices *cf.* Cicero, *Tusc.* iv. 10 *ex perturbationibus autem primum morbi conficiuntur. . . . Hoc loco nimium operae consumitur a Stoicis.*

in proportion as the hope of a greater gain has summoned it to action. If the existence of the passions is not in our own control, neither is the extent of their power; for if you once permit them to get a start, they will increase along with their causes, and they will be of whatever extent they shall grow to be. Moreover, no matter how small these vices are, they grow greater. That which is harmful never keeps within bounds. No matter how trifling diseases are at the beginning, they creep on apace; and sometimes the slightest augmentation of disease lays low the enfeebled body!

But what folly it is, when the beginnings of certain things are situated outside our control, to believe that their endings are within our control! How have I the power to bring something to a close, when I have not had the power to check it at the beginning? For it is easier to keep a thing out than to keep it under after you have let it in. Some men have made a distinction as follows, saying: "If a man has self-control and wisdom, he is indeed at peace as regards the attitude and habit of his mind, but not as regards the outcome. For, as far as his habit of mind is concerned, he is not perturbed, or saddened, or afraid; but there are many extraneous causes which strike him and bring perturbation upon him." What they mean to say is this: "So-and-so is indeed not a man of an angry disposition, but still he sometimes gives way to anger," and "He is not, indeed, inclined to fear, but still he sometimes experiences fear"; in other words, he is free from the fault, but is not free from the passion of fear. If, however, fear is once given an entrance, it will by frequent use pass over into a vice;[a] and anger, once admitted into the mind, will

animum admissa habitum illum ira carentis animi
16 retexet. Praeterea si non contemnit venientes extrinsecus causas et aliquid timet, cum fortiter eundum erit adversus tela, ignes, pro patria, legibus, libertate, cunctanter exibit et animo recedente. Non cadit
17 autem in sapientem haec diversitas mentis.

Illud praeterea iudico observandum, ne duo, quae separatim probanda sunt, misceamus. Per se enim colligitur unum bonum esse, quod honestum, per se rursus, ad vitam beatam satis esse virtutem. Si unum bonum est, quod honestum, omnes concedunt ad beate vivendum sufficere virtutem; e contrario non remittetur, si beatum sola virtus facit, unum bonum esse,
18 quod honestum est. Xenocrates et Speusippus putant beatum vel sola virtute fieri posse, non tamen unum bonum esse, quod honestum est. Epicurus quoque iudicat eum qui[1] virtutem habeat, beatum esse, sed ipsam virtutem non satis esse ad beatam vitam, quia beatum efficiat voluptas, quae ex virtute est, non ipsa virtus. Inepta distinctio. Idem enim negat umquam virtutem esse sine voluptate; ita si ei iuncta semper est atque inseparabilis, et sola satis est. Habet enim secum voluptatem, sine qua non
19 est, etiam cum sola est. Illud autem absurdum est, quod dicitur beatum quidem futurum vel sola virtute, non futurum autem perfecte beatum. Quod quem-

[1] *iudicat eum qui* Koch, on the authority of MSS. cited by Fickert; *iudicat cum* MSS.

---

[a] Representing the views of the Academic School.
[b] Frag. 508 Usener.

alter the earlier habit of a mind that was formerly free from anger. Besides, if the wise man, instead of despising all causes that come from without, ever fears anything, when the time arrives for him to go bravely to meet the spear, or the flames, on behalf of his country, his laws, and his liberty, he will go forth reluctantly and with flagging spirit. Such inconsistency of mind, however, does not suit the character of a wise man.

Then, again, we should see to it that two principles which ought to be tested separately should not be confused. For the conclusion is reached independently that that alone is good which is honourable, and again independently the conclusion that virtue is sufficient for the happy life. If that alone is good which is honourable, everyone agrees that virtue is sufficient for the purpose of living happily; but, on the contrary, if virtue alone makes men happy, it will not be conceded that that alone is good which is honourable. Xenocrates [a] and Speusippus [a] hold that a man can become happy even by virtue alone, not, however, that that which is honourable is the only good. Epicurus also decides [b] that one who possesses virtue is happy, but that virtue of itself is not sufficient for the happy life, because the pleasure that results from virtue, and not virtue itself, makes one happy. This is a futile distinction. For the same philosopher declares that virtue never exists without pleasure; and therefore, if virtue is always connected with pleasure and always inseparable therefrom, virtue is of itself sufficient. For virtue keeps pleasure in its company, and does not exist without it, even when alone. But it is absurd to say that a man will be happy by virtue alone, and yet not absolutely happy. I

admodum fieri possit, non reperio. Beata enim vita bonum in se perfectum habet, inexsuperabile. Quod si est, perfecte beata est.

Si deorum vita nihil habet maius aut melius, beata
autem vita divina est; nihil habet, in quod amplius
20 possit attolli. Praeterea si beata vita nullius est in-
digens, omnis beata vita perfecta est eademque est
et beata et beatissima. Numquid dubitas, quin beata
vita summum bonum sit? Ergo si summum bonum
habet, summe beata est. Quemadmodum summum
bonum adiectionem non recipit (quid enim supra
summum erit?), ita ne beata quidem vita, quae sine
summo bono non est. Quod si aliquem magis beatum
induxeris, induces et multo magis; innumerabilia discrimina summi boni facies, cum summum bonum in-
21 tellegam, quod supra se gradum non habet. Si est
aliquis minus beatus quam alius, sequitur, ut hic
alterius vitam beatioris magis concupiscat quam
suam. Beatus autem nihil suae praefert. Utrum-
libet ex his incredibile est: aut aliquid beato restare,
quod esse quam quod est malit, aut id illum non
malle, quod illo[1] melius est. Utique enim quo
prudentior est, hoc magis se ad id, quod est optimum,
extendet et id omni modo consequi cupiet. Quomodo
autem beatus est, qui cupere etiamnunc potest, immo
22 qui debet? Dicam, quid sit, ex quo veniat hic error:

[1] *illo* later MSS.; *illa* VPb.

cannot discover how that may be, since the happy life contains in itself a good that is perfect and cannot be excelled. If a man has this good, life is completely happy.

Now if the life of the gods contains nothing greater or better, and the happy life is divine, then there is no further height to which a man can be raised. Also, if the happy life is in want of nothing, then every happy life is perfect; it is happy and at the same time most happy. Have you any doubt that the happy life is the Supreme Good? Accordingly, if it possesses the Supreme Good, it is supremely happy. Just as the Supreme Good does not admit of increase (for what will be superior to that which is supreme?), exactly so the happy life cannot be increased either; for it is not without the Supreme Good. If then you bring in one man who is "happier" than another, you will also bring in one who is "much happier"; you will then be making countless distinctions in the Supreme Good; although I understand the Supreme Good to be that good which admits of no degree above itself. If one person is less happy than another, it follows that he eagerly desires the life of that other and happier man in preference to his own. But the happy man prefers no other man's life to his own. Either of these two things is incredible: that there should be anything left for a happy man to wish for in preference to what is, or that he should not prefer the thing which is better than what he already has. For certainly, the more prudent he is, the more he will strive after the best, and he will desire to attain it by every possible means. But how can one be happy who is still able, or rather who is still bound, to crave something else? I will tell you what is the

nesciunt beatam vitam unam esse. In optimo illam statu ponit qualitas sua, non magnitudo. Itaque in aequo est longa et brevis, diffusa et angustior, in multa loca multasque partes distributa et in unum coacta. Qui illam numero aestimat et mensura et partibus, id illi, quod habet eximium, eripit. Quid autem est in beata vita eximium? Quod plena est.
23 Finis, ut puto, edendi bibendique satietas est. Hic plus edit, ille minus; quid refert? Uterque iam satur est. Hic plus bibit, ille minus; quid refert? Uterque non sitit. Hic pluribus annis vixit, hic paucioribus; nihil interest, si tam illum multi anni beatum fecerunt quam hunc pauci. Ille, quem tu minus beatum vocas, non est beatus; non potest nomen inminui.

24 "Qui fortis est, sine timore est. Qui sine timore est, sine tristitia est. Qui sine tristitia est, beatus est." Nostrorum haec interrogatio est. Adversus hanc sic respondere conantur: falsam nos rem et controversiosam pro confessa vindicare, eum, qui fortis est, sine timore esse. "Quid ergo?" inquit, "fortis inminentia mala non timebit? Istuc dementis alienatique, non fortis est. Ille vero," inquit, "moderatissime timet, sed in totum extra metum non est."
25 Qui hoc dicunt, rursus in idem revolvuntur, ut illis

[a] The happy life constitutes virtue; and virtue, as Seneca says so often, is absolute, permitting neither increase nor diminution.

source of this error: men do not understand that the happy life is a unit; for it is its essence, and not its extent, that establishes such a life on the noblest plane. Hence there is complete equality between the life that is long and the life that is short, between that which is spread out and that which is confined, between that whose influence is felt in many places and in many directions, and that which is restricted to one interest. Those who reckon life by number, or by measure, or by parts, rob it of its distinctive quality. Now, in the happy life, what is the distinctive quality? It is its fulness.[a] Satiety, I think, is the limit to our eating or drinking. A eats more and B eats less; what difference does it make? Each is now sated. Or A drinks more and B drinks less; what difference does it make? Each is no longer thirsty. Again, A lives for many years and B for fewer; no matter, if only A's many years have brought as much happiness as B's few years. He whom you maintain to be "less happy" is not happy; the word admits of no diminution.

"He who is brave is fearless; he who is fearless is free from sadness; he who is free from sadness is happy." It is our own school which has framed this syllogism; they attempt to refute it by this answer, namely, that we Stoics are assuming as admitted a premiss which is false and distinctly controverted,—that the brave man is fearless. "What!" they say, "will the brave man have no fear of evils that threaten him? That would be the condition of a madman, a lunatic, rather than of a brave man. The brave man will, it is true, feel fear in only a very slight degree; but he is not absolutely free from fear." Now those who assert this are doubling back to their old argument, in that they regard

virtutum loco sint minora vitia. Nam qui timet quidem, sed rarius et minus, non caret malitia, sed leviore vexatur. "At enim dementem puto, qui mala imminentia non extimescit." Verum est, quod dicis, si mala sunt; sed si scit mala illa non esse et unam tantum turpitudinem malum iudicat, debebit secure pericula aspicere et aliis timenda contemnere. Aut si stulti et amentis est mala non timere, quo quis
26 prudentior est, hoc timebit magis. "Ut vobis," inquit, "videtur, praebebit se periculis fortis." Minime; non timebit illa, sed vitabit. Cautio illum decet, timor non decet. "Quid ergo?" inquit, "mortem, vincla, ignes, alia tela fortunae non timebit?" Non. Scit enim illa non esse mala, sed videri. Omnia ista
27 humanae vitae formidines[1] putat. Describe captivitatem, verbera, catenas, egestatem et membrorum lacerationes vel per morbum vel per iniuriam et quicquid aliud adtuleris: inter lymphatos metus numerat. Ista timidis timenda sunt. An id existimas malum, ad quod aliquando nobis nostra sponte veniendum est?

28 Quaeris quid sit malum? Cedere iis, quae mala vocantur, et illis libertatem suam dedere, pro qua

[1] Hense would add *inanes* after either *humanae* or *formidines*.

---

[a] *i.e.*, thereby allowing the aforesaid increase or diminution in virtue.

[b] For the argument compare *Ep.* lxxxii. 7 ff.—the topic, *contra mortem te praeparare.*

vices of less degree as equivalent to virtues.[a] For indeed the man who does feel fear, though he feels it rather seldom and to a slight degree, is not free from wickedness, but is merely troubled by it in a milder form. "Not so," is the reply, "for I hold that a man is mad if he does not fear evils which hang over his head." What you say is perfectly true, if the things which threaten are really evils; but if he knows that they are not evils and believes that the only evil is baseness, he will be bound to face dangers without anxiety and to despise things which other men cannot help fearing. Or, if it is the characteristic of a fool and a madman not to fear evils, then the wiser a man is the more he will fear such things! "It is the doctrine of you Stoics, then," they reply, "that a brave man will expose himself to dangers." By no means; he will merely not fear them, though he will avoid them. It is proper for him to be careful, but not to be fearful.[b] "What then? Is he not to fear death, imprisonment, burning, and all the other missiles of Fortune?" Not at all; for he knows that they are not evils, but only seem to be. He reckons all these things as the bugbears of man's existence. Paint him a picture of slavery, lashes, chains, want, mutilation by disease or by torture,—or anything else you may care to mention; he will count all such things as terrors caused by the derangement of the mind. These things are only to be feared by those who are fearful. Or do you regard as an evil that to which some day we may be compelled to resort of our own free will?

What then, you ask, is an evil? It is the yielding to those things which are called evils; it is the surrendering of one's liberty into their control, when really we ought to suffer all things in order to pre-

cuncta patienda sunt. Perit libertas, nisi illa contemnimus, quae nobis iugum inponunt. Non dubitarent, quid conveniret forti viro, si scirent, quid esset fortitudo. Non est enim inconsulta temeritas nec periculorum amor nec formidabilium adpetitio; scientia est distinguendi, quid sit malum et quid non sit. Diligentissima in tutela sui[1] fortitudo est et eadem patientissima eorum, quibus falsa species
29 malorum est. "Quid ergo? Si ferrum intentatur cervicibus viri fortis, si pars subinde alia atque alia suffoditur, si viscera sua in sinu suo vidit, si ex intervallo, quo magis tormenta sentiat, repetitur et per adsiccata viscera recens demittitur sanguis, non timet? Istum tu dices nec dolere?" Iste vero dolet. Sensum enim hominis nulla exuit virtus. Sed non timet; invictus ex alto dolores suos spectat. Quaeris quis tunc animus illi sit? Qui aegrum amicum adhortantibus.

30 "Quod malum est, nocet. Quod nocet, deteriorem facit. Dolor et paupertas deteriorem non faciunt; ergo mala non sunt." "Falsum est," inquit, "quod proponitis; non enim, si quid nocet, etiam deteriorem facit. Tempestas et procella nocet gubernatori, non
31 tamen illum deteriorem facit." Quidam e Stoicis ita adversus hoc respondent: deteriorem fieri guberna-

[1] *sui* later MSS.; *vi* VPb.

[a] Besides this definition (a standard Stoic one) of the third cardinal virtue, we also find "a knowledge of what to choose and what to avoid," "knowing how to endure things," and finally "the will to undertake great enterprises."

serve this liberty. Liberty is lost unless we despise those things which put the yoke upon our necks. If men knew what bravery was, they would have no doubts as to what a brave man's conduct should be. For bravery is not thoughtless rashness, or love of danger, or the courting of fear-inspiring objects; it is the knowledge which enables us to distinguish between that which is evil and that which is not.[a] Bravery takes the greatest care of itself, and likewise endures with the greatest patience all things which have a false appearance of being evils. "What then?" is the query; "if the sword is brandished over your brave man's neck, if he is pierced in this place and in that continually, if he sees his entrails in his lap, if he is tortured again after being kept waiting in order that he may thus feel the torture more keenly, and if the blood flows afresh out of bowels where it has but lately ceased to flow, has he no fear? Shall you say that he has felt no pain either?" Yes, he has felt pain; for no human virtue can rid itself of feelings. But he has no fear; unconquered he looks down from a lofty height upon his sufferings. Do you ask me what spirit animates him in these circumstances? It is the spirit of one who is comforting a sick friend.

"That which is evil does harm; that which does harm makes a man worse. But pain and poverty do not make a man worse; therefore they are not evils." "Your proposition," says the objector, "is wrong; for what harms one does not necessarily make one worse. The storm and the squall work harm to the pilot, but they do not make a worse pilot of him for all that." Certain of the Stoic school reply to this argument as follows: "The pilot becomes a worse pilot because of storms or

torem tempestate ac procella, quia non possit id, quod proposuit, efficere nec tenere cursum suum; deteriorem illum in arte sua non fieri, in opere fieri. Quibus Peripateticus "ergo," inquit, "et sapientem deteriorem faciet paupertas, dolor et quicquid aliud tale fuerit. Virtutem enim illi non eripiet, sed opera
32 eius inpediet." Hoc recte diceretur, nisi dissimilis esset gubernatoris condicio et sapientis. Huic enim propositum est in vita agenda non utique, quod temptat, efficere, sed omnia recte facere. Gubernatori propositum est utique navem in portum perducere. Artes ministrae sunt, praestare debent, quod promittunt. Sapientia domina rectrixque est; artes serviunt vitae, sapientia imperat.

33 Ego aliter respondendum iudico: nec artem gubernatoris deteriorem ulla tempestate fieri nec ipsam administrationem artis. Gubernator tibi non felicitatem promisit, sed utilem operam et navis regendae scientiam. Haec eo magis apparet, quo illi magis aliqua fortuita vis obstitit. Qui hoc potuit dicere "Neptune, numquam hanc navem nisi rectam," arti satis fecit; tempestas non opus gubernatoris impedit, sed succes-
34 sum. "Quid ergo?" inquit, "non nocet gubernatori ea res, quae illum tenere portum vetat, quae conatus eius inritos efficit, quae aut refert illum aut detinet

[a] *Cf.* Diogenes Laertius, ii. 79 *τοὺς τῶν ἐγκυκλίων παιδευμάτων μετασχόντας, φιλοσοφίας δὲ ἀπολειφθέντας, ὁμοίους ἔλεγεν εἶναι τοῖς τῆς Πηνελόπης μνηστῆρσιν.*

[b] The figure of the pilot is a frequent one in philosophy, from Plato down. See Seneca, *Ep.* viii. 4. The same argument, as applied to the musician, is found in *Ep.* lxxxvii. 12 ff.

squalls, inasmuch as he cannot carry out his purpose and hold to his course; as far as his art is concerned, he becomes no worse a pilot, but in his work he does become worse." To this the Peripatetics retort: "Therefore, poverty will make even the wise man worse, and so will pain, and so will anything else of that sort. For although those things will not rob him of his virtue, yet they will hinder the work of virtue." This would be a correct statement, were it not for the fact that the pilot and the wise man are two different kinds of person. The wise man's purpose in conducting his life is not to accomplish at all hazards what he tries, but to do all things rightly; the pilot's purpose, however, is to bring his ship into port at all hazards. The arts are handmaids;[a] they must accomplish what they promise to do. But wisdom is mistress and ruler. The arts render a slave's service to life; wisdom issues the commands.

For myself, I maintain that a different answer should be given: that the pilot's art is never made worse by the storm, nor the application of his art either. The pilot has promised you, not a prosperous voyage, but a serviceable performance of his task—that is, an expert knowledge of steering a ship. And the more he is hampered by the stress of fortune, so much the more does his knowledge become apparent. He who has been able to say, "Neptune, you shall never sink this ship except on an even keel,"[b] has fulfilled the requirements of his art; the storm does not interfere with the pilot's work, but only with his success. "What then," you say, "is not a pilot harmed by any circumstance which does not permit him to make port, frustrates all his efforts, and either carries him out to sea, or

et exarmat?" Non tamquam gubernatori, sed tamquam naviganti nocet; alioqui gubernator ille non est.
Gubernatoris[1] artem adeo non inpedit, ut ostendat;
tranquillo enim, ut aiunt, quilibet gubernator est.
Navigio ista obsunt, non rectori eius, qua rector est.
35 Duas personas habet gubernator: alteram communem
cum omnibus, qui eandem conscenderunt navem: ipse
quoque vector est; alteram propriam: gubernator
est. Tempestas tamquam vectori nocet, non tam-
36 quam gubernatori. Deinde gubernatoris ars alienum
bonum est: ad eos, quos vehit, pertinet, quomodo
medici ad eos, quos curat. Commune bonum est
sapientis[2]: est et eorum, cum quibus vivit, et proprium ipsius. Itaque gubernatori fortasse noceatur,[3]
cuius ministerium aliis[4] promissum tempestate in-
37 peditur; sapienti non nocetur a paupertate, non a
dolore, non ab aliis tempestatibus vitae. Non enim
prohibentur opera eius omnia, sed tantum ad
alios pertinentia; ipse semper in actu est, in
effectu tunc maximus, cum illi fortuna se opposuit.
Tunc enim ipsius sapientiae negotium agit, quam
38 diximus et alienum bonum esse et suum. Praeterea ne aliis quidem tunc prodesse prohibetur,
cum illum aliquae necessitates premunt. Propter
paupertatem prohibetur docere, quemadmodum
tractanda res publica sit, at illud docet, quemadmodum sit tractanda paupertas. Per totam vitam
opus eius extenditur.

Ita nulla fortuna, nulla res actus sapientis excludit.

[1] *alioqui gubernator ille non est. gubernatoris* Buecheler; *alioquin gubernatis* V; *alioqui ƀnatoris* P.

[2] *est sapientis* added by Hense.

[3] *noceatur* Schweighaeuser; *noceat* MSS.

[4] *aliis* later MSS.; *abiis* VP; *abhis* b.

holds the ship in irons, or strips her masts?" No, it does not harm him as a pilot, but only as a voyager; otherwise, he is no pilot. It is indeed so far from hindering the pilot's art that it even exhibits the art; for anyone, in the words of the proverb, is a pilot on a calm sea. These mishaps obstruct the voyage but not the steersman *qua* steersman. A pilot has a double rôle: one he shares with all his fellow-passengers, for he also is a passenger; the other is peculiar to him, for he is the pilot. The storm harms him as a passenger, but not as a pilot. Again, the pilot's art is another's good—it concerns his passengers just as a physician's art concerns his patients. But the wise man's good is a common good—it belongs both to those in whose company he lives, and to himself also. Hence our pilot may perhaps be harmed, since his services, which have been promised to others, are hindered by the storm; but the wise man is not harmed by poverty, or by pain, or by any other of life's storms. For all his functions are not checked, but only those which pertain to others; he himself is always in action, and is greatest in performance at the very time when fortune has blocked his way. For then he is actually engaged in the business of wisdom; and this wisdom I have declared already to be both the good of others, and also his own. Besides, he is not prevented from helping others, even at the time when constraining circumstances press him down. Because of his poverty he is prevented from showing how the State should be handled; but he teaches, none the less, how poverty should be handled. His work goes on throughout his whole life.

Thus no fortune, no external circumstance, can shut off the wise man from action. For the very

Id enim ipsum agit, quo alia agere prohibetur. Ad
utrosque casus aptus est: bonorum rector est, malo-
39 rum victor. Sic, inquam, se exercuit, ut virtutem
tam in secundis quam in adversis exhiberet nec
materiam eius, sed ipsam intueretur. Itaque nec
paupertas illum nec dolor nec quicquid aliud imperitos avertit et praecipites agit, prohibet. Tu illum
40 premi putas malis? Utitur. Non ex ebore tantum
Phidias sciebat facere simulacra; faciebat ex aere.
Si marmor illi, si adhuc viliorem materiam obtulisses,
fecisset, quale ex illa fieri optimum posset. Sic
sapiens virtutem, si licebit, in divitiis explicabit, si
minus, in paupertate; si poterit, in patria, si minus,
in exilio; si poterit, imperator, si minus, miles; si
poterit, integer, si minus, debilis. Quamcumque
fortunam acceperit, aliquid ex illa memorabile efficiet.
41 Certi sunt domitores ferarum, qui saevissima animalia et ad occursum expavescenda[1] hominem pati
subigunt[2] nec asperitatem excussisse contenti usque
in contubernium mitigant. Leonibus magister manum
insertat, osculatur tigrim suus custos, elephantum
minimus Aethiops iubet subsidere in genua et ambulare per funem. Sic sapiens artifex est domandi
mala. Dolor, egestas, ignominia, carcer, exilium

[1] *expavescenda* Gertz; *expavescentia* VPb.
[2] *subigunt* Ludwig von Jan; *sub iugum* VPb.

---

[a] *Cf. De Ben.* i. 5 *leonum ora a magistris inpune tractantur.*
[b] *Cf.* Suet. *Galba* 6: at the Floralia *Galba novum spectaculi genus elephantos funambulos edidit*; also *id. Nero*, 11, and Pliny, *N.H.* viii. 2.

thing which engages his attention prevents him from attending to other things. He is ready for either outcome: if it brings goods, he controls them; if evils, he conquers them. So thoroughly, I mean, has he schooled himself that he makes manifest his virtue in prosperity as well as in adversity, and keeps his eyes on virtue itself, not on the objects with which virtue deals. Hence neither poverty, nor pain, nor anything else that deflects the inexperienced and drives them headlong, restrains him from his course. Do you suppose that he is weighed down by evils? He makes use of them. It was not of ivory only that Phidias knew how to make statues; he also made statues of bronze. If you had given him marble, or a still meaner material, he would have made of it the best statue that the material would permit. So the wise man will develop virtue, if he may, in the midst of wealth, or, if not, in poverty; if possible, in his own country—if not, in exile; if possible, as a commander—if not, as a common soldier; if possible, in sound health—if not, enfeebled. Whatever fortune he finds, he will accomplish therefrom something noteworthy.

Animal-tamers are unerring; they take the most savage animals, which may well terrify those who encounter them, and subdue them to the will of man; not content with having driven out their ferocity, they even tame them so that they dwell in the same abode. The trainer puts his hand into the lion's mouth[a]; the tiger is kissed by his keeper. The tiny Aethiopian orders the elephant to sink down on its knees, or to walk the rope.[b] Similarly, the wise man is a skilled hand at taming evils. Pain, want, disgrace, imprisonment, exile,—these are universally to be

ubique horrenda, cum ad hunc pervenere, mansueta sunt. Vale.

LXXXVI.

Seneca Lvcilio svo salvtem

1 In ipsa Scipionis Africani villa iacens haec tibi scribo adoratis manibus eius et ara, quam sepulchrum esse tanti viri suspicor. Animum quidem eius in caelum, ex quo erat, redisse persuadeo mihi, non quia magnos exercitus duxit, hos enim et Cambyses furiosus ac furore feliciter usus habuit, sed ob egregiam moderationem pietatemque, quam magis in illo admirabilem iudico, cum reliquit patriam, quam cum defendit; aut Scipio Romae esse debebat aut Roma
2 in libertate. "Nihil," inquit, "volo derogare legibus, nihil institutis. Aequum inter omnes cives ius sit. Utere sine me beneficio meo, patria. Causa tibi libertatis fui, ero et argumentum; exeo, si plus quam tibi expedit, crevi."

3 Quidni ego admirer hanc magnitudinem animi, qua in exilium voluntarium secessit et civitatem exoneravit? Eo perducta res erat, ut aut libertas Scipioni aut Scipio libertati faceret iniuriam. Neutrum fas erat. Itaque locum dedit legibus et se

---

[a] See *Ep.* li. 11.

[b] *Cf.* Livy xxxviii. 53 *morientem rure eo ipso loco sepeliri se iussisse ferunt monumentumque ibi aedificari.*

[c] Herodotus iii. 25 ἐμμανής τε ἐὼν καὶ οὐ φρενήρης.

feared; but when they encounter the wise man, they are tamed. Farewell.

LXXXVI. ON SCIPIO'S VILLA

I am resting at the country-house which once belonged to Scipio Africanus[a] himself; and I write to you after doing reverence to his spirit and to an altar which I am inclined to think is the tomb[b] of that great warrior. That his soul has indeed returned to the skies, whence it came, I am convinced, not because he commanded mighty armies—for Cambyses also had mighty armies, and Cambyses was a madman[c] who made successful use of his madness—but because he showed moderation and a sense of duty to a marvellous extent. I regard this trait in him as more admirable after his withdrawal from his native land than while he was defending her; for there was the alternative: Scipio should remain in Rome, or Rome should remain free. "It is my wish," said he, "not to infringe in the least upon our laws, or upon our customs; let all Roman citizens have equal rights. O my country, make the most of the good that I have done, but without me. I have been the cause of your freedom, and I shall also be its proof; I go into exile, if it is true that I have grown beyond what is to your advantage!"

What can I do but admire this magnanimity, which led him to withdraw into voluntary exile and to relieve the state of its burden? Matters had gone so far that either liberty must work harm to Scipio, or Scipio to liberty. Either of these things was wrong in the sight of heaven. So he gave way

Liternum recepit tam suum exilium rei publicae inputaturus quam Hannibalis.

4 Vidi villam extructam lapide quadrato, murum circumdatum silvae, turres quoque in propugnaculum villae utrimque subrectas, cisternam aedificiis ac viridibus subditam, quae sufficere in usum vel exercitus posset, balneolum angustum, tenebricosum ex consuetudine antiqua; non videbatur maioribus nostris caldum nisi obscurum. Magna ergo me voluptas
5 subiit contemplantem mores Scipionis ac nostros. In hoc angulo ille Carthaginis horror, cui Roma debet, quod tantum semel capta est, abluebat corpus laboribus rusticis fessum. Exercebat enim opere se terramque, ut mos fuit priscis, ipse subigebat. Sub hoc ille tecto tam sordido stetit, hoc illum pavimentum tam vile sustinuit.

6 At nunc quis est, qui sic lavari sustineat? Pauper sibi videtur ac sordidus, nisi parietes magnis et pretiosis orbibus refulserunt, nisi Alexandrina marmora Numidicis crustis distincta sunt, nisi illis undique operosa et in picturae modum variata circumlitio praetexitur, nisi vitro absconditur camera, nisi Thasius lapis, quondam rarum in aliquo spectaculum templo, piscinas nostras circumdedit, in quas multa sudatione corpora exinanita[1] demittimus, nisi aquam argentea

[1] *exinanita* edd.; *exsaniata* Hense, with MSS.

[a] Livy's account (see above) dwells more on the unwillingness of Scipio and his friends to permit the great conqueror to suffer the indignities of a trial.

[b] A phrase frequent in Roman literature; see Lucretius iii. 1034 *Scipiadas, belli fulmen, Carthaginis horror.*

[c] Porphyry, basalt, etc.

[d] *i.e.*, the so-called *giallo antico*, with red and yellow tints predominating.

[e] A white variety, from Thasos, an island off the Thracian coast.

to the laws and withdrew to Liternum, thinking to make the state a debtor for his own exile no less than for the exile of Hannibal.[a]

I have inspected the house, which is constructed of hewn stone; the wall which encloses a forest; the towers also, buttressed out on both sides for the purpose of defending the house; the well, concealed among buildings and shrubbery, large enough to keep a whole army supplied; and the small bath, buried in darkness according to the old style, for our ancestors did not think that one could have a hot bath except in darkness. It was therefore a great pleasure to me to contrast Scipio's ways with our own. Think, in this tiny recess the "terror of Carthage,"[b] to whom Rome should offer thanks because she was not captured more than once, used to bathe a body wearied with work in the fields! For he was accustomed to keep himself busy and to cultivate the soil with his own hands, as the good old Romans were wont to do. Beneath this dingy roof he stood; and this floor, mean as it is, bore his weight.

But who in these days could bear to bathe in such a fashion? We think ourselves poor and mean if our walls are not resplendent with large and costly mirrors; if our marbles from Alexandria[c] are not set off by mosaics of Numidian stone,[d] if their borders are not faced over on all sides with difficult patterns, arranged in many colours like paintings; if our vaulted ceilings are not buried in glass; if our swimming-pools are not lined with Thasian marble,[e] once a rare and wonderful sight in any temple—pools into which we let down our bodies after they have been drained weak by abundant perspiration; and finally, if the water has not poured from silver

7 epitonia fuderunt. Et adhuc plebeias fistulas loquor; quid, cum ad balnea libertinorum pervenero? Quantum statuarum, quantum columnarum est nihil sustinentium, sed in ornamentum positarum inpensae causa! Quantum aquarum per gradus cum fragore labentium! Eo deliciarum pervenimus, ut nisi gemmas calcare nolimus.

8 In hoc balneo Scipionis minimae sunt rimae magis quam fenestrae muro lapideo exsectae, ut sine iniuria munimenti lumen admitterent; at nunc blattaria vocant balnea, si qua non ita aptata sunt, ut totius diei solem fenestris amplissimis recipiant, nisi et lavantur simul et colorantur, nisi ex solio agros ac maria prospiciunt. Itaque quae concursum et admirationem habuerant, cum dedicarentur, devitantur et in[1] antiquorum numerum reiciuntur, cum aliquid novi luxuria
9 commenta est, quo ipsa se obrueret. At olim et pauca erant balnea nec ullo cultu exornata. Cur enim exornaretur res quadrantaria et in usum, non in oblectamentum reperta? Non suffundebatur aqua nec recens semper velut ex calido fonte currebat, nec referre credebant, in quam perlucida sordes
10 deponerent. Sed, di boni, quam iuvat illa balinea intrare obscura et gregali tectorio inducta, quae scires

[1] *dedicarentur, devitantur et in* Hense; *dedicarentur et in* VPb.

---

[a] *Cf.* Pliny, *Ep.* ii. 17. 12 *piscina, ex qua natantes mare aspiciunt.*

spigots. I have so far been speaking of the ordinary bathing-establishments; what shall I say when I come to those of the freedmen? What a vast number of statues, of columns that support nothing, but are built for decoration, merely in order to spend money! And what masses of water that fall crashing from level to level! We have become so luxurious that we will have nothing but precious stones to walk upon.

In this bath of Scipio's there are tiny chinks—you cannot call them windows—cut out of the stone wall in such a way as to admit light without weakening the fortifications; nowadays, however, people regard baths as fit only for moths if they have not been so arranged that they receive the sun all day long through the widest of windows, if men cannot bathe and get a coat of tan at the same time, and if they cannot look out from their bath-tubs over stretches of land and sea.[a] So it goes; the establishments which had drawn crowds and had won admiration when they were first opened are avoided and put back in the category of venerable antiques as soon as luxury has worked out some new device, to her own ultimate undoing. In the early days, however, there were few baths, and they were not fitted out with any display. For why should men elaborately fit out that which costs a penny only, and was invented for use, not merely for delight? The bathers of those days did not have water poured over them, nor did it always run fresh as if from a hot spring; and they did not believe that it mattered at all how perfectly pure was the water into which they were to leave their dirt. Ye gods, what a pleasure it is to enter that dark bath, covered with a common sort of roof, knowing that therein your hero Cato,

Catonem tibi aedilem aut Fabium Maximum aut ex Corneliis aliquem manu sua temperasse? Nam hoc quoque nobilissimi aediles fungebantur officio intrandi ea loca, quae populum receptabant, exigendique munditias et utilem ac salubrem temperaturam, non hanc, quae nuper inventa est similis incendio, adeo quidem, ut convictum in aliquo scelere servum vivum lavari oporteat. Nihil mihi videtur iam interesse, ardeat balineum an caleat.

11 Quantae nunc aliqui rusticitatis damnant Scipionem, quod non in caldarium suum latis specularibus diem admiserat, quod non in multa luce decoquebatur et expectabat,[1] ut in balneo concoqueret. O hominem calamitosum! Nesciit[2] vivere. Non saccata aqua lavabatur, sed saepe turbida et, cum plueret vehementius, paene lutulenta. Nec multum eius intererat, an[3] sic lavaretur; veniebat enim ut
12 sudorem illic ablueret, non ut unguentum. Quas nunc quorundam voces futuras credis? "Non invideo Scipioni; vere in exilio vixit, qui sic lavabatur." Immo, si scias, non cotidie lavabatur. Nam, ut aiunt, qui priscos mores urbis tradiderunt, brachia et crura cotidie abluebant, quae scilicet sordes opere collegerant, ceterum toti nundinis lavabantur. Hoc loco dicet aliquis: "olim[4] liquet mihi inmundissimos fuisse. Quid putas illos oluisse?" Militiam, laborem,

[1] *expectabat* later MSS.; *spectabat* VPb.
[2] *nesciit* Gothofredus; *nescit* VPb.
[3] *an* later MSS.; *ac* VPb.
[4] *aliquis: olim* Hense; *aliquotis*, *aliquo*, *aliquis* MSS.

[a] *e.g.*, Varro, in the *Catus*: *balneum non cotidianum.*

as aedile, or Fabius Maximus, or one of the Cornelii, has warmed the water with his own hands! For this also used to be the duty of the noblest aediles —to enter these places to which the populace resorted, and to demand that they be cleaned and warmed to a heat required by considerations of use and health, not the heat that men have recently made fashionable, as great as a conflagration — so much so, indeed, that a slave condemned for some criminal offence now ought to be *bathed* alive! It seems to me that nowadays there is no difference between "the bath is on fire," and "the bath is warm."

How some persons nowadays condemn Scipio as a boor because he did not let daylight into his perspiring-room through wide windows, or because he did not roast in the strong sunlight and dawdle about until he could stew in the hot water! "Poor fool," they say, "he did not know how to live! He did not bathe in filtered water; it was often turbid, and after heavy rains almost muddy!" But it did not matter much to Scipio if he had to bathe in that way; he went there to wash off sweat, not ointment. And how do you suppose certain persons will answer me? They will say: "I don't envy Scipio; that was truly an exile's life—to put up with baths like those!" Friend, if you were wiser, you would know that Scipio did not bathe every day. It is stated by those[a] who have reported to us the old-time ways of Rome that the Romans washed only their arms and legs daily—because those were the members which gathered dirt in their daily toil—and bathed all over only once a week. Here someone will retort: "Yes; pretty dirty fellows they evidently were! How they must have smelled!" But they smelled of the camp, the farm, and heroism. Now that

virum. Postquam munda balnea inventa sunt, spur-
13 ciores sunt. Descripturus infamem et nimiis[1] notabilem deliciis Horatius Flaccus quid ait?

Pastillos Buccillus olet.[a]

Dares nunc Buccillum; proinde esset ac si hircum oleret, Gargonii loco esset, quem idem Horatius Buccillo opposuit. Parum est sumere unguentum, nisi bis die terque renovatur, ne evanescat in corpore. Quid, quod hoc odore tamquam suo gloriantur?

14 Haec si tibi nimium tristia videbuntur, villae inputabis, in qua didici ab Aegialo, diligentissimo patre familiae, is enim nunc huius agri possessor est, quamvis vetus arbustum posse transferri. Hoc nobis senibus discere necessarium est, quorum nemo non olivetum alteri ponit. Quod vidi illud arborum trimum
15 et quadrimum fastidiendi fructus aut deponere.[2] Te quoque proteget illa, quae

Tarda venit seris factura nepotibus umbram,

ut ait Vergilius noster, qui non quid verissime, sed quid decentissime diceretur aspexit nec agricolas
16 docere voluit, sed legentes delectare. Nam, ut alia omnia transeam, hoc quod mihi hodie necesse fuit deprehendere, adscribam:

[1] *nimiis* Lipsius; *nimis* VPb.
[2] The passage *quod vidi . . . aut deponere* is hopelessly corrupt.

---

[a] Horace calls him Rufillus (*Sat.* i. 2. 27): *pastillos Rufillus olet, Gargonius hircum.*
[b] This seems to be the general meaning of the passage.
[c] *Georgics*, ii. 58.

spick-and-span bathing establishments have been devised, men are really fouler than of yore. What says Horatius Flaccus, when he wishes to describe a scoundrel, one who is notorious for his extreme luxury? He says: "Buccillus[a] smells of perfume." Show me a Buccillus in these days; his smell would be the veritable goat-smell—he would take the place of the Gargonius with whom Horace in the same passage contrasted him. It is nowadays not enough to use ointment, unless you put on a fresh coat two or three times a day, to keep it from evaporating on the body. But why should a man boast of this perfume as if it were his own?

If what I am saying shall seem to you too pessimistic, charge it up against Scipio's country-house, where I have learned a lesson from Aegialus, a most careful householder and now the owner of this estate; he taught me that a tree can be transplanted, no matter how far gone in years. We old men must learn this precept; for there is none of us who is not planting an olive-yard for his successor. I have seen them bearing fruit in due season after three or four years of unproductiveness.[b] And you too shall be shaded by the tree which

> Is slow to grow, but bringeth shade to cheer
> Your grandsons in the far-off years,[c]

as our poet Vergil says. Vergil sought, however, not what was nearest to the truth, but what was most appropriate, and aimed, not to teach the farmer, but to please the reader. For example, omitting all other errors of his, I will quote the passage in which it was incumbent upon me to-day to detect a fault:

Vere fabis satio est: tunc te quoque, medica, putres
Accipiunt sulci, et milio venit annua cura.[a]

An uno[1] tempore ista ponenda sint et an utriusque verna sit satio, hinc aestimes licet: Iunius mensis est, quo tibi scribo, iam proclivis in Iulium; eodem die vidi fabam metentes, milium serentes.

17 Ad olivetum revertar, quod vidi duobus modis depositum[2]: magnarum arborum truncos circumcisis ramis et ad unum redactis pedem cum rapo suo transtulit amputatis radicibus, relicto tantum capite ipso, ex quo illae pependerant. Hoc fimo tinctum in scrobem demisit, deinde terram non adgessit tantum,
18 sed calcavit et pressit. Negat quicquam esse hac, ut ait, pisatione[b] efficacius; videlicet frigus excludit et ventum. Minus praeterea movetur et ob hoc nascentes radices prodire patitur ac solum adprendere, quas necesse est cereas[3] adhuc et precario haerentes levis quoque revellat agitatio. Rapum[4] autem arboris, antequam obruat, radit.[5] Ex omni enim materia, quae nudata est, ut ait, radices exeunt novae. Non plures autem super terram eminere debet truncus quam tres aut quattuor pedes. Statim enim ab imo vestietur nec magna pars quemadmodum in olivetis
19 veteribus arida et retorrida erit. Alter ponendi modus hic fuit: ramos fortes nec corticis duri, quales esse novellarum arborum solent, eodem genere

[1] *an uno* later MSS.; *annuo* VPb.
[2] *depositum* Gronovius; *dispositum* VPb.
[3] *cereas* later MSS.; *ceteras* (*caeteras*) MSS.; *teneras* Erasmus.
[4] *rapum* Ludwig von Jan; *parum* MSS.
[5] *radit* Pincianus; *radix* MSS.

[a] *Georgics*, i. 215 f.
[b] In Vitruvius vii. 1 G reads *pinsatione*, referring to the pounding of stones for flooring.

EPISTLE LXXXVI.

> In spring sow beans ; then, too, O clover plant,
> Thou'rt welcomed by the crumbling furrows ; and
> The millet calls for yearly care.[a]

You may judge by the following incident whether those plants should be set out at the same time, or whether both should be sowed in the spring. It is June at the present writing, and we are well on towards July; and I have seen on this very day farmers harvesting beans and sowing millet.

But to return to our olive-yard again. I saw it planted in two ways. If the trees were large, Aegialus took their trunks and cut off the branches to the length of one foot each; he then transplanted along with the ball, after cutting off the roots, leaving only the thick part from which the roots hang. He smeared this with manure, and inserted it in the hole, not only heaping up the earth about it, but stamping and pressing it down. There is nothing, he says, more effective than this packing process[b]; in other words, it keeps out the cold and the wind. Besides, the trunk is not shaken so much, and for this reason the packing makes it possible for the young roots to come out and get a hold in the soil. These are of necessity still soft; they have but a slight hold, and a very little shaking uproots them. This ball, moreover, Aegialus lops clean before he covers it up. For he maintains that new roots spring from all the parts which have been shorn. Moreover, the trunk itself should not stand more than three or four feet out of the ground. For there will thus be at once a thick growth from the bottom, nor will there be a large stump, all dry and withered, as is the case with old olive-yards. The second way of setting them out was the following: he set out in similar fashion branches that were strong and of soft bark, as those

deposuit. Hi paulo tardius surgunt, sed cum tamquam a planta processerint, nihil habent in se abhorridum aut triste.

20 Illud etiamnunc vidi, vitem ex arbusto suo annosam transferri; huius capillamenta quoque, si fieri potest, colligenda sunt, deinde liberalius sternenda vitis, ut etiam ex corpore radicescat. Et vidi non tantum mense Februario positas, sed etiam Martio exacto; tenent et
21 conplexae sunt non suas ulmos. Omnes autem istas arbores, quae, ut ita dicam, grandiscapiae sunt, ait aqua adiuvandas cisternina, quae si prodest, habemus pluviam in nostra potestate.

Plura te docere non cogito, ne quemadmodum Aegialus me sibi adversarium paravit, sic ego parem te mihi. Vale.

LXXXVII.

Seneca Lucilio suo salutem

1 Naufragium, antequam navem adscenderem, feci. Quomodo acciderit, non adicio, ne et hoc putes inter Stoica paradoxa ponendum, quorum nullum esse falsum nec tam mirabile quam prima facie videtur, cum volueris, adprobabo, immo etiam si nolueris. Interim hoc me iter docuit, quam multa haberemus supervacua et quam facile iudicio possemus deponere,

---

[a] An agricultural term not elsewhere found.

[b] *i.e.*, on my journey I travelled with almost as meagre an equipment as a shipwrecked man.

[c] *Cf. Ep.* lxxxi. 11 and note.

of young saplings are wont to be. These grow a little more slowly, but, since they spring from what is practically a cutting, there is no roughness or ugliness in them.

This too I have seen recently—an aged vine transplanted from its own plantation. In this case, the fibres also should be gathered together, if possible, and then you should cover up the vine-stem more generously, so that roots may spring up even from the stock. I have seen such plantings made not only in February, but at the very end of March; the plants take hold of and embrace alien elms. But all trees, he declares, which are, so to speak, "thick-stemmed,"[a] should be assisted with tank-water; if we have this help, we are our own rain-makers.

I do not intend to tell you any more of these precepts, lest, as Aegialus did with me, I may be training you up to be my competitor. Farewell.

LXXXVII. SOME ARGUMENTS IN FAVOUR OF THE SIMPLE LIFE

"I was shipwrecked before I got aboard."[b] I shall not add how that happened, lest you may reckon this also as another of the Stoic paradoxes;[c] and yet I shall, whenever you are willing to listen, nay, even though you be unwilling, prove to you that these words are by no means untrue, nor so surprising as one at first sight would think. Meantime, the journey showed me this: how much we possess that is superfluous; and how easily we can make up our minds to do away with things whose

quae, si quando necessitas abstulit, non sentimus ablata.

2 Cum paucissimis servis, quos unum capere vehiculum potuit, sine ullis rebus, nisi quae corpore nostro continebantur, ego et Maximus meus biduum iam beatissimum agimus. Culcita in terra iacet, ego in culcita. Ex duabus paenulis altera stragulum, altera
3 opertorium facta est. De prandio nihil detrahi potuit; paratum fuit non magis hora, nusquam sine caricis, numquam sine pugillaribus. Illae, si panem habeo, pro pulmentario sunt, si non habeo, pro pane. Cotidie mihi annum novum faciunt, quem ego faustum et felicem reddo bonis cogitationibus et animi magnitudine, qui numquam maior est, quam ubi aliena seposuit et fecit sibi pacem nihil timendo, fecit sibi
4 divitias nihil concupiscendo. Vehiculum, in quod inpositus sum, rusticum est; mulae vivere se ambulando testantur; mulio excalceatus, non propter aestatem. Vix a me obtineo, ut hoc vehiculum velim[1] videri meum. Durat adhuc perversa recti verecundia, et quotiens in aliquem comitatum lautiorem incidimus, invitus erubesco, quod argumentum est ista, quae probo, quae laudo, nondum habere certam sedem et inmobilem. Qui sordido vehiculo erubescit, pretioso gloriabitur.

5 Parum adhuc profeci. Nondum audeo frugalitatem palam ferre. Etiamnunc curo opiniones viatorum.

[1] *velim* V[2]; *nolim* V[1]Pb, etc.

---

[a] As Pliny the Elder (a man of the same inquiring turn of mind) did on his journeys, Pliny, *Ep.* iii. 5. 15.

[b] *Caricae* were sent as New Year gifts, implying by their sweetness the good wishes of the sender.

loss, whenever it is necessary to part with them, we do not feel.

My friend Maximus and I have been spending a most happy period of two days, taking with us very few slaves—one carriage-load—and no paraphernalia except what we wore on our persons. The mattress lies on the ground, and I upon the mattress. There are two rugs—one to spread beneath us and one to cover us. Nothing could have been subtracted from our luncheon; it took not more than an hour to prepare, and we were nowhere without dried figs, never without writing tablets.[a] If I have bread, I use figs as a relish; if not, I regard figs as a substitute for bread. Hence they bring me a New Year feast every day,[b] and I make the New Year happy and prosperous by good thoughts and greatness of soul; for the soul is never greater than when it has laid aside all extraneous things, and has secured peace for itself by fearing nothing, and riches by craving no riches. The vehicle in which I have taken my seat is a farmer's cart. Only by walking do the mules show that they are alive. The driver is barefoot, and not because it is summer either. I can scarcely force myself to wish that others shall think this cart mine. My false embarrassment about the truth still holds out, you see; and whenever we meet a more sumptuous party I blush in spite of myself—proof that this conduct which I approve and applaud has not yet gained a firm and steadfast dwelling-place within me. He who blushes at riding in a rattle-trap will boast when he rides in style.

So my progress is still insufficient. I have not yet the courage openly to acknowledge my thriftiness. Even yet I am bothered by what other travellers think of me. But instead of this, I should really

Contra totius generis humani opiniones mittenda vox erat: "Insanitis, erratis, stupetis ad supervacua, neminem aestimatis suo. Cum ad patrimonium ventum est, diligentissimi conputatores sic rationem ponitis singulorum, quibus aut pecuniam credituri estis aut beneficia, nam haec quoque iam expensa
6 fertis: late possidet, sed multum debet; habet domum formosam, sed alienis nummis paratam: familiam nemo cito speciosiorem producet, sed nominibus non respondet; si creditoribus solverit, nihil illi supererit. Idem in reliquis quoque facere debebitis, excutere quantum proprii quisque habeat."

7 Divitem illum putas, quia aurea supellex etiam in via sequitur, quia in omnibus provinciis arat, quia magnus kalendari liber volvitur, quia tantum suburbani agri possidet, quantum invidiose in desertis Apuliae possideret. Cum omnia dixeris, pauper est. Quare? Quia debet. "Quantum?" inquis. Omnia. Nisi forte iudicas interesse, utrum aliquis ab homine an a
8 fortuna mutuum sumpserit. Quid ad rem pertinent mulae saginatae unius omnes coloris? Quid ista vehicula caelata?

> Instratos ostro alipedes pictisque tapetis,
> Aurea pectoribus demissa monilia pendent,
> Tecti auro fulvom mandunt sub dentibus aurum.

Ista nec dominum meliorem possunt facere nec mulam

---

[a] *Nomen* in this sense means primarily the name entered in the ledger; secondarily, the item or transaction with which the name is connected.

[b] Vergil, *Aeneid*, vii. 277 ff., describing the gifts sent by King Latinus to Aeneas.

have uttered an opinion counter to that in which mankind believe, saying, "You are mad, you are misled, your admiration devotes itself to superfluous things! You estimate no man at his real worth. When property is concerned, you reckon up in this way with most scrupulous calculation those to whom you shall lend either money or benefits; for by now you enter benefits also as payments in your ledger. You say: 'His estates are wide, but his debts are large.' 'He has a fine house, but he has built it on borrowed capital.' 'No man will display a more brilliant retinue on short notice, but he cannot meet his debts.'[a] 'If he pays off his creditors, he will have nothing left.'" So you will feel bound to do in all other cases as well,—to find out by elimination the amount of every man's actual possessions.

I suppose you call a man rich just because his gold plate goes with him even on his travels, because he farms land in all the provinces, because he unrolls a large account-book, because he owns estates near the city so great that men would grudge his holding them in the waste lands of Apulia. But after you have mentioned all these facts, he is poor. And why? He is in debt. "To what extent?" you ask. For all that he has. Or perchance you think it matters whether one has borrowed from another man or from Fortune. What good is there in mules caparisoned in uniform livery? Or in decorated chariots and

> Steeds decked with purple and with tapestry,
> With golden harness hanging from their necks,
> Champing their yellow bits, all clothed in gold?[b]

Neither master nor mule is improved by such trappings.

9 M. Cato Censorius, quem tam e re publica fuit nasci quam Scipionem, alter enim cum hostibus nostris bellum, alter cum moribus gessit, cantherio vehebatur et hippoperis quidem inpositis, ut secum utilia portaret. O quam cuperem illi nunc occurrere aliquem ex his trossulis in via[1] cursores et Numidas et multum ante se pulveris agentem! Hic sine dubio cultior comitatiorque quam M. Cato videretur, hic, qui inter illos apparatus delicatos cum maxime dubi-
10 tat, utrum se ad gladium locet an ad cultrum. O quantum erat saeculi decus, imperatorem triumphalem, censorium, quod super omnia haec est, Catonem uno caballo esse contentum et ne toto quidem! Partem enim sarcinae ab utroque latere dependentes occupabant. Ita non omnibus obesis mannis et asturconibus et tolutariis praeferres unicum illum equum
11 ab ipso Catone defrictum? Video non futurum finem in ista materia ullum, nisi quem ipse mihi fecero. Hic itaque conticescam, quantum ad ista, quae sine dubio talia divinavit futura, qualia nunc sunt, qui primus appellavit "inpedimenta." Nunc volo paucissimas adhuc interrogationes nostrorum tibi reddere ad virtutem pertinentes, quam satisfacere vitae beatae contendimus.

12 "Quod bonum est, bonos facit. Nam et in arte musica quod bonum est, facit musicum. Fortuita

[1] After *via* Lipsius removed *divitibus*.

---

[a] For *trossuli* cf. *Ep.* lxxvi. 2, and footnote.
[b] *i.e.*, whether to turn gladiator or *bestiarius*.
[c] "Amblers" from Asturia in Spain.
[d] Horses with rapid steps, compared with *gradarii*, "slow pacers," *cf. Ep.* xl. 11.
[e] The literal meaning of *impedimenta*, "luggage."

EPISTLE LXXXVII.

Marcus Cato the Censor, whose existence helped the state as much as did Scipio's,—for while Scipio fought against our enemies, Cato fought against our bad morals,—used to ride a donkey, and a donkey, at that, which carried saddle-bags containing the master's necessaries. O how I should love to see him meet to-day on the road one of our coxcombs,[a] with his outriders and Numidians, and a great cloud of dust before him! Your dandy would no doubt seem refined and well-attended in comparison with Marcus Cato,—your dandy, who, in the midst of all his luxurious paraphernalia, is chiefly concerned whether to turn his hand to the sword or to the hunting-knife.[b] O what a glory to the times in which he lived, for a general who had celebrated a triumph, a censor, and what is most noteworthy of all, a Cato, to be content with a single nag, and with less than a whole nag at that! For part of the animal was preempted by the baggage that hung down on either flank. Would you not therefore prefer Cato's steed, that single steed, saddle-worn by Cato himself, to the coxcomb's whole retinue of plump ponies, Spanish cobs,[c] and trotters[d]? I see that there will be no end in dealing with such a theme unless I make an end myself. So I shall now become silent, at least with reference to superfluous things like these; doubtless the man who first called them "hindrances"[e] had a prophetic inkling that they would be the very sort of thing they now are. At present I should like to deliver to you the syllogisms, as yet very few, belonging to our school and bearing upon the question of virtue, which, in our opinion, is sufficient for the happy life.

"That which is good makes men good. For example, that which is good in the art of music makes the musician. But chance events do not make a

bonum non faciunt. Ergo non sunt bona." Adversus hoc sic respondent Peripatetici, ut quod primum
proponimus, falsum esse dicant. "Ab eo," inquiunt,
"quod est bonum, non utique fiunt boni. In musica
est aliquid bonum tamquam tibia aut chorda aut
organum aliquod aptatum ad usus canendi. Nihil
13 tamen horum facit musicum." Hic respondebimus:
"Non intellegitis, quomodo posuerimus quod bonum
est in musica. Non enim id dicimus, quod instruit
musicum, sed quod facit; tu ad supellectilem artis,
non ad artem venis. Si quid autem in ipsa arte
14 musica bonum est, id utique musicum faciet." Etiamnunc facere istuc[1] planius volo. Bonum in arte musica
duobus modis dicitur, alterum, quo effectus musici
adiuvatur, alterum, quo ars. Ad effectum pertinent
instrumenta, tibiae et organa et chordae, ad artem
ipsam non pertinent. Est enim artifex etiam sine
istis; uti forsitan non potest arte. Hoc non est
aeque duplex in homine; idem enim est bonum et
hominis et vitae.

15 "Quod contemptissimo cuique contingere ac
turpissimo potest, bonum non est. Opes autem et
lenoni et lanistae contingunt. Ergo non sunt bona."
"Falsum est," inquiunt, "quod proponitis. Nam et
in grammatice et in arte medendi aut gubernandi vi-
16 demus bona humillimis quibusque contingere." Sed
istae artes non sunt magnitudinem animi professae,

[1] *istuc* Hense; *is me* or *his me* MSS.

[a] *Cf.* Plato, *Phaedo* 86, where Socrates contrasts the material lyre with the "incorporeal, fair, divine" harmony which makes the music.

good man; therefore, chance events are not goods." The Peripatetics reply to this by saying that the premiss is false; that men do not in every case become good by means of that which is good; that in music there is something good, like a flute, a harp, or an organ suited to accompany singing; but that none of these instruments makes the musician. We shall then reply: "You do not understand in what sense we have used the phrase 'that which is good in music.' For we do not mean that which equips the musician, but that which makes the musician; you, however, are referring to the instruments of the art, and not to the art itself.[a] If, however, anything in the art of music is good, that will in every case make the musician." And I should like to put this idea still more clearly. We define the good in the art of music in two ways: first, that by which the performance of the musician is assisted, and second, that by which his art is assisted. Now the musical instruments have to do with his performance,—such as flutes and organs and harps; but they do not have to do with the musician's art itself. For he is an artist even without them; he may perhaps be lacking in the ability to practise his art. But the good in man is not in the same way twofold; for the good of man and the good of life are the same.

"That which can fall to the lot of any man, no matter how base or despised he may be, is not a good. But wealth falls to the lot of the pander and the trainer of gladiators; therefore wealth is not a good." "Another wrong premiss," they say, "for we notice that goods fall to the lot of the very lowest sort of men, not only in the scholar's art, but also in the art of healing or in the art of navigating." These arts, however, make no profession of greatness of

non consurgunt in altum nec fortuita fastidiunt. Virtus extollit hominem et super cara mortalibus conlocat; nec ea, quae bona, nec ea, quae mala vocantur, aut cupit nimis aut expavescit. Chelidon, unus ex Cleopatrae mollibus, patrimonium grande possedit. Nuper Natalis tam inprobae linguae quam inpurae, in cuius ore feminae purgabantur, et multorum heres fuit et multos habuit heredes. Quid ergo? Utrum illum pecunia inpurum effecit an ipse pecuniam inspurcavit? Quae sic in quosdam homines quomodo
17 denarius in cloacam cadit. Virtus super ista consistit. Suo aere censetur. Nihil ex istis quolibet incurrentibus bonum iudicat. Medicina et gubernatio non interdicit sibi ac suis admiratione talium rerum. Qui non est vir bonus, potest nihilominus medicus esse, potest gubernator, potest grammaticus tam mehercules quam cocus. Cui contingit habere rem non quamlibet, hunc non quemlibet dixeris; qualia quis-
18 que habet, talis est. Fiscus tanti est, quantum habet; immo in accessionem eius venit, quod habet. Quis pleno sacculo ullum pretium ponit nisi quod pecuniae in eo conditae numerus effecit? Idem evenit magnorum dominis patrimoniorum: accessiones illorum et appendices sunt.

Quare ergo sapiens magnus est? Quia magnum animum habet. Verum est ergo quod contemptis-
19 simo cuique contingit, bonum non esse. Itaque in-

[a] See *Ep.* lxxxviii., which is devoted to the development of this thought.

[b] *i.e.*, at its own worth.

soul; they do not rise to any heights nor do they frown upon what fortune may bring.[a] It is virtue that uplifts man and places him superior to what mortals hold dear; virtue neither craves overmuch nor fears to excess that which is called good or that which is called bad. Chelidon, one of Cleopatra's eunuchs, possessed great wealth; and recently Natalis—a man whose tongue was as shameless as it was dirty, a man whose mouth used to perform the vilest offices—was the heir of many, and also made many his heirs. What then? Was it his money that made him unclean, or did he himself besmirch his money? Money tumbles into the hands of certain men as a shilling tumbles down a sewer. Virtue stands above all such things. It is appraised in coin of its own minting;[b] and it deems none of these random windfalls to be good. But medicine and navigation do not forbid themselves and their followers to marvel at such things. One who is not a good man can nevertheless be a physician, or a pilot, or a scholar,—yes, just as well as he can be a cook! He to whose lot it falls to possess something which is not of a random sort, cannot be called a random sort of man; a person is of the same sort as that which he possesses. A strong-box is worth just what it holds; or rather, it is a mere accessory of that which it holds. Who ever sets any price upon a full purse except the price established by the count of the money deposited therein? This also applies to the owners of great estates: they are only accessories and incidentals to their possessions.

Why, then, is the wise man great? Because he has a great soul. Accordingly, it is true that that which falls to the lot even of the most despicable person is not a good. Thus, I should never regard

dolentiam numquam bonum dicam; habet illam cicada, habet pulex. Ne quietem quidem et molestia vacare bonum dicam; quid est otiosius verme? Quaeris, quae res sapientem faciat? Quae deum. Des oportet illi divinum aliquid, caeleste, magnificum. Non in omnes bonum cadit nec quemlibet possessorem pati-
20 tur. Vide

Et quid quaeque ferat regio et quid quaeque recuset:
Hic segetes, illic veniunt felicius uvae.
Arborei fetus alibi atque iniussa virescunt
Gramina. Nonne vides, croceos ut Tmolus odores,
India mittat ebur, molles sua tura Sabaei?
At Chalybes nudi ferrum.

21 Ista in regiones discripta sunt, ut necessarium mortalibus esset inter ipsos commercium, si invicem alius aliquid ab alio peteret. Summum illud bonum habet et ipsum suam sedem. Non nascitur, ubi ebur, nec ubi ferrum. Quis sit summi boni locus quaeris? Animus. Hic nisi purus ac sanctus est, deum non capit.

22 "Bonum ex malo non fit. Divitiae fiunt autem[1] ex avaritia. Divitiae ergo non sunt bonum." "Non est," inquit, "verum, bonum ex malo non nasci. Ex sacrilegio enim et furto pecunia nascitur. Itaque malum quidem est sacrilegium et furtum, sed ideo, quia plura mala facit quam bona. Dat enim lucrum, sed cum metu, sollicitudine, tormentis et animi et
23 corporis." Quisquis hoc dicit, necesse est recipiat

[1] *divitiae fiunt autem* Gemoll; *divitiae fiunt. fiunt autem* MSS.

---

[a] *Cf.* the argument in lxxvi. 9 f.
[b] *i.e.*, perfect reason and obedience to Nature.
[c] Vergil, *Georg.* i. 53 ff.

inactivity as a good; for even the tree-frog and the flea possess this quality.[a] Nor should I regard rest and freedom from trouble as a good; for what is more at leisure than a worm? Do you ask what it is that produces the wise man? That which produces a god.[b] You must grant that the wise man has an element of godliness, heavenliness, grandeur. The good does not come to every one, nor does it allow any random person to possess it. Behold

What fruits each country bears, or will not bear;
Here corn, and there the vine, grow richlier.
And elsewhere still the tender tree and grass
Unbidden clothe themselves in green. Seest thou
How Tmolus ships its saffron perfumes forth,
And ivory comes from Ind; soft Sheba sends
Its incense, and the unclad Chalybes
Their iron.[c]

These products are apportioned to separate countries in order that human beings may be constrained to traffic among themselves, each seeking something from his neighbour in his turn. So the Supreme Good has also its own abode. It does not grow where ivory grows, or iron. Do you ask where the Supreme Good dwells? In the soul. And unless the soul be pure and holy, there is no room in it for God.

"Good does not result from evil. But riches result from greed; therefore, riches are not a good." "It is not true," they say, "that good does not result from evil. For money comes from sacrilege and theft. Accordingly, although sacrilege and theft are evil, yet they are evil only because they work more evil than good. For they bring gain; but the gain is accompanied by fear, anxiety, and torture of mind and body." Whoever says this

sacrilegium, sicut malum sit, quia multa mala facit, ita bonum quoque ex aliqua parte esse, quia aliquid boni facit. Quo quid fieri portentuosius potest? Quamquam[1] sacrilegium, furtum, adulterium inter bona haberi prorsus persuasimus. Quam multi furto non erubescunt, quam multi adulterio gloriantur! Nam sacrilegia minuta puniuntur, magna in trium-
24 phis feruntur. Adice nunc, quod sacrilegium, si omnino ex aliqua parte bonum est, etiam honestum erit et recte factum vocabitur: nostra enim actio est.[2] Quod nullius mortalium cogitatio recipit.

Ergo bona nasci ex malo non possunt. Nam si, ut[3] dicitis, ob hoc unum sacrilegium malum est, quia multum mali adfert, si remiseris illi supplicia, si securitatem spoponderis, ex toto bonum erit. Atqui
25 maximum scelerum supplicium in ipsis est. Erras, inquam, si illa ad carnificem aut carcerem differs; statim puniuntur, cum facta sunt, immo dum fiunt. Non nascitur itaque ex malo bonum, non magis quam ficus ex olea. Ad semen nata respondent, bona degenerare non possunt. Quemadmodum ex turpi honestum non nascitur, ita ne ex malo quidem bonum. Nam idem est honestum et bonum.

26 Quidam ex nostris adversus hoc sic respondent: "Putemus pecuniam bonum esse undecumque sump-

[1] *quamquam* Gruter; *quam* Vb.
[2] Hense would read *vocabitur; honesta* (so Gemoll) *enim actio recta actio est.*
[3] *si ut* later MSS.; *sic ut* Vb.

[a] The good is absolute. The Stoics held that virtue and moral worth were identical, although those who followed the argument to its logical conclusion had to explain away many seeming inconsistencies. *Cf. Ep.* lxxxv. 17.

must perforce admit that sacrilege, though it be an evil because it works much evil, is yet partly good because it accomplishes a certain amount of good. What can be more monstrous than this? We have, to be sure, actually convinced the world that sacrilege, theft, and adultery are to be regarded as among the goods. How many men there are who do not blush at theft, how many who boast of having committed adultery! For petty sacrilege is punished, but sacrilege on a grand scale is honoured by a triumphal procession. Besides, sacrilege, if it is wholly good in some respect, will also be honourable and will be called right conduct; for it is conduct which concerns ourselves. But no human being, on serious consideration, admits this idea.

Therefore, goods cannot spring from evil. For if, as you object, sacrilege is an evil for the single reason that it brings on much evil, if you but absolve sacrilege of its punishment and pledge it immunity, sacrilege will be wholly good. And yet the worst punishment for crime lies in the crime itself. You are mistaken, I maintain, if you propose to reserve your punishments for the hangman or the prison; the crime is punished immediately after it is committed; nay, rather, at the moment when it is committed. Hence, good does not spring from evil, any more than figs grow from olive-trees. Things which grow correspond to their seed; and goods cannot depart from their class. As that which is honourable does not grow from that which is base, so neither does good grow from evil. For the honourable and the good are identical.[a]

Certain of our school oppose this statement as follows: "Let us suppose that money taken from any source whatsoever is a good; even though it is taken by

tam; non tamen ideo ex sacrilegio pecunia est, etiam si ex sacrilegio sumitur. Hoc sic intellege: in eadem urna et aurum est et vipera. Si aurum ex urna sustuleris, quia illic et vipera est, non ideo, inquam, mihi urna aurum dat, quia viperam habet, sed aurum dat, cum et viperam habeat. Eodem modo ex sacrilegio lucrum fit, non quia turpe et sceleratum est sacrilegium, sed quia et lucrum habet. Quemadmodum in illa urna vipera malum est, non aurum, quod cum vipera iacet, sic in sacrilegio malum est scelus, non
27 lucrum." A quibus dissentio[1]: dissimillima enim utriusque rei condicio est. Illic aurum possum sine vipera tollere, hic lucrum sine sacrilegio facere non possum. Lucrum istud non est adpositum sceleri, sed inmixtum.

28 "Quod dum consequi volumus, in multa mala incidimus, id bonum non est. Dum divitias autem consequi volumus, in multa mala incidimus; ergo divitiae bonum non sunt." "Duas," inquit, "significationes habet propositio vestra, unam: dum divitias consequi volumus, in multa nos mala incidere. In multa autem mala incidimus et dum virtutem consequi volumus. Aliquis dum navigat studii causa,
29 naufragium fecit, aliquis captus est. Altera significatio talis est: per quod in mala incidimus, bonum non est. Huic propositioni non erit consequens per

[1] *a quibus dissentio* later MSS.; *a quibus* VPb.

---

[a] That riches are not a good, but merely an advantage, was one of the Stoic paradoxes. In another passage (*Dial.* vii. 24. 5) Seneca speaks of them in a kindlier manner: *divitias nego bonum esse; nam si essent, bonos facerent. Ceterum et habendas esse et utiles et magna commoda vitae adferentis fateor. Cf.* § 36 of this letter.

an act of sacrilege, the money does not on that account derive its origin from sacrilege. You may get my meaning through the following illustration: In the same jar there is a piece of gold and there is a serpent. If you take the gold from the jar, it is not just because the serpent is there too, I say, that the jar yields me the gold—because it contains the serpent as well,—but it yields the gold in spite of containing the serpent also. Similarly, gain results from sacrilege, not just because sacrilege is a base and accursed act, but because it contains gain also. As the serpent in the jar is an evil, and not the gold which lies there beside the serpent; so in an act of sacrilege it is the crime, not the profit, that is evil." But I differ from these men; for the conditions in each case are not at all the same. In the one instance I can take the gold without the serpent, in the other I cannot make the profit without committing the sacrilege. The gain in the latter case does not lie side by side with the crime; it is blended with the crime.

"That which, while we are desiring to attain it, involves us in many evils, is not a good. But while we are desiring to attain riches, we become involved in many evils; therefore, riches are not a good." [a] "Your first premiss," they say, "contains two meanings; one is: we become involved in many evils while we are desiring to attain riches. But we also become involved in many evils while we are desiring to attain virtue. One man, while travelling in order to prosecute his studies, suffers shipwreck, and another is taken captive. The second meaning is as follows: that through which we become involved in evils is not a good. And it will not logically follow from our proposition that we become involved

divitias nos aut per voluptates in mala incidere; aut
si per divitias in multa mala incidimus, non tantum
bonum non sunt divitiae, sed malum sunt; vos autem
illas dicitis tantum bonum non esse. Praeterea,"
inquit, "conceditis divitias habere aliquid usus.
Inter commoda illas numeratis; atqui eadem ratione
ne [1] commodum quidem erunt. Per illas enim multa
30 nobis incommoda eveniunt." His quidam hoc respondent: "Erratis, qui incommoda [2] divitiis inputatis.
Illae neminem laedunt; aut sua nocet cuique stultitia
aut aliena nequitia, sic quemadmodum gladius neminem occidit; occidentis telum est. Non ideo divitiae
tibi nocent, si propter divitias tibi nocetur."

31 Posidonius, ut ego existimo, melius, qui ait divitias
esse causam malorum, non quia ipsae faciunt aliquid,
sed quia facturos inritant. Alia est enim causa effi-
ciens, quae protinus necesse est noceat, alia prae-
cedens. Hanc praecedentem causam divitiae habent;
inflant animos, superbiam pariunt, invidiam contra-
hunt et usque eo mentem alienant, ut fama pecuniae
32 nos etiam nocitura delectet. Bona autem omnia
carere culpa decet; pura sunt, non corrumpunt animos, non sollicitant. Extollunt quidem et dilatant,
sed sine tumore. Quae bona sunt fiduciam faciunt,
divitiae audaciam. Quae bona sunt magnitudinem

[1] *ne* inserted by Fickert.
[2] *qui incommoda* later MSS.; *qui commoda* Vb.

in evils through riches or through pleasure; otherwise, if it is through riches that we become involved in many evils, riches are not only not a good, but they are positively an evil. You, however, maintain merely that they are not a good. Moreover," the objector says, "you grant that riches are of some use. You reckon them among the advantages; and yet on this basis they cannot even be an advantage, for it is through the pursuit of riches that we suffer much disadvantage." Certain men answer this objection as follows: "You are mistaken if you ascribe disadvantages to riches. Riches injure no one; it is a man's own folly, or his neighbour's wickedness, that harms him in each case, just as a sword by itself does not slay; it is merely the weapon used by the slayer. Riches themselves do not harm you, just because it is on account of riches that you suffer harm."

I think that the reasoning of Posidonius is better: he holds that riches are a cause of evil, not because, of themselves, they do any evil, but because they goad men on so that they are ready to do evil. For the efficient cause, which necessarily produces harm at once, is one thing, and the antecedent cause is another. It is this antecedent cause which inheres in riches; they puff up the spirit and beget pride, they bring on unpopularity and unsettle the mind to such an extent that the mere reputation of having wealth, though it is bound to harm us, nevertheless affords delight. All goods, however, ought properly to be free from blame; they are pure, they do not corrupt the spirit, and they do not tempt us. They do, indeed, uplift and broaden the spirit, but without puffing it up. Those things which are goods produce confidence, but riches produce shamelessness. The things which are goods give us greatness of soul,

animi dant, divitiae insolentiam. Nihil autem aliud est insolentia quam species magnitudinis falsa.

33 "Isto modo," inquit, "etiam malum sunt divitiae, non tantum bonum non sunt." Essent malum, si ipsae nocerent, si, ut dixi, haberent efficientem causam; nunc praecedentem habent et quidem non inritantem tantum animos, sed adtrahentem. Speciem enim boni offundunt veri similem ac plerisque credi-

34 bilem. Habet virtus quoque praecedentem causam; adducit invidiam,[1] multis enim propter sapientiam, multis propter iustitiam invidetur. Sed nec ex se[2] hanc causam habet nec veri similem. Contra enim veri similior illa species hominum animis obicitur a virtute, quae illos in amorem et admirationem vocet.

35 Posidonius sic interrogandum ait: "quae neque magnitudinem animo dant nec fiduciam nec securitatem, non sunt bona. Divitiae autem et bona valetudo et similia his nihil horum faciunt; ergo non sunt bona." Hanc interrogationem magis etiamnunc hoc modo intendit: "quae neque magnitudinem animo dant nec fiduciam nec securitatem, contra autem insolentiam, tumorem, arrogantiam creant, mala sunt. A fortuitis autem in haec inpellimur;

[1] *adducit invidiam* Haase; *ad invidiam* Vb; *addunvidiam* P.
[2] *nec ex se* later MSS.; *necesse* VPb.

but riches give us arrogance. And arrogance is nothing else than a false show of greatness.

"According to that argument," the objector says, "riches are not only not a good, but are a positive evil." Now they would be an evil if they did harm of themselves, and if, as I remarked, it were the efficient cause which inheres in them; in fact, however, it is the antecedent cause which inheres in riches, and indeed it is that cause which, so far from merely arousing the spirit, actually drags it along by force. Yes, riches shower upon us a semblance of the good, which is like the reality and wins credence in the eyes of many men. The antecedent cause inheres in virtue also; it is this which brings on envy—for many men become unpopular because of their wisdom, and many men because of their justice. But this cause, though it inheres in virtue, is not the result of virtue itself, nor is it a mere semblance of the reality; nay, on the contrary, far more like the reality is that vision which is flashed by virtue upon the spirits of men, summoning them to love it and marvel thereat.

Posidonius thinks that the syllogism should be framed as follows: "Things which bestow upon the soul no greatness or confidence or freedom from care are not goods. But riches and health and similar conditions do none of these things; therefore, riches and health are not goods." This syllogism he then goes on to extend still further in the following way: "Things which bestow upon the soul no greatness or confidence or freedom from care, but on the other hand create in it arrogance, vanity, and insolence, are evils. But things which are the gift of Fortune drive us into these evil ways. Therefore these

36 ergo non sunt bona." "Hac," inquit, "ratione ne commoda quidem ista erunt." Alia est commodorum condicio, alia bonorum; commodum est, quod plus usus habet quam molestiae. Bonum sincerum esse debet et ab omni parte innoxium. Non est id bonum,
37 quod plus prodest, sed quod tantum prodest. Praeterea commodum et ad animalia pertinet et ad inperfectos homines et ad stultos. Itaque potest ei esse incommodum mixtum, sed commodum dicitur a maiore sui parte aestimatum; bonum ad unum sapientem pertinet; inviolatum esse oportet.

38 Bonum animum habere; unus tibi nodus, sed Herculaneus restat: "ex malis bonum non fit. Ex multis paupertatibus divitiae fiunt; ergo divitiae bonum non sunt." Hanc interrogationem nostri non agnoscunt, Peripatetici et fingunt illam et solvunt. Ait autem Posidonius hoc sophisma, per omnes dialecticorum scholas iactatum, sic ab Antipatro refelli:
39 "paupertas non per possessionem dicitur, sed per detractionem vel, ut antiqui dixerunt, orbationem. Graeci κατὰ στέρησιν dicunt. Non quod habeat dicit, sed quod non habeat.[1] Itaque ex multis inanibus nihil inpleri potest; divitias multae res faciunt, non

[1] Hense doubts the genuineness of *non quod . . . habeat.*

---

[a] The "knot of Hercules" is associated with the *caduceus* (twining serpents) in Macrob. *Sat.* i. 19. 16; and in Pliny, *N. H.* xxviii. 63, it has magic properties in the binding up of wounds.

[b] Frag. 54 von Arnim.

[c] *Per possessionem* translates the Greek καθ' ἕξιν, as *per orbationem* (or *detractionem*) translates κατὰ στέρησιν.

things are not goods." "But," says the objector, "by such reasoning, things which are the gift of Fortune will not even be advantages." No, advantages and goods stand each in a different situation. An advantage is that which contains more of usefulness than of annoyance. But a good ought to be unmixed and with no element in it of harmfulness. A thing is not good if it contains more benefit than injury, but only if it contains nothing but benefit. Besides, advantages may be predicated of animals, of men who are less than perfect, and of fools. Hence the advantageous may have an element of disadvantage mingled with it, but the word "advantageous" is used of the compound because it is judged by its predominant element. The good, however, can be predicated of the wise man alone; it is bound to be without alloy.

Be of good cheer; there is only one knot[a] left for you to untangle, though it is a knot for a Hercules: "Good does not result from evil. But riches result from numerous cases of poverty; therefore, riches are not a good." This syllogism is not recognized by our school, but the Peripatetics both concoct it and give its solution. Posidonius, however, remarks that this fallacy, which has been bandied about among all the schools of dialectic, is refuted by Antipater[b] as follows: "The word 'poverty' is used to denote, not the possession[c] of something, but the non-possession or, as the ancients have put it, deprivation, (for the Greeks use the phrase 'by deprivation,' meaning 'negatively'). 'Poverty' states, not what a man has, but what he has not. Consequently there can be no fulness resulting from a multitude of voids; many positive things, and not many deficiencies, make up riches.

multae inopiae. Aliter," inquit, "quam debes, paupertatem intellegis. Paupertas enim est non quae pauca possidet, sed quae multa non possidet; ita non ab eo dicitur, quod habet, sed ab eo, quod ei deest."

40 Facilius, quod volo, exprimerem, si Latinum verbum esset, quo ἀνυπαρξία significatur. Hanc paupertati Antipater adsignat; ego non video, quid aliud sit paupertas quam parvi possessio. De isto videbimus, si quando valde vacabit, quae sit divitiarum, quae paupertatis substantia; sed tunc quoque considerabimus, numquid satius sit paupertatem permulcere, divitiis demere supercilium quam litigare de verbis, quasi iam de rebus iudicatum sit.

41 Putemus nos ad contionem vocatos; lex de abolendis divitiis fertur. His interrogationibus suasuri aut dissuasuri sumus? His effecturi, ut populus Romanus paupertatem, fundamentum et causam imperii sui, requirat ac laudet,[1] divitias autem suas timeat, ut cogitet has se apud victos repperisse, hinc ambitum et largitiones et tumultus in urbem sanctissimam et temperantissimam inrupisse, nimis luxuriose ostentari gentium spolia, quod unus populus eripuerit omnibus, facilius ab omnibus uni eripi posse? Hanc

[1] *laudet* later MSS.; *laudes* VPb.

[a] Seneca here bursts into a diatribe on the corruption of Rome, a habit which we find in many other of his writings, especially in the *Naturales Quaestiones*.

You have," says he, "a wrong notion of the meaning of what poverty is. For poverty does not mean the possession of little, but the non-possession of much; it is used, therefore, not of what a man has, but of what he lacks." I could express my meaning more easily if there were a Latin word which could translate the Greek word which means "not-possessing." Antipater assigns this quality to poverty, but for my part I cannot see what else poverty is than the possession of little. If ever we have plenty of leisure, we shall investigate the question: What is the essence of riches, and what the essence of poverty; but when the time comes, we shall also consider whether it is not better to try to mitigate poverty, and to relieve wealth of its arrogance, than to quibble about the words as if the question of the things were already decided.

Let us suppose that we have been summoned to an assembly; an act dealing with the abolition of riches has been brought before the meeting. Shall we be supporting it, or opposing it, if we use these syllogisms? Will these syllogisms help us to bring it about that the Roman people shall demand poverty and praise it—poverty, the foundation and cause of their empire,—and, on the other hand, shall shrink in fear from their present wealth, reflecting that they have found it among the victims of their conquests, that wealth is the source from which office-seeking and bribery and disorder[a] have burst into a city once characterized by the utmost scrupulousness and sobriety, and that because of wealth an exhibition all too lavish is made of the spoils of conquered nations; reflecting, finally, that whatever one people has snatched away from all the rest may still more easily be snatched by all away from one? Nay, it

satius est suadere[1] et expugnare adfectus, non circumscribere. Si possumus, fortius loquamur; si minus, apertius. VALE.

LXXXVIII.

SENECA LVCILIO SVO SALVTEM

1 De liberalibus studiis quid sentiam, scire desideras: nullum suspicio, nullum in bonis numero, quod ad aes exit. Meritoria artificia sunt, hactenus utilia, si praeparant ingenium, non detinent. Tamdiu enim istis inmorandum est, quamdiu nihil animus agere maius
2 potest; rudimenta sunt nostra, non opera. Quare liberalia studia dicta sint, vides; quia homine libero digna sunt. Ceterum unum studium vere liberale est, quod liberum facit. Hoc est sapientiae, sublime, forte, magnanimum. Cetera pusilla et puerilia sunt; an tu quicquam in istis esse credis boni, quorum professores turpissimos omnium ac flagitiosissimos cernis? Non discere debemus ista, sed didicisse.

Quidam illud de liberalibus studiis quaerendum iudicaverunt, an virum bonum facerent; ne promittunt quidem nec huius rei scientiam adfectant.

[1] After *suadere* Hense added *re*.

[a] The regular round of education, ἐγκύκλιος παιδεία, including grammar, music, geometry, arithmetic, astrology, and certain phases of rhetoric and dialectic, are in this letter contrasted with liberal studies—those which have for their object the pursuit of virtue. Seneca is thus interpreting *studia liberalia* in a higher sense than his contemporaries would expect. Compare J. R. Lowell's definition of a university, "a place where nothing useful is taught."

were better to support this law by our conduct and to subdue our desires by direct assault rather than to circumvent them by logic. If we can, let us speak more boldly; if not, let us speak more frankly.

LXXXVIII. ON LIBERAL AND VOCATIONAL STUDIES

You have been wishing to know my views with regard to liberal studies.[a] My answer is this: I respect no study, and deem no study good, which results in money-making. Such studies are profit-bringing occupations, useful only in so far as they give the mind a preparation and do not engage it permanently. One should linger upon them only so long as the mind can occupy itself with nothing greater; they are our apprenticeship, not our real work. Hence you see why "liberal studies" are so called; it is because they are studies worthy of a free-born gentleman. But there is only one really liberal study,—that which gives a man his liberty. It is the study of wisdom, and that is lofty, brave, and great-souled. All other studies are puny and puerile. You surely do not believe that there is good in any of the subjects whose teachers are, as you see, men of the most ignoble and base stamp? We ought not to be learning such things; we should have done with learning them.

Certain persons have made up their minds that the point at issue with regard to the liberal studies is whether they make men good; but they do not even profess or aim at a knowledge of this particular

3 Grammaticus circa curam sermonis versatur et, si latius evagari vult, circa historias, iam ut longissime fines suos proferat, circa carmina. Quid horum ad virtutem viam sternit? Syllabarum enarratio et verborum diligentia et fabularum memoria et versuum lex ac modificatio? Quid ex his metum demit,
4 cupiditatem eximit, libidinem frenat? . . . Quaeritur[1] utrum doceant isti virtutem an non; si non docent, ne tradunt quidem. Si docent, philosophi sunt. Vis scire, quam non ad docendam virtutem consederint? Aspice, quam dissimilia inter se omnium studia sint; atqui similitudo esset idem docentium.

5 Nisi forte tibi Homerum philosophum fuisse persuadent, cum his ipsis, quibus colligunt, negent. Nam modo Stoicum illum faciunt, virtutem solam probantem et voluptates refugientem et ab honesto ne inmortalitatis quidem pretio recedentem, modo Epicureum, laudantem statum quietae civitatis et inter convivia cantusque vitam exigentis, modo Peripateticum, tria bonorum genera inducentem, modo Academicum, omnia incerta dicentem. Adparet nihil horum esse in illo, quia omnia sunt. Ista enim

[1] After *frenat* MSS. give *ad geometriam transeamus et ad musicen; nihil apud illas invenies, quod vetet timere, vetet cupere. Quisquis ignorat, alia frustra scit*, leaving an impossible syntax before *utrum*. *Videndum utrum* later MSS. *Quaeritur* would be a reasonable conjecture.

---

[a] *Grammaticus* in classical Greek means "one who is familiar with the alphabet"; in the Alexandrian age a "student of literature"; in the Roman age the equivalent of *litteratus*. Seneca means here a "specialist in linguistic science."

[b] *i.e.*, philosophy (virtue).

[c] This theory was approved by Democritus, Hippias of Elis, and the allegorical interpreters; Xenophanes, Heraclitus, and Plato himself condemned Homer for his supposed unphilosophic fabrications.

subject. The scholar[a] busies himself with investigations into language, and if it be his desire to go farther afield, he works on history, or, if he would extend his range to the farthest limits, on poetry. But which of these paves the way to virtue? Pronouncing syllables, investigating words, memorizing plays, or making rules for the scansion of poetry,—what is there in all this that rids one of fear, roots out desire, or bridles the passions? The question is: do such men teach virtue, or not? If they do not teach it, then neither do they transmit it. If they do teach it, they are philosophers. Would you like to know how it happens that they have not taken the chair for the purpose of teaching virtue? See how unlike their subjects are; and yet their subjects would resemble each other if they taught the same thing.[b]

It may be, perhaps, that they make you believe that Homer was a philosopher,[c] although they disprove this by the very arguments through which they seek to prove it. For sometimes they make of him a Stoic, who approves nothing but virtue, avoids pleasures, and refuses to relinquish honour even at the price of immortality; sometimes they make him an Epicurean, praising the condition of a state in repose, which passes its days in feasting and song; sometimes a Peripatetic, classifying goodness in three ways[d]; sometimes an Academic, holding that all things are uncertain. It is clear, however, that no one of these doctrines is to be fathered upon Homer, just because they are all there; for they are

[d] The *tria genera bonorum* of Cicero's *De Fin* v. 84. Cf. *ib*. 18, where the three proper objects of man's search are given as the desire for pleasure, the avoidance of pain, and the attainment of such natural goods as health, strength, and soundness of mind. The Stoics held that the good was absolute.

inter se dissident. Demus illis Homerum philosophum fuisse; nempe sapiens factus est, antequam carmina ulla cognosceret. Ergo illa discamus, quae Homerum fecere sapientem.

6 Hoc quidem me quaerere, uter maior aetate fuerit,
Homerus an Hesiodus, non magis ad rem pertinet
quam scire, cum minor Hecuba fuerit quam Helena,
quare tam male tulerit aetatem. Quid? Inquam,
annos Patrocli et Achillis inquirere ad rem existimas
7 pertinere? Quaeris, Vlixes ubi erraverit, potius
quam efficias, ne nos semper erremus? Non vacat
audire, utrum inter Italiam et Siciliam iactatus sit an
extra notum nobis orbem, neque enim potuit in tam
angusto error esse tam longus; tempestates nos
animi cotidie iactant et nequitia in omnia Vlixis mala
inpellit. Non deest forma, quae sollicitet oculos,
non hostis; hinc monstra effera et humano cruore
gaudentia, hinc insidiosa blandimenta aurium, hinc
naufragia et tot varietates malorum. Hoc me doce,
quomodo patriam amem, quomodo uxorem, quomodo
patrem, quomodo ad haec tam honesta vel naufragus
8 navigem. Quid inquiris, an Penelopa pudica[1] fuerit
an verba saeculo suo dederit? An Vlixem illum
esse, quem videbat, antequam sciret, suspicata sit

[1] *pudica* later MSS.; *inpudica* VPb.

---

[a] Summers compares Lucian, *Gall.* 17. Seneca, however does not take such gossip seriously.

[b] This sentence alludes to Calypso, Circe, the Cyclops and the Sirens.

[c] Unfavourable comment by Lycophron, and by Cicero *De Nat. Deor.* iii. 22 (*Mercurius*) *ex quo et Penelopa Pan natum ferunt.*

irreconcilable with one another. We may admit to these men, indeed, that Homer was a philosopher; yet surely he became a wise man before he had any knowledge of poetry. So let us learn the particular things that made Homer wise.

It is no more to the point, of course, for me to investigate whether Homer or Hesiod was the older poet, than to know why Hecuba, although younger than Helen,[a] showed her years so lamentably. What, in your opinion, I say, would be the point in trying to determine the respective ages of Achilles and Patroclus? Do you raise the question, "Through what regions did Ulysses stray?" instead of trying to prevent ourselves from going astray at all times? We have no leisure to hear lectures on the question whether he was sea-tost between Italy and Sicily, or outside our known world (indeed, so long a wandering could not possibly have taken place within its narrow bounds); we ourselves encounter storms of the spirit, which toss us daily, and our depravity drives us into all the ills which troubled Ulysses. For us there is never lacking the beauty to tempt our eyes, or the enemy to assail us; on this side are savage monsters that delight in human blood, on that side the treacherous allurements of the ear, and yonder is shipwreck and all the varied category of misfortunes.[b] Show me rather, by the example of Ulysses, how I am to love my country, my wife, my father, and how, even after suffering shipwreck, I am to sail toward these ends, honourable as they are. Why try to discover whether Penelope was a pattern of purity,[c] or whether she had the laugh on her contemporaries? Or whether she suspected that the man in her presence was Ulysses, before she knew it was he? Teach me

Doce me, quid sit pudicitia et quantum in ea bonum, in corpore an in animo posita sit.

9 Ad musicum transeo: doces me, quomodo inter se acutae ac graves consonent, quomodo nervorum disparem reddentium sonum fiat concordia; fac potius, quomodo animus secum meus consonet nec consilia mea discrepent. Monstras mihi, qui sint modi flebiles; monstra potius, quomodo inter adversa non
10 emittam flebilem vocem. Metiri me geometres docet latifundia potius quam doceat, quomodo metiar, quantum homini satis sit. Numerare docet me et avaritiae commodat digitos potius quam doceat nihil ad rem pertinere istas conputationes, non esse feliciorem, cuius patrimonium tabularios lassat, immo quam supervacua possideat, qui infelicissimus futurus est, si quantum habeat per se conputare cogetur.
11 Quid mihi prodest scire agellum in partes dividere, si nescio cum fratre dividere? Quid prodest colligere subtiliter pedes iugeri et conprendere etiam si quid decempedam effugit, si tristem me facit vicinus inpotens et aliquid ex meo abradens? Docet quomodo nihil perdam ex finibus meis; at ego discere
12 volo, quomodo totos hilaris amittam. "Paterno agro et avito," inquit, "expellor." Quid? Ante avum

[a] With *acutae* and *graves* supply *voces*.
[b] Perhaps the equivalent of a "minor."

rather what purity is, and how great a good we have in it, and whether it is situated in the body or in the soul.

Now I will transfer my attention to the musician. You, sir, are teaching me how the treble and the bass[a] are in accord with one another, and how, though the strings produce different notes, the result is a harmony; rather bring my soul into harmony with itself, and let not my purposes be out of tune. You are showing me what the doleful keys[b] are; show me rather how, in the midst of adversity, I may keep from uttering a doleful note. The mathematician teaches me how to lay out the dimensions of my estates; but I should rather be taught how to lay out what is enough for a man to own. He teaches me to count, and adapts my fingers to avarice; but I should prefer him to teach me that there is no point in such calculations, and that one is none the happier for tiring out the book-keepers with his possessions—or rather, how useless property is to any man who would find it the greatest misfortune if he should be required to reckon out, by his own wits, the amount of his holdings. What good is there for me in knowing how to parcel out a piece of land, if I know not how to share it with my brother? What good is there in working out to a nicety the dimensions of an acre, and in detecting the error if a piece has so much as escaped my measuring-rod, if I am embittered when an ill-tempered neighbour merely scrapes off a bit of my land? The mathematician teaches me how I may lose none of my boundaries; I, however, seek to learn how to lose them all with a light heart. "But," comes the reply, "I am being driven from the farm which my father and grandfather owned!" Well? Who owned the land before your grand-

tuum quis istum agrum tenuit? Cuius, non dico hominis, sed populi fuerit, expedire potes? Non dominus isto, sed colonus intrasti. Cuius colonus es? Si bene tecum agitur, heredis. Negant iurisconsulti quicquam usu capi[1] publicum; hoc, quod tenes, quod tuum dicis, publicum est et quidem generis humani.
13 O egregiam artem! Scis rotunda metiri, in quadratum redigis quamcumque acceperis formam, intervalla siderum dicis, nihil est, quod in mensuram tuam non cadat. Si artifex es, metire hominis animum. Dic quam magnus sit, dic quam pusillus sit. Scis, quae recta sit linea; quid tibi prodest, si quid in vita rectum sit ignoras?

14 Venio nunc ad illum, qui caelestium notitia gloriatur:

> Frigida Saturni sese quo stella receptet,
> Quos ignis caeli Cyllenius erret in orbes.

Hoc scire quid proderit? Ut sollicitus sim, cum Saturnus et Mars ex contrario stabunt aut cum Mercurius vespertinum faciet occasum vidente Saturno, potius quam hoc discam, ubicumque sunt ista, pro-
15 pitia esse, non posse mutari? Agit illa continuus ordo fatorum et inevitabilis cursus. Per statas vices remeant et effectus rerum omnium aut movent aut

[1] After *usu capi* the later MSS. give *publicum . . . dicis*; omitted by VPb.

---

[a] *i.e.*, for a certain term of years; see R. W. Leage, *Roman Private Law*, pp. 133 ff. Compare also Lucretius iii. 971, and Horace, *Ep*. ii. 2. 159.

[b] Vergil, *Georg*. i. 336 f.

[c] Saturn and Mars were regarded as unlucky stars. Astrology, which dates back beyond 3000 B.C. in Babylonia, was developed by the Greeks of the Alexandrian age and got a foothold in Rome by the second century B.C., flourished

father? Can you explain what people (I will not say what person) held it originally? You did not enter upon it as a master, but merely as a tenant. And whose tenant are you? If your claim is successful, you are tenant of the heir. The lawyers say that public property cannot be acquired privately by possession[a]; what you hold and call your own is public property—indeed, it belongs to mankind at large. O what marvellous skill! You know how to measure the circle; you find the square of any shape which is set before you; you compute the distances between the stars; there is nothing which does not come within the scope of your calculations. But if you are a real master of your profession, measure me the mind of man! Tell me how great it is, or how puny! You know what a straight line is; but how does it benefit you if you do not know what is straight in this life of ours?

I come next to the person who boasts his knowledge of the heavenly bodies, who knows

> Whither the chilling star of Saturn hides,
> And through what orbit Mercury doth stray.[b]

Of what benefit will it be to know this? That I shall be disturbed because Saturn and Mars are in opposition, or when Mercury sets at eventide in plain view of Saturn, rather than learn that those stars, wherever they are, are propitious,[c] and that they are not subject to change? They are driven along by an unending round of destiny, on a course from which they cannot swerve. They return at stated seasons; they either set in motion, or mark the

greatly under Tiberius. Cf. Horace, *Od.* i. 11. 1 f.; Juv. iii. 42 f., and F. Cumont, *Astrology and Religion among the Greeks and Romans* (trans.), esp. pp. 68 ff. and 84 ff.

notant. Sed sive quicquid evenit faciunt, quid inmutabilis rei notitia proficiet? Sive significant, quid refert providere quod effugere non possis? Scias
16 ista, nescias; fient.

> Si vero solem ad rapidum stellasque sequentes
> Ordine respicies, numquam te crastina fallet
> Hora nec insidiis noctis capiere serenae.

Satis abundeque provisum est, ut ab insidiis tutus
17 essem. "Numquid me crastina non fallit hora? Fallit enim quod nescienti evenit." Ego quid futurum sit, nescio; quid fieri possit, scio. Ex hoc nihil desperabo, totum expecto; si quid remittitur, boni consulo. Fallit me hora, si parcit, sed ne sic quidem fallit. Nam quemadmodum scio omnia accidere posse, sic scio et non utique casura. Utique secunda expecto, malis paratus sum.

18 In illo feras me necesse est non per praescriptum euntem. Non enim adducor, ut in numerum liberalium artium pictores recipiam, non magis quam statuarios aut marmorarios aut ceteros luxuriae ministros. Aeque luctatores et totam oleo ac luto constantem scientiam expello ex his studiis liberalibus; aut et unguentarios recipiam et cocos et ceteros[1] voluptatibus nostris ingenia accommodantes sua.

[1] *ceteros* later MSS.; *ceteris* VPb.

---

[a] Vergil, *Georg.* i. 424 ff.

[b] An allusion to the sand and oil of the wrestling-ring.

intervals of the whole world's work. But if they are responsible for whatever happens, how will it help you to know the secrets of the immutable? Or if they merely give indications, what good is there in foreseeing what you cannot escape? Whether you know these things or not, they will take place.

> Behold the fleeting sun,
> The stars that follow in his train, and thou
> Shalt never find the morrow play thee false,
> Or be misled by nights without a cloud.[a]

It has, however, been sufficiently and fully ordained that I shall be safe from anything that may mislead me. "What," you say, "does the 'morrow never play me false'? Whatever happens without my knowledge plays me false." I, for my part, do not know what is to be, but I do know what may come to be. I shall have no misgivings in this matter; I await the future in its entirety; and if there is any abatement in its severity, I make the most of it. If the morrow treats me kindly, it is a sort of deception; but it does not deceive me even at that. For just as I know that all things can happen, so I know, too, that they will not happen in every case. I am ready for favourable events in every case, but I am prepared for evil.

In this discussion you must bear with me if I do not follow the regular course. For I do not consent to admit painting into the list of liberal arts, any more than sculpture, marble-working, and other helps toward luxury. I also debar from the liberal studies wrestling and all knowledge that is compounded of oil and mud[b]; otherwise, I should be compelled to admit perfumers also, and cooks, and all others who lend their wits to the service of our

19 Quid enim, oro te, liberale habent isti ieiuni vomitores, quorum corpora in sagina, animi in macie et veterno sunt? An liberale studium istuc esse iuventuti nostrae credimus, quam maiores nostri rectam exercuerunt hastilia iacere, sudem torquere, equum agitare, arma tractare? Nihil liberos suos docebant, quod discendum esset iacentibus. Sed nec hae nec illae docent aluntve virtutem. Quid enim prodest equum regere et cursum eius freno temperare, adfectibus effrenatissimis abstrahi? Quid prodest multos vincere luctatione vel caestu, ab iracundia vinci?

20 "Quid ergo? Nihil nobis liberalia conferunt studia?" Ad alia multum, ad virtutem nihil. Nam et hae viles ex professo artes, quae manu constant, ad instrumenta vitae plurimum conferunt, tamen ad virtutem non pertinent. "Quare ergo liberalibus studiis filios erudimus?" Non quia virtutem dare possunt, sed quia animum ad accipiendam virtutem praeparant. Quemadmodum prima illa, ut antiqui vocabant, litteratura, per quam pueris elementa traduntur, non docet liberales artes, sed mox percipiendis locum parat, sic liberales artes non perducunt animum ad virtutem, sed expediunt.

---

[a] *Cf. Ep.* xv. 3 *copia ciborum subtilitas inpeditur.*

[b] In a strict sense; not, as in § 2, as Seneca thinks that the term should really be defined—the "liberal" study, *i.e.* the pursuit of wisdom.

[c] For the πρώτη ἀγωγή see Quintilian, ii. 1. 4.

pleasures. For what "liberal" element is there in these ravenous takers of emetics, whose bodies are fed to fatness while their minds are thin and dull?[a] Or do we really believe that the training which they give is "liberal" for the young men of Rome, who used to be taught by our ancestors to stand straight and hurl a spear, to wield a pike, to guide a horse, and to handle weapons? Our ancestors used to teach their children nothing that could be learned while lying down. But neither the new system nor the old teaches or nourishes virtue. For what good does it do us to guide a horse and control his speed with the curb, and then find that our own passions, utterly uncurbed, bolt with us? Or to beat many opponents in wrestling or boxing, and then to find that we ourselves are beaten by anger?

"What then," you say, "do the liberal studies contribute nothing to our welfare?" Very much in other respects, but nothing at all as regards virtue. For even these arts of which I have spoken, though admittedly of a low grade—depending as they do upon handiwork—contribute greatly toward the equipment of life, but nevertheless have nothing to do with virtue. And if you inquire, "Why, then, do we educate our children in the liberal studies?"[b] it is not because they can bestow virtue, but because they prepare the soul for the reception of virtue. Just as that "primary course,"[c] as the ancients called it, in grammar, which gave boys their elementary training, does not teach them the liberal arts, but prepares the ground for their early acquisition of these arts, so the liberal arts do not conduct the soul all the way to virtue, but merely set it going in that direction.

21 Quattuor ait esse artium Posidonius genera: sunt
volgares et sordidae, sunt ludicrae, sunt pueriles,
sunt liberales. Volgares opificum, quae manu constant et ad instruendam vitam occupatae sunt, in
quibus nulla decoris, nulla honesti simulatio est.
22 Ludicrae sunt, quae ad voluptatem oculorum atque
aurium tendunt. His adnumeres licet machinatores,
qui pegmata per se surgentia excogitant et tabulata
tacite in sublime crescentia et alias ex inopinato
varietates aut dehiscentibus, quae cohaerebant, aut
his, quae distabant, sua sponte coeuntibus aut his,
quae eminebant, paulatim in se residentibus. His
imperitorum feriuntur oculi omnia subita, quia causas
23 non novere, mirantium. Pueriles sunt et aliquid
habentes liberalibus simile hae artes, quas ἐγκυκλίους
Graeci, nostri autem liberales vocant. Solae autem
liberales sunt, immo, ut dicam verius, liberae, quibus
curae virtus est.

24 "Quemadmodum," inquit, "est aliqua pars philosophiae naturalis, est aliqua moralis, est aliqua rationalis,
sic et haec quoque liberalium artium turba locum
sibi in philosophia vindicat. Cum ventum est ad
naturales quaestiones, geometriae testimonio statur;
25 ergo eius, quam adiuvat, pars est." Multa adiuvant

---

[a] From what work of Posidonius Seneca is here quoting we do not know; it may perhaps be from the Προτρεπτικά, or *Exhortations*, indicating the training preliminary to philosophy.

[b] See note *a*, p. 348.

[c] *i.e.*, mathematics is a department of *philosophia naturalis*.

EPISTLE LXXXVIII.

Posidonius[a] divides the arts into four classes: first we have those which are common and low, then those which serve for amusement, then those which refer to the education of boys, and, finally, the liberal arts. The common sort belong to workmen and are mere hand-work; they are concerned with equipping life; there is in them no pretence to beauty or honour. The arts of amusement are those which aim to please the eye and the ear. To this class you may assign the stage-machinists, who invent scaffolding that goes aloft of its own accord, or floors that rise silently into the air, and many other surprising devices, as when objects that fit together then fall apart, or objects which are separate then join together automatically, or objects which stand erect then gradually collapse. The eye of the inexperienced is struck with amazement by these things; for such persons marvel at everything that takes place without warning, because they do not know the causes. The arts which belong to the education of boys, and are somewhat similar to the liberal arts, are those which the Greeks call the "cycle of studies,"[b] but which we Romans call the "liberal." However, those alone are really liberal —or rather, to give them a truer name, "free"— whose concern is virtue.

"But," one will say, "just as there is a part of philosophy which has to do with nature, and a part which has to do with ethics, and a part which has to do with reasoning, so this group of liberal arts also claims for itself a place in philosophy. When one approaches questions that deal with nature, a decision is reached by means of a word from the mathematician. Therefore mathematics is a department of that branch which it aids."[c] But many things

nos nec ideo partes nostri[1] sunt. Immo si partes essent, non adiuvarent. Cibus adiutorium corporis nec tamen pars est. Aliquid nobis praestat geometriae ministerium; sic philosophiae necessaria est, quomodo ipsi faber. Sed nec hic geometriae pars
26 est nec illa philosophiae. Praeterea utraque fines suos habet. Sapiens enim causas naturalium et quaerit et novit, quorum numeros mensurasque geometres persequitur et subputat. Qua ratione constent caelestia, quae illis sit vis quaeve natura, sapiens scit; cursus et recursus et quasdam observationes, per quas descendunt et adlevantur ac speciem interdum stantium praebent, cum caelestibus stare non
27 liceat, colligit mathematicus. Quae causa in speculo imagines exprimat, sciet sapiens; illud tibi geometres potest dicere, quantum abesse debeat corpus ab imagine et qualis forma speculi quales imagines reddat. Magnum esse solem philosophus probabit; quantus sit, mathematicus, qui usu quodam et exercitatione procedit; sed ut procedat, impetranda illi quaedam principia sunt. Non est autem ars sui
28 iuris, cui precarium fundamentum est. Philosophia nil ab alio petit, totum opus a solo excitat; mathematice, ut ita dicam, superficiaria est, in alieno aedificat. Accipit prima, quorum beneficio ad ul-

[1] *nostri* Madvig; *nostrae* MSS.

---

[a] This line of argument inversely resembles the criticism by Seneca of Posidonius in *Ep.* xc.—that the inventions of early science cannot be properly termed a part of philosophy.

[b] See *N.Q.* i. 4 ff.

[c] According to Roman law, *superficies solo cedit*, "the building goes with the ground."

aid us and yet are not parts of ourselves. Nay, if they were, they would not aid us. Food is an aid to the body, but is not a part of it. We get some help from the service which mathematics renders; and mathematics is as indispensable to philosophy as the carpenter is to the mathematician. But carpentering is not a part of mathematics, nor is mathematics a part of philosophy. Moreover, each has its own limits; for the wise man investigates and learns the causes of natural phenomena, while the mathematician follows up and computes their numbers and their measurements.[a] The wise man knows the laws by which the heavenly bodies persist, what powers belong to them, and what attributes; the astronomer merely notes their comings and goings, the rules which govern their settings and their risings, and the occasional periods during which they seem to stand still, although as a matter of fact no heavenly body can stand still. The wise man will know what causes the reflection in a mirror; but the mathematician can merely tell you how far the body should be from the reflection, and what shape of mirror will produce a given reflection.[b] The philosopher will demonstrate that the sun is a large body, while the astronomer will compute just how large, progressing in knowledge by his method of trial and experiment; but in order to progress, he must summon to his aid certain principles. No art, however, is sufficient unto itself, if the foundation upon which it rests depends upon mere favour. Now philosophy asks no favours from any other source; it builds everything on its own soil; but the science of numbers is, so to speak, a structure built on another man's land—it builds on alien soil.[c] It accepts first principles, and by their

teriora perveniat. Si per se iret ad verum, si totius mundi naturam posset conprendere, dicerem multum conlaturam mentibus nostris, quae tractatu caelestium crescunt trahuntque aliquid ex alto.[1] Una re consummatur animus, scientia bonorum ac malorum inmutabili; nihil[2] autem ulla ars alia de bonis ac malis quaerit.

29 Singulas lubet[3] circumire virtutes. Fortitudo contemptrix timendorum est; terribilia et sub iugum libertatem nostram mittentia despicit, provocat, frangit. Numquid ergo hanc liberalia studia corroborant? Fides sanctissimum humani pectoris bonum est, nulla necessitate ad fallendum cogitur, nullo corrumpitur praemio. "Ure," inquit, "caede, occide; non prodam, sed quo magis secreta quaeret dolor, hoc illa altius condam." Numquid liberalia studia hos animos facere possunt? Temperantia voluptatibus imperat, alias odit atque abigit, alias dispensat et ad sanum modum redigit nec umquam ad illas propter ipsas venit. Scit optimum esse modum cupitorum non quantum velis, sed quantum
30 debeas sumere. Humanitas vetat superbum esse adversus socios, vetat avarum. Verbis, rebus, adfectibus comem[4] se facilemque omnibus praestat. Nullum alienum malum putat. Bonum autem suum ideo maxime, quod alicui bono futurum est, amat. Numquid liberalia studia hos mores praecipiunt?

[1] *alto* Gruter; *alio* VP; *aliquo* b.

[2] Before *nihil* later MSS. give *quae soli philosophiae conpetit*; om. by the better MSS.

[3] *lubet* Muretus; *habet* VPb.

[4] *comem* later MSS.; *communem* VPb.

---

[a] Except philosophy.

[b] *i.e.*, in the more commonly accepted sense of the term.

favour arrives at further conclusions. If it could march unassisted to the truth, if it were able to understand the nature of the universe, I should say that it would offer much assistance to our minds; for the mind grows by contact with things heavenly, and draws into itself something from on high. There is but one thing that brings the soul to perfection—the unalterable knowledge of good and evil. But there is no other art [a] which investigates good and evil.

I should like to pass in review the several virtues. Bravery is a scorner of things which inspire fear; it looks down upon, challenges, and crushes the powers of terror and all that would drive our freedom under the yoke. But do "liberal studies" [b] strengthen this virtue? Loyalty is the holiest good in the human heart; it is forced into betrayal by no constraint, and it is bribed by no rewards. Loyalty cries: "Burn me, slay me, kill me! I shall not betray my trust; and the more urgently torture shall seek to find my secret, the deeper in my heart will I bury it!" Can the "liberal arts" produce such a spirit within us? Temperance controls our desires; some it hates and routs, others it regulates and restores to a healthy measure, nor does it ever approach our desires for their own sake. Temperance knows that the best measure of the appetites is not what you want to take, but what you ought to take. Kindliness forbids you to be over-bearing towards your associates, and it forbids you to be grasping. In words and in deeds and in feelings it shows itself gentle and courteous to all men. It counts no evil as another's solely. And the reason why it loves its own good is chiefly because it will some day be the good of another. Do "liberal studies" teach a man

Non magis quam simplicitatem, quam modestiam ac moderationem, non magis quam frugalitatem ac parsimoniam, non magis quam clementiam, quae alieno sanguini tamquam suo parcit et scit homini non esse homine prodige utendum.

31 "Cum dicatis," inquit, "sine liberalibus studiis ad virtutem non perveniri, quemadmodum negatis illa nihil conferre virtuti?" Quia nec sine cibo ad virtutem pervenitur, cibus tamen ad virtutem non pertinet. Ligna navi nihil conferunt, quamvis non fiat navis nisi ex lignis. Non est, inquam, cur aliquid putes eius adiutorio fieri, sine quo non potest fieri.
32 Potest quidem etiam illud dici: sine liberalibus studiis veniri ad sapientiam posse; quamvis enim virtus discenda sit, tamen non per haec discitur.

Quid est autem, quare existimem non futurum sapientem eum, qui litteras nescit, cum sapientia non sit in litteris? Res tradit, non verba, et nescio an certior memoria sit, quae nullum extra se sub-
33 sidium habet. Magna et spatiosa res est sapientia. Vacuo illi loco opus est. De divinis humanisque discendum est, de praeteritis de futuris, de caducis de aeternis, de tempore. De quo uno vide quam multa quaerantur: primum an per se sit aliquid; deinde an aliquid ante tempus sit sine tempore; cum

---

[a] This usage is a not infrequent one in Latin; cf. Petronius, *Sat.* 42 *neminem nihil boni facere oportet*; *id. ib.* 58; Verg. *Ecl.* v. 25, etc. See Draeger, *Hist. Syn.* ii. 75, and Roby, ii. 2246 ff.

[b] *Cf. Epp.* xxxi. 6 and lxxxi. 29 *aestimare res, de quibus . . . cum rerum natura deliberandum est.*

[c] The ancient Stoics defined Time as "extension of the world's motion." The seasons were said to be "alive" because they depended on material conditions. But the Stoics really acknowledged Time to be immaterial. The same problem of corporeality was discussed with regard to the "good.

such character as this? No; no more than they teach simplicity, moderation and self-restraint, thrift and economy, and that kindliness which spares a neighbour's life as if it were one's own and knows that it is not for man to make wasteful use of his fellow-man.

"But," one says, "since you declare that virtue cannot be attained without the 'liberal studies,' how is it that you deny that they offer any assistance to virtue?"[a] Because you cannot attain virtue without food, either; and yet food has nothing to do with virtue. Wood does not offer assistance to a ship, although a ship cannot be built except of wood. There is no reason, I say, why you should think that anything is made by the assistance of that without which it cannot be made. We might even make the statement that it is possible to attain wisdom without the "liberal studies"; for although virtue is a thing that must be learned, yet it is not learned by means of these studies.

What reason have I, however, for supposing that one who is ignorant of letters will never be a wise man, since wisdom is not to be found in letters? Wisdom communicates facts[b] and not words; and it may be true that the memory is more to be depended upon when it has no support outside itself. Wisdom is a large and spacious thing. It needs plenty of free room. One must learn about things divine and human, the past and the future, the ephemeral and the eternal; and one must learn about Time.[c] See how many questions arise concerning time alone: in the first place, whether it is anything in and by itself; in the second place, whether anything exists prior to time and without time; and again, did time

mundo coeperit an etiam ante mundum quia fuerit
34 aliquid, fuerit et tempus. Innumerabiles quaestiones sunt de animo tantum: unde sit, qualis sit, quando esse incipiat, quamdiu sit; aliunde alio transeat et domicilia mutet in[1] alias animalium formas aliasque coniectus, an non amplius quam semel serviat et emissus vagetur in toto; utrum corpus sit an non sit; quid sit facturus, cum per nos aliquid facere desierit, quomodo libertate sua usurus, cum ex hac effugerit cavea; an obliviscatur priorum et illinc[2] nosse se incipiat, unde corpori abductus in sublime secessit.

35 Quamcumque partem rerum humanarum divinarumque conprenderis, ingenti copia quaerendorum ac discendorum fatigaberis. Haec tam multa, tam magna ut habere possint liberum hospitium, supervacua ex animo tollenda sunt. Non dabit se in has angustias virtus; laxum spatium res magna desiderat. Expellantur omnia, totum pectus illi vacet.

36 "At enim delectat artium notitia multarum." Tantum itaque ex illis retineamus, quantum necessarium est. An tu existimas reprendendum, qui supervacua usibus conparat et pretiosarum rerum pompam in domo explicat, non putas eum, qui occupatus est in supervacua litterarum supellectile? Plus scire velle quam sit satis, intemperantiae genus

[1] *in* Koch; *ad* MSS.
[2] *illinc* Hense; *illi* (*ille*) (*illic*) *ne* MSS.

begin along with the universe, or, because there was something even before the universe began, did time also exist then? There are countless questions concerning the soul alone: whence it comes, what is its nature, when it begins to exist, and how long it exists; whether it passes from one place to another and changes its habitation, being transferred successively from one animal shape to another, or whether it is a slave but once, roaming the universe after it is set free; whether it is corporeal or not; what will become of it when it ceases to use us as its medium; how it will employ its freedom when it has escaped from this present prison; whether it will forget all its past, and at that moment begin to know itself when, released from the body, it has withdrawn to the skies.

Thus, whatever phase of things human and divine you have apprehended, you will be wearied by the vast number of things to be answered and things to be learned. And in order that these manifold and mighty subjects may have free entertainment in your soul, you must remove therefrom all superfluous things. Virtue will not surrender herself to these narrow bounds of ours; a great subject needs wide space in which to move. Let all other things be driven out, and let the breast be emptied to receive virtue.

"But it is a pleasure to be acquainted with many arts." Therefore let us keep only as much of them as is essential. Do you regard that man as blameworthy who puts superfluous things on the same footing with useful things, and in his house makes a lavish display of costly objects, but do not deem him blameworthy who has allowed himself to become engrossed with the useless furniture of learning? This desire to know more than is sufficient is a sort

37 est. Quid? Quod ista liberalium artium consectatio molestos, verbosos, intempestivos, sibi placentes facit et ideo non discentes necessaria, quia supervacua didicerunt. Quattuor milia librorum Didymus grammaticus scripsit. Misererer, si tam multa supervacua legisset. In his libris de patria Homeri quaeritur, in his de Aeneae matre vera, in his libidinosior Anacreon an ebriosior vixerit, in his an Sappho publica fuerit, et alia, quae erant dediscenda, si
38 scires. I nunc et longam esse vitam nega. Sed ad nostros quoque cum perveneris, ostendam multa securibus recidenda.

Magno impendio temporum, magna alienarum aurium molestia laudatio haec constat: O hominem litteratum! Simus hoc titulo rusticiore contenti: O
39 virum bonum! Itane est? Annales evolvam omnium gentium et quis primus carmina scripserit quaeram? Quantum temporis inter Orphea intersit et Homerum, cum fastos non habeam, computabo? Et Aristarchi ineptias, quibus aliena carmina conpunxit, recognoscam et aetatem in syllabis conteram? Itane in geometriae pulvere haerebo? Adeo mihi praeceptum illud salutare excidit: "Tempori parce"? Haec sciam? Et quid ignorem?

---

[a] Compare the schoolmaster of Juvenal (vii. 234 ff.), who must know

> Nutricem Anchisae, nomen patriamque novercae
> Anchemoli, dicat quot Acestes vixerit annis, etc.,

and Friedländer's note.

[b] A tradition, probably begun by the Greek comic writers, and explained by Professor Smyth (*Greek Melic Poets*, pp. 227 f.) as due to the more independent position of women among the Aeolians.

[c] Marking supposedly spurious lines by the *obelus*, and using other signs to indicate variations, repetitions, and interpolations. He paid special attention to Homer, Pindar, Hesiod, and the tragedians.

of intemperance. Why? Because this unseemly pursuit of the liberal arts makes men troublesome, wordy, tactless, self-satisfied bores, who fail to learn the essentials just because they have learned the non-essentials. Didymus the scholar wrote four thousand books. I should feel pity for him if he had only read the same number of superfluous volumes. In these books he investigates Homer's birthplace,[a] who was really the mother of Aeneas, whether Anacreon was more of a rake or more of a drunkard, whether Sappho was a bad lot,[b] and other problems the answers to which, if found, were forthwith to be forgotten. Come now, do not tell me that life is long! Nay, when you come to consider our own countrymen also, I can show you many works which ought to be cut down with the axe.

It is at the cost of a vast outlay of time and of vast discomfort to the ears of others that we win such praise as this: "What a learned man you are!" Let us be content with this recommendation, less citified though it be: "What a good man you are!" Do I mean this? Well, would you have me unroll the annals of the world's history and try to find out who first wrote poetry? Or, in the absence of written records, shall I make an estimate of the number of years which lie between Orpheus and Homer? Or shall I make a study of the absurd writings of Aristarchus, wherein he branded the text[c] of other men's verses, and wear my life away upon syllables? Shall I then wallow in the geometrician's dust[d]? Have I so far forgotten that useful saw "Save your time"? Must I know these things? And what may I choose not to know?

[d] The geometricians drew their figures in the dust or sand.

40 Apion grammaticus, qui sub C. Caesare tota circulatus[1] est Graecia et in nomen Homeri ab omnibus civitatibus adoptatus, aiebat Homerum utraque materia consummata, et Odyssia et Iliade, principium adiecisse operi suo, quo bellum Troianum complexus est. Huius rei argumentum adferebat, quod duas litteras in primo versu posuisset ex industria librorum
41 suorum numerum continentes. Talia sciat oportet, qui multa vult scire, non cogitare, quantum temporis tibi auferat mala valetudo, quantum occupatio publica, quantum occupatio privata, quantum occupatio cotidiana, quantum somnus. Metire aetatem tuam; tam multa non capit.

42 De liberalibus studiis loquor; philosophi quantum habent supervacui, quantum ab usu recedentis! Ipsi quoque ad syllabarum distinctiones et coniunctionum ac praepositionum proprietates descenderunt et invidere grammaticis, invidere geometris. Quicquid in illorum artibus supervacuum erat, transtulere in suam. Sic effectum est, ut diligentius loqui scirent
43 quam vivere. Audi, quantum mali faciat nimia subtilitas et quam infesta veritati sit. Protagoras ait de omni re in utramque partem disputari posse ex aequo et de hac ipsa, an omnis res in utramque partem disputabilis sit. Nausiphanes ait ex his, quae videntur
44 esse, nihil magis esse quam non esse. Parmenides

[1] *circulatus* a MS. of Lipsius; *circumlatus* Vb.

---

[a] Originally, rhapsodists who recited from Homer; in general, "interpreters and admirers—in short, the whole 'spiritual kindred'—of Homer" (D. B. Monro)

[b] An ancient explanation of the (now disproved) authorship by Homer of such poems as the *Cypria*, *Little Iliad Sack of Troy*, etc.

EPISTLE LXXXVIII.

Apion, the scholar, who drew crowds to his lectures all over Greece in the days of Gaius Caesar and was acclaimed a Homerid[a] by every state, used to maintain that Homer, when he had finished his two poems, the *Iliad* and the *Odyssey*, added a preliminary poem to his work, wherein he embraced the whole Trojan war.[b] The argument which Apion adduced to prove this statement was that Homer had purposely inserted in the opening line two letters which contained a key to the number of his books. A man who wishes to know many things must know such things as these, and must take no thought of all the time which one loses by ill-health, public duties, private duties, daily duties, and sleep. Apply the measure to the years of your life; they have no room for all these things.

I have been speaking so far of liberal studies; but think how much superfluous and unpractical matter the philosophers contain! Of their own accord they also have descended to establishing nice divisions of syllables, to determining the true meaning of conjunctions and prepositions; they have been envious of the scholars, envious of the mathematicians. They have taken over into their own art all the superfluities of these other arts; the result is that they know more about careful speaking than about careful living. Let me tell you what evils are due to over-nice exactness, and what an enemy it is of truth! Protagoras declares that one can take either side on any question and debate it with equal success—even on this very question, whether every subject can be debated from either point of view. Nausiphanes holds that in things which seem to exist, there is no difference between existence and non-existence. Parmenides maintains that nothing

ait ex his, quae videntur, nihil esse uno excepto[1] universo. Zenon Eleates omnia negotia de negotio deiecit: ait nihil esse. Circa eadem fere Pyrrhonei versantur et Megarici et Eretrici[2] et Academici, qui
45 novam induxerunt scientiam, nihil scire. Haec omnia in illum supervacuum studiorum liberalium gregem coice; illi mihi non profuturam scientiam tradunt, hi spem omnis scientiae eripiunt. Satius est supervacua scire quam nihil. Illi non praeferunt lumen, per quod acies derigatur ad verum; hi oculos mihi effodiunt. Si Protagorae credo, nihil in rerum natura est nisi dubium; si Nausiphani, hoc unum certum est, nihil esse certi; si Parmenidi, nihil est praeter unum; si Zenoni, ne unum quidem.

46 Quid ergo nos sumus? Quid ista, quae nos circumstant, alunt, sustinent? Tota rerum natura umbra est aut inanis aut fallax. Non facile dixerim, utris magis irascar, illis, qui nos nihil scire voluerunt, an illis, qui ne hoc quidem nobis reliquerunt, nihil scire. Vale.

LXXXIX

Seneca Lvcilio svo salvtem

1 Rem utilem desideras et ad sapientiam[3] prope-

[1] *uno excepto* inserted by Kalbfleisch; *nihil esse universo* Vb.

[2] *Eretrici* Lipsius; *cretici* Vb.

[3] *ad sapientiam* later MSS.; *sapientem* B.

---

[a] In other words, the unchangeable, perfect Being of the universe is contrasted with the mutable Non-Being of opinion and unreality.

[b] *i.e.*, the universe.

[c] See §§ 9 ff., which give the normal division.

exists of all this which seems to exist, except the universe alone.[a] Zeno of Elea removed all the difficulties by removing one; for he declares that nothing exists. The Pyrrhonean, Megarian, Eretrian, and Academic schools are all engaged in practically the same task; they have introduced a new knowledge, non-knowledge. You may sweep all these theories in with the superfluous troops of "liberal" studies; the one class of men give me a knowledge that will be of no use to me, the other class do away with any hope of attaining knowledge. It is better, of course, to know useless things than to know nothing. One set of philosophers offers no light by which I may direct my gaze toward the truth; the other digs out my very eyes and leaves me blind. If I cleave to Protagoras, there is nothing in the scheme of nature that is not doubtful; if I hold with Nausiphanes, I am sure only of this—that everything is unsure; if with Parmenides, there is nothing except the One[b]; if with Zeno, there is not even the One.

What are we, then? What becomes of all these things that surround us, support us, sustain us? The whole universe is then a vain or deceptive shadow. I cannot readily say whether I am more vexed at those who would have it that we know nothing, or with those who would not leave us even this privilege. Farewell.

LXXXIX. ON THE PARTS OF PHILOSOPHY[c]

It is a useful fact that you wish to know, one which is essential to him who hastens after wisdom

ranti necessariam, dividi philosophiam et ingens corpus eius in membra disponi. Facilius enim per partes in cognitionem[1] totius adducimur. Utinam quidem quemadmodum universa mundi facies in conspectum venit, ita philosophia tota nobis posset occurrere, simillimum mundo spectaculum. Profecto enim omnes mortales in admirationem sui raperet relictis iis, quae nunc magna magnorum ignorantia credimus. Sed quia contingere hoc non potest, est sic[2] nobis aspicienda,[3] quemadmodum mundi secreta cernuntur.

2 Sapientis quidem animus totam molem eius amplectitur nec minus illam velociter obit quam caelum acies nostra; nobis autem, quibus perrumpenda caligo est et quorum visus in proximo deficit, singula quaeque ostendi facilius possunt universi nondum capacibus. Faciam ergo quod exigis, et philosophiam in partes, non in frusta,[4] dividam. Dividi enim illam, non concidi, utile est. Nam conprehendere quem-
3 admodum maxima ita minima difficile est. Discribitur in tribus populus, in centurias exercitus. Quicquid in maius crevit, facilius agnoscitur, si discessit in partes, quas, ut dixi, innumerabiles esse et parvulas non oportet. Idem enim vitii habet nimia quod nulla divisio; simile confuso est, quidquid usque in pulverem sectum est.

[1] *cognitionem* later MSS.; *cogitationem* B.
[2] *est sic* Buecheler; *et sic* B; *et sic erit* later MSS.
[3] *aspicienda* Mentel.; *abscienda* B.
[4] *frusta* later MSS.; *frustra* B.

[a] See Plato, especially *Symposium* 211 ff.
[b] *i.e.*, an infinitely small *divisio* is the same as its opposite —*confusio.*

—namely, the parts of philosophy and the division of its huge bulk into separate members. For by studying the parts we can be brought more easily to understand the whole. I only wish that philosophy might come before our eyes in all her unity, just as the whole expanse of the firmament is spread out for us to gaze upon! It would be a sight closely resembling that of the firmament. For then surely philosophy would ravish all mortals with love for her[a]; we should abandon all those things which, in our ignorance of what is great, we believe to be great. Inasmuch, however, as this cannot fall to our lot, we must view philosophy just as men gaze upon the secrets of the firmament.

The wise man's mind, to be sure, embraces the whole framework of philosophy, surveying it with no less rapid glance than our mortal eyes survey the heavens; we, however, who must break through the gloom, we whose vision fails even for that which is near at hand, can be shown with greater ease each separate object even though we cannot yet comprehend the universe. I shall therefore comply with your demand, and shall divide philosophy into parts, but not into scraps. For it is useful that philosophy should be divided, but not chopped into bits. Just as it is hard to take in what is indefinitely large, so it is hard to take in what is indefinitely small. The people are divided into tribes, the army into centuries. Whatever has grown to greater size is more easily identified if it is broken up into parts; but the parts, as I have remarked, must not be countless in number and diminutive in size. For over-analysis is faulty in precisely the same way as no analysis at all; whatever you cut so fine that it becomes dust is as good as blended into a mass again.[b]

4 Primum itaque, si videtur[1] tibi, dicam, inter sapientiam et philosophiam quid intersit. Sapientia perfectum bonum est mentis humanae. Philosophia sapientiae amor est et adfectatio. Haec eo tendit,[2] quo illa pervenit. Philosophia unde dicta sit, apparet. Ipso enim nomine fatetur quid amet.[3]
5 Sapientiam quidam ita finierunt, ut dicerent divinorum et humanorum scientiam. Quidam ita: sapientia est nosse divina et humana et horum causas. Supervacua mihi haec videtur adiectio, quia causae divinorum humanorumque pars divinorum sunt. Philosophiam quoque fuerunt qui aliter atque aliter finirent. Alii studium illam virtutis esse dixerunt, alii studium corrigendae mentis, a quibusdam dicta
6 est adpetitio rectae rationis. Illud quasi constitit, aliquid inter philosophiam et sapientiam interesse. Neque enim fieri potest ut idem sit quod adfectatur et quod adfectat. Quomodo multum inter avaritiam et pecuniam interest, cum illa cupiat, haec concupiscatur, sic inter philosophiam et sapientiam. Haec enim illius effectus ac praemium est; illa venit, ad
7 hanc venitur.[4] Sapientia est, quam Graeci σοφίαν vocant. Hoc verbo Romani quoque utebantur, sicut philosophia nunc quoque utuntur. Quod et togatae

[1] *si videtur* Haase; *si ut videtur* MSS.
[2] *eo tendit* Cornelissen; *ostendit* B.
[3] *quid amet* Madvig; *quidam et* B.
[4] *venitur* Hense; *itur* MSS. W. Schultz argues that § 7 (*sapientia . . . Dossenni lege*) has by some error been transferred from its proper position after *quo illa pervenit* in § 4 to its present place, where it disturbs the sequence of the thought.

[a] "Love-of-Wisdom."
[b] Θείων τε καὶ ἀνθρωπίνων ἐπιστήμη, quoted by Plutarch, *De Plac. Phil.* 874 E.
[c] Cicero, *De Off.* ii. 2. 5.

In the first place, therefore, if you approve, I shall draw the distinction between wisdom and philosophy. Wisdom is the perfect good of the human mind; philosophy is the love of wisdom, and the endeavour to attain it. The latter strives toward the goal which the former has already reached. And it is clear why philosophy was so called. For it acknowledges by its very name the object of its love.[a] Certain persons have defined wisdom as the knowledge of things divine and things human.[b] Still others say: "Wisdom is knowing things divine and things human, and their causes also."[c] This added phrase seems to me to be superfluous, since the causes of things divine and things human are a part of the divine system. Philosophy also has been defined in various ways; some have called it "the study of virtue,"[d] others have referred to it as "a study of the way to amend the mind,"[e] and some have named it "the search for right reason." One thing is practically settled, that there is some difference between philosophy and wisdom. Nor indeed is it possible that that which is sought and that which seeks are identical. As there is a great difference between avarice and wealth, the one being the subject of the craving and the other its object, so between philosophy and wisdom. For the one is a result and a reward of the other. Philosophy does the going, and wisdom is the goal. Wisdom is that which the Greeks call σοφία. The Romans also were wont to use this word in the sense in which they now use "philosophy" also. This will be proved to your satisfaction by our old national

[d] The ἄσκησις ἀρετῆς of the earlier Stoics. Seneca (Frag. 17) also calls it *recta vivendi ratio*.

[e] *i.e.*, to make a *bona mens* out of a *mala mens*.

tibi antiquae probabunt et inscriptus Dossenni monumento titulus:

Hospes resiste et sophian Dossenni lege.

8 Quidam ex nostris, quamvis philosophia studium virtutis esset et haec peteretur, illa peteret, tamen non putaverunt illas distrahi posse. Nam nec philosophia sine virtute est nec sine philosophia virtus. Philosophia studium virtutis est, sed per ipsam virtutem; nec virtus autem esse sine studio sui potest nec virtutis studium sine ipsa. Non enim quemadmodum in iis, qui aliquid ex distanti loco ferire conantur, alibi est qui petit, alibi quod petitur. Nec quemadmodum itinera quae ad urbes perducunt, sic viae ad virtutem sunt[1] extra ipsam; ad virtutem venitur per ipsam; cohaerent inter se philosophia virtusque.

9 Philosophiae tres partes esse dixerunt et maximi et plurimi auctores: moralem, naturalem, rationalem. Prima conponit animum. Secunda rerum naturam scrutatur. Tertia proprietates verborum exigit et structuram et argumentationes, ne pro vero falsa subrepant. Ceterum inventi sunt et qui in pauciora

10 philosophiam et qui in plura diducerent. Quidam ex Peripateticis quartam partem adiecerunt[2] civilem, quia propriam quandam exercitationem desideret et

[1] *sic . . . sunt* added by Buecheler, giving the general sense; there is a lacuna in B, in which traces of a corrupt text can be made out.

[2] *adiecerunt* later MSS.; *adicerent* B.

---

[a] It is doubtful whether this was the name of a real person, or a mere "Joe Miller" type from the Fabula Atellana. The character in Horace, *Ep.* ii. 1. 173, is certainly the latter; and the testimony of Pliny (*N.H.* xiv. 15), who quotes a line from a play called *Acharistio*, is not reliable.

plays, as well as by the epitaph that is carved on the tomb of Dossennus[a]:

> Pause, stranger, and read the wisdom of Dossennus.

Certain of our school, however, although philosophy meant to them "the study of virtue," and though virtue was the object sought and philosophy the seeker, have maintained nevertheless that the two cannot be sundered. For philosophy cannot exist without virtue, nor virtue without philosophy. Philosophy is the study of virtue, by means, however, of virtue itself; but neither can virtue exist without the study of itself, nor can the study of virtue exist without virtue itself. For it is not like trying to hit a target at long range, where the shooter and the object to be shot at are in different places. Nor, as roads which lead into a city, are the approaches to virtue situated outside virtue herself; the path by which one reaches virtue leads by way of virtue herself; philosophy and virtue cling closely together.

The greatest authors, and the greatest number of authors, have maintained that there are three divisions of philosophy—moral, natural, and rational.[b] The first keeps the soul in order; the second investigates the universe; the third works out the essential meanings of words, their combinations, and the proofs which keep falsehood from creeping in and displacing truth. But there have also been those who divided philosophy on the one hand into fewer divisions, on the other hand into more. Certain of the Peripatetic school have added a fourth division, "civil philosophy," because it calls for a special sphere of activity and is interested in

[b] *i.e.*, logic.

circa aliam materiam occupata sit. Quidam adiecerunt his partem, quam οἰκονομικὴν vocant, ad-
ministrandae familiaris rei scientiam. Quidam et de
generibus vitae locum separaverunt. Nihil autem
horum non in illa[1] parte morali reperietur.
11 Epicurei duas partes philosophiae putaverunt
esse, naturalem atque moralem; rationalem remo-
verunt. Deinde cum ipsis rebus cogerentur ambigua
secernere, falsa sub specie veri latentia coarguere,
ipsi quoque locum, quem de iudicio et regula
appellant, alio nomine rationalem induxerunt, sed
eum accessionem esse naturalis partis existimant.
12 Cyrenaici naturalia cum rationalibus sustulerunt et
contenti fuerunt moralibus, sed hi quoque quae
removent, aliter inducunt. In quinque enim partes
moralia dividunt, ut una sit de fugiendis et petendis,
altera de adfectibus, tertia de actionibus, quarta de
causis, quinta de argumentis. Causae rerum ex
13 naturali parte sunt, argumenta ex rationali.[2] Ariston
Chius non tantum supervacuas esse dixit naturalem
et rationalem,[3] sed etiam contrarias. Moralem quo-

[1] *non in illa* the later MSS.; *non illa* B.

[2] *rationali* later MSS.; *morali* B. Buecheler thinks that a phrase *neutrum ex morali* may have dropped out—"neither belongs to the 'moral.'"

[3] *rationalem* later MSS.; *formalem* B.

---

[a] *i.e.*, "the management of the home."

[b] That is, of the various arts which deal with the departments of living, such as generalship, politics, business, etc.

[c] Frag. 242 Usener.

[d] Seneca by *de iudicio* is translating the Greek adjective δικανικός, "that which has to do with the courts of law," and by *de regula* the word κανονικός, "that which has to do with rules," here the rules of logic. The Epicureans used for logic κανονική, in contrast with Aristotle and his successors, who used λογική. The Latin *rationalis* is a translation of the latter.

a different subject matter. Some have added a department for which they use the Greek term "economics,"[a] the science of managing one's own household. Still others have made a distinct heading for the various kinds of life.[b] There is no one of these subdivisions, however, which will not be found under the branch called "moral" philosophy.

The Epicureans[c] held that philosophy was twofold, natural and moral; they did away with the rational branch. Then, when they were compelled by the facts themselves to distinguish between equivocal ideas and to expose fallacies that lay hidden under the cloak of truth, they themselves also introduced a heading to which they give the name "forensic and regulative,"[d] which is merely "rational" under another name, although they hold that this section is accessory to the department of "natural" philosophy. The Cyrenaic[e] school abolished the natural as well as the rational department, and were content with the moral side alone; and yet these philosophers also include under another title that which they have rejected. For they divide moral philosophy into five parts: (1) What to avoid and what to seek, (2) The Passions, (3) Actions, (4) Causes, (5) Proofs. Now the causes of things really belong to the "natural" division, the proofs to the "rational." Aristo[f] of Chios remarked that the natural and the rational were not only superfluous, but were also contradictory. He even limited the "moral," which was all that was

[e] Led by Aristippus of Cyrene. As the Cynics developed into the Stoics, so the Cyrenaics developed into the Epicureans.

[f] Frag. 357 von Arnim.

que, quam solam reliquerat, circumcidit; nam eum locum, qui monitiones continet, sustulit et paedagogi esse dixit, non philosophi, tamquam quidquam aliud sit sapiens quam humani generis paedagogus.

14 Ergo cum tripertita sit philosophia, moralem eius partem primum incipiamus disponere. Quam in tria rursus dividi placuit, ut prima esset inspectio suum cuique distribuens et aestimans quanto quidque dignum sit, maxime utilis. Quid enim est tam necessarium quam pretia rebus inponere? Secunda de impetu, de actionibus tertia.[1] Primum enim est, ut quanti[2] quidque sit iudices, secundum, ut impetum ad illa capias ordinatum temperatumque, tertium, ut inter impetum tuum actionemque conveniat, ut in omnibus istis tibi ipse consentias.

15 Quicquid ex tribus defuit, turbat et cetera. Quid enim prodest inter se[3] aestimata habere omnia, si sis in impetu nimius? Quid prodest impetus repressisse et habere cupiditates in tua[4] potestate, si in ipsa rerum actione tempora ignores nec scias quando quidque et ubi et quemadmodum agi debeat? Aliud est enim dignitates et pretia rerum nosse, aliud articulos, aliud impetus refrenare et ad agenda ire, non ruere. Tunc ergo vita concors sibi est, ubi actio non destituit impetum, impetus ex dignitate rei cuius-

[1] This is the order followed by Buecheler; B gives *secunda de actionibus tertia de impetu.*

[2] *quanti* Muretus; *quantum* B.

[3] *inter se* Gloeckner; *inter* B.

[4] *tua* later MSS.; *sua* B.

---

[a] Seneca translates θεωρητική.

[b] Ὁρμητική; the ὁρμαί, *impetus*, in the Stoic philosophy, are the natural instincts, which require training and regulation before they can be trusted.

[c] Πρακτική.

left to him; for he abolished that heading which embraced advice, maintaining that it was the business of the pedagogue, and not of the philosopher—as if the wise man were anything else than the pedagogue of the human race!

Since, therefore, philosophy is threefold, let us first begin to set in order the moral side. It has been agreed that this should be divided into three parts. First, we have the speculative[a] part, which assigns to each thing its particular function and weighs the worth of each; it is highest in point of utility. For what is so indispensable as giving to everything its proper value? The second has to do with impulse,[b] the third with actions.[c] For the first duty is to determine severally what things are worth; the second, to conceive with regard to them a regulated and ordered impulse; the third, to make your impulse and your actions harmonize, so that under all these conditions you may be consistent with yourself. If any of these three be defective, there is confusion in the rest also. For what benefit is there in having all things appraised, each in its proper relations, if you go to excess in your impulses? What benefit is there in having checked your impulses and in having your desires in your own control, if when you come to action you are unaware of the proper times and seasons, and if you do not know when, where, and how each action should be carried out? It is one thing to understand the merits and the values of facts, another thing to know the precise moment for action, and still another to curb impulses and to proceed, instead of rushing, toward what is to be done. Hence life is in harmony with itself only when action has not deserted impulse, and when impulse toward an

que concipitur proinde remissus vel acrior,[1] prout illa digna est peti.

16 Naturalis pars philosophiae in duo scinditur: corporalia et incorporalia. Utraque dividuntur in suos, ut ita dicam, gradus. Corporum locus in hos primum, in ea quae faciunt et quae ex his gignuntur; gignuntur autem elementa. Ipse de[2] elementis locus, ut quidam putant, simplex est, ut quidam, in materiam et causam omnia moventem et elementa dividitur.

17 Superest ut rationalem partem philosophiae dividam. Omnis oratio aut continua est aut inter respondentem et interrogantem discissa. Hanc διαλεκτικήν, illam ῥητορικὴν placuit vocari. Ῥητορικὴ verba curat et sensus et ordinem. Διαλεκτικὴ in duas partes dividitur, in verba et significationes, id est in res quae dicuntur et vocabula quibus dicuntur. Ingens deinde sequitur utriusque divisio. Itaque hoc loco finem faciam et

Summa sequar fastigia rerum;

alioqui si voluero facere partium partes, quaestionum
18 liber fiet. Haec, Lucili virorum optime, quo minus legas non deterreo, dummodo quicquid legeris,[3] ad mores statim referas.

Illos conpesce, marcentia in te excita, soluta constringe, contumacia doma, cupiditates tuas publicas-

[1] *vel acrior* some later MSS.; *acrior* B; *acriorque* other MSS.
[2] *ipse de* one later MS.; *de* is omitted by B and the rest.
[3] *legeris* later MSS.; *elegeris* B.

---

[a] Σωματική and ἀσώματος.
[b] Ποιητικά and παθητικά.
[c] *i.e.*, has no subdivisions.
[d] Vergil, *Aeneid*, i. 342.

object arises in each case from the worth of the object, being languid or more eager as the case may be, according as the objects which arouse it are worth seeking.

The natural side of philosophy is twofold: bodily and non-bodily.[a] Each is divided into its own grades of importance, so to speak. The topic concerning bodies deals, first, with these two grades: the creative and the created[b]; and the created things are the elements. Now this very topic of the elements, as some writers hold, is integral[c]; as others hold, it is divided into matter, the cause which moves all things, and the elements.

It remains for me to divide rational philosophy into its parts. Now all speech is either continuous, or split up between questioner and answerer. It has been agreed upon that the former should be called rhetoric, and the latter dialectic. Rhetoric deals with words, and meanings, and arrangement. Dialectic is divided into two parts: words and their meanings, that is, into things which are said, and the words in which they are said. Then comes a subdivision of each—and it is of vast extent. Therefore I shall stop at this point, and

> But treat the climax of the story;[d]

for if I should take a fancy to give the subdivisions, my letter would become a debater's handbook! I am not trying to discourage you, excellent Lucilius, from reading on this subject, provided only that you promptly relate to conduct all that you have read.

It is your conduct that you must hold in check; you must rouse what is languid in you, bind fast what has become relaxed, conquer what is obstinate, persecute your appetites, and the appetites of man-

que quantum potes vexa; et istis dicentibus "quo
19 usque eadem?" responde: "ego debebam dicere 'quo usque eadem peccabitis?'" Remedia ante vultis quam vitia desinere? Ego vero eo magis dicam et, quia recusatis, perseverabo. Tunc incipit medicina proficere, ubi in corpore alienato dolorem tactus expressit. Dicam etiam invitis profutura. Aliquando aliqua ad vos non blanda vox veniat, et quia verum singuli audire non vultis, publice audite.
20 Quo usque fines possessionum propagabitis? Ager uni domino, qui populum cepit, angustus est. Quo usque arationes vestras[1] porrigetis, ne provinciarum quidem spatio[2] contenti circumscribere praediorum modum? Inlustrium fluminum per privatum decursus est et amnes magni magnarumque gentium termini usque ad ostium a fonte vestri sunt. Hoc quoque parum est, nisi latifundiis vestris maria cinxistis, nisi trans Hadriam et Ionium Aegaeumque vester vilicus regnat, nisi insulae, ducum domicilia magnorum, inter vilissima rerum numerantur. Quam vultis late possidete, sit fundus quod aliquando imperium vocabatur; facite vestrum quicquid potestis, dum plus sit alieno.

21 Nunc vobiscum loquor, quorum aeque spatiose luxuria quam illorum avaritia diffunditur. Vobis

[1] *arationes vestras* Erasmus; *a rationib; vestris* B.
[2] *spatio* de Jan; *statione* B.

[a] For the thought compare Petronius, *Sat.* 48 *nunc coniungere agellis Siciliam volo, ut, cum Africam libuerit ire, per meos fines navigem.*

kind, as much as you can; and to those who say: "How long will this unending talk go on?" answer with the words: "I ought to be asking you 'How long will these unending sins of yours go on?'" Do you really desire my remedies to stop before your vices? But I shall speak of my remedies all the more, and just because you offer objections I shall keep on talking. Medicine begins to do good at the time when a touch makes the diseased body tingle with pain. I shall utter words that will help men even against their will. At times you should allow words other than compliments to reach your ears, and because as individuals you are unwilling to hear the truth, hear it collectively. How far will you extend the boundaries of your estates? An estate which held a nation is too narrow for a single lord. How far will you push forward your ploughed fields—you who are not content to confine the measure of your farms even within the amplitude of provinces?[a] You have noble rivers flowing down through your private grounds; you have mighty streams—boundaries of mighty nations—under your dominion from source to outlet. This also is too little for you unless you also surround whole seas with your estates, unless your steward holds sway on the other side of the Adriatic, the Ionian, and the Aegean seas, unless the islands, homes of famous chieftains, are reckoned by you as the most paltry of possessions! Spread them as widely as you will, if only you may have as a "farm" what was once called a kingdom; make whatever you can your own, provided only that it is more than your neighbour's!

And now for a word with you, whose luxury spreads itself out as widely as the greed of those to whom I have just referred. To you I say: "Will

dico: quo usque nullus erit lacus cui non villarum vestrarum fastigia immineant? Nullum flumen cuius non ripas aedificia vestra praetexant? Ubicumque scatebunt aquarum calentium venae, ibi nova deversoria luxuriae excitabuntur. Ubicumque in aliquem sinum litus curvabitur, vos protinus fundamenta iacietis[1] nec contenti solo nisi quod manu feceritis, mare[2] agetis introrsus. Omnibus licet locis tecta vestra resplendeant, aliubi inposita montibus in vastum terrarum marisque prospectum, aliubi ex plano in altitudinem montium educta, cum multa aedificaveritis, cum ingentia, tamen et singula corpora estis et parvola. Quid prosunt multa cubicula? In uno iacetis. Non est vestrum ubicumque non estis.

22 Ad vos deinde transeo, quorum profunda et insatiabilis gula hinc maria scrutatur, hinc terras, alia hamis, alia laqueis, alia retium variis generibus cum magno labore persequitur; nullis animalibus nisi ex fastidio pax est. Quantulum[3] ex istis epulis, quae per tot comparatis manus, fesso voluptatibus ore libatis? Quantulum ex ista fera periculose capta dominus crudus ac nauseans gustat? Quantulum ex tot conchyliis tam longe advectis per istum stomachum inexplebilem labitur? Infelices, ecquid[4] intellegitis maiorem vos famem habere quam ventrem?

23 Haec aliis dic, ut dum dicis, audias ipse; scribe,

[1] *iacietis* later MSS.; *facietis* B.
[2] *mare* a MS. of Gruter; *arme* B.
[3] *quantulum* later MSS.; *quantulum est* B.
[4] *ecquid* Gronovius; *esse quid* B.

---

[a] *i.e.*, by building embankments, etc. *Cf.* Horace, *Od.* ii. 18. 22 *parum locuples continente ripa.*

this custom continue until there is no lake over which the pinnacles of your country-houses do not tower? Until there is no river whose banks are not bordered by your lordly structures? Wherever hot waters shall gush forth in rills, there you will be causing new resorts of luxury to rise. Wherever the shore shall bend into a bay, there will you straightway be laying foundations, and, not content with any land that has not been made by art, you will bring the sea within your boundaries.[a] On every side let your house-tops flash in the sun, now set on mountain peaks where they command an extensive outlook over sea and land, now lifted from the plain to the height of mountains; build your manifold structures, your huge piles,—you are nevertheless but individuals, and puny ones at that! What profit to you are your many bed-chambers? You sleep in one. No place is yours where you yourselves are not.

"Next I pass to you, you whose bottomless and insatiable maw explores on the one hand the seas, on the other the earth, with enormous toil hunting down your prey, now with hook, now with snare, now with nets of various kinds; no animal has peace except when you are cloyed with it. And how slight a portion of those banquets of yours, prepared for you by so many hands, do you taste with your pleasure-jaded palate! How slight a portion of all that game, whose taking was fraught with danger, does the master's sick and squeamish stomach relish? How slight a portion of all those shell-fish, imported from so far, slips down that insatiable gullet? Poor wretches, do you not know that your appetites are bigger than your bellies?"

Talk in this way to other men,—provided that while you talk you also listen; write in this way,—

ut dum scribis, legas, omnia ad mores et ad sedandam rabiem adfectuum referens. Stude, non ut plus aliquid scias, sed ut melius. VALE.

XC

SENECA LVCILIO SVO SALVTEM

1 Quis dubitare, mi Lucili, potest, quin deorum immortalium munus sit quod vivimus, philosophiae quod bene vivimus? Itaque tanto plus huic nos debere quam dis, quanto maius beneficium est bona vita quam vita, pro certo haberetur, nisi ipsam philosophiam di tribuissent. Cuius scientiam nulli[1] de-
2 derunt, facultatem omnibus. Nam si hanc quoque bonum vulgare fecissent[2] et prudentes nasceremur, sapientia quod in se optimum habet, perdidisset: inter fortuita non esse.[3] Nunc enim hoc in illa pretiosum atque magnificum est, quod non obvenit, quod illam sibi quisque debet, quod non ab alio petitur.

Quid haberes quod in philosophia suspiceres, si
3 beneficiaria res esset? Huius opus unum est de divinis humanisque verum invenire.[4] Ab hac numquam recedit religio, pietas, iustitia et omnis alius comitatus virtutum consertarum et inter se cohaeren-

[1] *nulli* later MSS.; *ulli* B.
[2] *fecissent* later MSS.; *fecisset* B.
[3] *non esse* Gloeckner; *non esset* MSS.
[4] *invenire* later MSS.; *inveniri* B.

---

[a] *Cf.* § 18.
[b] *Cf.* Plato, *Crito* 48, "not life itself, but a good life, is chiefly to be desired."

provided that while you write you read, remembering that everything[a] you hear or read, is to be applied to conduct, and to the alleviation of passion's fury. Study, not in order to add anything to your knowledge, but to make your knowledge better. Farewell.

XC. ON THE PART PLAYED BY PHILOSOPHY IN THE PROGRESS OF MAN

Who can doubt, my dear Lucilius, that life is the gift of the immortal gods, but that living well[b] is the gift of philosophy? Hence the idea that our debt to philosophy is greater than our debt to the gods, in proportion as a good life is more of a benefit than mere life, would be regarded as correct, were not philosophy itself a boon which the gods have bestowed upon us. They have given the knowledge thereof to none, but the faculty of acquiring it they have given to all. For if they had made philosophy also a general good, and if we were gifted with understanding at our birth, wisdom would have lost her best attribute—that she is not one of the gifts of fortune. For as it is, the precious and noble characteristic of wisdom is that she does not advance to meet us, that each man is indebted to himself for her, and that we do not seek her at the hands of others.

What would there be in philosophy worthy of your respect, if she were a thing that came by bounty? Her sole function is to discover the truth about things divine and things human. From her side religion never departs, nor duty, nor justice, nor any of the whole company of virtues which cling

tium. Haec docuit colere divina, humana diligere, et penes deos imperium esse, inter homines consortium. Quod aliquandiu inviolatum mansit, antequam societatem avaritia distraxit et paupertatis causa etiam is, quos fecit locupletissimos, fuit. Desierunt[1] enim omnia possidere, dum volunt propria.

4 Sed primi mortalium quique ex his geniti naturam incorrupti sequebantur, eundem habebant et ducem et legem, commissi melioris arbitrio. Naturae est enim potioribus deteriora summittere. Mutis quidem gregibus aut maxima corpora praesunt aut vehementissima. Non praecedit armenta degener taurus, sed qui magnitudine ac toris ceteros mares vicit. Elephantorum gregem excelsissimus ducit; inter homines pro summo[2] est optimum. Animo itaque rector eligebatur, ideoque summa felicitas erat gentium, in quibus non poterat potentior esse nisi melior. Tuto[3] enim quantum vult potest, qui se nisi quod debet non putat posse.[4]

5 Illo ergo saeculo, quod aureum perhibent, penes sapientes fuisse regnum Posidonius iudicat. Hi con-

[1] *desierunt* later MSS.; *desiderium* B.
[2] *pro summo* ed. Ven. (1492); *proximo* or *pro maximo* MSS.
[3] *tuto* Buecheler; *toto* B; *tantum* others.
[4] *putat posse* some later MSS.; *putat esse* B.

---

[a] Compare the "knowledge of things divine and things human" of lxxxix. 5.

[b] The "Golden Age" motif was a frequent one in Latin literature. Compare, *e.g.*, Tibullus, i. 3. 35 ff., the passage beginning:

Quam bene Saturno vivebant rege, priusquam
Tellus in longas est patefacta vias!

Cf. § 46, summing up the message of Seneca's letter.

[c] While modern philosophy would probably side with Seneca rather than with Posidonius, it is interesting to know the opinion of Macaulay, who holds (Essay on Bacon) that

together in close-united fellowship. Philosophy has taught us to worship that which is divine, to love that which is human[a]; she has told us that with the gods lies dominion, and among men, fellowship. This fellowship remained unspoiled for a long time, until avarice tore the community asunder and became the cause of poverty, even in the case of those whom she herself had most enriched. For men cease to possess all things the moment they desire all things for their own.

But the first men and those who sprang from them, still unspoiled, followed nature, having one man as both their leader and their law, entrusting themselves to the control of one better than themselves. For nature has the habit of subjecting the weaker to the stronger. Even among the dumb animals those which are either biggest or fiercest hold sway. It is no weakling bull that leads the herd; it is one that has beaten the other males by his might and his muscle. In the case of elephants, the tallest goes first; among men, the best is regarded as the highest. That is why it was to the mind that a ruler was assigned; and for that reason the greatest happiness rested with those peoples among whom a man could not be the more powerful unless he were the better. For that man can safely accomplish what he will who thinks he can do nothing except what he ought to do.

Accordingly, in that age which is maintained to be the golden age,[b] Posidonius[c] holds that the government was under the jurisdiction of the wise.

there is much in common between Posidonius and the English inductive philosopher, and thinks but little of Seneca's ideas on the subject. *Cf.* W. C. Summers, *Select Letters of Seneca*, p. 312.

tinebant manus et infirmiorem a validioribus tuebantur, suadebant dissuadebantque et utilia atque inutilia monstrabant. Horum prudentia ne quid deesset suis providebat, fortitudo pericula arcebat, beneficentia augebat[1] ornabatque subiectos. Officium erat imperare, non regnum. Nemo quantum posset, adversus eos experiebatur, per quos coeperat posse, nec erat cuiquam aut animus in iniuriam aut causa, cum bene imperanti bene pareretur nihilque rex maius minari male parentibus posset, quam ut abirent[2] e regno.

6 Sed postquam subrepentibus vitiis in tyrannidem regna conversa sunt, opus esse legibus coepit, quas et ipsas inter initia tulere sapientes. Solon qui Athenas aequo iure fundavit, inter septem fuit[3] sapientia notos. Lycurgum si eadem aetas tulisset, sacro illi numero accessisset octavus. Zaleuci leges Charondaeque laudantur. Hi non in foro nec in consultorum atrio, sed in Pythagorae tacito illo sanctoque secessu didicerunt iura, quae florenti tunc Siciliae et per Italiam Graeciae ponerent.

7 Hactenus Posidonio adsentior; artes[4] quidem a philosophia inventas, quibus in cotidiano vita utitur, non concesserim nec illi fabricae adseram gloriam. "Illa," inquit, "sparsos et aut cavis tectos[5] aut aliqua

[1] *augebat* later MSS.; *agebat* B.

[2] *abirent* later MSS.; *abiret* B; *quam abire se regno* Gronovius.

[3] *fuit* Madvig; *cui* B.

[4] *adsentior; artes* Erasmus; *adsentio partes* (*artes*) MSS.

[5] *sparsos . . . tectos* Lipsius; *sparsose caucasis lectos* B.

[a] Cleobulus of Rhodes, Periander of Corinth, Pittacus of Mitylene, Bias of Priene, Thales of Miletus, Chilon of Sparta, and Solon of Athens. For some of these substitutions are made in certain lists.

[b] *Cf. Ep.* lxxxviii. 20 *ad alia multum, ad virtutem nihil.*

They kept their hands under control, and protected the weaker from the stronger. They gave advice, both to do and not to do; they showed what was useful and what was useless. Their forethought provided that their subjects should lack nothing; their bravery warded off dangers; their kindness enriched and adorned their subjects. For them ruling was a service, not an exercise of royalty. No ruler tried his power against those to whom he owed the beginnings of his power; and no one had the inclination, or the excuse, to do wrong, since the ruler ruled well and the subject obeyed well, and the king could utter no greater threat against disobedient subjects than that they should depart from the kingdom.

But when once vice stole in and kingdoms were transformed into tyrannies, a need arose for laws; and these very laws were in turn framed by the wise. Solon, who established Athens upon a firm basis by just laws, was one of the seven men renowned for their wisdom.[a] Had Lycurgus lived in the same period, an eighth would have been added to that hallowed number seven. The laws of Zaleucus and Charondas are praised; it was not in the forum or in the offices of skilled counsellors, but in the silent and holy retreat of Pythagoras, that these two men learned the principles of justice which they were to establish in Sicily (which at that time was prosperous) and throughout Grecian Italy.

Up to this point I agree with Posidonius; but that philosophy discovered the arts of which life makes use in its daily round[b] I refuse to admit, nor will I ascribe to it an artisan's glory. Posidonius says: "When men were scattered over the earth, protected by caves or by the dug-out shelter of a

rupe suffossa aut exesae arboris trunco docuit tecta moliri." Ego vero philosophiam iudico non magis excogitasse has machinationes tectorum supra tecta surgentium et urbium urbes prementium quam vivaria
8 piscium in hoc clausa, ut tempestatum periculum non adiret gula et quamvis acerrime pelago saeviente haberet luxuria portus suos, in quibus distinctos piscium greges saginaret. Quid ais? Philosophia homines docuit habere clavem et seram? Quid[1] aliud erat avaritiae signum dare? Philosophia haec cum tanto habitantium periculo inminentia tecta suspendit? Parum enim erat fortuitis tegi et sine arte et sine difficultate naturale invenire sibi aliquod receptaculum. Mihi crede, felix illud saeculum ante
9 architectos fuit, ante tectores.[2] Ista nata sunt iam nascente luxuria, in quadratum tigna decidere et serra per designata currente certa manu trabem scindere,

> Nam primi cuneis scindebant fissile lignum.

Non enim tecta cenationi epulum recepturae parabantur, nec in hunc usum pinus aut abies deferebatur longo vehiculorum ordine vicis intrementibus, ut ex illa lacunaria auro gravia penderent. Furcae
10 utrimque suspensae fulciebant casam. Spissatis ramalibus ac fronde congesta et in proclive disposita

[1] *quid* later MSS.; *quidquid* B.
[2] *ante architectos . . . ista* Hense; *antea architektos fuit. antetacteres. ista* B.

---

[a] Vergil, *Georg.* i. 144.
[b] *Cf.* Juvenal, iii. 254 ff.:

> Longa coruscat
> Serraco veniente abies, atque altera pinum
> Plaustra vehunt, nutant alte populoque minantur.

Compare also the "towering tenements" of § 8.

cliff or by the trunk of a hollow tree, it was philosophy that taught them to build houses." But I, for my part, do not hold that philosophy devised these shrewdly-contrived dwellings of ours which rise story upon story, where city crowds against city, any more than that she invented the fish-preserves, which are enclosed for the purpose of saving men's gluttony from having to run the risk of storms, and in order that, no matter how wildly the sea is raging, luxury may have its safe harbours in which to fatten fancy breeds of fish. What! Was it philosophy that taught the use of keys and bolts? Nay, what was that except giving a hint to avarice? Was it philosophy that erected all these towering tenements, so dangerous to the persons who dwell in them? Was it not enough for man to provide himself a roof of any chance covering, and to contrive for himself some natural retreat without the help of art and without trouble? Believe me, that was a happy age, before the days of architects, before the days of builders! All this sort of thing was born when luxury was being born,—this matter of cutting timbers square and cleaving a beam with unerring hand as the saw made its way over the marked-out line.

> The primal man with wedges split his wood.[a]

For they were not preparing a roof for a future banquet-hall; for no such use did they carry the pine-trees or the firs along the trembling streets[b] with a long row of drays—merely to fasten thereon panelled ceilings heavy with gold. Forked poles erected at either end propped up their houses. With close-packed branches and with leaves heaped up and laid

decursus imbribus quamvis magnis erat. Sub his tectis habitavere, sed securi. Culmus liberos texit, sub marmore atque auro servitus habitat.

In illo quoque dissentio a Posidonio, quod ferramenta fabrilia excogitata a sapientibus viris iudicat.
11 Isto enim modo dicat licet sapientes fuisse, per quos

> Tunc laqueis captare feras et fallere visco
> Inventum et magnos canibus circumdare saltus.

Omnia enim ista sagacitas hominum, non sapientia
12 invenit. In hoc quoque dissentio, sapientes fuisse qui ferri metalla et aeris invenerint, cum incendio silvarum adusta tellus in summo venas iacentis liquefactas[1] fudisset; ista[2] tales inveniunt, quales colunt.
13 Ne illa quidem tam suptilis mihi quaestio videtur quam Posidonio, utrum malleus in usu esse prius an forcipes coeperint. Utraque invenit aliquis excitati ingenii, acuti, non magni nec elati, et quicquid aliud corpore incurvato et animo humum spectante quaerendum est.

Sapiens facilis victu fuit, quidni? Cum hoc quoque saeculo esse quam expeditissimus cupiat.
14 Quomodo, oro te, convenit, ut et Diogenen mireris et Daedalum? Uter ex his sapiens tibi videtur? Qui serram commentus est, an ille qui cum vidisset puerum cava manu bibentem aquam, fregit protinus

[1] *liquefactas* later MSS.; *liquefacta* B.
[2] *ista* Pincianus; *ipsa* B.

---

[a] Vergil, *Georg.* i. 139 f.
[b] *Cf.* T. Rice Holmes, *Ancient Britain*, pp. 121 f., who concludes that the discovery of ore-smelting was accidental.

sloping they contrived a drainage for even the heaviest rains. Beneath such dwellings they lived, but they lived in peace. A thatched roof once covered free men; under marble and gold dwells slavery.

On another point also I differ from Posidonius, when he holds that mechanical tools were the invention of wise men. For on that basis one might maintain that those were wise who taught the arts

> Of setting traps for game, and liming twigs
> For birds, and girdling mighty woods with dogs.[a]

It was man's ingenuity, not his wisdom, that discovered all these devices. And I also differ from him when he says that wise men discovered our mines of iron and copper, "when the earth, scorched by forest fires, melted the veins of ore which lay near the surface and caused the metal to gush forth."[b] Nay, the sort of men who discover such things are the sort of men who are busied with them. Nor do I consider this question so subtle as Posidonius thinks, namely, whether the hammer or the tongs came first into use. They were both invented by some man whose mind was nimble and keen, but not great or exalted; and the same holds true of any other discovery which can only be made by means of a bent body and of a mind whose gaze is upon the ground.

The wise man was easy-going in his way of living. And why not? Even in our own times he would prefer to be as little cumbered as possible. How, I ask, can you consistently admire both Diogenes and Daedalus? Which of these two seems to you a wise man—the one who devised the saw, or the one who, on seeing a boy drink water from the hollow of his hand, forthwith took his cup from his wallet and

exemptum e perula calicem cum[1] hac obiurgatione sui: "quamdiu homo stultus supervacuas sarcinas habui!" qui se conplicuit in dolio et in eo cubitavit?

15 Hodie utrum tandem sapientiorem putas, qui invenit quemadmodum in inmensam altitudinem crocum latentibus fistulis exprimat, qui euripos subito aquarum impetu implet aut siccat et versatilia cenationum laquearia ita coagmentat, ut subinde alia facies atque alia succedat et totiens tecta quotiens fericula mutentur, an eum, qui et aliis et sibi hoc monstrat, quam nihil nobis natura durum ac difficile imperaverit, posse nos habitare sine marmorario ac fabro, posse nos vestitos esse sine commercio sericorum,[2] posse nos habere usibus nostris necessaria, si contenti fuerimus iis quae terra posuit in summo? Quem si audire humanum genus voluerit, tam super-

16 vacuum sciet sibi cocum esse quam militem. Illi sapientes fuerunt aut certe sapientibus similes, quibus expedita erat tutela corporis. Simplici cura constant necessaria; in delicias laboratur. Non desiderabis artifices; sequere naturam.

Illa noluit esse districtos. Ad quaecumque nos cogebat, instruxit. "Frigus intolerabilest corpori nudo." Quid ergo? Non pelles ferarum et aliorum animalium a frigore satis abundeque defendere queunt? Non corticibus arborum pleraeque gentes

[1] *cum* added by Baehrens.
[2] *sericorum* Fickert; *servorum* B.

---

[a] *Cf.* Diog. Laert. vi. 37 *θεασάμενός ποτε παιδίον ταῖς χερσὶ πῖνον, ἐξέῤῥιψε τῆς πήρας τὴν κοτύλην, εἰπών, Παιδίον με νενίκηκεν εὐτελείᾳ.*

[b] Compare the halls of Nero which Seneca may easily have had in mind: (Suet. *Nero* 31) *cenationes laqueatae tabulis eburneis versatilibus . . . praecipua cenationum rotunda, quae perpetuo diebus ac noctibus vice mundi circumageretur.*

broke it, upbraiding himself with these words:[a] "Fool that I am, to have been carrying superfluous baggage all this time!" and then curled himself up in his tub and lay down to sleep? In these our own times, which man, pray, do you deem the wiser—the one who invents a process for spraying saffron perfumes to a tremendous height from hidden pipes, who fills or empties canals by a sudden rush of waters, who so cleverly constructs a dining-room with a ceiling of movable panels that it presents one pattern after another, the roof changing as often as the courses,[b]—or the one who proves to others, as well as to himself, that nature has laid upon us no stern and difficult law when she tells us that we can live without the marble-cutter and the engineer, that we can clothe ourselves without traffic in silk fabrics, that we can have everything that is indispensable to our use, provided only that we are content with what the earth has placed on its surface? If mankind were willing to listen to this sage, they would know that the cook is as superfluous to them as the soldier. Those were wise men, or at any rate like the wise, who found the care of the body a problem easy to solve. The things that are indispensable require no elaborate pains for their acquisition; it is only the luxuries that call for labour. Follow nature, and you will need no skilled craftsmen.

Nature did not wish us to be harassed. For whatever she forced upon us, she equipped us. "But cold cannot be endured by the naked body." What then? Are there not the skins of wild beasts and other animals, which can protect us well enough, and more than enough, from the cold? Do not many tribes cover their bodies with the bark of

tegunt corpora? Non avium plumae in usum vestis conseruntur? Non hodieque magna Scytharum pars tergis vulpium induitur ac murum, quae tactu mollia

17 et inpenetrabilia ventis sunt? "Opus est tamen calorem solis aestivi umbra crassiore propellere." Quid ergo? Non vetustas multa dedit[1] loca, quae vel iniuria temporis vel alio quolibet casu excavata in specum recesserunt? Quid ergo? Non quilibet[2] virgeam cratem texuerunt manu et vili obliverunt luto, deinde stipula[3] aliisque silvestribus operuere fastigium, et pluviis per devexa labentibus hiemem transiere[4] securi? Quid ergo? Non in defosso latent Syrticae gentes quibusque propter nimios solis ardores nullum tegimentum satis repellendis caloribus solidum est nisi ipsa arens humus?

18 Non fuit tam inimica natura, ut, cum omnibus aliis animalibus facilem actum vitae daret, homo solus non posset sine tot artibus vivere. Nihil horum ab illa nobis imperatum est, nihil aegre quaerendum, ut possit vita produci. Ad parata nati sumus; nos omnia nobis difficilia facilium fastidio fecimus. Tecta tegimentaque et fomenta corporum et cibi et quae nunc ingens negotium facta sunt, obvia erant et

[1] *dedit* Madvig; *abdidit* MSS. Buecheler suspects the whole clause to be corrupt. H. Müller suggests *abdita dedit*.

[2] *quilibet* later MSS.; *quaelibet* B. G. Gemoll believes that the words *quid ergo . . . securi* should be placed at the head of § 17.

[3] *stipula* Hense et al.; *despicula* B; *de stipula* cod. Harl. followed by Haase.

[4] *transiere* later MSS.; *transire* B.

---

[a] *Cf.* Ovid, *Met.* i. 121 f.:

Domus antra fuerunt
Et densi frutices et vinctae cortice virgae.

trees? Are not the feathers of birds sewn together to serve for clothing? Even at the present day does not a large portion of the Scythian tribe garb itself in the skins of foxes and mice, soft to the touch and impervious to the winds? "For all that, men must have some thicker protection than the skin, in order to keep off the heat of the sun in summer." What then? Has not antiquity produced many retreats which, hollowed out either by the damage wrought by time or by any other occurrence you will, have opened into caverns? What then? Did not the very first-comers take twigs[a] and weave them by hand into wicker mats, smear them with common mud, and then with stubble and other wild grasses construct a roof, and thus pass their winters secure, the rains carried off by means of the sloping gables? What then? Do not the peoples on the edge of the Syrtes dwell in dug-out houses—and indeed all the tribes who, because of the too fierce blaze of the sun, possess no protection sufficient to keep off the heat except the parched soil itself?

Nature was not so hostile to man that, when she gave all the other animals an easy rôle in life, she made it impossible for him alone to live without all these artifices. None of these was imposed upon us by her; none of them had to be painfully sought out that our lives might be prolonged. All things were ready for us at our birth; it is we that have made everything difficult for ourselves, through our disdain for what is easy. Houses, shelter, creature comforts, food, and all that has now become the source of vast trouble, were ready at hand, free to

Among many accounts by Roman writers of early man, compare this passage of Ovid, and that in the fifth book of Lucretius.

gratuita et opera levi parabilia. Modus enim omnium prout necessitas erat; nos ista pretiosa, nos mira,[1] nos magnis multisque conquirenda artibus fecimus.

19 Sufficit ad id natura, quod poscit. A natura luxuria descivit, quae cotidie se ipsa incitat et tot saeculis crescit et ingenio adiuvat vitia. Primo supervacua coepit concupiscere, inde contraria, novissime animum corpori addixit et illius deservire libidini iussit. Omnes istae artes, quibus aut circitatur civitas aut strepit, corporis[2] negotium gerunt, cui omnia olim tamquam servo praestabantur, nunc tamquam domino parantur. Itaque hinc textorum, hinc fabrorum officinae sunt, hinc odores coquentium, hinc mollitia[3] molles corporis motus docentium mollesque cantus et infractos. Recessit enim ille naturalis modus desideria ope necessaria finiens; iam rusticitatis et miseriae est velle, quantum sat est.

20 Incredibilest, mi Lucili, quam facile etiam magnos viros dulcedo orationis abducat vero. Ecce Posidonius, ut mea fert opinio, ex is[4] qui plurimum philosophiae contulerunt, dum vult describere primum, quemadmodum alia torqueantur fila, alia ex molli solutoque ducantur, deinde quemadmodum tela suspensis

[1] *mira* Pincianus; *misera* B.
[2] *corporis* later MSS.; *corpori* BA.
[3] *mollitia* added by Capps.
[4] *is* Buecheler; *his* BA.

all, and obtainable for trifling pains. For the limit everywhere corresponded to the need; it is we that have made all those things valuable, we that have made them admired, we that have caused them to be sought for by extensive and manifold devices. Nature suffices for what she demands. Luxury has turned her back upon nature; each day she expands herself, in all the ages she has been gathering strength, and by her wit promoting the vices. At first, luxury began to lust for what nature regarded as superfluous, then for that which was contrary to nature; and finally she made the soul a bondsman to the body, and bade it be an utter slave to the body's lusts. All these crafts by which the city is patrolled —or shall I say kept in uproar—are but engaged in the body's business; time was when all things were offered to the body as to a slave, but now they are made ready for it as for a master. Accordingly, hence have come the workshops of the weavers and the carpenters; hence the savoury smells of the professional cooks; hence the wantonness of those who teach wanton postures, and wanton and affected singing. For that moderation which nature prescribes, which limits our desires by resources restricted to our needs, has abandoned the field; it has now come to this—that to want only what is enough is a sign both of boorishness and of utter destitution.

It is hard to believe, my dear Lucilius, how easily the charm of eloquence wins even great men away from the truth. Take, for example, Posidonius—who, in my estimation, is of the number of those who have contributed most to philosophy—when he wishes to describe the art of weaving. He tells how, first, some threads are twisted and some drawn out from the soft, loose mass of wool; next, how the

ponderibus rectum stamen extendat, quemadmodum subtemen insertum, quod duritiam utrimque[1] conprimentis tramae remolliat, spatha coire cogatur et iungi. Textrini quoque artem a sapientibus dixit inventam, oblitus postea repertum hoc subtilius genus, in quo

> Tela iugo vincta[2] est, stamen secernit harundo,
> Inseritur medium radiis subtemen acutis,
> Quod lato paviunt[3] insecti pectine dentes.

Quid, si contigisset illi adire[4] has nostri temporis telas, quibus[5] vestis nihil celatura conficitur, in qua non dico nullum corpori auxilium, sed nullum pudori est?

21 Transit deinde ad agricolas nec minus facunde describit proscissum aratro solum et iteratum,[6] quo solutior terra facilius pateat radicibus, tunc sparsa semina et collectas manu herbas, ne quid fortuitum et agreste succrescat, quod necet segetem. Hoc quoque opus ait esse sapientium, tamquam non nunc quoque plurima cultores agrorum nova inveniant, per
22 quae fertilitas augeatur. Deinde non est contentus his artibus, sed in pistrinum sapientem summittit. Narrat enim quemadmodum rerum naturam imitatus panem coeperit facere. "Receptas," inquit, "in os fruges concurrens inter se duritia dentium frangit,

[1] *utrimque* later MSS.; *utrumque* BA.
[2] *vincta* (with Ovid) a later MS.; *iuncta* BA.
[3] *paviunt* Gruter; *pariunt* BA.
[4] *adire* later MSS.; *addere* BA.
[5] *quibus* later MSS.; *in quibus* BA.
[6] *iteratum* Pincianus; *inter aratrum* BA.

---

[a] Ovid, *Met.* vi. 55 ff.
[b] Professor Summers calls attention to the similarity of this passage and Cicero, *De Nat. Deor.* ii. 134 ff. *dentibus manditur . . . a lingua adiuvari videtur . . . in alvo . . . calore . . . in reliquum corpus dividantur.*

upright warp keeps the threads stretched by means of hanging weights; then, how the inserted thread of the woof, which softens the hard texture of the web which holds it fast on either side, is forced by the batten to make a compact union with the warp. He maintains that even the weaver's art was discovered by wise men, forgetting that the more complicated art which he describes was invented in later days—the art wherein

> The web is bound to frame; asunder now
> The reed doth part the warp. Between the threads
> Is shot the woof by pointed shuttles borne;
> The broad comb's well-notched teeth then drive it home.[a]

Suppose he had had the opportunity of seeing the weaving of our own day, which produces the clothing that will conceal nothing, the clothing which affords —I will not say no protection to the body, but none even to modesty!

Posidonius then passes on to the farmer. With no less eloquence he describes the ground which is broken up and crossed again by the plough, so that the earth, thus loosened, may allow freer play to the roots; then the seed is sown, and the weeds plucked out by hand, lest any chance growth or wild plant spring up and spoil the crop. This trade also, he declares, is the creation of the wise,—just as if cultivators of the soil were not even at the present day discovering countless new methods of increasing the soil's fertility! Furthermore, not confining his attention to these arts, he even degrades the wise man by sending him to the mill. For he tells us how the sage, by imitating the processes of nature, began to make bread. "The grain,"[b] he says, "once taken into the mouth, is crushed by the flinty teeth, which meet in hostile encounter, and

et quicquid excidit, ad eosdem dentes lingua refertur; tunc vero miscetur, ut facilius per fauces lubricas transeat. Cum pervenit in ventrem, aequali eius fervore concoquitur, tunc demum corpori accedit.
23 Hoc aliquis secutus exemplar lapidem asperum aspero inposuit ad similitudinem dentium, quorum pars immobilis motum alterius exspectat; deinde utriusque attritu grana franguntur et saepius reguntur, donec ad minutiam frequenter trita redigantur. Tum farinam aqua sparsit et adsidua tractatione perdomuit finxitque panem, quem primo cinis calidus et fervens testa percoxit, deinde furni paulatim reperti et alia genera, quorum fervor serviret arbitrio." Non multum afuit, quin sutrinum quoque inventum a sapientibus diceret.

24 Omnia ista ratio quidem, sed non recta ratio commenta est. Hominis enim, non sapientis inventa sunt, tam mehercules quam navigia, quibus amnes quibusque maria transimus aptatis ad excipiendum ventorum impetum velis et additis a tergo gubernaculis, quae huc atque illuc cursum navigii torqueant. Exemplum a piscibus tractum est, qui cauda reguntur et levi eius in utrumque momento velocita-
25 tem suam flectunt. "Omnia," inquit, "haec sapiens quidem invenit; sed minora quam ut ipse tractaret,

whatever grain slips out the tongue turns back to the selfsame teeth. Then it is blended into a mass, that it may the more easily pass down the slippery throat. When this has reached the stomach, it is digested by the stomach's equable heat; then, and not till then, it is assimilated with the body. Following this pattern," he goes on, "someone placed two rough stones, the one above the other, in imitation of the teeth, one set of which is stationary and awaits the motion of the other set. Then, by the rubbing of the one stone against the other, the grain is crushed and brought back again and again, until by frequent rubbing it is reduced to powder. Then this man sprinkled the meal with water, and by continued manipulation subdued the mass and moulded the loaf. This loaf was, at first, baked by hot ashes or by an earthen vessel glowing hot; later on ovens were gradually discovered and the other devices whose heat will render obedience to the sage's will." Posidonius came very near declaring that even the cobbler's trade was the discovery of the wise man.

Reason did indeed devise all these things, but it was not right reason. It was man, but not the wise man, that discovered them; just as they invented ships, in which we cross rivers and seas—ships fitted with sails for the purpose of catching the force of the winds, ships with rudders added at the stern in order to turn the vessel's course in one direction or another. The model followed was the fish, which steers itself by its tail, and by its slightest motion on this side or on that bends its swift course. "But," says Posidonius, "the wise man did indeed discover all these things; they were, however, too petty for him to deal with himself and so he entrusted them

sordidioribus ministris dedit." Immo non aliis excogitata ista sunt quam quibus hodieque curantur. Quaedam nostra demum prodisse[1] memoria scimus, ut speculariorum usum perlucente testa clarum transmittentium lumen, ut suspensuras balneorum et inpressos parietibus tubos, per quos circumfunderetur calor, qui ima simul ac summa foveret aequaliter. Quid loquar marmora, quibus templa, quibus domus fulgent? Quid lapideas moles in rotundum ac leve formatas, quibus porticus et capacia populorum tecta suscipimus? Quid verborum notas, quibus quamvis citata excipitur oratio et celeritatem linguae manus sequitur? Vilissimorum mancipiorum ista commenta
26 sunt; sapientia altius sedet nec manus edocet, animorum magistra est.

Vis scire, quid illa eruerit, quid effecerit? Non decoros[2] corporis motus nec varios per tubam ac tibiam cantus, quibus exceptus spiritus aut in exitu aut in transitu formatur in vocem. Non arma nec muros nec bello[3] utilia molitur, paci favet et genus
27 humanum ad concordiam vocat. Non est, inquam, instrumentorum ad usus necessarios opifex. Quid illi tam parvola adsignas? Artificem vides vitae. Alias quidem artes sub dominio habet. Nam cui

[1] *prodisse* later MSS.; *prodidisse* BA.
[2] *decoros* later MSS.; *dedecoros* BA.
[3] *bello* Madvig; *bella* BA.

---

[a] Besides *lapis specularis* (window-glass) the Romans used alabaster, mica, and shells for this purpose.

[b] Suetonius tells us that a certain Ennius, a grammarian of the Augustan age, was the first to develop shorthand on a scientific basis, and that Tiro, Cicero's freedman, had invented the process. He also mentions Seneca as the most scientific and encyclopaedic authority on the subject.

to his meaner assistants." Not so; these early inventions were thought out by no other class of men than those who have them in charge to-day. We know that certain devices have come to light only within our own memory—such as the use of windows which admit the clear light through transparent tiles,[a] and such as the vaulted baths, with pipes let into their walls for the purpose of diffusing the heat which maintains an even temperature in their lowest as well as in their highest spaces. Why need I mention the marble with which our temples and our private houses are resplendent? Or the rounded and polished masses of stone by means of which we erect colonnades and buildings roomy enough for nations? Or our signs[b] for whole words, which enable us to take down a speech, however rapidly uttered, matching speed of tongue by speed of hand? All this sort of thing has been devised by the lowest grade of slaves. Wisdom's seat is higher; she trains not the hands, but is mistress of our minds.

Would you know what wisdom has brought forth to light, what she has accomplished? It is not the graceful poses of the body, or the varied notes produced by horn and flute, whereby the breath is received and, as it passes out or through, is transformed into voice. It is not wisdom that contrives arms, or walls, or instruments useful in war; nay, her voice is for peace, and she summons all mankind to concord. It is not she, I maintain, who is the artisan of our indispensable implements of daily use. Why do you assign to her such petty things? You see in her the skilled artisan of life. The other arts, it is true, wisdom has under her

vita, illi vitam ornantia quoque[1] serviunt; ceterum ad beatum statum tendit, illo ducit, illo vias aperit.
28 Quae sint mala, quae videantur ostendit, vanitatem exuit mentibus, dat magnitudinem solidam, inflatam vero et ex inani speciosam reprimit, nec ignorari sinit inter magna quid intersit et tumida, totius naturae notitiam ac suae tradit. Quid sint di qualesque declarat, quid inferi, quid lares et genii, quid in secundam numinum[2] formam animae perpetuatae,[3] ubi consistant, quid agant, quid possint, quid velint.

Haec eius initiamenta sunt, per quae non municipale sacrum, sed ingens deorum omnium templum, mundus ipse reseratur, cuius vera simulacra verasque facies cernendas[4] mentibus protulit. Nam ad specta-
29 cula tam magna hebes visus est. Ad initia deinde rerum redit aeternamque rationem toti inditam et vim omnium seminum singula proprie figurantem. Tum de animo coepit inquirere, unde esset, ubi, quamdiu, in quot membra divisus Deinde a corporibus se ad incorporalia transtulit veritatemque et

[1] *vitam ornantia quoque* Hense; *vitae quoque ornantia* MSS.

[2] *numinum* Erasmus; *nominum* BA.

[3] *perpetuatae* Schweighaeuser; *perpetitae* MSS. and Hense.

[4] *cernendas* later MSS.; *cernendis* BA.

---

[a] Possibly either the *manes* or the *indigitamenta* of the early Roman religion.

[b] *i.e.*, λόγος.

control; for he whom life serves is also served by the things which equip life. But wisdom's course is toward the state of happiness; thither she guides us, thither she opens the way for us. She shows us what things are evil and what things are seemingly evil; she strips our minds of vain illusion. She bestows upon us a greatness which is substantial, but she represses the greatness which is inflated, and showy but filled with emptiness; and she does not permit us to be ignorant of the difference between what is great and what is but swollen; nay, she delivers to us the knowledge of the whole of nature and of her own nature. She discloses to us what the gods are and of what sort they are; what are the nether gods, the household deities, and the protecting spirits; what are the souls which have been endowed with lasting life and have been admitted to the second class of divinities,[a] where is their abode and what their activities, powers, and will.

Such are wisdom's rites of initiation, by means of which is unlocked, not a village shrine, but the vast temple of all the gods—the universe itself, whose true apparitions and true aspects she offers to the gaze of our minds. For the vision of our eyes is too dull for sights so great. Then she goes back to the beginnings of things, to the eternal Reason[b] which was imparted to the whole, and to the force which inheres in all the seeds of things, giving them the power to fashion each thing according to its kind. Then wisdom begins to inquire about the soul, whence it comes, where it dwells, how long it abides, into how many divisions it falls. Finally, she has turned her attention from the corporeal to the incorporeal, and has closely examined truth and the

argumenta eius excussit, post haec quemadmodum discernerentur vitae aut vocis ambigua, in utraque enim falsa veris inmixta sunt.

30 Non abduxit, inquam, se, ut Posidonio videtur, ab istis artibus sapiens, sed ad illas omnino non venit. Nihil enim dignum inventu iudicasset, quod non erat dignum perpetuo usu iudicaturus. Ponenda non sumeret.

31 "Anacharsis," inquit, "invenit rotam figuli, cuius circuitu vasa formantur." Deinde quia apud Homerum invenitur figuli rota, malunt [1] videri versus falsos esse quam fabulam. Ego nec Anacharsim auctorem huius rei fuisse contendo et, si fuit, sapiens quidem hoc invenit, sed non tamquam sapiens, sicut multa sapientes faciunt, qua homines sunt, non qua sapientes. Puta velocissimum esse sapientem; cursu omnes anteibit, qua velox est, non qua sapiens. Cuperem Posidonio aliquem vitrearium ostendere, qui spiritu vitrum in habitus plurimos format, qui vix diligenti manu effingerentur. Haec inventa sunt, postquam sapientiam [2] invenire desîmus.

[1] *malunt* MSS. ; *mavult* several editors.
[2] *sapientiam* Buecheler ; *sapientem* BA.

---

[a] Seneca, himself one of the keenest scientific observers in history (witness the *Nat. Quaest.*, *Epp.* lvii., lxxix., etc.), is pushing his argument very far in this letter. His message is clear enough ; but the modern combination of natural science, psychology, and philosophy shows that Posidonius had some justification for his theories. Cf. also Lucretius, v. 1105-7 ff.

[b] This Scythian prince and friend of Solon, who visited Athens in the sixth century B.C., is also said to have invented the bellows and the anchor. Cf., however, *Iliad* xviii. 600 f. *ὡς ὅτε τις τροχὸν ἄρμενον ἐν παλάμῃσιν ἑζόμενος κεραμεὺς πειρήσεται*, and Leaf's comment: "The potter's wheel was

marks whereby truth is known, inquiring next how that which is equivocal can be distinguished from the truth, whether in life or in language; for in both are elements of the false mingled with the true.

It is my opinion that the wise man has not withdrawn himself, as Posidonius thinks, from those arts which we were discussing, but that he never took them up at all.[a] For he would have judged that nothing was worth discovering that he would not afterwards judge to be worth using always. He would not take up things which would have to be laid aside.

"But Anacharsis," says Posidonius, "invented the potter's wheel, whose whirling gives shape to vessels."[b] Then because the potter's wheel is mentioned in Homer, people prefer to believe that Homer's verses are false rather than the story of Posidonius! But I maintain that Anacharsis was not the creator of this wheel; and even if he was, although he was a wise man when he invented it, yet he did not invent it *qua* "wise man"—just as there are a great many things which wise men do as men, not as wise men. Suppose, for example, that a wise man is exceedingly fleet of foot; he will outstrip all the runners in the race by virtue of being fleet, not by virtue of his wisdom. I should like to show Posidonius some glass-blower who by his breath moulds the glass into manifold shapes which could scarcely be fashioned by the most skilful hand. Nay, these discoveries have been made since we men have ceased to discover wisdom.

known in pre-Mycenean times, and was a very ancient invention to the oldest Epic poets." Seneca is right.

32 "Democritus," inquit, "invenisse dicitur fornicem, ut lapidum curvatura paulatim inclinatorum medio saxo alligaretur." Hoc dicam falsum esse; necesse est enim ante Democritum et pontes et portas fuisse,
33 quarum fere summa curvantur. Excidit porro vobis eundem Democritum invenisse, quemadmodum ebur molliretur, quemadmodum decoctus calculus in zmaragdum converteretur, qua hodieque coctura inventi lapides in[1] hoc utiles colorantur. Ista sapiens licet invenerit, non qua sapiens erat, invenit; multa enim facit, quae ab inprudentissimis aut aeque fieri videmus[2] aut peritius atque exercitatius.

34 Quid sapiens investigaverit, quid in lucem protraxerit, quaeris? Primum verum naturamque, quam non ut cetera animalia oculis secutus est tardis ad divina. Deinde vitae legem, quam ad universa derexit, nec nosse tantum sed sequi deos docuit et accidentia non aliter excipere quam imperata. Vetuit parere opinionibus falsis et quanti quidque esset, vera aestimatione perpendit. Damnavit mixtas paenitentia voluptates et bona semper placitura laudavit et palam fecit felicissimum esse cui felicitate

[1] *in* added by Schweighaeuser.
[2] *videmus* Erasmus; *vidimus* BA.

[a] Seneca (see next sentence) is right again. The arch was known in Chaldaea and in Egypt before 3000 B.C. Greek bee-hive tombs, Etruscan gateways, and early Roman remains, testify to its immemorial use.

[b] The ancients judged precious stones merely by their colour; their *smaragdus* included also malachite, jade, and several kinds of quartz. Exposure to heat alters the colour of some stones; and the alchemists believed that the "angelical stone" changed common flints into diamonds, rubies, emeralds, etc. See G. F. Kunz, *The Magic of Jewels and Charms*, p. 16. It was also an ancient superstition that emeralds were produced from jasper.

But Posidonius again remarks: "Democritus is said to have discovered the arch,[a] whose effect was that the curving line of stones, which gradually lean toward each other, is bound together by the key-stone." I am inclined to pronounce this statement false. For there must have been, before Democritus, bridges and gateways in which the curvature did not begin until about the top. It seems to have quite slipped your memory that this same Democritus discovered how ivory could be softened, how, by boiling, a pebble could be transformed into an emerald,[b] —the same process used even to-day for colouring stones which are found to be amenable to this treatment! It may have been a wise man who discovered all such things, but he did not discover them by virtue of being a wise man; for he does many things which we see done just as well, or even more skilfully and dexterously, by men who are utterly lacking in sagacity.

Do you ask what, then, the wise man has found out and what he has brought to light? First of all there is truth, and nature; and nature he has not followed as the other animals do, with eyes too dull to perceive the divine in it. In the second place, there is the law of life, and life he has made to conform to universal principles; and he has taught us, not merely to know the gods, but to follow them, and to welcome the gifts of chance precisely as if they were divine commands. He has forbidden us to give heed to false opinions, and has weighed the value of each thing by a true standard of appraisement. He has condemned those pleasures with which remorse is intermingled, and has praised those goods which will always satisfy; and he has published the truth abroad that he is most happy who has no

non opus est, potentissimum esse qui se habet in potestate.

35 Non de ea philosophia loquor, quae civem extra patriam posuit, extra mundum deos, quae virtutem donavit voluptati, sed de illa,[1] quae nullum bonum putat nisi quod honestum est, quae nec hominis nec fortunae muneribus deleniri[2] potest, cuius hoc pretium est, non posse pretio capi. Hanc philosophiam fuisse illo rudi saeculo, quo adhuc artificia deerant et ipso usu discebantur utilia, non credo.

36 Secutast[3] fortunata tempora, cum in medio iacerent beneficia naturae promiscue utenda, antequam avaritia atque luxuria dissociavere mortales et ad rapinam ex consortio discurrere.[4] Non erant illi sapientes viri,

37 etiam si faciebant facienda sapientibus. Statum quidem generis humani non alium quisquam suspexerit magis, nec si cui permittat deus terrena formare et dare gentibus mores, aliud probaverit quam quod apud illos fuisse memoratur, apud quos

> Nulli subigebant arva coloni,
> Ne signare quidem aut partiri limite campum
> Fas erat ; in medium quaerebant, ipsaque tellus
> Omnia liberius nullo poscente ferebat.

38 Quid hominum illo genere felicius ? In commune rerum natura fruebantur ; sufficiebat illa ut parens

[1] *de illa* attested by Pincianus ; *illa* BA.
[2] *deleniri* Muretus ; *deleri* BA.
[3] *secutast* Buecheler ; *sicutaut* BA.
[4] After *discurrere* Buecheler suggested *docuere.*

---

[a] *i.e.*, the Epicureans, who withdrew from civil life and regarded the gods as taking no part in the affairs of men.
[b] *i.e.*, live according to nature.
[c] Verg. *Georg.* i. 125 ff.

need of happiness, and that he is most powerful who has power over himself.

I am not speaking of that philosophy which has placed the citizen outside his country and the gods outside the universe, and which has bestowed virtue upon pleasure,[a] but rather of that philosophy which counts nothing good except what is honourable,—one which cannot be cajoled by the gifts either of man or of fortune, one whose value is that it cannot be bought for any value. That this philosophy existed in such a rude age, when the arts and crafts were still unknown and when useful things could only be learned by use,—this I refuse to believe.

Next there came the fortune-favoured period when the bounties of nature lay open to all, for men's indiscriminate use, before avarice and luxury had broken the bonds which held mortals together, and they, abandoning their communal existence, had separated and turned to plunder. The men of the second age were not wise men, even though they did what wise men should do.[b] Indeed, there is no other condition of the human race that anyone would regard more highly; and if God should commission a man to fashion earthly creatures and to bestow institutions upon peoples, this man would approve of no other system than that which obtained among the men of that age, when

> No ploughman tilled the soil, nor was it right
> To portion off or bound one's property.
> Men shared their gains, and earth more freely gave
> Her riches to her sons who sought them not.[c]

What race of men was ever more blest than that race? They enjoyed all nature in partnership. Nature sufficed for them, now the guardian, as before

ita tutela[1] omnium, haec erat publicarum opum secura possessio. Quidni ego illud locupletissimum mortalium genus dixerim, in quo pauperem invenire non posses?

Inrupit in res optime positas avaritia et, dum seducere aliquid cupit atque in suum vertere, omnia fecit aliena et in angustum se ex inmenso redegit.[2] Avaritia paupertatem intulit et multa concupiscendo
39 omnia amisit. Licet itaque nunc conetur reparare[3] quod perdidit, licet agros agris adiciat vicinum vel pretio pellens[4] vel iniuria, licet in provinciarum spatium rura dilatet et possessionem vocet per sua longam peregrinationem, nulla nos finium propagatio eo reducet unde discessimus.

Cum omnia fecerimus, multum habebimus;
40 universum habebamus. Terra ipsa fertilior erat inlaborata et in usus populorum non diripientium larga. Quidquid natura protulerat, id non minus invenisse quam inventum monstrare alteri voluptas erat. Nec ulli aut superesse poterat aut deesse; inter concordes dividebatur. Nondum valentior inposuerat infirmiori manum, nondum avarus abscondendo quod sibi iaceret, alium necessariis quoque excluserat; par erat alterius
41 ac sui cura. Arma cessabant incruentaeque humano

[1] *ita tutela* Buecheler; *in tutela* or *in tutelam* MSS.
[2] *redegit* Buecheler and a late MS.; *redacti* BA.
[3] *conetur reparare* Buecheler and Gloeckner; *concurrere parare* BA.
[4] *pellens* a late MS.; *pelleris* BA.

she was the parent, of all; and this her gift consisted of the assured possession by each man of the common resources. Why should I not even call that race the richest among mortals, since you could not find a poor person among them?

But avarice broke in upon a condition so happily ordained, and, by its eagerness to lay something away and to turn it to its own private use, made all things the property of others, and reduced itself from boundless wealth to straitened need. It was avarice that introduced poverty and, by craving much, lost all. And so, although she now tries to make good her loss, although she adds one estate to another, evicting a neighbour either by buying him out or by wronging him, although she extends her country-seats to the size of provinces and defines ownership as meaning extensive travel through one's own property,—in spite of all these efforts of hers, no enlargement of our boundaries will bring us back to the condition from which we have departed.

When there is no more that we can do, we shall possess much; but we once possessed the whole world! The very soil was more productive when untilled, and yielded more than enough for peoples who refrained from despoiling one another. Whatever gift nature had produced, men found as much pleasure in revealing it to another as in having discovered it. It was possible for no man either to surpass another or to fall short of him; what there was, was divided among unquarrelling friends. Not yet had the stronger begun to lay hands upon the weaker; not yet had the miser, by hiding away what lay before him, begun to shut off his neighbour from even the necessities of life; each cared as much for his neighbour as for himself. Armour lay

sanguine manus odium omne in feras verterant. Illi quos aliquod nemus densum a sole protexerat, qui adversus saevitiam hiemis aut imbris vili receptaculo tuti sub fronde vivebant, placidas transigebant sine suspirio noctis. Sollicitudo nos in nostra purpura versat et acerrimis excitat stimulis; at quam mollem
42 somnum illis dura tellus dabat! Non inpendebant caelata laquearia, sed in aperto iacentes sidera superlabebantur et insigne spectaculum noctium mundus in praeceps agebatur silentio tantum opus ducens.[1] Tam interdiu illis quam nocte patebant[2] prospectus huius pulcherrimae domus. Libebat intueri signa ex media caeli parte vergentia, rursus ex occulto alia
43 surgentia. Quidni iuvaret vagari inter tam late sparsa miracula? At vos ad omnem tectorum pavetis sonum et inter picturas vestras, si quid increpuit, fugitis adtoniti. Non habebant domos instar urbium. Spiritus ac liber inter aperta perflatus et levis umbra rupis aut arboris et perlucidi fontes rivique non opere nec fistula nec ullo coacto itinere obsolefacti, sed sponte currentes et prata sine arte formosa, inter haec agreste domicilium rustica politum manu. Haec erat secundum naturam domus, in qua libebat

[1] *ducens* later MSS.; *dicens* BA.
[2] *patebant* MSS.; *patebat* an old reading found by Pincianus.

[a] *Cf.* Horace, *Ep.* i. 10. 20 f.:

Purior in vicis aqua tendit rumpere plumbum
Quam quae per pronum trepidat cum murmure rivum?

unused, and the hand, unstained by human blood, had turned all its hatred against wild beasts. The men of that day, who had found in some dense grove protection against the sun, and security against the severity of winter or of rain in their mean hiding-places, spent their lives under the branches of the trees and passed tranquil nights without a sigh. Care vexes us in our purple, and routs us from our beds with the sharpest of goads; but how soft was the sleep the hard earth bestowed upon the men of that day! No fretted and panelled ceilings hung over them, but as they lay beneath the open sky the stars glided quietly above them, and the firmament, night's noble pageant, marched swiftly by, conducting its mighty task in silence. For them by day, as well as by night, the visions of this most glorious abode were free and open. It was their joy to watch the constellations as they sank from mid-heaven, and others, again, as they rose from their hidden abodes. What else but joy could it be to wander among the marvels which dotted the heavens far and wide? But you of the present day shudder at every sound your houses make, and as you sit among your frescoes the slightest creak makes you shrink in terror. *They* had no houses as big as cities. The air, the breezes blowing free through the open spaces, the flitting shade of crag or tree, springs crystal-clear and streams not spoiled by man's work, whether by water-pipe [a] or by any confinement of the channel, but running at will, and meadows beautiful without the use of art,—amid such scenes were their rude homes, adorned with rustic hand. Such a dwelling was in accordance with nature; therein it was a joy to live, fearing neither the dwelling itself nor for its safety. In

habitare nec ipsam nec pro ipsa timentem; nunc magna pars nostri metus tecta sunt.

44 Sed quamvis egregia illis vita fuerit et carens fraude, non fuere sapientes, quando hoc iam in opere maximo nomen est. Non tamen negaverim fuisse alti spiritus viros et, ut ita dicam, a dis recentes. Neque enim dubium est, quin meliora mundus nondum effetus ediderit. Quemadmodum autem omnibus indoles fortior fuit et ad labores paratior, ita non erant ingenia omnibus consummata. Non enim dat
45 natura virtutem; ars est bonum fieri. Illi quidem non aurum nec argentum nec perlucidos lapides [1] in [2] ima terrarum faece quaerebant parcebantque adhuc etiam mutis [3] animalibus; tantum aberat ut [4] homo hominem non iratus, non timens, tantum spectaturus occideret. Nondum vestis illis erat picta, nondum texebatur aurum, adhuc nec eruebatur.

46 Quid ergo est [5]? Ignorantia rerum innocentes erant. Multum autem interest, utrum peccare aliquis nolit an [6] nesciat. Deerat illis iustitia, deerat prudentia, deerat temperantia ac fortitudo. Omnibus his virtutibus habebat similia quaedam rudis vita; virtus non contingit animo nisi instituto et edocto et ad summum adsidua exercitatione perducto. Ad hoc quidem, sed sine hoc nascimur et in optimis

[1] *lapides* later MSS.; omitted by BA.
[2] *in* added by Schweighaeuser.
[3] *mutis* later MSS.; *multis* BA.
[4] *ut* later MSS.; omitted by BA.
[5] *est* added by Feige.
[6] *an* later MSS.; *aut* BA.

[a] Because virtue depends upon reason, and none but voluntary acts should meet with praise or blame.

these days, however, our houses constitute a large portion of our dread.

But no matter how excellent and guileless was the life of the men of that age, they were not wise men; for that title is reserved for the highest achievement. Still, I would not deny that they were men of lofty spirit and—if I may use the phrase—fresh from the gods. For there is no doubt that the world produced a better progeny before it was yet worn out. However, not all were endowed with mental faculties of highest perfection, though in all cases their native powers were more sturdy than ours and more fitted for toil. For nature does not bestow virtue; it is an art to become good. They, at least, searched not in the lowest dregs of the earth for gold, nor yet for silver or transparent stones; and they still were merciful even to the dumb animals—so far removed was that epoch from the custom of slaying man by man, not in anger or through fear, but just to make a show! They had as yet no embroidered garments nor did they weave cloth of gold; gold was not yet even mined.

What, then, is the conclusion of the matter? It was by reason of their ignorance of things that the men of those days were innocent; and it makes a great deal of difference whether one wills not to sin or has not the knowledge to sin.[a] Justice was unknown to them, unknown prudence, unknown also self-control and bravery; but their rude life possessed certain qualities akin to all these virtues. Virtue is not vouchsafed to a soul unless that soul has been trained and taught, and by unremitting practice brought to perfection. For the attainment of this boon, but not in the possession of it, were we born;

quoque, antequam erudias, virtutis materia, non virtus est. VALE.

XCI

SENECA LVCILIO SVO SALVTEM

1 Liberalis noster nunc tristis est nuntiato incendio, quo Lugdunensis colonia exusta est. Movere hic casus quemlibet posset, nedum hominem patriae suae amantissimum. Quae res effecit, ut firmitatem animi sui quaerat, quam videlicet ad ea, quae timeri posse putabat, exercuit. Hoc vero tam inopinatum malum et paene inauditum non miror si sine metu fuit, cum esset sine exemplo. Multas enim civitates incendium vexavit, nullam abstulit. Nam etiam ubi hostili manu in tecta [1] ignis inmissus est, multis locis deficit,[2] et quamvis subinde excitetur, raro tamen sic cuncta depascitur, ut nihil ferro relinquat. Terrarum quoque vix umquam tam gravis et perniciosus fuit motus, ut tota oppida everteret. Numquam denique tam infestum ulli exarsit incendium, ut nihil alteri
2 superesset incendio. Tot pulcherrima opera, quae singula inlustrare urbes singulas possent, una nox stravit, et in tanta pace quantum ne bello quidem timeri potest accidit. Quis hoc credat? Ubique

[1] *in tecta* Erasmus; *iniecta* MSS.
[2] *deficit* later MSS.; *defecit* BA.

[a] In spite of the *centesimus annus* of § 14 (*q.v.*), the most probable date of this letter, based on Tac. *Ann.* xvi. 13 and other general evidence, is July–September 64 A.D. 58 A.D. would be too early for many reasons—among them that "peace all over the world" would not be a true statement until January of 62. (See the monographs of Jonas, O. Binder, Peiper, and Schultess.)

and even in the best of men, before you refine them by instruction, there is but the stuff of virtue, not virtue itself. Farewell.

XCI. ON THE LESSON TO BE DRAWN FROM THE BURNING OF LYONS[a]

Our friend Liberalis[b] is now downcast; for he has just heard of the fire which has wiped out the colony of Lyons. Such a calamity might upset anyone at all, not to speak of a man who dearly loves his country. But this incident has served to make him inquire about the strength of his own character, which he has trained, I suppose, just to meet situations that he thought might cause him fear. I do not wonder, however, that he was free from apprehension touching an evil so unexpected and practically unheard of as this, since it is without precedent. For fire has damaged many a city, but has annihilated none. Even when fire has been hurled against the walls by the hand of a foe, the flame dies out in many places, and although continually renewed, rarely devours so wholly as to leave nothing for the sword. Even an earthquake has scarcely ever been so violent and destructive as to overthrow whole cities. Finally, no conflagration has ever before blazed forth so savagely in any town that nothing was left for a second. So many beautiful buildings, any single one of which would make a single town famous, were wrecked in one night. In time of such deep peace an event has taken place worse than men can possibly fear even in time of war. Who can believe

[b] Probably Aebutius Liberalis, to whom the treatise *De Beneficiis* was dedicated.

armis quiescentibus, cum toto orbe terrarum diffusa securitas sit, Lugudunum, quod ostendebatur in Gallia, quaeritur.

Omnibus fortuna, quos publice adflixit, quod passuri erant, timere permisit. Nulla res magna non aliquod habuit ruinae suae spatium; in hac una nox interfuit inter urbem maximam et nullam. Denique diutius illam tibi perisse quam perît narro.

3 Haec omnia Liberalis nostri adfectum inclinant[1] adversus sua firmum et erectum. Nec sine causa concussus est; inexpectata plus adgravant; novitas adicit calamitatibus pondus, nec quisquam mortalium non magis quod etiam miratus est, doluit.

4 Ideo nihil nobis inprovisum esse debet. In omnia praemittendus[2] animus cogitandumque non quidquid solet, sed quicquid potest fieri. Quid enim est, quod non fortuna, cum voluit, ex florentissimo detrahat? Quod non eo magis adgrediatur et quatiat, quo speciosius fulget? Quid illi arduum quidve difficile
5 est? Non una via semper, ne tota quidem incurrit, modo nostras in nos manus advocat, modo suis contenta viribus invenit pericula sine auctore. Nullum tempus exceptum est; in ipsis voluptatibus causae

[1] *inclinant* cod. Harl.; *inclinandum* BA.
[2] *praemittendus* later MSS.; *permittendus* BA.

[a] That Lyons, situated at the junction of the Arar and the Rhone, was of especial prominence in Gaul, may be also gathered from the fact that it boasted a government mint and the *Ara Augusti*—a shrine established for the annual worship of all the Gallic states. Moreover, the Emperor Claudius delivered his famous address in that city (see Tac. *Ann.* xi. 23 f.).

it? When weapons are everywhere at rest, and when peace prevails throughout the world, Lyons, the pride of Gaul,[a] is missing!

Fortune has usually allowed all men, when she has assailed them collectively, to have a foreboding of that which they were destined to suffer. Every great creation has had granted to it a period of reprieve before its fall; but in this case, only a single night elapsed between the city at its greatest and the city non-existent. In short, it takes me longer to tell you it has perished than it took for the city to perish.

All this has affected our friend Liberalis, bending his will, which is usually so steadfast and erect in the face of his own trials. And not without reason has he been shaken; for it is the unexpected that puts the heaviest load upon us. Strangeness adds to the weight of calamities, and every mortal feels the greater pain as a result of that which also brings surprise.

Therefore, nothing ought to be unexpected by us. Our minds should be sent forward in advance to meet all problems, and we should consider, not what is wont to happen, but what can happen. For what is there in existence that Fortune, when she has so willed, does not drag down from the very height of its prosperity? And what is there that she does not the more violently assail the more brilliantly it shines? What is laborious or difficult for her? She does not always attack in one way, or even with her full strength; at one time she summons our own hands against us; at another time, content with her own powers, she makes use of no agent in devising perils for us. No time is exempt; in the midst of our very pleasures there spring up causes of suffering.

doloris oriuntur. Bellum in media pace consurgit et auxilia securitatis in metum transeunt; ex amico inimicus, hostis ex socio. In subitas tempestates hibernisque maiores agitur aestiva tranquillitas. Sine hoste patimur hostilia, et cladis causas, si alia deficiunt, nimia sibi felicitas invenit. Invadit temperantissimos morbus, validissimos phthisis, innocentissimos poena, secretissimos tumultus.

Eligit aliquid novi casus, per quod velut oblitis
6 vires suas ingerat. Quidquid longa series multis laboribus, multa deum indulgentia struxit, id unus dies spargit ac dissipat. Longam moram dedit malis properantibus, qui diem dixit; hora[1] momentumque temporis evertendis imperiis sufficit. Esset aliquod inbecillitatis nostrae solacium rerumque nostrarum, si tam tarde perirent[2] cuncta quam fiunt[3]; nunc incrementa lente exeunt, festinatur in damnum.
7 Nihil privatim, nihil publice stabile est; tam hominum quam urbium fata volvuntur. Inter placidissima terror existit nihilque extra tumultuantibus causis mala, unde minime exspectabantur, erumpunt. Quae domesticis bellis steterant regna, quae externis, inpellente nullo ruunt. Quota quaeque felicitatem civitas pertulit?

Cogitanda ergo sunt omnia et animus adversus ea,

[1] *hora* Gruter; *horam* BA.
[2] *tam tarde perirent* later MSS.; *tanta reperirent* BA.
[3] *fiunt* later MSS.; *finiunt* BA.

---

[a] *Cf. Ep.* iv. 7, esp. the words *noli huic tranquillitati confidere: momento mare evertitur.*

War arises in the midst of peace, and that which we depended upon for protection is transformed into a cause of fear; friend becomes enemy, ally becomes foeman. The summer calm is stirred into sudden storms, wilder than the storms of winter.[a] With no foe in sight we are victims of such fates as foes inflict, and if other causes of disaster fail, excessive good fortune finds them for itself. The most temperate are assailed by illness, the strongest by wasting disease, the most innocent by chastisement, the most secluded by the noisy mob.

Chance chooses some new weapon by which to bring her strength to bear against us, thinking we have forgotten her. Whatever structure has been reared by a long sequence of years, at the cost of great toil and through the great kindness of the gods, is scattered and dispersed by a single day. Nay, he who has said "a day" has granted too long a postponement to swift-coming misfortune; an hour, an instant of time, suffices for the overthrow of empires! It would be some consolation for the feebleness of our selves and our works, if all things should perish as slowly as they come into being; but as it is, increases are of sluggish growth, but the way to ruin is rapid. Nothing, whether public or private, is stable; the destinies of men, no less than those of cities, are in a whirl. Amid the greatest calm terror arises, and though no external agencies stir up commotion, yet evils burst forth from sources whence they were least expected. Thrones which have stood the shock of civil and foreign wars crash to the ground though no one sets them tottering. How few the states which have carried their good fortune through to the end!

We should therefore reflect upon all contingencies,

8 quae possunt evenire, firmandus. Exilia, tormenta morbi,[1] bella, naufragia meditare.[2] Potest te patriae, potest patriam tibi casus eripere, potest te in solitudines abigere,[3] potest hoc ipsum, in quo turba suffocatur, fieri solitudo. Tota ante oculos sortis humanae condicio ponatur, nec quantum frequenter evenit, sed quantum plurimum potest evenire, praesumamus animo, si nolumus opprimi nec illis inusitatis velut novis obstupefieri; in plenum cogitanda fortuna est.

9 Quotiens Asiae, quotiens Achaiae urbes uno tremore ceciderunt? Quot oppida in Syria, quot in Macedonia devorata sunt? Cypron quotiens vastavit haec clades? Quotiens in se Paphus corruit? Frequenter nobis nuntiati sunt totarum urbium interitus, et nos inter quos ista frequenter nuntiantur, quota pars omnium sumus?

Consurgamus itaque adversus fortuita et quicquid inciderit, sciamus non esse tam magnum quam
10 rumore iactetur. Civitas arsit opulenta ornamentumque provinciarum, quibus et inserta erat et excepta, uni tamen inposita et huic non latissimo[4]

[1] *morbi* BA; *morbos* later MSS.
[2] *meditare* later MSS.; *meditari* BA.
[3] *abigere* Matthiae; *abicere* BA.
[4] *latissimo* Buecheler; *altissimo* BA.

---

[a] The passage bears a striking resemblance to the words of Theseus in an unknown play of Euripides (Nauck, Frag. 964) quoted by Cicero, *Tusc.* iii. 14. 29, and by Plutarch, *Consolation to Apollonius*, 112 d.

[b] Seneca (*N.Q.* vi. 26) speaks of Paphos (on the island of Cyprus) as having been more than once devastated. We know of two such accidents—one under Augustus and another under Vespasian. See the same passage for other earthquake shocks in various places.

[c] Lyons held an exceptional position in relation to the

and should fortify our minds against the evils which may possibly come. Exile, the torture of disease, wars, shipwreck,—we must think on these.[a] Chance may tear you from your country or your country from you, or may banish you to the desert; this very place, where throngs are stifling, may become a desert. Let us place before our eyes in its entirety the nature of man's lot, and if we would not be overwhelmed, or even dazed, by those unwonted evils, as if they were novel, let us summon to our minds beforehand, not as great an evil as oftentimes happens, but the very greatest evil that possibly can happen. We must reflect upon fortune fully and completely.

How often have cities in Asia, how often in Achaia, been laid low by a single shock of earthquake! How many towns in Syria, how many in Macedonia, have been swallowed up! How often has this kind of devastation laid Cyprus[b] in ruins! How often has Paphos collapsed! Not infrequently are tidings brought to us of the utter destruction of entire cities; yet how small a part of the world are we, to whom such tidings often come!

Let us rise, therefore, to confront the operations of Fortune, and whatever happens, let us have the assurance that it is not so great as rumour advertises it to be. A rich city has been laid in ashes, the jewel of the provinces, counted as one of them and yet not included with them[c]; rich though it was, nevertheless it was set upon a single hill,[d] and that

three Gallic provinces; it was a free town, belonging to none and yet their capital, much like the city of Washington in relation to the United States.

[d] A fact mentioned merely to suggest Rome with her seven hills.

monti; omnium istarum civitatium, quas nunc magnificas ac nobiles audis, vestigia quoque tempus eradet. Non vides, quemadmodum in Achaia clarissimarum urbium iam fundamenta consumpta sint nec quicquam
11 extet, ex quo[1] appareat illas saltim fuisse? Non tantum manu facta labuntur, nec tantum humana arte atque industria posita vertit dies; iuga montium diffluunt, totae desedere regiones, operta sunt fluctibus quae procul a conspectu maris stabant. Vasta vis[2] ignium colles, per quos relucebat, erosit et quondam altissimos vertices, solacia navigantium ac speculas, ad humile deduxit. Ipsius naturae opera vexantur et ideo aequo animo ferre debemus urbium
12 excidia. Casurae stant.[3] Omnes hic exitus manet, sive interna vis flatusque praeclusa via violenti pondus,[4] sub quo tenentur, excusserint, sive torrentium impetus[5] in abdito vastior obstantia effregerit, sive flammarum violentia conpaginem soli ruperit, sive vetustas, a qua[6] nihil tutum est, expugnaverit minutatim, sive gravitas caeli egesserit populos et situs deserta corruperit. Enumerare omnes fatorum vias longum est. Hoc unum scio: omnia mortalium

[1] *quo* later MSS.; *qua* BA.
[2] *vasta vis* Haupt; *vastavit* BA.
[3] *casurae stant* Haupt; *casura exstant* BA.
[4] *sive . . . pondus* H. Mueck; *sive . . . preclusa violenti pondus* MSS.
[5] *impetus* added by Buecheler.
[6] *a qua* Erasmus; *in qua* BA.

---

[a] For example, Mycenae and Tiryns.

not very large in extent. But of all those cities, of whose magnificence and grandeur you hear to-day, the very traces will be blotted out by time. Do you not see how, in Achaia, the foundations of the most famous cities have already crumbled to nothing, so that no trace is left to show that they ever even existed?[a] Not only does that which has been made with hands totter to the ground, not only is that which has been set in place by man's art and man's efforts overthrown by the passing days; nay, the peaks of mountains dissolve, whole tracts have settled, and places which once stood far from the sight of the sea are now covered by the waves. The mighty power of fires has eaten away the hills through whose sides they used to glow, and has levelled to the ground peaks which were once most lofty — the sailor's solace and his beacon. The works of nature herself are harassed; hence we ought to bear with untroubled minds the destruction of cities. They stand but to fall! This doom awaits them, one and all; it may be that some internal force, and blasts of violence which are tremendous because their way is blocked, will throw off the weight which holds then down; or that a whirlpool of raging currents, mightier because they are hidden in the bosom of the earth, will break through that which resists its power; or that the vehemence of flames will burst asunder the framework of the earth's crust; or that time, from which nothing is safe, will reduce them little by little; or that a pestilential climate will drive their inhabitants away and the mould will corrode their deserted walls. It would be tedious to recount all the ways by which fate may come; but this one thing I know: all the works of mortal man have been doomed to

opera mortalitate damnata sunt, inter peritura vivimus.

13 Haec ergo atque eiusmodi solacia admoveo Liberali nostro incredibili quodam patriae suae amore flagranti, quae fortasse consumpta est, ut in melius excitaretur. Saepe maiori fortunae locum fecit iniuria. Multa ceciderunt, ut altius surgerent. Timagenes felicitati urbis inimicus aiebat Romae sibi incendia ob hoc unum dolori esse, quod sciret meliora surrectura
14 quam arsissent. In hac quoque urbe veri simile est certaturos omnes, ut maiora certioraque quam amisere restituantur.[1] Sint utinam diuturna et melioribus auspiciis in aevum longius condita! Nam huic coloniae ab origine sua centensimus annus est, aetas ne homini quidem extrema. A Planco deducta in hanc frequentiam[2] loci opportunitate convaluit, quot tamen gravissimos casus intra spatium humanae senectutis tulit.[3]

15 Itaque formetur animus ad intellectum patientiamque sortis suae et sciat[4] nihil inausum esse fortunae, adversus imperia illam idem habere iuris quod adversus imperantes, adversus urbes idem posse quod adversus homines. Nihil horum indignandum

[1] *restituantur* Buecheler, who thought it the reading of BA, which is more probably *restituant*, according to Hense.
[2] *in hanc frequentiam* later MSS. ; *in hac frequentia* BA.
[3] *tulit* added by Buecheler.
[4] *sciat* later MSS. ; *sciant* BA.

[a] Probably the writer, and intimate friend of Augustus, who began life in Rome as a captive from Egypt. Falling into disfavour with the Emperor, he took refuge with the malcontent Asinius Pollio at Tusculum, and subsequently died in the East. Cf. Seneca, *De Ira*, iii. 23.

[b] It was in 43 B.C. that Plancus led out the colonists who were chiefly Roman citizens driven from Vienna. Seneca would have been more accurate had he said "one hundred and eighth (or seventh)." Buecheler and Schultess would

mortality, and in the midst of things which have been destined to die, we live!

Hence it is thoughts like these, and of this kind, which I am offering as consolation to our friend Liberalis, who burns with a love for his country that is beyond belief. Perhaps its destruction has been brought about only that it may be raised up again to a better destiny. Oftentimes a reverse has but made room for more prosperous fortune. Many structures have fallen only to rise to a greater height. Timagenes,[a] who had a grudge against Rome and her prosperity, used to say that the only reason he was grieved when conflagrations occurred in Rome was his knowledge that better buildings would arise than those which had gone down in the flames. And probably in this city of Lyons, too, all its citizens will earnestly strive that everything shall be rebuilt better in size and security than what they have lost. May it be built to endure and, under happier auspices, for a longer existence! This is indeed but the hundredth year since this colony was founded—not the limit even of a man's lifetime.[b] Led forth by Plancus, the natural advantages of its site have caused it to wax strong and reach the numbers which it contains to-day; and yet how many calamities of the greatest severity has it endured within the space of an old man's life!

Therefore let the mind be disciplined to understand and to endure its own lot, and let it have the knowledge that there is nothing which fortune does not dare—that she has the same jurisdiction over empires as over emperors, the same power over cities as over the citizens who dwell therein. We must

(unnecessarily) emend to read *centesimus septimus.* But Seneca was using round numbers.

est. In eum intravimus mundum, in quo his legibus vivitur. Placet; pare. Non placet; quacumque vis, exi. Indignare, si quid in te iniqui proprie constitutum est; sed si haec summos imosque necessitas alligat, in gratiam cum fato revertere, a quo omnia
16 resolvuntur. Non est quod nos tumulis metiaris et his monumentis, quae viam disparia praetexunt; aequat omnes cinis. Inpares nascimur, pares morimur. Idem de urbibus quod de urbium incolis dico: tam Ardea capta quam Roma est. Conditor ille iuris humani non natalibus[1] nos nec nominum claritate distinxit, nisi dum sumus. Ubi vero ad finem mortalium ventum est, "discede," inquit, "ambitio! omnium, quae terram premunt, siremps[2] lex esto." Ad omnia patienda pares sumus; nemo altero fragilior est, nemo in crastinum sui certior.

17 Alexander Macedonum rex discere geometriam coeperat, infelix, sciturus, quam pusilla terra esset, ex qua minimum occupaverat. Ita dico: infelix ob hoc, quod intellegere debebat falsum se gerere cognomen. Quis enim esse magnus in pusillo potest? Erant illa, quae tradebantur, suptilia et diligenti intentione discenda, non quae perciperet vesanus homo

[1] *natalibus* later MSS.; *non talibus* BA.
[2] *siremps* Cuiacius; *seremiles* B; *sere miles* A.

---

[a] Ardea, the earliest capital of Latium, and Rome, the present capital of the empire. Seneca probably refers to Ardea's capture and destruction by the Samnites in the fourth century; Rome was captured by the Celts in 390 B.C. The former greatness of Ardea was celebrated by Vergil, *Aeneid*, vii. 411 ff.:

> et nunc magnum manet Ardea nomen,
> Sed fortuna fuit.

[b] *Siremps* (or *sirempse*—Plaut. *Amph.* 73), an ancient

not cry out at any of these calamities. Into such a world have we entered, and under such laws do we live. If you like it, obey; if not, depart whithersoever you wish. Cry out in anger if any unfair measures are taken with reference to you individually; but if this inevitable law is binding upon the highest and the lowest alike, be reconciled to fate, by which all things are dissolved. You should not estimate our worth by our funeral mounds or by these monuments of unequal size which line the road; their ashes level all men! We are unequal at birth, but are equal in death. What I say about cities I say also about their inhabitants: Ardea was captured as well as Rome.[a] The great founder of human law has not made distinctions between us on the basis of high lineage or of illustrious names, except while we live. When, however, we come to the end which awaits mortals, he says: "Depart, ambition! To all creatures that burden the earth let one and the same[b] law apply!" For enduring all things, we are equal; no one is more frail than another, no one more certain of his own life on the morrow.

Alexander, king of Macedon, began to study geometry[c]; unhappy man, because he would thereby learn how puny was that earth of which he had seized but a fraction! Unhappy man, I repeat, because he was bound to understand that he was bearing a false title. For who can be "great" in that which is puny? The lessons which were being taught him were intricate and could be learned only by assiduous application; they were not the kind to be

legal term, is derived by Festus from *similis re ipsa*; but Corssen explains it as from *sic rem pse*.

[c] *i.e.*, surveying. See *Ep.* lxxxviii. 10.

et trans oceanum cogitationes suas mittens. "Facilia," inquit, "me doce." Cui praeceptor "ista,"
18 inquit, "omnibus eadem sunt, aeque difficilia." Hoc puta rerum naturam dicere: "ista, de quibus quereris, omnibus eadem sunt. Nulli dare faciliora possum,[1] sed quisquis volet, sibi ipse[2] illa reddet faciliora." Quomodo? Aequanimitate. Et doleas oportet et sitias et esurias et senescas, si tibi longior contigerit inter homines mora, et aegrotes et perdas aliquid et
19 pereas. Non est tamen quod istis, qui te circumstrepunt, credas; nihil horum malum est, nihil intolerabile aut durum. Ex consensu istis metus est. Sic mortem times quomodo famam. Quid autem stultius homine verba metuente? Eleganter Demetrius noster solet dicere eodem loco sibi esse voces inperitorum, quo ventre redditos crepitus. "Quid enim," inquit, "mea,[3] susum isti an deosum
20 sonent?" Quanta dementia est vereri, ne infameris ab infamibus? Quemadmodum famam extimuistis sine causa, sic et illa, quae numquam timeretis, nisi fama iussisset. Num quid detrimenti faceret vir
21 bonus iniquis rumoribus sparsus? Ne morti quidem hoc apud nos[4] noceat; et haec malam olitionem habet. Nemo eorum, qui illam accusant,[5] expertus est.

[1] *possum* Buecheler; *possunt* BA.
[2] *ipse* Haase; *ipsi* BA.
[3] *mea susum* B corr.; *mea refert susum* B; *meas refert usum* A.
[4] *nos* later MSS.; *vos* BA.
[5] *accusant* later MSS.; *accusat* BA.

---

[a] *i.e.*, Ὠκεανός, the stream which encircles the earth.
[b] This plain-living, plain-speaking philosopher appears also in *Epp.* xx. 9 and lxii. 3. Seneca refers to him as *seminudum, quanto minus quam stramentis incubantem.*

comprehended by a madman, who let his thoughts range beyond the ocean.[a] "Teach me something easy!" he cries; but his teacher answers: "These things are the same for all, as hard for one as for another." Imagine that nature is saying to us: "Those things of which you complain are the same for all. I cannot give anything easier to any man, but whoever wishes will make things easier for himself." In what way? By equanimity. You must suffer pain, and thirst, and hunger, and old age too, if a longer stay among men shall be granted you; you must be sick, and you must suffer loss and death. Nevertheless, you should not believe those whose noisy clamour surrounds you; none of these things is an evil, none is beyond your power to bear, or is burdensome. It is only by common opinion that there is anything formidable in them. Your fearing death is therefore like your fear of gossip. But what is more foolish than a man afraid of words? Our friend Demetrius[b] is wont to put it cleverly when he says: "For me the talk of ignorant men is like the rumblings which issue from the belly. For," he adds, "what difference does it make to me whether such rumblings come from above or from below?" What madness it is to be afraid of disrepute in the judgment of the disreputable! Just as you have had no cause for shrinking in terror from the talk of men, so you have no cause now to shrink from these things, which you would never fear had not their talk forced fear upon you. Does it do any harm to a good man to be besmirched by unjust gossip? Then let not this sort of thing damage death, either, in our estimation; death also is in bad odour. But no one of those who malign death has made trial of it.

Interim temeritas est damnare, quod nescias. At illud scis, quam multis utilis sit, quam multos liberet tormentis, egestate, querellis, suppliciis, taedio. Non sumus in ullius potestate, cum mors in nostra potestate sit. VALE.

XCII

SENECA LVCILIO SVO SALVTEM

1 Puto, inter me teque conveniet externa corpori adquiri, corpus in honorem animi coli, in animo esse partes ministras, per quas movemur alimurque, propter ipsum principale nobis datas. In hoc principali est aliquid inrationale, est et rationale. Illud huic servit, hoc unum est, quod alio non refertur, sed omnia ad se refert.[1] Nam illa quoque divina ratio omnibus praeposita est, ipsa sub nullo est; et haec autem nostra eadem est, quia[2] ex illa
2 est. Si de hoc inter nos convenit, sequitur ut de illo quoque conveniat, in hoc uno positam esse beatam vitam, ut in nobis ratio perfecta sit. Haec enim sola non submittit animum, stat contra fortunam; in quolibet rerum habitu securos[3] servat. Id autem unum bonum est, quod numquam defringitur. Is est, inquam, beatus quem nulla res minorem facit;

[1] *refert* a later MS. and Madvig; *perfert* BA.
[2] *quia* later MSS.; *quae* BA.
[3] *securos* later MSS.; *servitus* BA.

---

[a] The reader will find this topic treated at greater length in Seneca's *De Vita Beata*.

[b] *i.e.*, the soul. See Aristotle, *Eth.* i. 13: "It is stated that the soul has two parts, one irrational and the other possessing reason." Aristotle further subdivides the irrational part into (1) that which makes for growth and increase, and (2) desire (which will, however, obey reason). In this passage Seneca uses "soul" in its widest sense.

Meanwhile it is foolhardy to condemn that of which you are ignorant. This one thing, however, you do know—that death is helpful to many, that it sets many free from tortures, want, ailments, sufferings, and weariness. We are in the power of nothing when once we have death in our own power! Farewell.

XCII. ON THE HAPPY LIFE[a]

You and I will agree, I think, that outward things are sought for the satisfaction of the body, that the body is cherished out of regard for the soul, and that in the soul there are certain parts which minister to us, enabling us to move and to sustain life, bestowed upon us just for the sake of the primary part of us.[b] In this primary part there is something irrational, and something rational. The former obeys the latter, while the latter is the only thing that is not referred back to another, but rather refers all things to itself. For the divine reason also is set in supreme command over all things, and is itself subject to none; and even this reason which we possess is the same, because it is derived from the divine reason. Now if we are agreed on this point, it is natural that we shall be agreed on the following also—namely, that the happy life depends upon this and this alone: our attainment of perfect reason. For it is naught but this that keeps the soul from being bowed down, that stands its ground against Fortune; whatever the condition of their affairs may be, it keeps men untroubled. And that alone is a good which is never subject to impairment. That man, I declare, is happy whom nothing makes

tenet summa, et ne ulli quidem nisi sibi innixus. Nam qui aliquo auxilio sustinetur, potest cadere. Si aliter est, incipient multum in nobis valere non nostra. Quis autem vult constare fortunam[1] aut quis se prudens ob aliena miratur?

3 Quid est beata vita? Securitas et perpetua tranquillitas. Hanc dabit animi magnitudo, dabit constantia bene iudicati tenax. Ad haec quomodo pervenitur? Si veritas tota perspecta est; si servatus est in rebus agendis ordo, modus, decor, innoxia voluntas ac benigna, intenta rationi nec umquam ab illa recedens, amabilis simul mirabilisque. Denique ut breviter tibi formulam scribam, talis animus esse sapientis viri debet, qualis deum deceat.
4 Quid potest desiderare is, cui omnia honesta contingunt? Nam si possunt aliquid non honesta conferre ad optimum statum, in his erit beata vita, sine quibus honesta.[2] Et quid turpius stultiusve quam bonum rationalis animi ex inrationalibus
5 nectere? Quidam tamen augeri summum bonum iudicant, quia parum plenum sit fortuitis repugnantibus. Antipater quoque inter magnos sectae huius auctores aliquid se tribuere dicit externis, sed exiguum admodum. Vides autem quale sit die non[3] esse contentum, nisi aliquis igniculus adluxerit. Quod potest in hac claritate solis habere scintilla

[1] *fortunam* Buecheler; *fortuna* BA.
[2] *honesta* Hense; *non est* BA.
[3] *die non* Erasmus; *zenon* BA.

[a] Certain of the Peripatetic and Academic school.
[b] Probably due to the criticism of the Stoics by Carneades, who said that everything which is according to nature should be classed among the goods.

less strong than he is; he keeps to the heights, leaning upon none but himself; for one who sustains himself by any prop may fall. If the case is otherwise, then things which do not pertain to us will begin to have great influence over us. But who desires Fortune to have the upper hand, or what sensible man prides himself upon that which is not his own?

What is the happy life? It is peace of mind, and lasting tranquillity. This will be yours if you possess greatness of soul; it will be yours if you possess the steadfastness that resolutely clings to a good judgment just reached. How does a man reach this condition? By gaining a complete view of truth, by maintaining, in all that he does, order, measure, fitness, and a will that is inoffensive and kindly, that is intent upon reason and never departs therefrom, that commands at the same time love and admiration. In short, to give you the principle in brief compass, the wise man's soul ought to be such as would be proper for a god. What more can one desire who possesses all honourable things? For if dishonourable things can contribute to the best estate, then there will be the possibility of a happy life under conditions which do not include an honourable life. And what is more base or foolish than to connect the good of a rational soul with things irrational? Yet there are certain philosophers who hold that the Supreme Good admits of increase because it is hardly complete when the gifts of fortune are adverse.[a] Even Antipater,[b] one of the great leaders of this school, admits that he ascribes some influence to externals, though only a very slight influence. You see, however, what absurdity lies in not being content with the daylight unless it is increased by a tiny fire. What importance can

6 momentum? Si non es sola honestate[1] contentus, necesse est aut quietem adici velis, quam ἀοχλησίαν vocant Graeci, aut voluptatem. Horum alterum utcumque recipi potest. Vacat enim animus molestia liber ad inspectum universi, nihilque illum avocat a contemplatione naturae. Alterum illud, voluptas, bonum pecoris est. Adicimus rationali inrationale, honesto inhonestum. Ad hanc vitam[2] facit titil-
7 latio corporis; quid ergo dubitatis dicere bene esse homini, si palato bene est? Et hunc tu, non dico inter viros numeras, sed inter homines, cuius summum bonum saporibus et coloribus[3] sonisque[4] constat? Excedat ex hoc animalium numero pulcherrimo ac dis secundo: mutis adgregetur animal pabulo laetum.

8 Inrationalis pars animi duas habet partes, alteram animosam, ambitiosam, inpotentem, positam in adfectionibus, alteram humilem, languidam, voluptatibus deditam; illam effrenatam, meliorem tamen, certe fortiorem ac digniorem viro reliquerunt, hanc necessariam beatae vitae putaverunt, et ener-
9 vem[5] et abiectam. Huic rationem servire iusserunt et fecerunt animalis generosissimi summum[6] bonum demissum et ignobile, praeterea mixtum portentosumque et ex diversis ac male[7] con-

[1] *honestate* later MSS.; *honesta* B¹A.
[2] *ad hanc vitam* Buecheler; *magno vitam* B; *magnevitam* A.
[3] *coloribus* later MSS.; *caloribus* BA.
[4] *sonisque* Windhaus; *sonis* or *solis* MSS.
[5] *et enervem* Rossbach; *inenervem* BA.
[6] *generosissimi summum* Buecheler; *generosissimum* (or *-i*) MSS.
[7] *ac male* Schweighaeuser; *animalis* BA.

---

[a] If we call pleasure a good.
[b] *Cf.* § 1 of this letter. Plato gives three divisions—the

a spark have in the midst of this clear sunlight? If you are not contented with only that which is honourable, it must follow that you desire in addition either the kind of quiet which the Greeks call "undisturbedness," or else pleasure. But the former may be attained in any case. For the mind is free from disturbance when it is fully free to contemplate the universe, and nothing distracts it from the contemplation of nature. The second, pleasure, is simply the good of cattle. We are but adding [a] the irrational to the rational, the dishonourable to the honourable. A pleasant physical sensation affects this life of ours; why, therefore, do you hesitate to say that all is well with a man just because all is well with his appetite? And do you rate, I will not say among heroes, but among men, the person whose Supreme Good is a matter of flavours and colours and sounds? Nay, let him withdraw from the ranks of this, the noblest class of living beings, second only to the gods; let him herd with the dumb brutes—an animal whose delight is in fodder!

The irrational part of the soul is twofold [b]: the one part is spirited, ambitious, uncontrolled; its seat is in the passions; the other is lowly, sluggish, and devoted to pleasure. Philosophers have neglected the former, which, though unbridled, is yet better, and is certainly more courageous and more worthy of a man, and have regarded the latter, which is nerveless and ignoble, as indispensable to the happy life. They have ordered reason to serve this latter; they have made the Supreme Good of the noblest living being an abject and mean affair, and a monstrous hybrid, too, composed of various members

λογιστικόν, the ἐπιθυμητικόν, and the θυμοειδές which obeys either the first or the second. See his *Republic*, 440.

gruentibus membris. Nam ut ait Vergilius noster in Scylla

> Prima hominis facies et pulchro pectore virgo
> Pube tenus, postrema inmani corpore pistrix
> Delphinum caudas utero commissa luporum.

Huic tamen Scyllae fera animalia adiuncta sunt,
horrenda, velocia; at isti sapientiam ex quibus
10 conposuere portentis! Prima ars hominis est ipsa
virtus; huic committitur inutilis caro et fluida,
receptandis tantum cibis habilis, ut ait Posidonius.
Virtus illa divina in lubricum desinit et superioribus
eius partibus venerandis atque caelestibus animal
iners ac marcidum adtexitur. Illa utcumque altera
quies nihil quidem ipsa praestabat animo, sed
inpedimenta removebat; voluptas ultro dissolvit et
omne robur emollit. Quae invenietur tam discors
inter se iunctura corporum? Fortissimae rei inertis-
sima adstruitur, severissimae parum seria, sanctissimae
11 intemperans usque ad incesta.[1] "Quid ergo?"
inquit, "si virtutem nihil inpeditura sit bona valitudo
et quies et dolorum vacatio,[2] non petes illas?"
Quidni petam? Non quia bona sunt, sed quia
secundum naturam sunt, et quia bono a me iudicio
sumentur. Quid erit tunc in illis bonum? Hoc
unum, bene eligi. Nam cum[3] vestem qualem decet,

[1] *incesta* Gruter; *ingesta* BA.
[2] *vacatio* later MSS.; *vagatio* BA.
[3] *cum* omitted in A and supplied by a late hand in B. Buecheler suggests *nam vestem qualem decet cum sumo.*

---

[a] *Aeneid*, iii. 426 ff.

which harmonize but ill. For as our Vergil, describing Scylla, says[a]:

> Above, a human face and maiden's breast,—
> A beauteous breast,—below, a monster huge
> Of bulk and shapeless, with a dolphin's tail
> Joined to a wolf-like belly.

And yet to this Scylla are tacked on the forms of wild animals, dreadful and swift; but from what monstrous shapes have these wiseacres compounded wisdom! Man's primary art is virtue itself; there is joined to this the useless and fleeting flesh, fitted only for the reception of food, as Posidonius remarks. This divine virtue ends in foulness, and to the higher parts, which are worshipful and heavenly, there is fastened a sluggish and flabby animal. As for the second desideratum, — quiet, — although it would indeed not of itself be of any benefit to the soul, yet it would relieve the soul of hindrances; pleasure, on the contrary, actually destroys the soul and softens all its vigour. What elements so inharmonious as these can be found united? To that which is most vigorous is joined that which is most sluggish, to that which is austere that which is far from serious, to that which is most holy that which is unrestrained even to the point of impurity. "What, then," comes the retort, "if good health, rest, and freedom from pain are not likely to hinder virtue, shall you not seek all these?" Of course I shall seek them, but not because they are goods,—I shall seek them because they are according to nature and because they will be acquired through the exercise of good judgment on my part. What, then, will be good in them? This alone,—that it is a good thing to choose them. For when I don suitable attire, or

sumo, cum ambulo ut oportet, cum ceno quemadmodum debeo, non cena aut ambulatio aut vestis
bona sunt, sed meum in iis propositum servantis in
12 quaque re rationi convenientem modum. Etiamnunc
adiciam: mundae vestis electio adpetenda est
homini. Natura enim homo mundum[1] et elegans
animal est. Itaque non est bonum per se munda
vestis, sed mundae vestis electio, quia non in re
bonum est, sed in electione quali. Actiones nostrae
13 honestae sunt, non ipsa quae aguntur. Quod de
veste dixi, idem me dicere de corpore existima.
Nam hoc quoque natura ut quandam vestem animo
circumdedit; velamentum eius est. Quis autem
umquam vestimenta aestimavit arcula? Nec bonum
nec malum vagina gladium facit. Ergo de corpore
quoque idem tibi respondeo: sumpturum quidem
me, si detur electio, et sanitatem et vires, bonum
autem futurum iudicium de illis meum, non ipsa.

14 "Est quidem," inquit, "sapiens beatus; summum
tamen illud bonum non consequitur, nisi illi et
naturalia instrumenta respondeant. Ita miser quidem esse, qui virtutem habet, non potest, beatissimus
autem non est, qui naturalibus bonis destituitur ut
15 valitudine, ut membrorum integritate." Quod incredibilius videtur, id concedis, aliquem in maximis
et continuis doloribus non esse miserum, esse etiam
beatum; quod levius est, negas, beatissimum esse.

[1] *mundum* later MSS.; *mundus* BA.

walk as I should, or dine as I ought to dine, it is not my dinner, or my walk, or my dress that are goods, but the deliberate choice which I show in regard to them, as I observe, in each thing I do, a mean that conforms with reason. Let me also add that the choice of neat clothing is a fitting object of a man's efforts; for man is by nature a neat and well-groomed animal. Hence the choice of neat attire, and not neat attire in itself, is a good; since the good is not in the thing selected, but in the quality of the selection. Our actions are honourable, but not the actual things which we do. And you may assume that what I have said about dress applies also to the body. For nature has surrounded our soul with the body as with a sort of garment; the body is its cloak. But who has ever reckoned the value of clothes by the wardrobe which contained them? The scabbard does not make the sword good or bad. Therefore, with regard to the body I shall return the same answer to you,—that, if I have the choice, I shall choose health and strength, but that the good involved will be my judgment regarding these things, and not the things themselves.

Another retort is: "Granted that the wise man is happy; nevertheless, he does not attain the Supreme Good which we have defined, unless the means also which nature provides for its attainment are at his call. So, while one who possesses virtue cannot be unhappy, yet one cannot be perfectly happy if one lacks such natural gifts as health, or soundness of limb." But in saying this, you grant the alternative which seems the more difficult to believe,—that the man who is in the midst of unremitting and extreme pain is not wretched, nay, is even happy; and you deny that which is much less

Atqui si potest virtus efficere, ne miser aliquis sit, facilius efficiet, ut beatissimus sit. Minus enim intervalli a beato[1] ad beatissimum restat quam a misero ad beatum. An quae res tantum valet, ut ereptum calamitatibus inter beatos locet, non potest adicere quod superest, ut beatissimum faciat? In
16 summo deficit clivo? Commoda sunt in vita[2] et incommoda, utraque extra nos. Si non est miser vir bonus, quamvis omnibus prematur incommodis, quomodo non est beatissimus, si aliquibus commodis deficitur? Nam quemadmodum incommodorum onere usque ad miserum non deprimitur, sic commodorum inopia non deducitur a beatissimo, sed tam sine commodis beatissimus est, quam non est sub incommodis miser; aut potest illi eripi bonum suum, si potest minui.

17 Paulo ante dicebam igniculum nihil conferre lumini solis. Claritate enim eius quicquid sine illo luceret absconditur. "Sed quaedam," inquit, "soli quoque opstant." At sol integer est[3] etiam inter opposita, et quamvis aliquid interiacet, quod nos prohibeat eius aspectu, in opere est, cursu suo fertur. Quotiens inter nubila eluxit, non est sereno minor,

[1] *a beato* later MSS.; *beato* BA.
[2] *in vita* later MSS.; *invicta* BA.
[3] *at sol integer est* Buecheler; *ipsamasole integra est* BA.

---

[a] § 5.

serious,—that he is completely happy. And yet, if virtue can keep a man from being wretched, it will be an easier task for it to render him completely happy. For the difference between happiness and complete happiness is less than that between wretchedness and happiness. Can it be possible that a thing which is so powerful as to snatch a man from disaster, and place him among the happy, cannot also accomplish what remains, and render him supremely happy? Does its strength fail at the very top of the climb? There are in life things which are advantageous and disadvantageous,—both beyond our control. If a good man, in spite of being weighed down by all kinds of disadvantages, is not wretched, how is he not supremely happy, no matter if he does lack certain advantages? For as he is not weighted down to wretchedness by his burden of disadvantages, so he is not withdrawn from supreme happiness through lack of any advantages; nay, he is just as supremely happy without the advantages as he is free from wretchedness though under the load of his disadvantages. Otherwise, if his good can be impaired, it can be snatched from him altogether.

A short space above,[a] I remarked that a tiny fire does not add to the sun's light. For by reason of the sun's brightness any light that shines apart from the sunlight is blotted out. "But," one may say, "there are certain objects that stand in the way even of the sunlight." The sun, however, is unimpaired even in the midst of obstacles, and, though an object may intervene and cut off our view thereof, the sun sticks to his work and goes on his course. Whenever he shines forth from amid the clouds, he is no smaller, nor less punctual either, than when

ne tardior quidem, quoniam multum interest, utrum
18 aliquid obstet tantum, an inpediat. Eodem modo virtuti opposita nihil detrahunt; non est minor, sed minus fulget. Nobis forsitan non aeque apparet ac nitet, sibi eadem est et more solis obscuri in occulto vim suam exercet. Hoc itaque adversus virtutem possunt calamitates et damna et iniuriae, quod adversus solem potest nebula.

19 Invenitur, qui dicat sapientem corpore parum prospero usum nec miserum esse nec beatum. Hic quoque fallitur, exaequat enim fortuita virtutibus et tantundem tribuit honestis quantum honestate carentibus. Quid autem foedius, quid indignius quam comparari veneranda contemptis? Veneranda enim sunt iustitia, pietas, fides, fortitudo, prudentia; e contrario vilia sunt, quae saepe contingunt pleniora vilissimis, crus solidum et lacertus et dentes et
20 tororum[1] sanitas firmitasque. Deinde si sapiens, cui corpus molestum est, nec miser habebitur nec beatus, sed in medio[2] relinquetur, vita quoque eius nec adpetenda erit nec fugienda. Quid autem tam absurdum quam sapientis vitam adpetendam non esse? Aut quid tam extra fidem quam esse aliquam vitam nec adpetendam nec fugiendam? Deinde si

[1] *tororum* Capps; *horum* MSS.; *ceterorum* Buecheler; *nervorum* Kronenberg.
[2] *in medio* later MSS.; *medio* BA

he is free from clouds; since it makes a great deal of difference whether there is merely something in the way of his light or something which interferes with his shining. Similarly, obstacles take nothing away from virtue; it is no smaller, but merely shines with less brilliancy. In our eyes, it may perhaps be less visible and less luminous than before; but as regards itself it is the same and, like the sun when he is eclipsed, is still, though in secret, putting forth its strength. Disasters, therefore, and losses, and wrongs, have only the same power over virtue that a cloud has over the sun.

We meet with one person who maintains that a wise man who has met with bodily misfortune is neither wretched nor happy. But he also is in error, for he is putting the results of chance upon a parity with the virtues, and is attributing only the same influence to things that are honourable as to things that are devoid of honour. But what is more detestable and more unworthy than to put contemptible things in the same class with things worthy of reverence! For reverence is due to justice, duty, loyalty, bravery, and prudence; on the contrary, those attributes are worthless with which the most worthless men are often blessed in fuller measure, — such as a sturdy leg, strong shoulders, good teeth, and healthy and solid muscles. Again, if the wise man whose body is a trial to him shall be regarded as neither wretched nor happy, but shall be left in a sort of half-way position, his life also will be neither desirable nor undesirable. But what is so foolish as to say that the wise man's life is not desirable? And what is so far beyond the bounds of credence as the opinion that any life is neither desirable nor undesirable? Again, if bodily

damna corporis miserum non faciunt, beatum esse patiuntur. Nam quibus potentia non est in peiorem transferendi[1] statum, ne interpellandi quidem optimum.

21 "Frigidum," inquit, "aliquid et calidum novimus, inter utrumque tepidum est; sic aliquis beatus est, aliquis miser, aliquis nec beatus nec miser." Volo hanc contra nos positam imaginem excutere. Si tepido illi plus frigidi ingessero, fiet frigidum. Si plus calidi adfudero, fiet novissime calidum. At huic nec misero nec beato quantumcumque ad miserias adiecero, miser non erit, quemadmodum
22 dicitis; ergo imago ista dissimilis est. Deinde trado tibi hominem nec miserum nec beatum. Huic adicio caecitatem; non fit miser. Adicio debilitatem; non fit miser. Adicio dolores continuos et graves; miser non fit. Quem tam multa mala in miseram vitam non transferunt, ne ex beata quidem educunt.
23 Si non potest, ut dicitis, sapiens ex beato in miserum decidere, non potest in non beatum. Quare enim qui labi coepit,[2] alicubi subsistat? Quae res illum non patitur ad imum devolvi, retinet in summo. Quidni non possit beata vita rescindi? Ne remitti quidem potest, et ideo virtus ad illam per se ipsa satis est.

24 "Quid ergo?" inquit, "sapiens non est beatior,

[1] *transferendi* later MSS.; *transiendi* BA.
[2] *qui labi coepit* Muretus; *qui illa coepit* BA.

[a] Answering the objection raised in § 14.

ills do not make a man wretched, they consequently allow him to be happy. For things which have no power to change his condition for the worse, have not the power, either, to disturb that condition when it is at its best.

"But," someone will say, "we know what is cold and what is hot; a lukewarm temperature lies between. Similarly, A is happy, and B is wretched, and C is neither happy nor wretched." I wish to examine this figure, which is brought into play against us. If I add to your lukewarm water a larger quantity of cold water, the result will be cold water. But if I pour in a larger quantity of hot water, the water will finally become hot. In the case, however, of your man who is neither wretched nor happy, no matter how much I add to his troubles, he will not be unhappy, according to your argument; hence your figure offers no analogy. Again, suppose that I set before you a man who is neither miserable nor happy. I add blindness to his misfortunes; he is not rendered unhappy. I cripple him; he is not rendered unhappy. I add afflictions which are unceasing and severe; he is not rendered unhappy. Therefore, one whose life is not changed to misery by all these ills is not dragged by them, either, from his life of happiness. Then if, as you say, the wise man cannot fall from happiness to wretchedness, he cannot fall into non-happiness. For how, if one has begun to slip, can one stop at any particular place? That which prevents him from rolling to the bottom, keeps him at the summit. Why, you urge, may not a happy life possibly be destroyed? It cannot even be disjointed; and for that reason virtue is itself of itself sufficient for the happy life.[a]

"But," it is said, "is not the wise man happier if

qui diutius vixit, quem nullus avocavit dolor, quam ille, qui cum mala fortuna semper luctatus est?" Responde mihi: numquid et melior est et honestior? Si haec non sunt, ne beatior quidem est. Rectius vivat oportet, ut beatius vivat; si rectius non potest, ne beatius quidem.[1] Non intenditur virtus, ergo ne beata quidem vita, quae ex virtute est. Virtus enim tantum bonum est, ut istas accessiones minutas non sentiat, brevitatem aevi et dolorem et corporum varias offensiones. Nam voluptas non est digna, ad
25 quam respiciat. Quid est in virtute praecipuum? Futuro non indigere nec dies suos computare; in quantulo libet tempore bona aeterna consummat. Incredibilia nobis haec videntur et supra humanam naturam excurrentia. Maiestatem enim eius ex nostra inbecillitate metimur[2] et vitiis nostris nomen virtutis inponimus. Quid porro? Non aeque incredibile videtur aliquem in summis cruciatibus positum dicere "beatus sum"? Atqui haec vox in ipsa officina voluptatis audita est. "Beatissimum," inquit, "hunc et hunc diem ago" Epicurus, cum illum hinc urinae difficultas torqueret, hinc insana-
26 bilis exulcerati dolor ventris. Quare ergo incredibilia ista sint aput eos, qui virtutem colunt, quom[3] aput eos quoque reperiantur,[4] aput quos voluptas imperavit? Hi quoque degeneres et humillimae mentis aiunt in summis doloribus, in summis calamitatibus sapientem

[1] *ne beatius quidem* later MSS.; *ne beatus quidem* BA.
[2] *metimur* later MSS.; *mentimur* BA.
[3] *quom* O. Rossbach; *cum* BA.
[4] *reperiantur* later MSS.; *aperiantur* BA.

---

[a] *Cf. Ep.* lxxi. 16 *non intenditur virtus.* The Stoic idea of *tension* may be combined here with the raising of a note to a higher pitch.

[b] Frag. 138 Usener. *Cf.* Sen. *Ep.* lxvi. 47.

he has lived longer and has been distracted by no pain, than one who has always been compelled to grapple with evil fortune?" Answer me now,—is he any better or more honourable? If he is not, then he is not happier either. In order to live more happily, he must live more rightly; if he cannot do that, then he cannot live more happily either. Virtue cannot be strained tighter,[a] and therefore neither can the happy life, which depends on virtue. For virtue is so great a good that it is not affected by such insignificant assaults upon it as shortness of life, pain, and the various bodily vexations. For pleasure does not deserve that virtue should even glance at it. Now what is the chief thing in virtue? It is the quality of not needing a single day beyond the present, and of not reckoning up the days that are ours; in the slightest possible moment of time virtue completes an eternity of good. These goods seem to us incredible and transcending man's nature; for we measure its grandeur by the standard of our own weakness, and we call our vices by the name of virtue. Furthermore, does it not seem just as incredible that any man in the midst of extreme suffering should say, "I am happy"? And yet this utterance was heard in the very factory of pleasure, when Epicurus said:[b] "To-day and one other day have been the happiest of all!" although in the one case he was tortured by strangury, and in the other by the incurable pain of an ulcerated stomach. Why, then, should those goods which virtue bestows be incredible in the sight of us, who cultivate virtue, when they are found even in those who acknowledge pleasure as their mistress? These also, ignoble and base-minded as they are, declare that even in the midst of excessive pain and mis-

nec miserum futurum nec beatum. Atqui hoc quoque incredibile est, immo incredibilius. Non video enim, quomodo non in infimum[1] agatur e fastigio suo deiecta virtus. Aut beatum praestare debet, aut si ab hoc depulsa est, non prohibebit fieri miserum. Stans non potest mitti; aut vincatur oportet aut vincat.

27 "Dis," inquit, "inmortalibus solis et virtus et beata vita contigit, nobis umbra quaedam illorum bonorum et similitudo. Accedimus ad illa, non pervenimus." Ratio vero dis hominibusque communis est; haec in illis consummata est, in nobis consum-
28 mabilis. Sed ad desperationem nos vitia nostra perducunt; nam ille alter secundus est ut aliquis parum constans ad custodienda optima, cuius iudicium labat etiamnunc et incertum est. Desideret oculorum atque aurium sensum, bonam valitudinem et non foedum aspectum corporis et habitu manente suo
29 aetatis praeterea longius spatium. Per hanc potest non paenitenda agi vita, at[2] inperfecto viro huic malitiae vis quaedam inest, quia animum habet mobilem ad prava. Illa apparens malitia et exagitata[3] abest[4]; non est adhuc bonus, sed in bonum fingitur. Cuicumque autem deest aliquid ad bonum, malus est.

[1] *non in infimum* vulg.; *non in imum* Buecheler; *non infirmum* BA.

[2] *agi vita at* Buecheler; *agitavit* BA.

[3] *apparens malitia et exagitata* Buecheler; *aitarens malitia et ea agitata* BA.

[4] A and B give *de bono* after *abest*; in B the words are added at the end of the line.

fortune the wise man will be neither wretched nor happy. And yet this also is incredible,—nay, still more incredible than the other case. For I do not understand how, if virtue falls from her heights, she can help being hurled all the way to the bottom. She either must preserve one in happiness, or, if driven from this position, she will not prevent us from becoming unhappy. If virtue only stands her ground, she cannot be driven from the field; she must either conquer or be conquered.

But some say: "Only to the immortal gods is given virtue and the happy life; we can attain but the shadow, as it were, and semblance of such goods as theirs. We approach them, but we never reach them." Reason, however, is a common attribute of both gods and men; in the gods it is already perfected, in us it is capable of being perfected. But it is our vices that bring us to despair; for the second class of rational being, man, is of an inferior order,—a guardian, as it were, who is too unstable to hold fast to what is best, his judgment still wavering and uncertain. He may require the faculties of sight and hearing, good health, a bodily exterior that is not loathsome, and, besides, greater length of days conjoined with an unimpaired constitution. Though by means of reason he can lead a life which will not bring regrets, yet there resides in this imperfect creature, man, a certain power that makes for badness, because he possesses a mind which is easily moved to perversity. Suppose, however, the badness which is in full view, and has previously been stirred to activity, to be removed; the man is still not a good man, but he is being moulded to goodness. One, however, in whom there is lacking any quality that makes for goodness, is bad.

Sed

Si cui virtus animusque in corpore praesens,

hic deos aequat, illo tendit originis suae memor.
30 Nemo inprobe eo conatur ascendere, unde descenderat. Quid est autem cur non existimes in eo divini aliquid existere, qui dei pars est? Totum hoc, quo continemur, et unum est et deus; et socii sumus eius et membra. Capax est noster animus, perfertur illo, si vitia non deprimant. Quemadmodum corporum nostrorum habitus erigitur et spectat in caelum, ita animus, cui in quantum vult licet porrigi, in hoc a natura rerum formatus est, ut paria dis vellet. Et si utatur suis viribus ac se in spatium suum extendat, non aliena via[1] ad summa nititur.
31 Magnus erat labor ire in caelum; redit. Cum hoc iter nactus est, vadit audaciter contemptor omnium nec ad pecuniam respicit aurumque et argentum illis, in quibus iacuere, tenebris dignissima, non ab hoc aestimat splendore,[2] quo inperitorum[3] verberant oculos, sed a vetere caeno,[4] ex quo illa secrevit cupiditas nostra et effodit.

Scit, inquam, aliubi positas esse divitias quam quo congeruntur; animum impleri debere, non arcam.
32 Hunc inponere dominio rerum omnium licet, hunc in possessionem rerum naturae inducere, ut sua

[1] *via* Schweighaeuser; *vita* BA.
[2] *ab hoc aestimat splendore* Rubenius; *ad hoc aestimat splendorem* BA.
[3] *inperitorum* cod. Velz.; *inperitior* B; *inpericior* A.
[4] *a vetere caeno* Rubenius; *avertero caelo* BA.

---

[a] Vergil, *Aeneid*, v. 363. Vergil MSS. read *pectore*.
[b] *i.e.*, to participation in the divine existence.

But

> He in whose body virtue dwells, and spirit
> E'er present,[a]

is equal to the gods; mindful of his origin, he strives to return thither. No man does wrong in attempting to regain the heights from which he once came down. And why should you not believe that something of divinity exists in one who is a part of God? All this universe which encompasses us is one, and it is God; we are associates of God; we are his members. Our soul has capabilities, and is carried thither,[b] if vices do not hold it down. Just as it is the nature of our bodies to stand erect and look upward to the sky, so the soul, which may reach out as far as it will, was framed by nature to this end, that it should desire equality with the gods. And if it makes use of its powers and stretches upward into its proper region it is by no alien path that it struggles toward the heights. It would be a great task to journey heavenwards; the soul but returns thither. When once it has found the road, it boldly marches on, scornful of all things. It casts no backward glance at wealth; gold and silver—things which are fully worthy of the gloom in which they once lay—it values not by the sheen which smites the eyes of the ignorant, but by the mire of ancient days, whence our greed first detached and dug them out.

The soul, I affirm, knows that riches are stored elsewhere than in men's heaped-up treasure-houses; that it is the soul, and not the strong-box, which should be filled. It is the soul that men may set in dominion over all things, and may install as owner of the universe, so that it may limit its riches only

orientis occidentisque terminis finiat[1] deorumque ritu cuncta possideat,[2] cum opibus suis divites superne despiciat, quorum nemo tam suo laetus est
33 quam tristis alieno. Cum se in hanc sublimitatem tulit, corporis quoque ut[3] oneris necessarii non amator, sed procurator est nec se illi, cui inpositus est, subicit. Nemo liber est, qui corpori servit. Nam ut alios dominos, quos nimia pro illo sollicitudo invenit, transeas, ipsius morosum imperium delica-
34 tumque est. Ab hoc modo aequo animo exit, modo magno prosilit, nec quis deinde relicti eius futurus sit exitus quaerit. Sed ut ex barba capilloque tonsa neglegimus, ita ille divinus animus egressurus hominem, quo receptaculum suum conferatur, ignis illud exurat an lapis includat[4] an terra contegat an ferae distrahant, non magis ad se iudicat pertinere quam secundas ad editum infantem. Utrum proiectum aves differant, an consumatur

Canibus data praeda marinis,[5]

35 quid ad illum, qui nullus est[6]? Sed tunc quoque, cum inter homines est, non timet ullas[7] post mortem minas eorum, quibus usque ad mortem timeri parum est. Non conterret, inquit, me nec uncus nec proiecti

[1] *finiat* later MSS.; *fiat* BA.
[2] *possideat* later MSS.; *possideant* BA.
[3] *ut* Buecheler; *vel* or *velut* BA.
[4] After *illud* Rossbach reads *exurat an lapis includat an terra*, etc.; *illud excludat an terra* BA; *exurat* (for *excludat*) later MSS.
[5] *praeda Latinis* Vergil.
[6] *qui nullus est* Hense; *qui nullus* BA.
[7] *est, non timet ullas* Buecheler; *est timet ullas* BA.

[a] Vergil, *Aeneid*, ix. 485.

by the boundaries of East and West, and, like the gods, may possess all things; and that it may, with its own vast resources, look down from on high upon the wealthy, no one of whom rejoices as much in his own wealth as he resents the wealth of another. When the soul has transported itself to this lofty height, it regards the body also, since it is a burden which must be borne, not as a thing to love, but as a thing to oversee; nor is it subservient to that over which it is set in mastery. For no man is free who is a slave to his body. Indeed, omitting all the other masters which are brought into being by excessive care for the body, the sway which the body itself exercises is captious and fastidious. Forth from this body the soul issues, now with unruffled spirit, now with exultation, and, when once it has gone forth, asks not what shall be the end of the deserted clay. No; just as we do not take thought for the clippings of the hair and the beard, even so that divine soul, when it is about to issue forth from the mortal man, regards the destination of its earthly vessel—whether it be consumed by fire, or shut in by a stone, or buried in the earth, or torn by wild beasts—as being of no more concern to itself than is the afterbirth to a child just born. And whether this body shall be cast out and plucked to pieces by birds, or devoured when

> thrown to the sea-dogs as prey,[a]

how does that concern him who is nothing? Nay, even when it is among the living, the soul fears nothing that may happen to the body after death; for though such things may have been threats, they were not enough to terrify the soul previous to the moment of death. It says: "I am not frightened

ad contumeliam cadaveris laceratio foeda visuris. Neminem de supremo officio rogo, nulli reliquias meas commendo. Ne quis insepultus esset, rerum natura prospexit.[1] Quem saevitia proiecerit, dies condet.[2] Diserte Maecenas ait :

Nec tumulum curo. Sepelit natura relictos.

Alte cinctum putes dixisse. Habuit enim ingenium et grande et virile, nisi illud secundis discinxisset.[3] VALE.

[1] *prospexit* Buecheler ; *prospicit* BA.
[2] *condet* later MSS. ; *condit* BA.
[3] *secundis discinxisset* later MSS. ; *secundis cinxisset* BA.

---

[a] *Cf.* Juvenal, x. 65 *Seianus ducitur unco spectandus.* The bodies of criminals were dragged by the hook through the city to the *Scalae Gemoniae*, down which they were flung.
[b] Frag. 6 Lunderstedt.

by the executioner's hook,[a] nor by the revolting mutilation of the corpse which is exposed to the scorn of those who would witness the spectacle. I ask no man to perform the last rites for me; I entrust my remains to none. Nature has made provision that none shall go unburied. Time will lay away one whom cruelty has cast forth." Those were eloquent words which Maecenas uttered:

> I want no tomb; for Nature doth provide
> For outcast bodies burial.[b]

You would imagine that this was the saying of a man of strict principles. He was indeed a man of noble and robust native gifts, but in prosperity he impaired these gifts by laxness.[c] Farewell.

[c] The figure is taken from the Roman dress,—one who was "girt high" (*alte cinctus*), ready for vigorous walking, being contrasted with the loosely-girdled person (*discinctus*), indolent or effeminate. On the character of Maecenas see *Epp.* cxiv. 4 ff., xix. 9, cxx. 19.

APPENDIX

containing some new readings found in the Codex Quirinianus (Q), a MS. of the ninth or tenth century, published at Brescia by Achilles Beltrami in 1916. The MS. includes *Epp.* I–LXXXVIII.

I. 5. *superest, sat est* vulg.
de homine moderato sat est Q.
da hominem moderatum: sat est Beltrami.

VIII. 7. *differetur* Q.
differtur vulg.

XIV. 17. *adde* Q, confirming L^1; *ede* rell.

XXV. 2. *perfecturus* Q; *profecturus* vulg.

XXXIII. 9. *quid est quod a(r) te* Q; *quid est quare et* Hense; etc.

XLVIII. 1. *quae tam longa quam* Q; *tam longam quam* rell

LXV. 22. *vindicet* Q; *ducet* vulg.

LXVI. 32. *virtuti: nihil enim aliud est virtus quam recta ratio. omnes virtutes rationes sunt* Q, confirming Schweighaeuser.

LXXI. 7. Before *nisi qui omnia bona exaequaverit,* Q adds *nisi qui omnia prior i(p)se contempserit.*

LXXI. 12. *de hoc cursu* Q; *ex h. c.* vulg.

LXXII. 3. Q adds (after *philosophandum est*) *sed ut philosopheris vacandum est.*

LXXV. 1. *desideremus* Q; *sederemus* vulg.

LXXVI. 20. Q adds (after *calcasse*) *inventus est qui divitias proiceret.*

LXXVII. 17. Q adds (after *doleas*) *amicos scis enim amicus esse.*

LXXVIII. 9. *longior impetus mora* Q ; *impetus mora* rell.

LXXXI. 8. *esse grati* Q ; *esse* rell.

LXXXI. 21. Q adds (after *urget*) *nemo sibi gratus est qui alteri non fuit. hoc me putas dicere qui ingratus est miser erit.*

LXXXII. 11. *sed ille Rutilius qui fortiore vultu in exilium iit quam misisset* Q ; *ut quam misisset* MSS.

LXXXIII. 2. Q adds (after *cogitamus*) *et id raro; quid fecerimus non cogitamus.*

LXXXIV. 11. Q adds *nihil vitaverimus nisi ratione suadente,* with a twelfth-century MS.

LXXXVII. 26. After *sustuleris* Q adds *non ideo sustuleris.*

LXXXVIII. 41. *non vis cogitare* Q, with some later MSS. ; *non cogitare* rell.

INDEX OF PROPER NAMES

INDEX

INDEX